Precious Moments with the Master

Dale Manternach

Copyright © 2011 by Dale Manternach

Precious Moments with the Master
by Dale Manternach

Printed in the United States of America

ISBN 9781613796108

All rights reserved solely by the author. The author guarantees all contents are original and do not infringe upon the legal rights of any other person or work. No part of this book may be reproduced in any form without the permission of the author. The views expressed in this book are not necessarily those of the publisher.

Unless otherwise indicated, Bible quotations are taken from the New King James Version. Copyright © 1982 by Thomas Nelson Inc.

www.xulonpress.com

January 1

Life must go on!

An American January 1, New Years Day, has typically been one of closed business on main street, a day of quiet rest for many, declaration of new resolutions for the year ahead, a special day of football "bowls" on TV, the parade of roses in California, lots of family gatherings, and often some community parties, like skating and skiing and snowmobiling in the northern climates. After a busy December of advent gatherings, public school and Sunday school programs, choir cantatas, and Christmas Eve worship, most pastors and churches are glad to rest on New Years Day.

Some of us will look back and rejoice over the new babies, the baptisms, the birthday celebrations, along with the anniversaries. A great time to remember Psalm 46:10: "Be still and know that I am God." As we reflect on the past, we take our new calendar down and plan for the days ahead. A good time to stand on Proverbs 3:5-6: "Trust in the Lord with all your heart, and lean not unto your own understanding; acknowledge Him in all your ways, and He will direct your paths." A good time to forget the negatives the old nature insists that we must contend with and turn to Philippians 4:6: "Be careful for nothing, but by prayer and supplication, with thanksgiving, let your requests be made known unto God and the peace of God which passes all understanding will keep your hearts and minds in Christ Jesus."

Before we realize it, day number one of the New Year has literally evaporated into the darkness of evening, and we hear Paul, "forgetting the things which are behind, and reaching forward to those things which are ahead, I press toward the goal for the prize of the upward call of God in Christ Jesus." Philippians 3:13.

"I wish above all things that you may prosper and be in health even as your soul prospers."!!! John 2.

January 2

"A merry heart does good, like a medicine..." Proverbs 17:22

He was "a kickin' up his heels," King David was, totally immersed in a joyful spirit. His more dignified wife, Michal, looked through a window and saw King David "leaping and whirling before the Lord, and she despised him." II Samuel 16:7. Jealous, embarrassed, or false humility? Or was it legalism I've been chastised within the days of my youth, when I, too, "kicked up my heals" in the fun and exercise of dancing, without the stomach full of liquor, nor the heart full of lust, however. Shame, shame for a Christian!! Sarcastically, I suspect, when wife Michal spewed out "How glorious was the King of Israel today uncovering himself in the eyes of the maids of his servants..." Vs. 20. David replied: "It was before the Lord, Who chose to appoint me ruler over the people of the Lord, over Israel. Therefore, I will play music before the Lord." Vs.21 And maybe first springing from his inner man, the like of prophet Nehemiah: "The joy of the Lord is my strength." Nehemiah 3:10

In my circle of Christian friendships, I love to laugh from a light heart, while sometimes I see a long, sad, "plastic-like" face in the crowd, a face that would surely crack if it tried to laugh, or even smile.

I am so appreciative of the two mates I've enjoyed with lots of laughter within our home. And for all the laughter my children manifested, especially at the dinner table. We teased, pulled pranks, and often heard a spur-of-the-moment comical expression from one of the eight around our table. They learned to "give and take" too, at game playing times, a mixture of serious competition and laughter.

"A merry heart is like a medicine...it's soothing for your sadness, gives you joy; so lift your voice and let your spirit soar...the happiness is yours, without alloy." (Hess).

"Laugh and the world laughs with you..." a simple song for either the worldly or the Christian.

From one who agrees with a slogan: "Wholesome laughter has great FACE value. A countenance shows it!"

January 3

"...but joy comes in the morning." Psalm 30:3

Because I was a curious young boy on the Montana prairies, always an early riser, I could often enjoy the radiant, colorful hours of the sun in the eastern sky long before the sun itself would appear on the horizon. Even more interesting was seeing and hearing all of nature begin to shuffle on the farm: the rooster crowing, the cattle and sheep began to stir with a low bellow and a snappy bleat in the springtime as they "spoke" to their babies. Certain birds would rustle in the shelter belt and begin to sing as if to alert all of nature that "sunrise is on the way" for another day. The grass was often wet with dew, waiting for the sun's warmth to dry. The quiet ripple of the nearby stream blessed the frogs, now awakened, only to "squawk" again into the late evening at sunset. The deer and the antelope become aroused at the water's edge for a good drink and on their way to the grazing on the adjacent pastures. And most beautiful of all, the Chinese pheasant cockerels ambling slowly out of the shelter belt just in time to see the brilliant, huge, round sun appear on the far horizon to give light for the newborn day.

I hear King David from Psalm 30:1: "I will extol You, oh Lord, for You have lifted me up...weeping may endure for a night, but JOY comes in the morning."

In Luke 1 we read of patient, dedicated, faithful "old Zacharias" praising God as he waited for the promised Messiah, Jesus, to be born. As I looked eagerly for, and listened intently, for a sunrise on the prairies, Zacharias listened daily for a spiritual sunrise, the Son coming into full view over the eastern horizon, ushering in the day of grace for humanity to feast on and drink in freely. Quoting from Malachi 4:2: "The Dayspring (sunrise) from on high has visited us, to give light to those who sit in darkness."

The Messiah ("Light of the world") came from heaven to earth, died for our sins, and shed His blood to bathe us clean "Though your sins be as scarlet, they shall be white as snow, though they be crimson red, they shall be like wool" Isaiah 1:18. He was resurrected and ascended back to heaven with the promise: "I will come again and take you unto Myself." John 14:3. "I will never leave you, nor forsake you"

From one determined to: "...bless the Lord at all times; His praise shall continually be in my mouth. My soul shall make its boast in the Lord; and the humble shall hear of it, and be glad. Come, let us magnify the Lord. Let us exalt His name together." Psalm 34:3.

January 4

"He makes me to lie down in green pastures..." Psalm 23:1.

I am one who thanks and praises God for that wonderful gift of memory that He created us with, one of those "good and perfect gifts from above." James 1:17. I remember well that quiet, sunny, summer afternoon as a boy in the 1930's on the plains of Montana when I lay on a side hill watching over our flock of sheep. The joy of the setting strengthened my inner man, while the unbelievable peace of God surrounded me and a hunger for more of the psalms and the gospels pleased me, and the Word encouraged me out there in my carefree leisure time. It was like as with Mary and Martha, and Jesus had stopped by, and I was sitting at His feet that pleasant afternoon. Maybe He showed me a bit of Psalm 37, so appropriate for the setting where I love to rehearse vs. 3-7: "Trust in the Lord and do good; dwell in the land and feed on His faithfulness. Delight yourself in the Lord, and He shall give you the desires of your heart. Commit your way to the Lord; Trust also in Him, and He shall bring it to pass. He shall bring forth your righteousness as the light, and your justice as the noonday. Rest in the Lord and wait patiently for Him."

Then I could occasionally hear the bleating of a mother, and the response of her lamb as the flock would quietly pass by, diligently nipping off the blades of grass.

Sometimes it's necessary to step away from the noisy pressures of life and spend undistracted time with Jesus, as He purposely gives us those personal moments with Him, precious moments of heart-to-heart fellowship that refreshes and renews the spirit, soul, and body. "One thing is needed, and Mary has chosen that good part, which will not be taken away from her." Jesus, Luke 10:42

As I lay on that warm hillside overlooking the wide Poplar Valley, the river running in its very midst, and the vast acreage that spread out for miles in every direction, my sanctuary for the afternoon, I could appreciate that I had "the best seat in the house" on life's stage.

Psalmist David and I had similar testimonies when he penned Psalm 23, where we enjoy the quietness of Godly pastures: "The Lord is my shepherd; I shall not want. He makes me to lie down in green pastures; He leads me beside the still waters. He restores my soul, He leads me in the paths of righteousness for His name's sake..."

From one who enjoys the privilege and security of: "...we are His people, the sheep of His pasture..." Ps. 100:3.

January 5

"I have a dream..." Martin Luther King, Jr.

"I have a dream" cried out Martin Luther King, Jr. during the days of the civil rights birth forty years ago. Likewise, I have a vision, a picture, today of the Roman soldier decked out in full armor in his part in the birthing of Christendom at the cross at Calvary. When Paul described the full armor every believer needs spiritually for defense in this world, he fashioned it after the Roman soldier's armor that he dressed in every morning.

I see the Roman soldier without armor, and the Christian likewise, as an unprotected lamb out on the range, surrounded by coyotes. However, I also see both, decked out in their full available armor, capable of taking on the whole world as they leave their dwelling in the morning. To put on the armor with child-like faith in the Almighty God literally saturating it, is like putting garments on the clay body to protect it from the elements, and just as necessary every morning. To "gird my waist with truth" I listen to Jesus in John 17: 17: "Sanctify them by Your truth, Your Word is truth." "My son, give attention to My Words...they are life unto those who find them, and health unto their flesh." Proverbs 4:20. Be armed with Jesus in the heart, the Living Word, the ultimate Truth.

"The breastplate of righteousness" is the impenetrable blood of Jesus, that pure, clean, innocent, sinless blood we bathe the inner man with as we come daily to the cross, so that "though your sins are as scarlet, they shall be white like snow; though they be as crimson red, they shall be like wool." Isaiah 1:18. Because of child-like faith in the covering of the blood, "No weapon formed against me shall prosper this day." Isaiah 54:17. "When the enemy comes in like a flood, the Spirit of the Lord will raise up a standard against him." Isaiah 59:19.

Like a pony shod with a horse shoe to protect his feet for a peaceful journey with his rider over rugged terrain, so is Matthew 5:44 for a man's soul as he daily carries with him the author of peace, Jesus: "I say, love your enemies, bless them that curse you, do good for them that hate you; and pray for them that spitefully use you, and persecute you."

We see helmets worn by football players, cyclists, and construction workers to protect their head, inside of which is the mind, which the enemy loves to use as its workshop and playground by way of temptation for evil. The helmet of salvation, coupled with the "sword of the Spirit" gives us the identical weapon Jesus used to overcome temptation: "It is written." And then, three times He quoted scripture and the enemy left Him. "God's Word is living, powerful, and sharper than a double-edged sword..." Hebrews 4:12.

Faith in the Jesus who "descended into the bowels of the earth and overcame powers and principalities, and made an open show of them, triumphing over them in the victory He had just had on the cross" Colossians. 2:15, make Him a shield that protects us from the top of the head to the tip of the toe from the deadly, poisonous darts of the enemy. Let us remember: "The thief does not come but for to kill, to steal, and to destroy. I have come to give life, and to give life abundantly." Jesus, John 10:10.

Jesus, the Living Word, is my full armor this morning, and I pray and trust yours, too.

January 6

"...Consider your ways." Haggai 1:5, 7.

Well do I remember, with skepticism, the counsel from old Tom, my farmer neighbor of my dad's generation, when he said to me that a farmer never has any extra cash in his pocket until he retires. I was an arrogant young punk out to show an old jigger like that, until after fifty three years, at my retirement, I humbly remembered and respected old Tom as a man of truth and wisdom I once scoffed at. He was right on. In both of our lifetime's generations, any surplus cash we might have enjoyed went for expansion, updating equipment, keeping up on livestock inventory, and then times of coping with drought, hail, grasshoppers, and poor prices for our products. Neighbor Tom was right; farmers are the biggest legalized gamblers in the world!!

As I look back on my days since retirement, I see what a blessing my mate and I enjoyed spiritually as we feasted on God's Word and prayer in our troubled times. I wonder what unchecked prosperity might have done for us, both for the now and for eternity.

And here I consider the Israelites as they fared forty years of wilderness life before crossing the Jordan River to a land of "milk and honey", a land of prosperity. In Deuteronomy 8, Moses seemed more afraid of the coming prosperity than the past rigors of the wilderness desert.

So he wrote: "The Lord your God is bringing you into a good land, a land of brooks of water...a land in which you will eat bread without scarcity, in which you will lack nothing...when you have eaten and are full, then you shall bless the Lord your God for the good land He has given you. Beware that you do not forget the land...lest when you have eaten and are full, and have built beautiful houses and dwell in them; and when your herds and your flocks multiply, and your silver and gold multiply, and all that you have is multiplied; when your heart is lifted up...you shall remember the Lord your God, for it is He who has given you power to get wealth..." Deuteronomy 8:18.

What a message for America who in pre-WWII days found most people without much prosperity, filling our churches for worship every Sunday. But the uncanny prosperity of post-WWII days has emptied our churches by and large, and alienated many of the wealthy from God. Moses would share with us: "Therefore you shall keep the commandments of the Lord your God, to walk in His ways, and to fear Him." Deuteronomy 8:6.

"How much better to get wisdom than gold, and to get understanding is to be chosen rather than silver." Proverbs 16: 16.

From one who hears the warning of Haggai: "Thus says the Lord of hosts: consider your ways."

January 7

"Sufficient for the day..."

Good morning, friends, sitting up to the breakfast table prepared for the inner man at the Lord's invitation: "Therefore, come boldly before the throne of grace to obtain mercy, and to find grace to help in time of need." Hebrews 4:16. "My grace is sufficient for you," one day at a time, even today.

Ranchers out in the hills and valleys under the Big Sky in Montana learn early in the winter how many bales of hay or pounds of grain pellets to unload for the herd's consumption for just one day, while allowing for that day's temperature. If a rancher should carry two or three day's supply onto the feeding area, good, green, lush alfalfa hay would become expensive bedding, since the herd would eat its fill and then lay overnight on the remainder, making it unpalatable. "Sufficient unto the day is the evil thereof." Matthew 6:34

So we find Moses and the Israelites in a similar situation immediately after coming out of Egypt and across the Red Sea, manna from above daily, sufficient for that day only, a manna that would spoil if hoarded even for one day ahead. I remember well the day Jesus dealt with me regarding that "me-first syndrome" and greed in the early days of building an "empire" at any cost. There is something about the ugly spirit of greed and hoarding that destroys the sweet, sweet spirit of faith and trust.

God spoke to Paul similar wisdom and exhortation in II Corinthians 12:9: "My grace is sufficient for you for my strength is made perfect in weakness." "Out of your need will I provide and make your faith strong as you rely on Me daily, one day at a time" the Lord is clearly saying to us here. I have never seen this better lived out than with George Mueller of nineteenth century London, who managed a large orphanage most of his adult life, and never knew even a day ahead where the food would come from. But, not a single meal was missing on the hour it was needed. His faith in God and his time on his knees proved "sufficient for the day" for out of his weakness was the Lord's strength made perfect.

Jesus taught us to pray: "Give us this day our daily bread," His desire is to give us each day as we trust Him, and we will never see want. "Seek ye first the kingdom of God and all these things (food, housing, and raiment) shall be added unto you: Therefore, do not worry about tomorrow, for tomorrow will worry about its own things. Sufficient for the day is its own trouble." Matthew 6:33-34.

January 8

All it takes is one!

I opened the letter and found a survey I was asked to sign and return within seventy-two hours. My natural thought: "Will this ONE more return really make any difference?" It takes a hundred pennies to make a full dollar; and it takes twelve eggs to make a dozen; and eleven men to fill out a complete football team in the NFL.

Being a history buff, I remember Aaron Burr was short only one electoral vote to become a U.S. President. One positive vote brought

Texas into the Union, and one vote kept President Andrew Jackson from impeachment.

Martin Luther was one bold, fearless, single man of passion and conviction when he nailed the ninety-five thesis to the church door in Wittenberg, Germany, and gave us the Protestant theology: "For by grace are you saved through faith, not of your own, but a gift from God, not of works, lest anyone should boast." Ephesians 2:8-9.

Getting back to myself, I thought of that ONE person in my life most responsible for my eternal life...my mother, who first acquainted me with Jesus, and then insisted on Sunday School, Church every Sunday without fail, confirmation, and Bible camp experience many summers.

Of all the young, pure, maidservants in Galilee to choose from, the angel Gabriel was sent to Nazareth, to a virgin, of the house of David. Her name was Mary: "Then the angel said to her 'Do not be afraid, Mary, for you have found favor with God.'" Luke 1:30. "You will conceive and bring forth a Son, and shall call His name Jesus." Vs. 31. "For with God nothing will be impossible." Vs. 37.

In God's plan for humanity along the way, Abraham, Gideon, Moses, Noah, Hannah, David, Daniel, Paul, Peter, James, and John, when called of God, might hear the same as Mary heard: "With God nothing will be impossible" as He convinced them to take charge of their post on this earth.

Are you ready to grasp the truth that you be the ONE consecrated to Jesus for ONE special chore under God's anointing?

From one who prays daily "Use me, oh Lord; make me a blessing to You."

January 9

God's Word, full of "stone memorials."

On many lawns in Sioux Falls are large, heavy rocks, some of which I am sure are placed as a memorial of the old family farm that a son or daughter wants to remember.

My mate, Alice, has one such large rock out in the pasture of her childhood farm days in Iowa. Many missionaries had visited her parent's farm home when she was growing up, and the exciting stories from Africa and other mission fields stirred her heart to become a missionary when grown up. At age eleven, she had a lamb of her own, and when she sold the lamb's fleece, she bought her first Bible... now well on her way to becoming a REAL missionary. Out in the pasture, alongside a pond of water where the cows lay on a sunny day, chewing their cud, their eyes half asleep, and Alice, sitting on a large rock with her Bible on her lap, practiced preaching to a pretty sleepy congregation. The rock will always be a memorial of her preaching, and she claims, the origin of the "holy cow."

God's Word is full of "stone" memorials. One such one is found in I Samuel which came into being "When the Philistine leaders heard about the great crowds at Mizpah, and they mobilized their army and advanced. The Israelis were badly frightened. "Plead with God to save us!" they cried to Samuel. Just as Samuel was sacrificing the burnt offering, the Philistines arrived from battle; but the Lord spoke with a mighty voice of thunder from Heaven, and they were thrown into confusion." Vs. 7-10.

"The Lord frustrates the devices of the crafty before their hands can carry out their plans. " Job 5:12.

"The Israelis routed them and chased them...killing them along the way." Vs. 11. "Samuel then took a stone and placed it between Mizpah and Ashanah, and named it Ebenezer (meaning "the stone of Help")...for the Lord has certainly helped us." Vs. 12.

From the plains of Montana, from one who knows both the blessing and the curse of a large rock.

January 10

"...Lord, remember me..." Luke 23:42

Sometime during the teens of the last century, a man immigrated from Europe to America, married a pretty young woman, and accumulated a family of nine by the time of the depression days of the 1930's. He then developed cancer, left his family to make a final visit to his homeland, after saying goodbye to his young mate and family. Whether he promised to return or not I do not know, but I can imagine his loved ones craved to see him one more time, but his cancer took his life instead. One of the brood later shared bitterly with me how he had felt deserted as a little boy in such troublesome times for his mother's heavy responsibility.

So it must have been for Joseph in Genesis 40, deserted by the promise of a butler in a prison in Pharaoh's Egypt. Joseph was not only innocently incarcerated, but jilted by his friend, whose dream Joseph had interpreted, and for the favor, a promise to plead for Joseph's release when he suddenly was set free. But two more years passed by because the butler failed to remember his promise.

But there is One who never forgets even the least of us. On that Good Friday afternoon, while Jesus hung on a cross between two thieves, a miracle happened. Something magnetic about Jesus caused one of the thieves to cry out: "Remember me..." And Jesus immediately promised: "Today will you be with Me in Paradise." And Jesus kept His promise. And that thief's name now is written in the Lamb's book of life. From eternal death unto life; from bitterness to joy; an impenetrable, stony heart exchanged for a heart of flesh." Ezekiel 36:26.

"For I am not ashamed of the gospel of Christ, for it is the power of God unto salvation." Romans 1:16.

Like the thief, I am one who has tasted of Jeremiah 33:3: "Call upon Me and I will answer you, and show you great and mighty things you do not know."

January 11

"For one's life does not consist in the abundance of things he possesses." Luke 12:15

Nevertheless, I am one who is always encouraged to see a farmer succeed, young or old, large acreage or small, rich or poor. One day when I drove by one of the farmland acreage's I left behind in Montana, I was surprised and encouraged to find my three steel bins with a total of nine thousand bushels capacity gone, and replaced by two steel bins with a total capacity of fifty two thousand bushels. The young brothers have bought many more acres all around, and my farm acreage is the center, along a good, year-round highway. I am encouraged that the two hardworking brothers, super managers, are doing so well.

Then, when I drove by another acreage, I found several steel bins with a capacity of fifteen thousand bushels cuddled up beside my single little bin, one a "hopper bottom" bin for easy unloading.

A few years ago a farmer I mingled with in Montana retired, and with an imaginary problem. He couldn't empty the full Quonset in his view because wheat was a poor price. Sometime later, the price increased considerably, but he couldn't sell then without facing an income tax problem. In my unsympathetic frame of mind, that rich man wanted the best of both worlds!!

"Thy Word have I hidden in my heart..." Psalm 139:11, and out it popped as I considered these three farmers: Then Jesus spoke a parable to them from Luke 12: "The ground of a certain rich man yielded plentifully, and he thought within himself, saying, 'What shall I do, since I have no room to store my crops?...I will pull down my barns and build greater, and will store all my crops...And I will say to my soul... take your ease; eat, drink, and be merry.' But God said to him: 'Fool!! This night your soul will be required of you; then, whose will those things be...?'" "So is he who lays up treasure for himself, and is not rich toward God." Luke 12:16-21.

"Beloved, I pray that you may prosper in all things, and be in health, just as your soul prospers." 111 John 1:2...by sharing generously your time, talent, and treasure.

From one who stands daily on James 1:17: "Every good gift and every perfect gift is from above..."

January 12

"My son, give attention to My Words...they are life unto those who find them and health unto their flesh." Proverbs 4:20-21.

Good counsel that even my herd of cows on the Montana ranch could say "Amen" to—food and water handed to them on a silver platter every morning!!!—would arise very early on a cold, cold January morning, prepare a meal from God's Word for the radio broadcast, enjoy a warm breakfast at my dining room table, and head out to the herd of cows a mile and a half to the south, to give them their ration of hay for the day. Daily, I would see them rise up from their steaming bed of straw, and begin to follow my tractor loaded with a large bale of nice green hay, a long, single queue headed for the hillside or, on a windy day, into a deep ravine to satisfy their hunger. Only a short while later, the same parade back to the corral for a drink of water, a ritual that lasted all day long, and all winter long, a manna for the belly and living water for the thirst. Feed and water, not only "life unto those who found it, and health unto their flesh," but also for the little baby they were carrying in the womb, so that in the springtime each mother could proudly show off her calf, also full of "life and health," like our inner man when fed God's Word.

Our daily devotional time ought to be like that: regular, filled with God's Word, satisfying to the soul, with praise and prayer providing living water to satisfy the thirsty soul looking for "life and health" which only God Himself can provide as He lays Himself out before us.

"Wild Bill," my Montana neighbor, picked up a Bible in a motel room one evening, and for the first time in his many years of life opened its pages, was fed generously, drank of the living water, shed tears from a truly repentant heart—repentant of alcoholism, gambling, fighting, greed and a long list of ungodliness, and by morning was "a brand new creation, old things passed away, all things become new," truly born again, a true testimony of the power of the Word of God, "life unto those find it and health unto their flesh."

"Be thankful to Him, and bless His name, for the Lord is good, His mercy is everlasting and His truth endures to all generations." Psalm 100:4-5.

January 13

"For the poor you have with you always," Matthew 26:11, Jesus speaking.

I remember so well that picture of five widows, grandmothers, including my own, sitting outdoors on an old wooden bench, perhaps at a community picnic. It was during the depression days of the early 1930's, on a hot, sunny, dry day during the long drought in Montana. Their birthdays dated back to the 1850's, their faces stern and weathered by long years of what we would today call "hardship," all of them farm wives. As it was with most oldsters in those days, their home was now with a son or daughter and family, in the absence of "old folk's homes", assisted living facilities, nursing homes. In most cases, their assets were not much more than their clothes on their backs. They lived in the "horse and buggy" days of senior citizens care in America. I remember what I thought, but what does God think and say about caring for the grandpas and grandmas all around us?

We read from Exodus 22:22-23: "You shall not afflict any widow or fatherless child. If you afflict them in any way, and they cry out to Me, I will surely hear their cry; and My wrath will become hot..."

From the street of a northern city in India we hear the cry of a seventy year old widow, a mother who says: "My son tells me: 'You have grown old. Now who is going to feed you? Go away.'" She cries out: "What do I do? My pain has no limit." Tragic!! "No place to hang her hat."

But Jesus, who searches every heart, tells it like this in Matthew 25:34: "Then the King will say to those on His right hand, 'Come, you blessed of My Father, inherit the kingdom prepared for you, for I was hungry and you gave Me food; I was thirsty and you gave Me drink; I was a stranger and you took Me in; I was naked and you clothed Me; I was sick and you visited Me..." And the crowd asked in so many Words: "When did we do all this to You?" And Jesus answered and said: "Inasmuch as you did it to one of the least of these ... you did it to Me."

Let us imitate our Father and hear the cries of our needy as He hears them, be they needs of the flesh or needs of the inner man.

January 14

"A friend in need is a friend indeed." A cliché.

About three weeks after my wife Lois' demise in **August 19**95, I and my combine crew came home at dark to find a nice meal laid out before us on the cupboard. Imagine the joy of a small group of hungry harvesters!! Attached to the aluminum foil wrap was the married name of one foreign to me, but soon discovered as a young lady from twenty five miles away who had remembered me as a Bible study teacher years earlier. That manifestation of friendship is still lingering after these fourteen years.

I recently read: "A friend is the first person who comes in when the whole world has gone out." Amen and Amen!!

In I Samuel 30 we find David drawing much encouragement from Jonathan while demented King Saul hunted him down like a hound dog. Jonathan had an inside track as Saul's son and said to David: "If it pleases my father to do you evil, then I will report to you and send you away, that you may go safely." I Samuel 20:13. "Now Jonathan loved him (David); for he loved him as he loved his own soul." Vs. 17.

That's sacrificial love like Jesus manifested on that cross at Calvary. "What a friend we have in Jesus; All our sins and griefs to bear!...Do thy friends despise, forsake thee? Take it to the Lord in prayer." A favorite hymn.

From one who cherishes my many genuine friends as against the "fairweather" ones.

January 15

"The Lord talked to you face to face" Deuteronomy 5:4

Yes, that was the day He shared Paul's letter to the Ephesians from chapter 2: "You He made alive who were born dead in trespasses and sins, in which you once walked according to the course of this world, according to the prince of the air, the spirit who now works in the sons of disobedience, among whom also we all once conducted ourselves in the lusts of our flesh, fulfilling the desires of the flesh and of the mind, and were by nature children of wrath, just as like others. But God who is rich in mercy because of His great love with which He loved us, even when we were dead in trespasses, made us alive together with Christ (by grace you have been saved), and raised up together, and made us sit together in heavenly places in Christ. For by grace you have been saved, not of yourselves, it is a gift of God, not of works, lest any man shall boast."

An anonymous writer puts it like this with a testimony entitled:

I MET THE MASTER, FACE TO FACE
I had walked life's path with an easy tread
Had followed where comfort and pleasure led;
And then one day in a quiet place, I met the Master face to face.
With station and rank and wealth for a goal,
Much thought for the body, not much for the soul;
I had thought to win in life's mad race,
When I met the Master, face to face.
I met Him and knew Him, and blushed to see
That His eyes filled with sorrow were turned on me;
And I faltered and fell at His feet that day,
While all my castles melted away.
Melted and vanished, and in their place
I saw nothing else but my Master's face;
And I cried aloud, "Make me meet
To follow the path of Thy wounded feet."
And now my thoughts are for the souls of men
I've lost my life, to find it again,
For since that day in a quiet place,
I met the Master face to face.

January 16

Jesus Christ—God's dream manifested

"Hush!" I shouted to the congregation of men gathered around me in my dream. "Listen to that voice I hear on the radio." The men burst into laughter and asked: "Don't you recognize that voice? You should. It's yours." Then I awakened that spring morning of 1975. I tucked the dream away into my memory bank, not even sharing with my mate. Our group of men had accumulated many good, reputable teaching tapes during those charismatic days, and one day in late summer I suggested "This is too good for us to keep to ourselves.

Let us put them on KCGM radio, a new service to our community, an FM station with power to reach out about one hundred miles, even into Canada." The men unanimously agreed, and offered to finance it. I was delegated to visit the radio administrator, and we were received well and given prime time. Months later, when we had exhausted our supply of good tapes, I was asked to go on live every weekday morning, since I had already been editing the tapes each morning. Hence, Gospel Good News was born, and is still alive after almost thirty-three years, at fifteen minutes per day.

I write this today on Martin Luther King's birthday, the man who also had a dream, a dream to set the black man free in America from the bondage of slavery and racism.

What a blessing for our nation as black men and women have been taken out of bondage as they individually choose, and have risen to the "top" in politics, in banking, in theatre, in sports, in music, in education, in government, in the medical world, the writer's world, and in the evangelistic thrust of our nation.

Martin Luther King, Jr. was assassinated for his dream, but his people were set free.

Joseph, too, had a dream. "There we were binding sheaves in the field. Then, behold, my sheaf arose and also stood upright; and indeed your sheaves stood all around and bowed down to my sheaf" Genesis 37:17. Out of jealousy, his brothers sold him to "a company of Ishmaelites" on the way to Egypt, where he spent thirteen years in prison because of a conjured up sexual assault case.

His dream of yesteryear finalized when a terrible famine overcame Israel, and Joseph, now second in command in Egypt under the Pharaoh, saw his brothers bow down to him for food like his dream had revealed, a blessing for the hungry outer man like mine was for the hungry, thirsty, inner man.

"The Spirit of the Lord is upon Me, because I have been anointed to preach good news to the poor, to heal the broken hearted, to set the captives free, to restore sight to the blind, and to set free them that are bruised." Jesus, Luke 4:18.

Is not Jesus God's "dream" manifested?

January 17

"The Lord is my light and my salvation..." Psalms 27:1

    It was bedtime the other evening when we heard an electrical breaker snap off about two blocks away, casting absolute pure darkness in and around our home, jet black darkness all over the immediate neighborhood. Later reflection caused me to rehearse Genesis 1:3: "Then God said, 'let there be light; and there was light. And God saw the light, that it was good; and God divided the light from the darkness, and God called the light day, and the darkness He called night." Can you imagine with me the density of darkness when "the earth was without form and void" Vs. 2. That is surely the same density of the inner-man, born from a mother's womb, each of us an heir of inherent sin. As God said "let there be light for the secular world," I hear Him say "let there be light for the inner-man" when the Holy Spirit acts like a magnet to pull, lift one out of the world of darkness, death, and destruction, into the world of light as we come with childlike faith to the foot of the cross with a genuine confession of sin from a truly repentant heart. David had experienced this wonderful gift of salvation, and sang out in Psalm 30: "I will extol You, oh Lord, for You have lifted me up...You have brought my soul up from the grave... weeping may endure for a night, but joy comes in the morning." From eternal darkness in Hell to eternal joy and light in Heaven.
    "The Lord is my light and my salvation; whom shall I fear" Psalm 27:1.
    "Truly the light is sweet, and it is pleasant for the eyes to behold the sun..." Eccl. 11:7.
    "Thy Word is a lamp unto my feet, and a light unto my path." Psalm 119:105.

January 18

"Let her glean among the sheaves ..." Boaz. Ruth 2:15

    Early in my grain-farming career I learned about "gleaning" of grain much like Ruth learned from Naomi's relative, Boaz. Ruth 2.

Annually, at harvest time, my neighbor that I harvested with had Michigan relatives come to visit. They paid close attention to every stop we harvesters made out in the field of grain. The "return grain auger" would occasionally plug on the little Case combine for various reasons, and the vertical auger required opening a door at the bottom, close to the ground, out of which would pour up to a half-bushel of cracked grain, hulls, chaff, green weeds, and good, whole grain. At every stop the Michigan gleaners would come with a "gunny" sack and a small shovel to retrieve the grain for chicken food in the winter months ahead. Out West, our practice was to leave the little piles for the deer, antelope, pheasants, and other birds to eat.

"Love your hurting neighbor" was the gist of God's command in the days of bare-hand harvest by going over the crop only once and leave the "waste" for the gleaners from town. He put it like this from Deuteronomy 24:20-22: "When you beat your olive trees, do not go over the boughs again; it shall be for the fatherless, the stranger, and the widow. When you gather your grapes from the vineyard, you shall not glean it afterward; it shall be for the fatherless, the stranger, the widow."

To this day, "Let each one give as he purposes in his heart, not grudgingly or of necessity; for God loves a cheerful giver." II Corinthians 9:7.

Praise God for His abundance here in America!

January 19

".. and the Lord said to Elijah...on the third year I will send rain on the earth." I Kings 18:1

My first trial in the business world came in 1937, at the ripe old age of eleven years. It was the final year of severe drought in Montana, and almost the end of the "great depression." No grass sprouted in the springtime, and no seeded crops took root. Consequently, there was no pasture for grazing, no harvest of feed or grain crops. The government had an emergency program whereby ranchers could sell their livestock to the government and get paid a meager penny per pound. I can still vividly remember the hour my five year old, fifteen hundred pound cow went up a loading chute into a truck to be hauled away, a cow my dad had given me earlier, intended to be my start of a herd someday. But now she is gone, my first business venture, sold for a cent per pound, fifteen dollars. My dad wept with me, but never offered to replace the cow. He taught me to "take it on the chin." What a character builder I can now see that was!

A terrible flood on July 13 of that year broke the drought cycle, and from 1938 on, normal rainfall returned, after eight years of severe drought.

So it was with Elijah and a widow of Zarephath we read of in I Kings 17. During a three year drought, Prophet Elijah's source of water completely dried up, the Brook of Chereth, and one day God directed him to seek out a widow of Zarephath for help. For those who trust and obey God always has a way: a bit of faith, a heart of obedience, a tiny measure of flour, a few drops of oil, and a compassionate heart for the man of God miraculously extended these three lives, and soon the famine ended. Later the son's dead body was resurrected as the Prophet ministered to him, and the Lord used the Prophet abundantly for ministry throughout the land.

"Trust in the Lord with all your heart...acknowledge Him in ALL your ways, and He will direct your paths." Proverbs 3:5-6. Tried and tested!

January 20

"Out of the abundance of the heart the mouth speaks." Matthew 12:34

It was a dark, miserably cold evening when my unsaved friend sat within a group of campers on the bank of the Hungry Horse River in western Montana, the first day of Bible camp, unknown by any of the men around him. His truly born again spouse had encouraged him to come with her, knowing his need. Out of the abundance of his fleshy heart spewed "murmuring and complaining" from an attitude that led a sheepskin—covered man to look at him and say; "You need Jesus!" My friend's proud, sullen rebellious heart raised the silent question: "What does that "sheepherder" know about what I need?" Within twenty-four hours, ministry had delivered him from demonic forces deep within, and he became a "brand new creature, old things passed away, all things become new." I Corinthians 5:17. Justified!! Now ready for a lot of sanctification! "Then I will sprinkle clean water on you...I will give you a new heart, and put a new spirit within you, I will take the heart of stone out of you and give you a heart of flesh. I will put my Spirit within you." Ezekiel 36:25-26. What a transformation for that one "who will open the door and let Me in." Revelation 3:20.

My friend experienced the necessary confession of sin from a truly repentant heart, as did King David, "the apple of God's eye," we read of from 2 Samuel 12. Both appreciated and accepted correction. David's parade of sins started from a housetop, with lust for Bathsheba, a night of fornication and adultery, the murder of her husband, and the conception of an illegitimate son.

A loyal friend with a heart full of love is God in action..."You need Jesus!" So the Lord sent Prophet Nathan to David with a concocted story to illustrate David's sin; whereby a rich man in town owned a flock of sheep, while a neighbor owned only one ewe lamb, a pet of the family. To prepare a "lamb chop" meal for a friend passing by, the rich man stole the only sheep of his neighbor. On that note, David became angry and shouted out: "As the Lord lives, this man shall surely die! And he shall restore four-fold for the lamb because he did this thing; because he had no pity." Then Nathan said to David: "You are the man!" After much chastising from the Lord, He said: "For you did it secretly, but I will expose you to all of Israel." David said to Nathan: "I have sinned against the Lord." And Nathan said to David: "The Lord has put away your sin; you shall not die."

"If we confess our sin, God is faithful and just to forgive our sin, and to cleanse us from all unrighteousness." I John 1:9. "You can be sure your sin will find you out." Numbers 32:23.

January 21

"Are they (angels) not all ministering spirits...?" Hebrews 1:14.

I surely accepted angels as such one late fall afternoon in Montana. It was hunting season, and it had rained many days, so that all the earth was soaking wet. A couple teen-age hunters stuck their pickup into a soft field of my neighbor's and walked to my tractor a few miles away, and at night, stuck it also while trying to retrieve their pickup. On the morrow, upon hearing of the fiasco, a friend and I took my four-wheel drive farm tractor to the scene, and while I backed the tractor toward the stuck pickup, my friend stood between the two vehicles to hook the chain, and at a precise moment I discovered my throw-out bearing was gone out so the tractor would not stop. I immediately shut down the ignition, sparing my friend's body from being crushed. To God be the glory as I credited angelic power for the miracle.

Then I heard from God's Word: "For He shall give His angels charge over you to keep you in all your ways. In their hands they shall bear you up, lest you should dash your foot against a stone." Psalm 91:11-12. How good to know that we sinners on this earth can be blessed by the same promise as sinless Jesus we find in Matthew 4:6 when Satan tempted Jesus to jump off from a high pinnacle, and Jesus could stand on that same promise, in both cases because of the love of God for both His adopted sons and His "only begotten Son."

So often, if our eyes are open and our faith active, we see how an angel saves lives, and protects us from injury or death. So it was with Salaam we find in Numbers 22:31: "Then the Lord opened Salaam's eyes, and he saw the Angel of the Lord standing in his way with a drawn sword in his hand...and the angel of the Lord said to him 'Why have you struck your donkey three times? Behold, I have come out to stand against you because your way is perverse against Me. The donkey saw Me and turned aside from Me these three times. If she had not turned aside from Me, surely I would have killed you and let her live.' And Salaam said to the Angel of the Lord, 'I have sinned, for I did not know You stood against me. Now, therefore, if it displeases You, I will turn back.'" What extreme God will go to bring a man to confession and repentance!!

"You can be sure your sin will find you out." Numbers 32:23.

From one who can hardly wait for the Lord to show me how many times angels played into my life.

January 22

"My grace is sufficient for you..." II Corinthians 12:9

"Therefore, come boldly before the throne of grace to obtain mercy, and to find grace to help in time of need." Hebrews 4:16. Strangely, this invitation became especially significant this Christmas season when I was reminded again that there had to be a birth before there could be a death, the manifestation of "grace". It all began at Bethlehem and culminated at Calvary where a perfect sacrifice was made to cover humanity's sin, when on that cross Christ's body was broken and His side pierced to flow pure, clean, innocent, sinless blood to wash away sin for the truly repentant heart. That's grace. I was praying, with supplication, for help for a serious physical need, and I heard; "My grace is sufficient for you, for My strength is made perfect in weakness." The same Word Paul received when he "pleaded three times that it (a thorn in the flesh) might depart from me." II Corinthians 12:8. I marveled and learned a lesson in the way Paul accepted God's stern Word: "Therefore, I take pleasure in infirmities..." Vs. 10.

Then I joyfully remembered all the trials and tribulations He had already pulled me through because of that wonderful power of "grace" and how many times grace worked in my life that I am not at all cognizant of over these eighty-four years, years when I enjoyed the love, joy, peace, hope, and security we all covet.

I learn so much from Paul, and now I can see how he lived through and fared so well when I read from II Corinthians 11, where we read of his trials and tribulations, proving to me that walking with God as close as Paul did after Damascus is not always a "bed of roses" which many people expect. "I speak as a fool...in labors more abundant, in stripes beyond measure, in prisons frequently, in death more often. From the Jews I received forty stripes minus one. Three times I was beaten with rods; three times stoned; three times I was shipwrecked; a night and a day I have been in the deep; in journeys often, in perils of waters, in perils of robbers, in perils of my own countrymen, in perils of the Gentiles, in perils of the city, in perils in the wilderness, in perils in the sea, in perils among false brethren, in weariness and toil, in sleeplessness often, in hunger and in thirst, in fastings often, in cold and nakedness."

"Bless the Lord, oh my soul, and all that is within me, bless His holy name."

January 23

"Yet it pleased the Lord...to put Him to death." Isaiah 53:5.

I remember well that May day in the 1930's when our neighbor to the west, Fisher, went out to prepare his garden for seeding with only a spade, a hoe, and a few matches to first burn off the thrash from last year. The east wind carried the fire out into the valleys and over the hills of his neighbor's pastures and fields. Every neighbor dropped what they were doing to fight the fire in absence of rural fire-fighting equipment in those days. Tractors went out with plows to turn up black, wet barriers, and soon the fire was over. There was no wonder as to who had started it, but only forgiveness for the man short of equipment, and with a large family to care for. Retaliation and lawsuits were unheard of on the western prairies, as was the "blame game."

How many times since 9/11 have we turned on our TV to see a large fire belching black smoke into the clouds over Iraq, perpetrated by America's enemy in that Asian world? Proud of their dastardly act of killing and burning down walls of buildings, someone always steps out to "claim the blame", or shall we say "take the credit."

Over the years I have heard so many people blame the angry Romans for killing Jesus; but guess what? God takes the blame, in that it was a central theme of God's plan for the salvation of lost humanity's inherent sin problem. Only a perfect sacrifice would satisfy God, One put through the fire. The prophet Isaiah foretold the death of the promised Messiah like this: "He was wounded for our transgressions, He was bruised for our iniquities; the chastisement for our peace was upon Him, and by His stripes we are healed...yet it pleased the Lord to bruise Him; He has put Him to grief." Isaiah 53:5, 10.

God claimed responsibility for the death of His son so that anyone can claim the forgiveness from His Son, and the blessing of Isaiah 1 :18: "...Though your sins be as scarlet, they shall be as white as snow; though they be crimson red, they shall be like wool."

It was not because of carelessness, nor of anger and retaliation, but out of a heart of love that God sacrificed His Son: "For God so loved the world that He gave His only begotten Son, that whosoever believes in Him shall not perish, but have everlasting life." John 3:16

"Thank You, Jesus!!"

January 24

"Do not fear or be dismayed, for the battle is not yours, but God's." II Chronicles 20:15

"Breaking News" suddenly flashed across the TV screen, followed almost instantly with a picture of a forced plane landing on the Hudson River in New York. The experienced, alert pilot, with mechanical problems, was forced down for a perfect water landing. He alone was responsible for many lives. For occupants on either shore, the appearance of a plane was sudden, unexpected, and nondestructive. It looked like everything was "made to order," as it was so quiet and perfect.

So it was that evening when "Jesus told His disciples to get into the boat and cross to the other side of the lake." Matthew 14:22. And so it was, that suddenly and unexpected, after night fell, "the disciples were in trouble, for the winds had risen and they were fighting heavy seas." Vs. 24. But their loving, experienced, wise, "Pilot", Jesus, suddenly came to their rescue, walking unrecognized on the waves..."they thought He was a ghost." Vs. 36. Jesus, their "pilot" spoke to them: "Be of good cheer! It is I, do not be afraid." "And when they (Jesus and Peter) got into the boat, the wind ceased." Vs. 32. A perfect landing with no casualties!!

Breaking News: "Pilot Jesus quiets the waves...no casualties."

"No trial has overtaken you but such as is common to man (in the air, on land, or sea), but God is faithful, Who will not allow you to be tried beyond what you are able to stand, but with the trial will also make a way of escape, that you may be able to bear it." I Corinthians 10:13. (Parenthesis mine).

"God is our refuge and our strength; a very present help in trouble." Psalm 46:1.

From one who is trusting Jesus to safely "pilot" me into the eternal haven above....

January 25

"Rejoice with those who rejoice, and weep with those who weep." Romans 12:15

It was a bleak spring day in 1902 when the saddle horse came back to my Grandpa's ranch, dragging my twelve year old Uncle Henry. His foot had slipped through the uncovered saddle stirrup, evidently as he tried to dismount some place out there on the wide open prairies, or as he tried to get back into the saddle after a short rest, or maybe a "potty call." I've tried hard to imagine the fear and helplessness and hopelessness that attacked his young mind when that horse took those first steps, his small body literally hanging, and his head bouncing on the hard grassland roots. I can picture the tears flowing like a river, and his pleading for the horse to stop at his command. Then the fear of evident death as he perhaps quickly gauged the miles back home. Finally, the time of delirium and the loss of consciousness before the final sting of death as he passed into eternity. Can you imagine the pioneer parents and the ten siblings without a neighbor, nor a mortician, pastor or even a cemetery within sixty miles? So, they made a wooden box, dressed him in his "best", and buried him on a side hill near the farmstead. Years later, when a town emerged nearby, they "resurrected" the body and moved it into the community cemetery.

And here I think of the day when Jesus was literally "dragged" through the streets of Jerusalem, bearing His own cross, on their way to crucify Him on that cross at Calvary. Excruciating pain, unbearable fatigue, physical weakness, drenching perspiration, blood flowing freely from the stripes on His back, surely with each step, the distance left. Humanly speaking, the Divine Man, must have experienced hopelessness and helplessness, but "for the joy that was set before Him, He endured the cross." Hebrews 12:2. I've tried to imagine the shocking pain when they drove the huge spikes through His hands and feet to fasten Him to that cross. And then that dark Good Friday afternoon, how His body's weight must have almost shut off His breathing. But, most painful of all, when the cup of sin was poured over His head and His Father turned His back, causing a broken heart to cry out: "My God, My God, why have You forsaken Me?" Then the time of physical delirium and His last Word after "He gave up His Spirit—'It is finished'".

The family's "resurrection" of Henry's body and God's resurrection of Jesus' body have nothing in common. One has stayed dead to this hour, while the Other rose up alive forever. Hallelujah!! At the one "resurrection" there was only a sad rehearsal, while at the Other, the best good news ever told: "He is risen."

"I know that my Redeemer lives ... how my heart yearns within me." Job 19:25, 27.

January 26

"...I die daily." Paul, I Corinthians 15:31

One warm, quiet evening at a river near Richland, Montana, I sat embarrassed, fleshly proud, humiliated, and even wanting to laugh. We charismatics had just come from a Sunday church service where it was suggested this foot-washing. I watched the enthusiastic ones while I refused, like Peter in John 13:8. I was ignorant, so that it looked to me like works and foolishness. However, thirty years later while us six deacons at Abiding Savior washed each other's feet on the platform before the congregation, I concurred, because I had heard Jesus in the meantime from God's Word: "He poured water into a basin and began to wash the disciples' feet and to wipe them with a towel."

From John 13:5 I began to see some sense, some value, some power, and even a necessity when He proceeded, and then settled a rebuff from Peter: "You shall never wash my feet!" Vs. 8. Peter, like me, was perhaps also embarrassed, proud, humiliated, and ignorant of Jesus' purpose. Jesus quickly convinced him: "If I do not wash your feet, you have no part with me." Vs. 8. Convicted Peter lost no time: "Lord, not my feet only, but also my hands and my head." Vs. 9. When Jesus then explained perhaps the theology of it, that: once you are bathed in the blood of Jesus, your inherent sin is now "white like snow", Isaiah 1:18. Your daily washing keeps you "all clean." Jesus: "He who is bathed needs only to wash his feet..." Vs. 10. In those days two thousand years ago, the bare-foot man dirtied his feet as he traveled the dusty trails, and, like me, is so prone to dirty his heart because of temptation, and the weakness of the "old flesh nature."

Brother Paul puts it like this in I Corinthians 15:31: "I affirm...I die daily."

We all need to pray and repent with Peter's final humility: "Search me, oh Lord, and know my heart, try me and know my thoughts, and see if there be any wicked way within me."David, Psalm 139:23.

From one who needs "to know wisdom and instruction, to receive Words of understanding..." Proverbs 1:2.

January 27

"If we confess our sin ..." 1 John 1:9...a bridge is built.

The heavy rains descended from above, and the flood waters arose and washed out the bridge on Highway #13, leaving a wide, deep gulch. Until bridge builders came on the scene days later, the north and south sides had no communication, making the highway useless.

Today's news channel told of another bridge that was appropriately put in place when Letterman stepped up on TV to face the whole world and apologize to Governor Sarah Palin, whose daughters had unnecessarily suffered shame and disgrace by a "cute", sarcastic joke he spelled out recently over his show. I PTL (Praise the Lord) that heartfelt conviction drove him to come like a gentleman to build a bridge of communication. She graciously accepted the apology.

As a child, a parent, and a friend, I've been on both sides...sometimes a bridge destroyer and sometimes a builder. Sometimes the new bridge was even stronger and more beautiful than the original.

There is one bridge that's missing at our birth in every person's life "for all have sinned and fall short of the glory of God" Romans 3:23. For eternity's sake, that bridge is a MUST since "the wages of sin is death..." Romans 6:23. But Paul puts a bright and shining spotlight on the tragedy when he writes "But you He made alive who were dead in trespass and sins," Ephesians 2:1. A truth that caused David to sing out in Psalm 30:3: "...You have brought my soul up from the grave; You have kept me alive that I should not go down to the pit." Born dead because of inherent sin, alienated from God!!! However, "...for to every man has God dealt the measure of faith." Romans 12:3, so "Faith comes by hearing, and hearing by the Word of God." Romans 1:17.

It's a wonderful bridge that lasts a lifetime as found in Ephesians 2:8-9: "For by grace are you saved through faith; not of yourself, but it is a gift of God, not of works, lest any man should boast."

"Amazing grace, how sweet the sound that saved a wretch like me;" when I came to the cross on bended knee and with a truly repentant heart, confessed my sin, and Jesus set me free!! And that beautiful cross now afforded me a "bridge" to span the deep gulf that alienated me from God, so that I can now enter the throne room, because "the veil was rent from top to bottom" that Good Friday afternoon at Calvary.

Now I can sing with David from Psalm 91:1: "I will dwell in the secret place of the Most High, and abide under the shadow of the Almighty, I will say of the Lord, You are my Refuge, my Fortress."

I've crossed the bridge where the tonnage sign reads: "Unlimited weight."

January 28

"Allow the little children to come unto Me..." Matthew 19:14.

Sixty years ago when a young family of five and their Norwegian neighbor, Ivar, met on Main Street, my soft heart was always touched. There the little ones stood all huddled around Ivar with outstretched hands, knowing full well that he would drop a coin into each of their little hands, enough for a candy bar or an ice cream cone. I could see that the old gentleman enjoyed the giving as much as they enjoyed the receiving.

"Allow the little children to come unto Me, and forbid them not..." Jesus, Matthew 19: 14. And for a similar reason...He had a coveted gift for them, "that He might put His hand on them and pray." Vs. 13.

Oh how many Gideon brothers have we seen come back from a distribution blitz of Bibles in a foreign land, etched deeply into their minds and hearts the sight of yet many, many outstretched hands when the supply they had was exhausted. We PTL (Praise the Lord) for those who received, and pray for another opportunity for those who did not receive.

Disciple Andrew said to Jesus: "There is a lad here who has five loaves and two small fish ..." John 6:9a. The day was spent, the crowd was hungry, and only a little boy, and surely his mother back home, had prepared for the evening meal. Can't you imagine the pride and sense of importance that rose up within him at such a strategic time, as he volunteered his lunch? "But what is that among so many?" Vs. 9b.

As Ivar was to the little ones on main street, and my Gideon brothers to the spiritually hungry across the oceans, so was Jesus to the famished multitude when He blessed the tiny meal and was miraculously able to fill every extended hand, perhaps fifteen thousand people, leaving also twelve baskets of "leftovers."

"And my God shall supply all your needs according to His riches in glory by Christ Jesus", Philippians 4: 19, a promise prefaced by a compliment from Paul for the generous, giving hearts. Vs. 14-15.

"Give, and it will be given to you: good measure, pressed down, shaken together, running over shall men put into your bosom. For with the same measure that you use, it will be measured back to you ..."—love, joy, peace, hope, and encouragement included.

From one who knows that "God loves a cheerful giver." I Corinthians 9:7.

January 29

"Prepare the way of the Lord..." Mark 1:3.

What a pleasant impression was mine when in April 1945 the 16th Armored Division I was attached to drive on those straight, wide, paved roads in Germany, beautified on either side with very tall green trees. I saw a product of Hitler's plan to wage war on most of Europe with that road advantage. Our own General Eisenhower, commander of U.S. forces in Europe, later became U.S. President, and saw such advantage in those "super highways" in case of war, that our own interstate web was born in the 1950's.

My own community in eastern Montana knew of a similar need in change to modernize a forty-seven mile road as horse and buggy days phased into the motor vehicle era. In 1932 horses and scrapers, caterpillars and dozers came on deck to make radical changes. The old dirt roads, simply an elaborate trail with a shallow ditch on either side, went conveniently thither and yon through alkali river bottoms, up to the hilltops, over shallow ravines and narrow, improvised river crossings and crooked, sudden turns, requiring strict attention and slow speeds. Roads definitely unfit for the age just ahead.

So, the state of Montana engineered raised-up, wide, hardtop, fairly snow-free resistant highways. They straightened them out, cut down the hills and filled the ravines, shortened them considerably, and built concrete-based steel bridges across the rivers. Highway #13 is now state maintained for repair and for snow removal. A marvelous change that now called for speed limit signs!

Like Hitler planned in Germany's 1930's, so did ancient kings plan in their desires to conquer neighboring nations by having "super highways" for quick, safe entrance in and out for troops and equipment.

So the prophet Isaiah was inspired by God to see it like this in Isaiah 40:3-4: "...make straight in the desert a highway for our God. Every valley shall be exalted and every mountain and hill brought low; the crooked places shall be made straight, and the rough places smooth..."

I can imagine that it was a roadway like Isaiah described when John the Baptist cried out for the people to repent while baptizing at the River Jordan, and he looked up and saw Jesus coming: "Prepare the way of the Lord, make His paths straight." Mark 1:3.

PTL for the "road" Jesus claimed to be: "I am the Way, the Truth, and the Life; no man comes to the Father but by me." John 14:6.

January 30

"... count it all joy when you fall into various trials, knowing that the testing of your faith produces patience." James 1:2.

Trials! Patience! Joy! God had asked of me during the severe drought on my Montana farm the decade of the eighties...no rain, no crop, no grass for the livestock in summer nor foliage for winter. Living and operating costs, taxes, and land payments fell short of meeting the budget. One year the added cost even of a trip to the Rockies five hundred miles away for summer pasture. Two years of severe grasshopper infestation. Joy? Patience? My soul literally bathed in Psalm 42:1 — —"As the deer pants for the water brooks, so pants my soul for You, oh God," my only resource for help as I daily had to cope with the: "Why are you cast down, oh my soul, and why are you disquieted within me?" Vs. 5a.

The seasons wore on, and one day, through a personal ministry from an evangelist friend, I heard: "Though the fig tree may not blossom, nor fruit be on the vines; though the labor of the olive may fail; and the field yield no food; though the flock may be cut off from the fold and there be no herd in the stalls— —yet I will rejoice in the Lord, I will joy in the God of my salvation." Habakkuk 3:17-19.

Such Divine backing for my child-like faith gave me the patience of James 1:2, and the rains began to fall and prices for our goods increased just as the day of reckoning approached, and with it the joy of James 1:2. The trial subsided, and my faith in God expanded, and I sang out loud and clear: "I will extol You, Oh Lord, for You have lifted me up. You have not allowed the enemy to rejoice over me." David, Psalm 30:1

Sorely tried and tested Wayne Myers, an evangelist acquaintance, puts it this way: "God is never late, but He misses a lot of opportunities to be early."

From one who has learned that patience pays big dividends, and that "The joy of the Lord is my strength." Nehemiah 10:8.

January 31

"Pure love has no fear." II Timothy 1:7

I've discovered, as I have mingled with them, that squirrels are like people—some trust me and some are afraid of me. People who walk with Jesus tend to love me, and like my occasional fellowship. But, the atheist and agnostic I come across can't get away from me fast enough because there seems to be an automatic spiritual warfare and discomfort.

Reminds me of two squirrels I've known. My neighbor Stan and I have spent hours sitting in the coolness of summer shade of his garage, sometimes watching a healthy-looking squirrel come right up to my friend who would feed him nuts out of his hand. But, that's not all; he fed him daily on the corn kernels placed at the base of the big tree on the boulevard. The friendly squirrel seemed to know and appreciate those favors with no fear, but with pure trust and love in his heart. I never got such intimacy from that rodent even though my pickup, standing nearby, sometimes treated him to a "tasty" drink as he chewed holes in my brake line twice. The difference? We just didn't connect. He knew Stan personally by his charity. My "drink offering" for him was like Dave's, who made a clever device to hang a cob of corn on occasionally for the squirrel's daily ration, it's giver totally unknown, and hence a squirrel's spirit of fear toward that donor, since they never connected.

Some people are like that with God as they run from Him in fear of a spanking. They don't know that He loves them, forgives, and richly provides them with everything for their need and enjoyment in life on this earth.

"...for He makes His sun rise on the good and on the evil, and sends rain on the just and the unjust." Matthew 5:45.

Psalmist David's intimacy with God caused him to praise God and out of a loving, thankful, fearless heart comes Psalm 65:9-13: "You visit the earth and water it...You water its ridges abundantly, You settle its furrows; You make soft with showers, You bless its growth. You crown the year with Your goodness, and Your paths drip with abundance...The pastures are clothed with flocks, the valleys also are covered with grain; they shout for joy, they also sing."

From one who loves the Man "from Whom all blessings flow, praise Him all creatures here below; praise Him above you heavenly host, praise Father, Son, and Holy Ghost." A doxology.

February 1

".. it is hard for a rich man to enter the kingdom of heaven" Jesus, Matthew 19:23.

One Sunday morning, as a young adult, I stood outside the church only a few minutes after an adult class had completed what I called: "The ten easy lessons on becoming a Lutheran." The class had just been confirmed. One of them was a young, already fairly wealthy, successful farmer. I shook his hand and congratulated him on his achievement. He responded with an arrogant, old-nature pride snicker, indicating to me the foolishness of it all. He had accomplished church membership in case he or his family needed it, but with no evident change of heart. However, about sixty years later, on his deathbed, at the encouragement and ministry of a truly born-again pastor, he accepted the Lord as his Savior. PTL!

In Revelation 3 we read of a whole church full of people like my friend, full of wealth, and consequently a delusion of self-sufficiency, and an "I don't need God" attitude. America today, starting with post-WWII, is another Laodicea, a land of sensual glitter, easy to purchase. America's Christian culture of yesteryear has allowed a culture of idolatry to creep in and literally take it over. Why then Jesus?

Jesus rebuked the Laodicean church, calling them "lukewarm ... wretched, miserable, poor, blind, and naked." Vs. 16-17. But oh for the power of God's love for even such blatant sinners, when in Vs. 19 Jesus says: "As many as I love, I rebuke and chasten. Therefore, be zealous and repent."

My Montana friend spent sixty miserable years without Jesus' fellowship. He divorced his wife and watched his family disintegrate. He didn't hear Jesus speak from Vs. 20: "Behold, I stand at the door and knock. If anyone hears My voice and opens the door, I will come in to him, and dine with him and he with Me."

The Psalmist puts it this way: "Blessed is the man who walks not in the counsel of the ungodly...he shall be like a tree planted by the rivers of water, that brings forth its fruit in its season, whose leaf also shall not wither; and whatever he does shall prosper." Psalm 1:1, 3.

February 2

"Put Me in remembrance..." Isaiah 43:26

Moses had died, and the Lord commanded Joshua to replace him. His immediate chore was to usher the Israelites across the Jordan River even though the springtime waters overflowed the river's banks. When all the people had miraculously crossed over the Jordan, the Lord spoke to Joshua: "Take twelve men— —one from every tribe, and command them: 'take twelve stones ...out of the midst of the Jordan, from where the priests' feet (with the arc of the Lord in hand) stood firm...that this may be a sign to your descendants that the waters of the Jordan were cut off...these stones a memorial to the children of Israel'" Vs. 3, 5-7. What a day to remember...the Lord's banking up the river on both sides so they could cross over on dry land, "that they may know, that as I was with Moses, so shall I be with you." Joshua 3:7.

In my hometown in Montana is a certain spot on a certain street that I see as my Jordan River crossing. I was in the dairy business, delivering milk, house to house seven days a week, a "workaholic", bent on building an agricultural "empire." Whenever I drive over a certain spot on the north end of that street, I still remember that warm, sunny, quiet, Sunday morning when cars lined both sides of the street for blocks...Lutherans and Catholics each at their worship service.

My lonely, empty heart sank as the Lord convicted me of idolatry, a false god. I didn't know I Samuel 7:3 at that time, but a similar message I heard: "If you return to the Lord with ALL your heart, then put away the foreign gods from among you, and prepare your heart for the Lord, and serve Him only, He will deliver you." I was a "workaholic" and needed deliverance. I stopped Sunday delivery that very day.

There I erected a memorial, not of wood, stone, or brick, but of a chastising from the Lord whenever I pass over that exact spot which has meant so much to me down to this very day. Perhaps this writing will be my "stone" erected for my descendants to occasionally visit as my memorial of that experience in my early life.

I am thankful that He spoke and that I heard.

I love that greatest memorial of all, that we can all celebrate together the Lord's Supper, and Jesus Word to us: "...Do this in remembrance of Me..." Luke 22:69. "How could I forget You, oh Lord?"

February 3

The late Paul Harvey and I, contemporaries, had much in common I've gleaned from his radio broadcasts and his writings, both of us proud to be a part of the "Greatest Generation." These were the days when rural life dominated in America, and with it, dirt roads, he described like this:

"There is not a problem in America today...crime, drugs, education, divorce, or delinquency, that wouldn't be remedied if we just had more dirt roads, because dirt roads give character. People who live at the end of dirt roads learn early on that life is a bumpy ride. That it can jar you right down to your teeth, sometimes, but it's worth it if, at the end a loving spouse, happy kids, and a dog.

We wouldn't have near the trouble with our educational system if our kids got their exercise walking a dirt road to school with other kids from whom they learn how to get along. There was less crime on our streets before they were paved. Criminals didn't walk two dusty miles to rob or rape, if they knew they would be welcomed by five barking dogs and a double barrel shotgun. And there were no drive-by shootings. Our values were better when our roads were worse.

People did not worship their cars more than their kids, and motorists were more courteous. They didn't tailgate by riding the bumper because the guy in front would choke you with dust, and bust your windshield with rocks. Dirt roads taught patience.

Dirt roads were environmentally friendly, because you didn't hop into your car for a quart of milk, as you walked to the barn to get your milk. For your mail, you walked to the mailbox.

What if it rained, and the dirt road washed out? That was the best part, because then you stayed home, and had some family time... roasted marshmallows, and popcorn. You'd pony ride on daddy's shoulders, and learn how to make pretty quilts.

At the end of the dirt road you soon learned that bad words tasted like soap. Most paved roads lead to trouble and dirt roads more likely lead to a fishing pond or a swimming hole on a hot summer day.

At the end of a dirt road, the only time we ever locked our car was in August so that some neighbor wouldn't fill it with too much zucchini. At the end of the dirt road, there was always extra springtime income when the city dude would get stuck, and you'd have to harness and hitch up a team of horses and pull them out. Usually a dollar and always a new friend at the end of the dirt road, where sometimes a husky young man on each corner of the old Model "T" Ford would carry it out." By Paul Harvey.

February 4

"God frustrates the devices of the crafty..." Job 5:12

If there is a message of hope in these perilous times we Christians, we Americans as a whole, are living in today, it MUST BE in the power of the Lord's presence. God tells us in Jeremiah 29:11: "I know the thoughts I think toward you, thoughts of peace, not of evil; I give you a future, I give you a hope..." — the presence of God.

But how can I really sense His presence now in 2009? How can I see testimony of His intimate, genuine presence in the "now" when it comes to protecting me from another terrorist attack, or protection over my finances, or even protection over my possible loss of faith in these perilous times?

The testimonies of many men and women we find in God's Word — their trial God brought them through with a principal and a promise at work have been etched deeply into my heart and soul, faith builders, so that my empathy with them has been a bulwark of strength for my child-like faith.

We can walk with Abraham, Jacob, Joseph, Joshua, Moses, Gideon, David, Daniel, the three Hebrew children, Elijah, Ruth, Hannah, and Paul, and many other faith-building testimonies, everyone patterned to prove God's presence is with us, even in perilous times.

For example, God promised Israel's leader, Joshua, after crossing the Jordan River, where he overcame twenty-nine enemy nations "not in my power, but as the Lord goes with me." And he stood on God's promise: "There shall not any men be able to stand before you all the days of your life; as I was with Moses, so I will be with you; I will not fail you nor forsake you; be strong and of good courage;" Joshua 1:5. God's presence close at hand.

I believe that anyone can have and enjoy the presence of God if he will just pray daily, even hourly, for God's anointing on His Word from Proverbs 3:5-6: "Trust in the Lord with all your heart; lean not unto your own understanding. Acknowledge Him in all your ways and trust Him to direct your paths."

Since September 11, 2001, God has proven to us the power of His presence with us who stand firmly on Job 5:12: "God frustrates the devices of the crafty so that their hand cannot carry out their plans." It's 24/7!! Our prisons are populated with everyone caught in the act since 9/11.

"God is our refuge and strength, a very PRESENT help in trouble." Psalm 46:1. (Emphasis mine).

February 5

"But seek first the kingdom of God..." Matthew 6:33

When I first came into the Charismatic movement which swept across America in the 1960's and '70's, I heard many, many of those "exciting", almost supernatural testimonies of how certain people came to their born-again experience. I coveted a testimony like that, and their special opportunity to share with large crowds of people. How childish!! Some were set free from all kinds of addictions; some prison terms where they had heard the Word of God taught or preached for the first time, and they became truly born-again. They were convicted of sin and confessed it with a truly repentant heart. They reminded me of Paul in Acts 9. Their testimony spread like wild-fire, and they were frequently asked to share at gatherings which were full of hungry, spiritually starved men and women.

I can remember well the evening when Janet literally ran to the altar at the invitation, and tearfully laid her life on the line, and surrendered to Jesus. She brought with her a long pedigree of immorality and a heavy load of sin she was convicted of.

I thought to myself: "I wish I had an exciting testimony like that", even though I never coveted what they had to go through, the life they had lived to "earn" that privilege. My testimony seemed so boring and lacking in luster.

Then one day the Lord showed me that I had the best testimony of all in His sight. Something like Stephen's against Saul's in Acts 6-7. It seemed to me that I came slowly, little by little, starting in early childhood and culminating in my teen years when I surrendered to Jesus at a Bible camp where we were encouraged to consecrate our whole being—our head, heart, hands, feet, and our time, talent, and treasure to Jesus.

Today I am satisfied with my testimony as I see it borne out in Mark 4:26: "And He said, the kingdom of God is as if a man should scatter seed on the ground ...and the seed should...first be the blade, then the head, after that the full grain in the head. But when the grain ripens, immediately he puts in the sickle because the harvest has come." The fruit is evident, as it came on little by little, over a whole season.

"Some planted seed in my heart, others then watered it, and it bore fruit in its own season." I Corinthians 3:6.

A proper testimony is powerful: "They overcame him (Satan) by the blood of the Lamb and the Word of their testimony." Revelation 12:11.

February 6

"My God, My God, why have You forsaken Me?" Matthew 27:46

Jesus' driest "dry spell"

Having lived in Montana for my first seventy three years, engaged primarily in the world of agriculture, I saw some "dry spells", weather-wise. After the flourishing 1920's, came almost a decade of drought, ending in 1938. In 1937 my neighbor begged the banker to foreclose on his farm, to clear his name, and release him to move on. Totally discouraged!! The banker refused, sent him back to the farm, and the weather pattern immediately changed. The old gent and his wife retired ten years later, sold the farm, and lived out their life financially sound. From the flourishing days, through the drought, to the mountain top when the "dry spell" ended.

Off and on for the next sixty years it was a season of good moisture followed by a "dry spell"—prosperity to poverty, feast to famine.

As dry spells come to the farmer, so they come to the inner man in its season, most usually after a mountain top experience.

Bold prophet Elijah fell one day from a mountain top of incredible success into the pit of despair, a dry spell. He had successfully called fire down from heaven that consumed his animal sacrifice along with twelve barrels of water encasing the grate, humiliating 450 unsuccessful prophets of Baal. God's people fell down on their faces and worshiped the God of Heaven. Almost simultaneously, with faith in God's power, he prayed down rain to end a long drought. He also outran King Ahab's chariot over many miles, successes God's power blessed him with, seemingly undauntable.

In the very hour of his blessings, popularity, and spiritual revelation, he plunged deep into despair when Queen Jezebel threatened to kill him for his destroying her prophets of Baal at the "barbecue" contest. I Kings 19.

In a single day, he fell into depression, a "dry spell" so severe that he begged God to take his life, sitting alone under a tree, wallowing in self pity.

I can just hear God speaking a positive note to Elijah like He spoke to me during a similar dry spell: "I know the thoughts I think toward you, thoughts of peace, not of evil. I give you a future, I give you a hope" Jeremiah 29: 11.

Elijah and I both heard: "Get busy! Go out in My name. You're not alone."

February 7

"..there will be weeping and gnashing of teeth." Matthew 8:12

One evening I saw on TV news a lady on tape hurry up to the ticket counter at an airport, only to find that she was too late, her plane had left on scheduled time and left her behind. Immediately, in a fit of desperation, she cried, she screamed, she fell to the floor and kicked like a small child. She pounded on the floor with her fists, totally absorbed in a severe, uncomfortable moment of futility. It was all recorded on a camera. Bill O'Reilly saw her that evening as a "pinhead," while I immediately saw her as one of millions who will be left behind at Jesus' return one of these days, suddenly realizing that "it's all over," too late, no more time, headed down the slippery, broad path to Hell and eternal death "as it was in the days of Noah."

The truth of Matthew 24:36-42 began running through my mind. "But of that hour and day, no one knows...but as the days of Noah were, so also will the coming of the Son of Man be...they were eating and drinking, marrying and giving in marriage...and did not know until the flood came and took them all away,...so also will the coming of the Son of Man be...watch therefore, for you do not know what hour your Lord is coming."

I can see the mad rush toward Noah's ark when reality set in, much like the crying eighty five year old lady in the nursing home I saw running behind her family with that pitiful look, only to find the door was locked.

The Japanese woman "leaned on her own understanding" to be on time, ready to "fly away." Solomon tells us to "Trust the Lord ... acknowledge Him ... and He will direct your path." He will have us believers ready to "flyaway" on time when He returns in the clouds to take us home. I Thessalonians 4:1-7.

Waiting patiently for His return, and the door will be open.

February 8

"The name of the Lord is a strong tower; the righteous runs into it, and is safe." Proverbs 18:10

Paul writes in Philippians 2:9: "God also has exalted Him, and given Him the name which is above every name, that at the name of Jesus every knee shall bow..." Since we are living in a spirit-driven world, I see this "bowing knee" no better illustrated than with my farmer friend across the International boundary in Sask., Canada. He owned a Holstein bull, which he contained in a steel pen in his barn. Holstein bulls are temperamental, one day friend to man, and another a foe not to be trusted. While feeding and watering the animal in his pen, my friend suddenly found himself hurled against the wall. The bull receded and stood like a statue ready to lunge again. No time for the godly man to pray, so he simply cried out "Jesus, Jesus, Jesus", without stopping, as he made his way to climb out of the pen. After finding his feet planted on solid ground, he ceased his chant, and the bull hit the steel panel like a bullet. Yes, the name of the Lord is a strong tower for the godly to find refuge in.

Yes, we are living in a spirit-driven world!! We see that in action in Matthew 20 where Jesus entered into Gadarene country and found two demon possessed men, dangerous men, living in a cave. Spiritual warfare broke out quickly when the omnipotent Jesus was recognized by the demons as the Son of God, tormenting the demonic spirit within them. So, the demons begged: "'If You cast us out, send us into that herd of swine.' 'Be gone!' said Jesus, and they came out and entered into the swine, driving them over a cliff, where they drowned in the water below."

"Every knee shall bow at the name of Jesus..." Philippians 2:9.

The two delivered men, set free, had just experienced: "The name of the Lord is a strong tower, and the righteous runs into it and is safe."

"I have been anointed to deliver those in bondage..." Jesus, Luke 4:18.

Delivered, and set free!

February 9

The curse of that "me-first" syndrome.

A few days ago when a man at a Wal-Mart store in New York city was trampled to death by human feet as he opened a door on Black Friday, trampled by people hungering for the glitter of this world, I thought of a situation I once lived next door to in Montana. My old bachelor, widowed neighbor, about seventy five years of age, one day in late fall, went to the barnyard to do his daily livestock chores. There stood his herd of cows, waiting to be let out to feed. As he unlatched the long, heavy barbed wire gate, he suffered a fatal heart attack and fell to the ground. The cows rushed out, but not one of them stepped on his dead clay body. Does the animal world instinctively have more respect for human life than humanity itself has?

Could there have been an angel from heaven standing over that Godly, Christian man's dead body? In Numbers 22 God sent an angel to direct a donkey's steps with evil Balaam on his back. Three times the angel diverted the donkey while his rider was blind as to what was going on. Finally, after three beatings, the Lord caused the donkey to speak to Balaam: "What have I done that deserves your beating me these three times?" Vs. 28.

King Saul, on the other hand, a human leader, would gladly, purposely trample young David under foot in his jealous rage, like the greedy shoppers at Wal-Mart, saturated with that me-first syndrome. "Saul kept a jealous watch on David." I Samuel 18:9. "A tormenting spirit from God overwhelmed Saul and he began to rave like a madman...Saul, fiddling with his spear, suddenly hurled it at David, intending to pin him to the wall...for Saul was afraid of him and jealous...", like the crowd at Wal-Mart, afraid and jealous! !

"Then Jesus said to His disciples, 'If anyone desires to come after Me, let him deny himself, take up his cross, and follow Me.'" Matthew 16:24. In other Words "get rid of that me-first syndrome."

Was my old neighbor's dead body spared trampling because of an angel's watch over him, while the man in New York was destroyed by that human me-first syndrome? "...love one another as I have loved you..." Jesus. John 24:34.

February 10

How dark is Hell?!!

Can you imagine how a young GI like me, who loves lots of light, hated those cloudy, jet-black nights out on the Atlantic Ocean in a convoy of ships headed for France in WWII days? Indescribably black!! Unimaginable darkness and solitude on the deck of that huge ship during four hours of "guard duty." So dark and quiet that my relief could not find me—four black hours that seemed like eternity.

Until Jesus, the Light of Heaven, came to earth in the flesh, the entire world was in that same impenetrable darkness, spiritually speaking; a heavy black cloud hanging over every man's head because of inherent sin we are all born with, alienated from Jesus, and continues to burden us down in untold darkness until we say "yes" to Jesus, "the Light of the world." Like the unsaved rich man in Luke 16: "The rich man died and was buried...And being in torments in Hades, he lifted up his eyes...cried...and said, 'Father Abraham, have mercy on me,'" The verdict? "Too late."

Rural America, except for the moonshine and starlight, was that dark at night until REA brought in electricity, and the homes and farmsteads, barns, and shops lighted up, and the light shone through the windows and yard lights. And we hear David's response for such light from the heart: "I will extol You, oh Lord, for you have lifted me up...You have brought my soul up out of the grave, and You have kept me alive, that I should not fall into the pit..."

A statistic I read recently tells that 90% of the world is still living in the darkness of night in the spirit world, since only 10% of our 6.2 billion people on earth today are of the Christian flock, whose Shepherd Himself declares in John 14:6: "I am the way, the truth, and the life; no man comes to the Father but by Me." The world of false gods, idols, and old nature flesh are living spiritually with the likeness of a flashlight whose batteries are failing, and only dim light for a very short time. Their light is like a wax candle which lasts only a few hours and then vanishes. Like the light of a campfire that must be extinguished lest it burn up a forest.

God's Word tells us that Hell is a place of hopeless torment and darkness like experienced on the Atlantic Ocean. Think of that for ETERNITY!—so dark that no one can find you, lasting not for only four hours, but for ETERNITY.

"I am the Light of the world. He who follows Me shall not walk in darkness, but have the Light of Life." Jesus, John 8:12.

February 11

"When I look up into the night skies and see the work of Your fingers..." Psalm 8:3a

It was a moderately foggy night when I drove over the crest of a hill about one-half mile south of the well-known "Bridges" oil well alongside of highway 13 in northeast Montana. A gas-burning flame at the well site, mixed with the substance of the fog, portrayed a beauty I have never seen before, nor since—a panorama, I believe, of every color known to man, beautifully woven together, too gorgeous to describe with human Words. I stopped and soaked up the unbelievable beauty for a long time, and wondered if that could be at least the tip of an iceberg of the beauty of heaven, described in part in Revelation 22: "...pure water of life, clear as crystal...tree of life bearing twelve fruits, loaded with leaves. There shall be no night there, no lamp, nor light of sun, for the glory of the Lord gives them light that will reign forever and ever." I believe I saw a taste of that "glory of the Lord" that night, as I looked up into the night skies to see the works of God's creative fingers.

I was equally blessed on that autumn morning when I first saw my oldest daughter occupying an incubator shortly after her birth. She weighed only 4 lbs. 11 oz., a full-term baby floundering energetically with both arms and legs. How could a person with such tiny fingers, toes, arms, and legs ever be ready for life on this earth? "But with God nothing shall be impossible." The angel to Mary, Luke 1:3. What a marvelous sight to a brand new mother and dad as we looked on with joy!!

"I cannot understand how You can bother with mere man, to pay attention to him! And yet, You have made him only a little lower than the angels, and have placed a crown of glory and honor upon his head." Psalm 8:4-5.

Is it possible to grab the finest beauty of nature here on earth and hope it is but a semblance of what we will see in heaven when we come over the crest of that hill for the first time, a sight that will last forever?

It is written: "Eye has not seen, nor ear heard; nor have entered into the heart of man the things which God has prepared for those who love Him." II Corinthians 2:9.

Heaven bound!!!

February 12

"...But he (the rich man) took the poor man's lamb..." II Samuel 12:4

The young brothers, having taken their deceased father's farm holdings, were struggling to get established, to be able to pay their daily expense accounts. They were strong, ambitious, honest, young men. They stored their tractor diesel fuel in a large overhead tank on their farmstead. The alert young men had reason to suspect that someone was stealing fuel from the tank. They had reason also to suspect an older man, a millionaire neighbor. They set a trap: making it widely known in their community that on a certain day they would be gone traveling, and made sure that the suspect would be advised.

Instead of leaving on that designated day, they quietly hid out in their quonset building and waited. The wealthy suspect drove his pickup into their farmstead, and up to the diesel fuel tank. The brothers came out and caught the rich man in the act of stealing. They could point their finger at him confidently: "You are the man!"

One day when God wanted King David to confess his sin of literally stealing Bathsheba from Uriah, her husband, He used Nathan to set a trap. Nathan told David of a rich man who had a flock of sheep, but stole his poor neighbor's only lamb to prepare a meal for a traveler who had come to his home. "So David's anger was greatly aroused against the rich man, and he said to Nathan; "As the Lord lives, the man who has done this shall surely die! And he shall restore fourfold for the lamb..." Then Nathan said to David 'You are the man!'" Thus says the Lord...I anointed you king over Israel and delivered you from the hand of Saul..." On and on God reminded David, the rich man, of the many blessings God had showered upon him over his lifetime. The trap worked, and David said to Nathan; "1 have sinned against the Lord." And Nathan said to David; "The Lord has put away your sin; you shall not die." II Samuel 13,

"Though your sin be as scarlet, it shall be white as snow; though your sin be crimson red, it shall be like wool." Isaiah 1: 18.

David confessed and was forgiven, while the millionaire who stole the fuel died, cursing God on his deathbed. "...except you repent, you shall perish." Luke 13:5.

February 13

"I will extol You, oh Lord, for You have lifted me up; You have not made my enemies to rejoice over me. Oh Lord my God, I cried out to You, and You lifted me, You have brought my soul up from the grave; You have kept me alive, that I should not go down to the pit." Ps. 30:1

The severe, unexpected, blinding, February snowstorm, coming from the southeast, lasted six 24-hour days, plugging all the roads, and taking its toll on a rancher's large herd of cows huddled behind a tall, steep embankment a mile from the farmstead. Six days without feed or water. Even snowmobiles were no help. To this day, the dry bones of the perished animals lay exposed, the bones of eighteen brood cows.

When I sometimes drive by that valley on the nearby pavement, I visualize again the unpleasant memory of that storm, and I think of "the valley of dry bones" we become acquainted with in Ezekiel 37.

There was a reason for the valley of dry bones. "...when the house of Israel dwelt in their own land, they defiled it by their own ways and deeds." Ch. 36:17. "Therefore, I poured out My wrath on them for the blood they had shed on the land, and for their idols..."Vs. 18. "I judged them according to their ways and deeds." Vs. 19. "They profaned My holy name..." Vs. 20. God's wrath and judgment, like the snowstorm, filled a valley with dry bones because of sin, unrepentance, and consequently unforgiveness,

But God's deep love for His people set up a means of return. He prophesied in Vs. 26-27: "I will give you a new heart and put a new spirit within you, I will take the heart of stone out of your flesh, and give you a heart of flesh, I will put My Spirit within you and cause you to walk in My statutes..."

Prophet Ezekiel saw in the valley the same dryness and darkness we are each born into because of inherent sin, "dead in trespass and sin", alienated from God, dead in our spirit being. Can we not see and experience an analogy of what happened in that valley when the Word of the Lord comes to us with this truth of Calvary, Christ, the cross, and the resurrection? "If any man be in Christ Jesus he is a brand new creation, old things passed away, all things become new." Cor. 5:17.

Praise God that dead, dry "bones" can be restored to life!! "Behold, oh my people, I will open your graves, raise you up...and bring you into the land of Israel." Vs. 12

February 14

"Who can find a virtuous wife?" Proverbs 31: 10

Have you heard it said, "Roses are red, violets are blue; sugar is sweet and so are you"? Hey fellas, it's Valentine's Day, an opportune time to let the "fairest" lady of your life know how deep your love for her really is.

God's priceless love letter to all humanity (the Bible), from which we read of the deep love God manifested in John 3: 16, "For God so loved the world that He gave His only begotten Son, that whosoever believes on Him, shall not perish, but have everlasting life."

As a young third grade boy, with my first bible in hand, I soon noticed that the letters in red were verses spoken by Jesus; a blood-red intended to put emphasis on His spoken Words. And here I think specifically of Luke 22:20, "This cup is the new covenant in My blood, which is shed for you." What a contrast is Jesus' agape manifested love toward us compared to our human, "puppy love" toward one another as we try to carry out His command to "love one another."

God's plan was written in red...written with the precious blood of Christ, as of "a Lamb without blemish and without spot." 1 Peter 1:19

Oh, yes, we set aside in February a day to celebrate human love, but long before this day, our God sent us a love letter with eternal, everlasting, sign of canceled debt.

So today we sing, "Turn your eyes upon Jesus, look full in His wonderful face, and the things of earth will grow strangely dim, in the light of His glory and grace."

February 15

"...fathers, do not provoke your children to wrath, but bring them up in the admonition and training of the Lord." Ephesians 6:4.

It was mom and dad's anniversary, and six-year old Brandon decided that Saturday morning to bake pancakes for his parents. He found a big bowl and a spoon, pulled a chair to the counter, opened the cupboard, and pulled out the heavy flour canister, spilling it on the floor. He scooped some of the flour into the bowl with his hands, mixed in most of a cup of milk, and added some sugar, leaving a floury trail on the floor which by now had a few tracks from the kitten, too. Brandon was covered with flour and frustrated. He wanted this to be something special for mom and dad, but it was getting worse by the minute. He didn't know whether to put it in the oven or on top of the stove, not knowing how to operate either.

Suddenly, he saw his kitten licking from the bowl of mix and reached to push her away and knocked the eggs to the floor. Frantically, he tried to clean up this terrible mess, getting his pajamas white and sticky. Just then he saw dad standing at the door and big tears welled up in his eyes. All he had wanted to do was good, but then this mess! He waited for a scolding or maybe even a spanking, but his father just watched. Then, walking through the mess, dad picked up his crying son, hugged him and loved him, while his own pajamas became messy in the ordeal.

That's how God deals with us in a sticky marriage, or an insulting friend, a work we hate, or a health problem. Sometimes we just stand there in tears, and that's when God picks us up and loves us and forgives us, even though our mess gets all over Him. So, let's just keep on making pancakes. "My grace is sufficient for you, for My strength is made perfect in weakness." II Corinthians 12:9.

"...he (Job) would rise up early in the morning and offer burnt offerings according to the number of them all (his ten children). For Job said: 'It may be that my sons have sinned and cursed God in their hearts'. This Job did regularly." Job 1:5. (Parenthesis mine)

Dad, can you do any less for your son or daughter?

Happy anniversary to all you Dads and Moms out there who celebrate today.

February 16

"... deny yourself, take up your cross, and follow Me..." Matthew 16:24.

My bumper sticker reads, in blue letters on white: "Are You Following Jesus This Close?" To some, it draws a smile, to others a scowl. What mental and emotional stress a cozy rear bumper driver puts on me when I think of the possibility of having to make a sudden stop even at thirty-five miles per hour. Seat belt or no seat belt, it's dangerous!! Many believers in Jesus love the sticker's question and respect the gist of the message, while, I suspect, from daily evidence, others hate it and ride all the closer because they simply hate Jesus, my Lord and Savior.

Having spent seventy-three years of my life in a rather quiet, laid-back culture as a rancher in rural Montana, the rush of interstate and city street driving is foreign to me. I don't really fare too well in the rush of today's culture in general.

Then I ask myself: "What would Jesus do, what would Jesus think?" And I am drawn to Luke 19 and Jesus taking time in a busy day to minister to Zacchaeus, a rich tax collector who needed help in the inner man. A multitude of people were to go on a certain route Zacchaeus knew well, following Jesus, and I can just imagine some of them in a hurry to keep on keeping on. Perhaps some-shouted: "Why give this dishonest, rich tax collector, a sinner of sinners, even the time of day?" "Let's rush on" But I can also just see patient Jesus: "He looked up and saw him (Zacchaeus) sitting in a sycamore tree because he was short of stature." He didn't want to miss seeing Jesus in person. We get here a real feel of how the Holy Spirit works in lives to prepare them for the great miracle of salvation like He has done with all of us who believe. So, the whole procession stopped, even the would-be bumper riders. How would the impatient, "rush crowd" now react when they heard Jesus: "Zacchaeus, make haste, come down, for today I must stay at your house." What? Not just a short interlude, but...."For today I must STAY at your house." This taxed the rush crowd to the limit. "You mean ALL day, Jesus?" Here, my old guitarist, composer brother from Montana would play and sing: "Take a little time for Jesus, 'cuz He took time for you." It's like many people today trying to beat the red stop light at the intersection. "Me! Wait forty-five seconds?" But oh what a blessing for the loving, patient Jesus to see and hear the changed heart; "Look, Lord, I give half of my goods to the poor, and if I have taken anything from anyone by false accusation, I restore four-fold." Vs. 8.

"Let him deny himself, (lay aside that me-first syndrome), take up his cross, (crucify his old flesh), and follow Me." (A following that would take Zacchaeus to Calvary) and his soul's first bath in the shed blood of Jesus. And then hear Jesus: "Today, salvation has come to this house..." Vs. 9, 7

To deny oneself, to nail that flesh to a cross like Zacchaeus did, takes quiet time with the Lord.

February 17

"Time bomb enclosed!"

The other evening when I squeezed the little plastic bottle of eye drops to hit the "bull's eye," and deposit the drop perfectly, I misjudged, and it ran down my cheek. That really bugs me, not because of the running, but because of the waste of a very expensive commodity. Every drop counts because there aren't many in the little container, and when it's empty, it's another trip to the pharmacy, and another good dent in the check book.

This morning I thought of another precious commodity given FREELY to me as I began to prepare my radio message, given to me every day on a silver platter...time. And as I thought of the way I try so hard to never waste a drop of eye medication, I asked myself: "If I had to buy time, would there be any difference in the way I spend it? Would I be so upset over one little eye drop if it were free on the market? Because hours, days, and weeks are given freely to us, does that give us license to waste them, or rather to invest them wisely?"

"And to one he (master over servants) gave five talents, to another two, and to another, one, to each according to his own ability..." Jesus, in a parable, Matthew 25. When he returned, he was pleased that the two given most invested theirs and doubled their investment. The third: "I was afraid, and went and hid your talent in the ground." Vs. 25. "...take the talent from him...and cast the unprofitable servant into outer darkness. There will be weeping and gnashing of teeth" Vs. 28, 30. A "time bomb" explosion!

My Bible says our days are numbered. Psalm 90:10, 12. There are only so many of them, carefully meted out to us, purposed to return that commodity back to Him with big dividends because we have invested wisely in His work here on earth during our lifespan.

I am so thankful that God does not sell time, but gives it freely, with the invitation "...come boldly before the throne of grace to obtain mercy and to find grace to help in time of need." Hebrews 4:16.

Yes, time is precious! "Handle with care."

"We do not know how long we have till time for us is past, so let us live as if this day is going to be our last." Dennis De Haan.

"Take a little time for Jesus, 'cause He took time for you," a song written by an old friend up in Montana.

February 18

"I have set before you life & death..." Deut. 30:19

Listen carefully in the spirit, doorbells are ringing at both front and back doors of the heart at the same time, awakening you out of your slumber. You have to make an instant decision: "which door shall I go to first?" The inner being suggests "Go first to the front door," and there you will see Jesus in Person, His proffered hand ready to take yours as He patiently explains His mission...that "God so loves you and all humanity that He sent Jesus from heaven in the flesh, One who would go to any extreme, even to death on a cross, to redeem a lost soul. Jesus, perfectly clean, innocent, and sinless like His Father, is to shamefully die on a cross and shed His blood at Calvary, just outside Jerusalem." Good news! It's a historical fact that on that dark Good Friday afternoon He would supernaturally take all the accumulated sin of all mankind upon His body to make a one time blood sacrifice, to pay a onetime ransom to bring back to God any and all who would come to that cross with child-like faith, lay down his sin and bathe the inner man in the blood of Jesus. That sinner is now truly born again, resurrected from inherent death. Why all this "That none should perish for eternity but that all should have everlasting life. " John 3:16.

While Jesus is at the front door of our hearts "to give life and give it abundantly" (John 10:10), Satan is ringing the back door bell. Bright lights are flashing to lure, entice, play with the old flesh nature, beckoning to "come eat, drink and make merry. Wallow in the glamorous world of sin that has come to kill, steal, and destroy." John 10:10.

King David opened the back door and got one whiff of worldliness that almost destroyed him as lust, adultery, sex, deceit, and murder came boldly to "kill, steal, and destroy." Except for sweet conviction, confession, and repentance, and his plea "take not Your Holy Spirit from me" (Psalm 51: 11) he was headed for disaster that would steal away the love, joy, peace, and security God had blessed him with since his teenage years.

We make a choice this morning; "Which am I going to open my life to today?" If the one at the back door who has come to destroy, a curse that leads to eternal destruction; or open to the One Who has promised "to give life and give it abundantly," a blessing that begins here and now today with a quantity and quality of hope, love, joy, peace and security that will be an eternal blessing in the very presence of Jesus.

What an eternal difference a single choice NOW can make!

Consider your choice, life or death "...I have set before you life and death, blessing and cursing; therefore, choose life, that both you and your descendants might live. " Deuteronomy 30:19.

February 19

"... for the joy of the Lord is your strength." Nehemiah 8:10

"Is that seat taken?" I asked a pleasant looking man at the crowded Dallas-Ft. Worth airport waiting room, and he promptly said: "No, it's just for you." Immediately I saw him as "my kind of guy," and we had a blast for several minutes until interrupted. Another plunked himself beside me a few days ago with a long, poker face I thought would surely crack if he smiled. Immediately his bitter tongue railed out at farmers and "their greed for government subsidies." The little boy inside of him was angry and upset and it showed unpleasantly on his face. Not "my type of guy."

I love to study people, and it doesn't take long to see what kind of influence a stranger can have on my life, positive or negative. The voice, the look in the eye, the response to a kindly greeting reflects on the face, or other body action which quickly tells me a brief resume of that person.

Think of the powerful influence Jesus had on three of His disciples on the mount of Transfiguration, where it says in Matthew 17:2 "His face shone like the sun, and His clothes dazzling white" That pleased His Father Who then bellowed out across the universe: "This is My beloved Son in whom I am well pleased. Hear Him!" A positive influence!

And there was Moses, likewise, who had been in the immediate presence of God for several days receiving the Ten Commandments, and when he came back to his people, his face "glowed brilliantly" and three million people could see he had been in the very intimate presence of God. Something shows.

When Jesus was born in Bethlehem "there were shepherds out in the fields, keeping watch over their flocks by night"; and one dark night "an angel of the Lord shone around them." The angels face, fresh from heaven, aglow with supernatural light as he shared the best good news ever told to man, reflecting love, joy, hope, peace, and security from his face and godly personality. "...an angel of the Lord stood before them, and the glory of the Lord shone around them...bring you good tidings of great joy which shall be to all people. For there is born to you this day a Savior, Who is Christ the Lord." Luke 2:9-11. .

Friends, our face is what people see, the one part of our body uncovered, showing the world like it really is for me personally. Our face is important in our daily walk with Jesus because it reflects the actual goings on of the little boy or girl inside, the real me. Our face is a mirror of what's going on inside, a joyous little boy or girl reflecting on the exposed part of the outer man, a mirror of the inner man, and it blesses people.

Can someone see on your face today that you've been in the intimate presence of God?

"A merry heart makes a cheerful countenance." Proverbs 15:13.

February 20

Before I left my Montana ranch, a little ninety-year old lady, along with her children and some grandchildren came to "find" her early-day farmstead, a lady who, in the early days of our community, before my time, had lived on a farm I now owned, the Pepper Place it was always known as. I guided them to the exact spot of their former dwelling, only a basement and the windmill still visible, situated at the foothills overlooking the Poplar River. As she slowly, quietly, meditated for some time from her wheelchair that sunny afternoon, looking across the wide, long valley, I could just sense her memory bank at work: the neighbor's names, the tough times without electricity or any conveniences, the livestock that grazed the prairies, the horse and buggy days, some years of drought, the old country school just around the corner of a ridge of hills to the south. Finally, she asked, as she looked across the valley, "Which place was the Olson farm, the Haug farm, and the Billy Kraft's horse ranch?" I pointed them out as she became more talkative with her kinfolk at hand.

This biblical experience came to my mind as my imagination stirred a bit, wondering what must have gone through the apostle John's mind out there on the lonely Isle of Patmos by himself. The other eleven were gone, and perhaps John wondered about some of them now, surely a lonely man after all the exciting days with Jesus a few years earlier. Have we not seen pictures of that rugged, remote island that help us to imagine the old disciple "whom Jesus loved", quietly meditating in his forced isolation, as he daily walked those rugged, quiet, beautiful shores where the waves licked at the rocks? John must have gazed out over the blue waters toward Jerusalem many miles away, a longing in his heart, Jerusalem, where he saw Jesus weep, where he mixed with the crowd at the Passover, where he watched Jesus ride into town on a donkey on Palm Sunday. He surely could not shake off remembering the horrific events that led up to the crucifixion and the resurrection of Jesus. He maybe wept when he remembered standing at the foot of the cross that Good Friday afternoon, caressing Mary, the weeping mother of Jesus, to his bosom with soft words of comfort and hope. And, oh yes, that footrace he and Peter had to reach the empty tomb, and the conversation with angelic guardians. And finally, he must have relived over and over again his own suffering and pain he had endured as a spreader of the gospel, facing angry enemies after telling what he and his friends had witnessed about their Lord and Savior Jesus.

I can just see Jeremiah 29:11 in effect here in John's life, God speaking: "I know the thoughts I have toward you, thoughts of peace, not of evil. I give you a future, I give you a hope." And here is John's bold and confident testimony: "It is I, your brother John, a fellow sufferer for the Lord's sake, who is writing this letter to you. I, too, have shared the patience Jesus gives, and we shall share His kingdom." Revelation 1:9.

I believe that because of John's faith and love for Jesus it can be said of him like it was said of Jesus: "...Who for the joy that was set before Him, He endured..." Hebrews 12:2

"I will bless the Lord at all times; His praise shall continually be in my mouth." Psalm 34:1.

February 21

"For by grace are you saved through faith." Ephesians 2:8

Have you ever wondered why there is such a contrast between Christianity, a message of love, and all other "religions" based on works? Why does the Koran of the Muslim faith teach "Kill and destroy every Jew and every Christian on sight"? Or, "Maim them by dismembering their appendages." On and on go the desires of the works of hatred, a spiritual warfare. Works?? "For by grace are you saved through faith...not of works..." Ephesians 2:8-9.

As I have played on this thought, I see it's because with Christianity there must be a change of the heart, which is a miracle. "We are all born with a heart dead in trespass and sin," (Ephesians

2:1) born with a heart alienated from God; a time now to drop the hand of Satan and place it in the hand of Jesus, Who tells us in Matthew 5:44: "but I say to you, love your enemies, bless them that curse you, do good to them that hate you; and pray for those who spitefully use you, and persecute you." Quite a contrast, eh?

It's all summed up in Ezekiel 36:26: "I will remove your stony heart from within you, and put a new heart within you, a heart of flesh; I will put My Spirit within you." The essence of a truly born-again person. I know from experience that a "stone" is impenetrable, and that flesh is not such, in any man's hand, including God's hand. All other faiths are based on works for their salvation. But Paul tells Christendom; "For by grace are you saved through faith...not of works..."

So, it's easy, natural, to live by the desires, the consent, and demands of our old, untamed nature.

We Christians hear Jesus from Mark 8:34; "If any would come after Me, let him deny himself, take up his cross, and follow Me." Get rid of that old "me-first syndrome" and nail that old-nature flesh to a cross, the intent of any cross in those days, to die in the flesh.

PTL that we can serve a living, resurrected Jesus, while all false gods that men serve and worship, have died, and are now only a pile of bones in an earthen grave.

"Weeping may endure for a night, but joy comes in the morning." Psalm 30:5.

Only because the "Light of the world has come" can we find the "joy of the morning."

February 22

"I once was lost, but now am found." Vs.1 "Amazing Grace"

What a fitting testimony for that young twelve-year old Boy Scout in N.C. reported lost in the mountains and forests on Saturday and found Tuesday morning. There were tears of joy in that boy's home, in that community, in that Boy Scout troop, and around the nation as we all joined together in prayer from compassionate hearts. I can just picture the boy as a captive to his own environment, enveloped by a thick forest of tall trees and steep mountain sides. I can imagine the fear that taunted him night and day, the hunger and thirst pangs, the dread of loneliness, and the darkness of night with its low temperatures and no comfortable place to lay his head. Surely, too, the possibility of death must have crossed his mind in that hopeless, helpless, unfriendly environment. Oh, that he might hear God from Isaiah 41:10 to kindle hope, love, joy, peace and security as he trudged along aimlessly: "Fear not, for I am with you; be not dismayed, for I am your God. I will strengthen you; yes, I will help you, I will uphold you with My righteous right hand." That Word from the Lord would be like a helicopter overhead, ready to land and physically retrieve the boy.

During these final Lenten season days, I've appreciated the analogy we are imitating on our way to the celebration of the resurrection from our bondage and lost state of the little boy or girl living inside of each of us, "born dead in trespass and sin," ambling in a wilderness, lost. Like that Boy Scout, we, too, were captive in our dark, dangerous, fearsome, hopeless environment. Cold, starving, continually seeking, but to no avail, an inner vacuum crying out to be found alive. Without our realizing it, we were reaching out with a restless, tormented heart for the comfort and peace of a Word from the mouth of God we hear in Psalm 27: "The Lord is my light and my salvation; Whom shall I fear? The Lord is the strength of my life; of whom shall I be afraid?"

As the helicopter chopped overhead, I can just see that Boy Scout clamoring for an open space in the forest to expose himself in the light, waving his arms for attention. But, there was evidently none. I sense that each one of us who are truly born-again also heard the call from above when we were lost. And on that day we realized our true lost state, and pleaded to be found, and made ourselves exposed to the light. Both our plight and our victory are perfectly described in Ephesians 2 "...dead in trespass and sin" Vs. 1. Then Paul describes our hopeless, helpless picture "you once walked...according to the prince of the air (Satan)...the spirit of disobedience...fulfilling the desires of the flesh and the mind...by nature children of wrath" Vs. 2-3. Lost in the wilderness of sin!!

Then comes the joy of being found in Vs. 4: "But God,...rich in mercy...loved us even when we were dead in trespasses, made us alive together with Christ...For by grace have you been saved through faith...a gift of God, not of works..." Vs. 4-9.

"I will extol You, oh Lord, for You have lifted me up; You've not made my enemies to rejoice over me...I cried unto You and You brought my soul up from the grave; You have kept me alive that I should not go down to the pit...Weeping may endure for a night, but joy comes in the morning." Psalm 30:1-3; 5b.

February 23

"...find a donkey tied, and a colt with her..." Matthew 21:2

Years ago, on a day of meditating from Matt. 21 during the Lenten season, the Lord spoke to me by way of the Holy Spirit, and suddenly: "You are that donkey!"

Jesus said to two disciples as they trod toward Jerusalem: "Go into the village...loose them (donkeys) and bring them to Me." Vs. 2. One day in my early years, Jesus sent an evangelist from Minnesota into my rural community in Montana. He preached the truth from God's Word and I, tied to a post called heritage and tradition, was untied and set free, having heard the truth, and a call from Jesus to take His Word "unto the uttermost parts of the earth." Jesus knew the time was ripe for me to be unloosed, as He also did with the donkey and the colt. Now was the time to be loosed and become available for Jesus. The evangelist's work was to me like the two disciples were to Jesus: "Go...unloose her and her colt"...go and unloose that man and his family. I and three of my sons and my mate were set free to go out and carry Jesus "into the Jerusalems" in our realm of influence. When the evangelist preached, we knew that the Holy Spirit was at work to set us free and to make us ready to share, lay out before Him, unselfishly, our time, talent, and treasure with our generation.

Like the people with Jesus that day on their way into Jerusalem, we, too, enjoyed praise and worship in a brand new way. We, too, could now sing from the heart: "Hosanna to the Son of David;

Hosanna to the Highest." Vs. 9. We had welcomed Jesus into our hearts like they welcomed Him into Jerusalem. We then spread out before Him our unselfish portion of our gifts and possessions on hand as they did with the branches and the garments.

"If anyone desires to come after Me, let him deny himself, and take up his cross and follow Me." Matt. 16:24. There's the key: the flesh to die, the spirit to rise up alive. Crucifixion and resurrection!! And those following behind Jesus end up with Calvary, the crucifixion, and the resurrection, not only for Jesus, but for the untied donkey and his family. "Believe on the Lord Jesus Christ, and you will be saved, you and your household." Paul: Acts 26:31.

It means the end of being tied to that "me-first syndrome." It means allowing the old nature flesh to be crucified on a cross, giving up the bondage of sin. And then the realization: "If any man be in Christ Jesus, he is a new creation; old things have passed away; behold, all things have become new" for the precious inner man, the God part of us, the spirit and soul. II Cor 5:17.

Yes, I saw myself as a donkey, my family alongside, as the colt, willing and obedient to be set free for a Divine, eternal, purpose.

"I will bless the Lord at all times; His praise shall continually be in my mouth. My soul shall make its boast in the Lord; the humble shall hear of it and be glad. Come now, let us magnify the Lord, let us exalt His name together." Ps 34:1-3

PTL (Praise the Lord) for the light that that first resurrection of ours shines upon a dark soul in bondage to sin. Eph. 2:1-9

February 24

"...Do not be afraid nor dismayed...for the battle is not yours, but God's." II Chronicles 20:15

Trials are purposed to drive us into God's Word, and I appreciate that, my antidote to usually unpleasant life experiences.

One day in my desperate search, King Jehosophat and I became real close brothers in the Lord as I found II Chronicles 20 my antidote. We each had three enemies knocking at our door to destroy us. He had the armies of Moab, Ammon, and Mt. Seir surrounding him like a band of coyotes surrounds a flock of sheep, maneuvering for the kill. I had the three enemies of long-time drought, severe infestation of grasshoppers, and exceedingly high interest on borrowed money, devastating my farm and ranch operation.

When I heard from the heart of God "Do not fear nor be dismayed, for the battle is not yours but God's," a heavy load fell from my back instantly, and I eagerly went on to satisfy my hunger for more instruction God gives to His people in a trial I could empathize with.

God intimated to the king and to me that there is no armor for the backside, so do not run away, but face your enemy, not in your own strength and power, but in God's.

"As I was with Moses, so I will be with you" God to Joshua, Joshua 1:5. "Surely I will be with you, and you shall defeat the Midianites as one man." God to Gideon, Judges 6: 16. "This day the Lord will deliver you into my hand." David to Goliath, I Sam. 17:46.

So, with child-like faith I listened from II Chronicles 20: "Tomorrow, go down against them...you will not need to fight. Position yourselves, stand still, and see the salvation of the Lord... go out against them for the Lord is with you." Vs. 16-17.

I positioned myself in the same world as the King and his people, stood still and waited upon the Lord as that trial drug on for almost a decade. I learned the power of praise from a thankful heart along the way like Jehosophat and his people learned and practiced: "Now, when they began to sing and to praise, thy Lord set ambushes against the people of Ammon, Moab, and Mt. Seir...and they were defeated." Vs. 22.

"God frustrates the devices of the crafty so that their hands cannot carry out their plans." Job 5: 12.

"So when Judah came to a place overlooking the wilderness... there were the dead bodies...no one had escaped." Vs. 24.

As I patiently waited in prayer and praise, the skies began to pour out rain, the grasshoppers vanished to this very day, interest rates descended quickly, and the price of grain came upward at the market place.

The title to the ranch was saved, "Not by might, not by power, but by My Spirit" says the Lord." Zechariah 4:6.

"Because of Your mercies, I am not consumed, because Your compassions never fail; they are new every morning; great is Your faithfulness." Lamentations 3:23-24

February 25

"...sealed for the day of redemption..." Ephesians 4:30b

Canning garden vegetables and fruit, beef, pork, and chicken raised on a typical Midwest farm blessed the dinner table of farm households delightfully in the cold of winter in generations past. My mother spent literally years of her life standing over the hot old coal range, watching over the pressure cooker filled with glass jars full of produce raised on the farm. That was the day before deep freezers or even locker plants on most small town main streets. It was the pioneer day's means of food preservation. Most of the quart jars were capped with a light tin cap placed on top of a rubber seal and pressed down with a threaded ring. Then, throughout the evening, as the jars stood on the cupboard top, we could hear one lid "pop" after another, guaranteeing the seal of that jar now ready to be put away for the winter, or perhaps even winters ahead.

Most of us adults remember standing before an altar in a church where we sealed our marriage with vows originating in the heart and verbalized with the voice, a marriage made in Heaven, sealed "til death do we part."

All this for protection and preservation.

I see each of us at our birth like a raw product, subject to everlasting spoilage because of inherent sin, like raw products of the old farmstead, ready to spoil because of bacteria and decay. But one verse of scripture preserves every believer as Jesus declares in John 10:28: "And I give them eternal life; and they shall never perish; neither shall anyone snatch them out of my hand." Why? Because of the assurance: "The Spirit of truth...you know, for He dwells with you and will be in you." John 14:17.

When we've been through the heat of the old "pressure cooker," the Holy Spirit walking alongside us to nudge us to make a choice—life or death—we come to a point of surrender to Jesus. Then the Holy Spirit moves into our clay frame and attaches Himself like a Siamese twin to our inner man. I Corinthians 6:19. Then are we "sealed for the day of redemption."

Halleluiah for that resurrection day when the sealed lid "pops" open and we've been preserved for an eternity in the bosom of Jesus.

"I will extol You, oh Lord, for You have lifted me up..." David, Psalm 30:1.

February 26

"Eli, Eli, lama sabachthani?" Matthew 27:46

My rancher son and I found a big, young, healthy cow with a bloated belly; she looked like a barrel with hide over it. We locked her head into a headstall and did what any layman in the cow business would do. We injected a garden hose down her esophagus, into her stomach. That got no response, so we injected a trocar into the middle of a triangular area just ahead of the hipbone, an operation that lets smelly, gaseous, material escape, but to no avail. So, we loaded her into a stock trailer and hurried to the local vet for help. To get her into his barn where the vet wanted to secure her head in his big metal headstall, she had to pass through a regular walk-in door that was so much too narrow that even a blind rancher with common sense could see the plight of the innocent beast. The proud, professional vet, decked out with western hat, tight jeans, and sharp, high healed cowboy boots, climbed the corral fence, straddled the cow and punched her bloated belly with his heels until she fell down and died.

Every time I think of that innocent animal being put to death like that by a man's physical abuse, a manifestation of indecent anger, I think of Jesus at Calvary. There, too, was an innocent One the madness of this world, put to death in a most inhumane way

From Matthew 27 we read of how Pilate scourged Jesus, then delivered Him to be crucified. They stripped Him of His clothing, and twisted a crown of thorns upon His head, and placed a reed in His right hand. They spat on Him and with the reed struck Him on the head. They taunted and mocked Him, drawing blood from His back with severe whipping. They gave Him sour wine mixed with gall to drink. Then they crucified Him by nailing His hands and feet to a cross with huge spikes, and when the cross was raised up and the base dropped into a hole, there was excruciating pain and nearly impossible lung function as His weight bore down on the spikes.

As the innocent cow gave her life at the hand of an intemperate veterinarian, so Jesus, innocent of sin, became the sacrifice for every man's sin at the hands of intemperate Roman soldiers. The significant difference, however, poured from Jesus' love-filled heart: "Father, forgive them for they know not what they do." Luke 23:34. The spikes hurt His flesh, but surely His greatest pain erupted when He forced Himself: "My God, My God, why have You forsaken Me?" Mark 15:34. "Eli, Eli, lama, sabachthani?"

By His resurrection from the tomb He proved for us: "Weeping may endure for a night, but joy comes in the morning." Psalm 30:5.

"It was for the joy that was set before Him that He endured the cross." Hebrews 12:2.

Any of our suffering for Him is meager compared to His suffering for us!!

February 27

"...old things passed away, all things become new..." II Corinthians 5:17

On Main Street in a small western town, a Baptist church and a bar stood side by side. On an evening when the church called Mavis to worship or to a Bible study, the bar beckoned Stan to come and enjoy the "glitter of this world." Winter and summer, since church dismissed hours before the bar had to legally close, she waited for Stan, praying all that time against the forces of evil and for his salvation. Many years of this tested her patience, her love, her perseverance until one Sunday morning when he dressed up and escorted her to the little Baptist church, from which he received Jesus as his

Savior, and immediately Lord of his life, a "brand new creation, old things passed way and all things become new."

As the charismatic movement came through that area, it drew many of us together for special evangelistic meetings and for many of us a week together at a Bible camp in the Rockies.

A couple years passed by and Mavis was suddenly taken home as her heart failed her. A hushed bit of gossip began to float in and out of both the bar and the church: "Now, will Stan keep his faith?" the church wondered, while the bar crowd was sure they would get him back in that small community where everybody knows everybody.

Stan stood strong, kept his faith, and in time married a former high school classmate. The Christian community rejoiced and stood by him with prayer, love, and great fellowship.

The couple retired from farming only a short time later, and on their way to their new home in the Rockies, a vehicle accident claimed the wife's life, an accident where he stood by and with several others watched her burn to death. He then married a third time and they lived in that retirement home in the Rockies, very close to the Bible camp where I last saw Stan, still surrendered to Jesus, worshiping Him in spirit, soul, and body.

Stan reminds me of Job, pelted on every side by trials for nine long months. He lost his family, his wealth, his health, the loyalty of three close friends, and the patience of his spouse.

Men like Job and Stan are blessed when they can "pass through the waters and the rivers and walk through the fires..." Isaiah 43:3, and still leave a testimony to the world like Job left in chapter 19:25: "For I know that my Redeemer lives. And He shall stand at last on the earth ...that in my flesh I shall see God...how my heart yearns within me."

As praise was with Job and my friend Stan, so it was with David in Psalm 30:1: "I will extol You, oh Lord, for You have lifted me up. You have not allowed my enemies to rejoice over me."

February 28

"Loose him and bring him here...because the Lord has need of him" Luke 10:30

One day years ago during my Holy Week meditation on Luke 19:30 those Words grabbed my special attention, the Lord here speaking of a colt on His way to Jerusalem on Palm Sunday. I pictured myself as that colt tied to a post when I heard Jesus speak to His disciples. The colt was tied to a post in Jerusalem just ahead, presumably eating hay or grass, or sleeping, or perhaps nursing, or just basking in the comforts of his animal nature's world. Maybe he was waiting for his mother to loose him and take him out into the hills where he could kick up his heels. Here he was just simply a young, useless beast of burden that day, tied to a post, going nowhere in life. Jesus said to two of His disciples: "Go into the village...you'll find a colt...loose him and bring him here." Jesus spoke here as One with authority, and might as well have said: "Loose him for he is Mine to loose." Jesus laid claim to the colt for a season for a specific purpose. As I read and meditated, I thought: "Am I not like that colt in the eyes of Jesus?" standing by without much worth unless Jesus calls me out for a specific purpose. Am I not tied to a post of "heritage and tradition" in this dead church body I am part of? Am I not tied to the awful secular world's posts all around me?—my own inherent flesh, and even the temptations of Satan? Am I not tied to that "me-first" syndrome, and deaf to Christ's call on my life? "...if you would come after Me, deny yourself, take up your cross, and follow Me." Has not Jesus full claim to me, the One who loved me with Agape love before I was conceived, sanctified me before I was born, anointed me to be saved one day to spend eternity in Heaven with Him, created in His image, a spirit being? He gave me a normal birth into an earthly family, living in a Christian-based nation where I can claim with David: "Blessed are You, Lord God, my Father FOREVER AND EVER!" addressing the real, only God, the God of creation and salvation, while most of the world is worshiping a false god.

I love that phrase: "The Lord has need of him"—need of even a colt tied to a post. "Then they brought him (the colt) to Jesus." One evening at a gathering of truly born-again believers when I saw I needed what they had, Jesus used "disciples" to unloose me for a ride I could give Jesus when they prayed for me, and brought this "colt" to Jesus for a specific purpose. "Then they brought him to

Jesus. And they threw their own garments on the colt, and they set Jesus on him." No saddle, but garments, a saddle blanket for His comfort. That evening of prayer for this "colt" put on me the robe of righteousness, the belt of truth, the sandals of peace, and the helmet of salvation, and loosed the Holy Spirit unto liberty and freedom in my life, now ready to give Jesus a ride first into my own little Jerusalem, and then into Judea and Samaria, and to the uttermost parts of the earth: into many cities and countrysides as I would now unselfishly share my time, talent and treasure with Him.

My friend, Jesus is looking for your availability like that colt even more so than your ability.

March 1

"Oh what a beautiful morning, Oh, what a beautiful day. I've got a wonderful feeling everything's a goin' my way"... a refrain from the play "Oklahoma" that entertained for many months on Broadway during WWII. The second cast of that play found its way to France, where, on a nice, warm, summer evening about twilight, I was blessed as a GI in the army. The refrain acted as a good meal to my lonely soul as it took me so glibly back to the freedom I enjoyed as a boy on the Montana prairies, now echoed and acted out on similar prairies of Oklahoma. I can still see that male singer riding so freely down that old gravel road in his horse-drawn "surrey with the fringe on top", singing as carefree as a bird.

It reminds me today of vs. 1-2 of Psalm 100: "Make a joyful sound unto the Lord all you lands; Serve the Lord with gladness; Come before His presence with singing..."

When I think of that refrain from Oklahoma, and what it did for me, I think of Joseph, Jacob's younger son, the apple of his eye, who was abused by his jealous brothers in the absence of his father out on the prairies of Canaan, and thrown into a deep pit to die. But immediately was then sold as a slave to some foreigners who came by. Talk about his loneliness, lonely for his freedom of boyhood days, rejected now like many experience in a divorce from their mate. Trial and tribulation continued when he was hired by Potiphar to care for some chores around his home, and suddenly was accused of seducing Potiphar's wife. She conjured up a lie to deceive her husband. Joseph was imprisoned and literally forgot about for thirteen years. Sometime later, when his brothers came back into his life, humbled by a famine in Canaan, ashamed of their jealousy of bygone days, we hear from Joseph, now Pharaoh's second in command, "You meant if for bad, but God meant it for good." Kind, forgiving, generous, Godly Joseph must surely have rejoiced in his inner man the day he was reconciled with his brothers with "Oh, what a beautiful morning, oh, what a beautiful day, I've got a wonderful feeling, everything's going my way."

"For we know that all things work together for good for those who love God, to those who are the called according to His purpose" Romans 8:28. And His purpose is that such man be conformed to the image of Jesus, like Joseph kept himself throughout the trials. Vs. 29.

I believe Joseph's testimony from his mouth and from his blessed actions was so genuine because he trusted from day one in Proverbs 3:5-6: "Trust in the Lord with all your heart, and lean not on your own understanding; in all your ways acknowledge Him, And He shall direct your paths."

"Oh, what a beautiful morning...beautiful day..." when we hear the invitation of Jeremiah 33:3 ringing in our ear: "Call upon Me and I will answer you, and show you great and mighty things you do not know." To this Joseph would say "Amen."

From one who can sing with David this morning: "I will extol You, oh Lord, for You have lifted me up." Psalm 30:1

March 2

"The thief has not come but to kill, steal and destroy; but I have come to give life and give it abundantly." John 10:10

My brother and I, high school students, sat one evening at the dining room table doing our school homework. Suddenly very suddenly, a severe headache came upon me, and, alarmed, I noticed my brother slumped over and both of my parents passed out in the living room. Impulsively!!! "Gas fumes," and I rushed to open doors and windows, and to awaken my family. In our basement, a Delco, 32-volt light plant ran occasionally in those pre-REA days to keep the huge batteries charged that supplied electricity for our farmstead. Upon investigation, the exhaust pipe had broken off, consequently retaining in our home the deadly exhaust intended to be expelled outdoors. The enemy had come to "kill, steal and destroy" four lives, but our Lord intervened at exactly the proper moment and "gave life abundantly."

I am reminded of the Israelites in a similar dire need which God also took care of "just in time"—their coming to the Red Sea on their way to freedom—a life or death matter, and on either side of them unscaleable natural walls, an unaffordable sea in front, and an enemy behind, bent on one thing: "to kill, steal, and destroy." But "just in time," God acted upon the prayer of Moses and opened up the Red Sea for His three million or so people, dried its floor, and hustled His people to safety, "just in time" to destroy the enemy stepping into that same riverbed only minutes later. Exodus 14:21

"Out of the mouths of babes and infants You have ordered strength, because of your enemies, that you may silence the enemy and the avenger". Psalm 8:3.

From my mouth over these past sixty five years has frequently come praise and thanks for our deliverance that evening, a song, much like Moses and his family sang from Exodus 15:1, just as appropriate as he, too; and his Israelite family escaped death at the exact needed moment when God intervened. Then Moses and the children of Israel sang this song to the Lord:

"I will sing to the Lord,
For He has triumphed gloriously!
The horse and its rider
He has thrown into the sea!
The Lord is my strength and song,
And He has become my salvation.
He is my God. And I will praise Him...
My father's God, and I will exalt Him
...Pharaoh's chariots He has cast into the sea,
His chosen captains also are
Drowned in the Red Sea,
The depths have covered them,
They sank to the bottom like a stone."

My personal testimony rings out from Psalm 37:25: "I have been young, and now am old; yet I have not seen the righteous forsaken..." I praise God that "Greater is He that is in me than he that is in the world" I John 4:4.

Praise flows naturally from a grateful heart "in the morning, at noontime, and when the sun goes down."

March 3

"You can be sure your sin will find you out." Numbers 32:23.

Most of us as mischievous little children got "caught with our hand in the cookie jar." But how many grownups have been caught with their daughter in a grain bin? A "light-fingered," very husky couple in Montana placed a scoop shovel into their pickup box, piled into the cab with their teenage daughter and drove to a remote bin of wheat out in the hills away from mainstream traffic or civilization. They backed up to the bin, opened the door, and the husky young daughter climbed into the bin and put the shovel into gear, intending to fill the pickup box and head for the grain elevator in town. "You can be sure your sin will find you out" when the owner of the wheat drives into the yard. The parents, sorely shocked, fled the scene, leaving the daughter with the shovel in the bin. They let kleptomania, the passion of the flesh, get them into trouble, even though the odds were highly against their being "found out."

"But the eyes of the Lord run to and fro throughout the whole earth..." 2 Chronicles 16:9. "His own iniquities entrap the wicked man, and he is caught in the cords of his sin" Proverbs 5:22.

One evening King David walked on the roof of his house, and allowed his eyes to fall on beautiful, naked Bathsheba bathing next door. Uncontrollable lust for her arose, and he foolishly arranged for a night with her at his house. She conceived a child, and then began David's cover-up. Her husband, Uriah, was ordered home from the war-front with David's intent to give him a special furlough, and time for him to be with his wife. Uriah refused such a favor when he arrived home, loyal to his buddies on the front line. Since "Plan A" failed, David engaged "Plan B"—to kill Uriah "in action" on the front line so he could legally marry Bathsheba and claim the baby as his own, a deceitful cover-up. "But the thing that David had done displeased the Lord." 2 Samuel 11:26.

"The eyes of the Lord are in every place, keeping watch on the evil and the good." Proverbs 15:3.

"The Lord sent Nathan to David...and with him, a parable to bring David to his knees in repentance. There were two men...one with many flocks of sheep and one with only one ewe lamb. A guest came to the rich man's house. The man with many flocks refused to butcher one of his own but chose to steal the poor man's only lamb to feed his guest. And angry David rose up, 'As the Lord lives, the man who has done this shall surely die...and restore fourfold... because he had no pity.'" 2 Samuel 12:5-6. "Then Nathan said to David, 'You are the man...Then David said to Nathan, 'I have sinned against the Lord. And Nathan said to David, 'The Lord has put away your sin, you shall not die.'"

"If we confess our sins, He is faithful and just to forgive us our sins, and to cleanse us from all unrighteousness." 1 John 1:9. "For the eyes of the Lord are on the righteous, and His ears are open to their prayers." 1 Peter 3:12.

March 4

Ever since I was a very young boy out on the prairies, I have heard the "ring of freedom" and I have known my heritage as very secure, my liberty guaranteed. My brother and I, scaling the hills and crossing the valleys, on horseback or on foot, occasionally met horse-drawn wagon-loads of Indians or Gypsies, and without any fear, when they would stop and visit with us. As a first grader in the old country school in 1932, I saw on my classroom walls the large portraits of Lincoln and Washington, and not only at our school, but hundreds of others across the land in that era. Seven or eight decades ago, fresh on the heels of our WWI victory, public school kids were proud of the political and military heroes of our history, and had instilled in our young, fresh, innocent, curious minds a decent respect for our inherited, traditional values stemming from an uncanny sense of freedom and liberty in religious, as well as social, political, economic, and educational worlds. We learned to love America and to pledge allegiance to the flag from joyous hearts without any opposition. We bowed our heads in prayer and sang with gusto those old familiar Deep South spirituals of our black brothers. I became especially attached to Abraham Lincoln, my hero as a pioneer, a man of God eventually, with extremely powerful traits of character, a love for humanity, especially for the down-and-out in our society, and finally as President of the U.S. Today, he is still my most respected hero. I was born sixty years too late, however, to ever get to know him in person, so that all I have is what Herndon and other historians and biographers have recorded.

And you know something? That's exactly how it is with many, many professing believers in Jesus this morning...knowing Jesus and facts of salvation, the intellectual part, without knowing Him as Savior personally. One day John 17:3, an integral part of Jesus' lengthy prayer, became a point for me to sincerely contend with daily in my Christian walk, where Jesus prayed: "This is eternal life, that they may know You, the only true God, and Jesus Christ whom You have sent." If God were to quiz believers on Christianity in general today, many would score well on such questions as "Did

Christ die for your sins? Did He rise from the dead? Is He coming back to earth?" Or, do you trust Him for your every day keep or your checking account? What about the "toughies" like these: "Will you trust Me with your life? Will you entrust yourself to My church family? Will you serve Me by genuinely sharing from your heart, your time, talent, and treasure, as you get involved with ministries?" "You search the scriptures, for in them you think you have eternal life; and these are they which testify of Me. But, you are not willing to come to Me, that you may have life." John 5:39-40. Can you agree with many facts in the written Word, but haven't yet surrendered your heart to Jesus, the Living Word?

This devotion coming from one who knows the facts of salvation, and the freedom and liberty it brings to life, but also one who knows the Savior, the Author of that freedom and liberty.

March 5

"And the light shines in the darkness..." John 1:5.

The deep post holes were dug, the cement poured, the tall, steel uprights in place, the welding completed, the electrical wires in place and the switches installed. Weeks had passed by, and all the volunteers now on deck. I remember well that dark evening when I was cultivating my field, and suddenly the city built on a hill six miles away lit up and the new baseball diamond was ready to host the state of Montana Legion baseball tournament, which our team won that year.

Reminds me of another dark night when the sky lighted up suddenly: "Now there were in the same country (Bethlehem) shepherds living out in the fields, keeping watch over their flock by night. And behold...the glory of the Lord shone around them..." Luke 2:8-9. The "glory of the Lord" is a light so bright as to put to shame the mechanical electric power; so bright that all of heaven is lighted 24/7 with that radiant glory of God. God had come to earth in the Person of His Son Jesus, Who went directly to a cross at Calvary to shine on all humanity as He took our dark sin upon Himself, and shed His blood to wash our inner being clean.

"You He...made alive who were dead in trespasses and sins..." Ephesians 2:1. "...You brought my soul up from the grave..." Psalm 30:3. Spiritually alienated from God we were from birth. But now: "the light shines in the darkness." John 1:5.

"I will extol You, oh Lord, for you have lifted me up; You have not allowed my enemy to rejoice over me...weeping may endure for a night, but joy comes in the morning." Psalm 30:1, 5.

Whether from a physically lighted baseball diamond in Montana or from a divine light over a lowly manger in Bethlehem, I hear Jesus: "I am the Light of the world..." John 8:12.

March 6

"The Crown of Life..." Rev. 2:10

I enjoyed an evening of the SD State AA basketball tournament for consolation winner and the championship. Only one team, of course, captured the trophy for state champion, an undefeated team in tournament play. A lengthy ordeal preceded the big crowning as players, coaches, and team managers of several teams paraded across the gym floor to receive their respective trophies as they placed in the tourney. Trophies, trophies, trophies...handshakes, congratulations, news media and TV personnel capturing the hour via camera. What a thrill it must have been for those teenage boys, the coaches, the cheer leaders, school superintendents and principals, and, yes, the parents and school fans.

Then, I thought to myself, "Can this be a miniature of the hour when the "crown of life" will be neatly placed on the head of each winner on God's team, those who played the game of life by the grace of God and now have won the championship award?"

"Trust in the Lord with all your heart...acknowledge Him in all your ways, and He will direct your paths." Proverbs 3:5-6,

It was in the Easter season when Jesus captured His crown of life for His work of love and obedience while here on earth, His big victory was that Good Friday afternoon at Calvary, and that early Easter morning when He was raised from the tomb, alive, never again to die! And we recall His last Word from the cross: "It is finished." No more necessary, His big crowning victory we find in Colossians 2:15 when His spirit descended into the bowels of the earth and "overcame powers and principalities, made an open show of them, and triumphed over His victory on the cross." Jesus the champion!!

It was the eternal "joy that was set before Him" that compelled Jesus to win, the joy of now having sacrificed His perfect body and pure, clean, innocent, sinless blood to pay for the sins of all of humanity. It was a real genuine, God-pleasing, acceptable sacrifice for the inherent sin problem. And now, also, the joy of knowing that all who would accept Him and His work on Calvary will be crowned as a winner, and spend eternity with Him. "...for whosoever believes on Him shall not perish, but have everlasting life." John 3:16. A double trophy of joy...one for Coach Jesus and one for you and me, His team.

The losers of the game of life are Satan and "anyone not found written in the Book of Life was cast into the lake of fire." Revelation 20:15.

When the last buzzer sounds and the clock shows zero time left, all will know whose team we were playing on: "And they that be wise shall shine as the brightness of the firmament..." Daniel 12:3. A crown of bright, shining stars?? Sparkling diamonds??

March 7

"The Lord, He is God" I Kings 18:39

"Whoa! Stop!" cries out a helpless old-timer of yesteryear while pulling on the steering wheel with all his might when he made his transfer from horse and buggy days to the old model T Ford which failed to respond like a horse and sometimes ran into a river, through a garage wall, or sometimes into a snowbank or a pile of rocks or quicksand. Almost as nerve-wrecking and pressured as was my trip to the airport the other day, starting a bit late, stopping on red at almost every stoplight, waiting patiently for a slow train to pass by, and finally, unexpected road construction. The return trip, on the other hand, was almost a continuous flow of green lights from the airport to my driveway. Such is life, I thought to myself—some smooth travel, some rough.

And here I think of prophet Elijah from 1 Kings 18 where one day he enjoyed a mountain top experience when his "barbecue," cooked by the fire from Heaven, proved to the false prophets of Baal that Elijah's God was One of power while their god was powerless. "Now, when all the people saw it they fell on their faces; and they said: 'The Lord, He is God! The Lord, He is God'" The false prophets were seized and executed, and on his escape from angry Queen Jezebel, hot on his heels, to a peaceful recourse with Elisha and the transfer of anointing; Elijah hit several stop and go lights under some pressure, running for his life to Beersheba, and then after a day's journey, depressed and tired, stopped and sat under a juniper tree, waiting, waiting for the stop light to turn green, begging God: "Lord, take my life, for I am no better than my fathers." Vs. 19:4. The light turned green as an angel ministered food and water to him, and the light turned red as he lay down and slept again. The light turned green again as the angel returned, touched him and said: "'Arise and eat...the journey is too great for you.' So he arose, and ate and drank, and he went on in the strength of that food for forty days and forty nights as far as Horeb, the mountain of God." The stop light turned red and he went into a cave and spent the night. When the Lord spoke to him, wallowing in self-pity. "What are you doing here, Elijah?" The light turned green at God's command and he went out on a mountain side where he felt a hurricane wind go by, and then an earthquake, and then a fire, but the Lord was in none of these scary storms. Then he heard God in a quiet, gentle voice, "What are you doing here, Elijah?" The light turned green and he desperately fled from there, found Elisha plowing in a field, passed by him and threw his mantle on him, transferring power of prophecies twice fold. Our lives, too, are as a roller coaster, full of starts and stops as we learn to walk in Proverbs 3:5-8: "Trust the Lord with all your heart and lean not unto your own understanding; acknowledge Him in all your ways, and He will direct your paths."

The stops and starts, the red and green lights in our lives, trials galore, will make us, too, ready to pass our tried and tested mantel on to the next generation as God's work continues until His return.

March 8

"If anyone desires to come after Me, let him deny himself...and follow Me." Matt. 16:24.

    To follow Jesus takes a faith that costs something, complete surrender of time, talent, and treasure, sacrifice of spirit, soul, and body as they are brought unto discipline. "Deny himself" Jesus said, bury that innate "me-first syndrome". "And take up his cross", a means of execution was Jesus implying, a death of the old self, the old nature we are all born with, death to that which separates us from God...unconfessed sin, the world around us, the flesh part of our inner man like as He gave up His physical life (flesh) and shed His blood. His body was broken, sacrificed...His flesh for your sin and mine; to stand in our place before a just God to declare our innocence as truly born-again people, while the man of the world will stand alone at the White Throne Judgment, pleading his own merits which the prophet tells us is "as filthy rags" in the sight of God. His pure, clean, innocent, sinless blood poured from His pierced side to become a detergent for the inner man's first bath. And we can hear from Isaiah 1:18: "Come now, let us reason together, says the Lord: Though your sins be as scarlet, they shall be white as snow; though they are red like crimson, they shall be as wool."
    From 11 Tim. 2, we find four word pictures portraying perseverance of service that magnify Jesus' command "deny yourself." First, "You must endure hardship as a good soldier"...one who leaves family, friends, vocation, or school to please his nation now at war. Vs. 3-4.
    "An athlete is not crowned unless he plays by the rules" Vs. 5. I've seen basketball, baseball, and hockey players expelled for bad conduct, sent to the shower room.
    The farmer, a hardworking, disciplined man of Paul's day, cut the grain with a scythe, and picked it up in their arms to tie in a bundle, which later was flailed, beaten to remove the ripe seeds. A sacrifice of long hours and human energy.

The fourth picture is of Paul himself in Vs. 8: "I suffer trouble as an evildoer, even to the point of chains", a jailed evangelist, "...enduring all things for the sake of the elect..."

This devotion coming from one who has learned that the sharing of time, talent, and treasure must be sacrificial to satisfy our Lord. His was!! Is yours?

March 9

"Look for a thing where you dropped it." A true proverb.

"I looked for him, but I did not-find him." Song of Solomon 3: 1.

Oh, how many times I dropped a washer, a bolt, a nut, a fine spring, a cotter key or a drift key onto the ground, into stubble or cultivated dirt while lying under the tractor, the combine, the baler, or the implement I was trying to repair out in the field. I looked for the "thing" where I thought I had dropped it, sometimes to no avail until I prayed. PTL for such a "magnetic force", a magnifying glass, extra keen eyesight when the Lord became "Reachable Jesus," reachable because the Holy Spirit living within us and about us, reachable as we put our hand and our trust in His hand with child-like faith, and today walk another mile across this old earth as a pilgrim headed for a promised land, traveling on a bumpy road just like Jesus traveled on across this same planet. He, too, was headed back to His promised land where He has prepared a room for every believer that His hand has led "Reachable Jesus." "...if I go to prepare a place for you, I will come again and receive you to Myself, that where I am, there you may be also." John 14:3. Reachable Jesus forever!!!

But for some, He may not still be a "reachable Jesus" because coziness with Him has been replaced with aloofness along the bumpy trek of life. Have you quit praying on a daily, disciplined visit to the closet? It is there you must return to find Him. Or, has His reach escaped you because of sin? Confession and repentance are your way back. "If we confess our sin, He is faithful and just to forgive our sin, and to cleanse us from all unrighteousness..." I John 1:9. "If My people which are called by Name will humble themselves and pray and seek My face and turn from their wicked ways,

I will hear them from Heaven, I will forgive their sin, and I will heal their land." II Chronicles 7:14

"Look for a thing where you dropped it," lest you too, must confess with the author of Song of Solomon 3:1: "I looked for Him, but I did not find Him" a discouraging, deplorable grievance which also is eternal.

I praise God this morning that "In the beginning was the Word, and the Word was with God, and the Word was God...and the Word became flesh and dwelt among us...full of grace and truth." John 1:1, 14.

As a shepherd who walked before my flock of sheep on the ranch, so is Jesus to me this day, "reachable Jesus," my shepherd I love and seek to follow.

March 10

Keep your eyes upon Jesus!

I hear from Heaven this morning the chorus: "Turn your eyes upon Jesus, look full in His wonderful face; and the things of earth will grow strangely dim in the light of His glory and grace." Oh how much of our attention and fellowship with Jesus is blurred at devotional time, during Bible study time, or when the anointed message is flowing from the pulpit, all because we allow our minds and hearts to wander to the dinner just ahead, or the afternoon game of baseball or golf, or the fishing trip to the lake, or the dealing on a new car or piece of real estate in the mix. One day I took a trip with Peter, James, and John who followed Jesus to the Mount of Transfiguration where "His face shone like the sun and His garments dazzling white" as He stood there conversing with Elijah "the prophet" and Moses, "the law" and suddenly Peter's imaginative mind and his fleshly eye veered from the scene, a carelessness that caused God to bellow across the universe: "This is My beloved Son in whom I am well pleased. HEAR HIM!"—a powerful, unexpected voice that put the disciples on their faces on the ground, their hearts full of fear. A moment later Jesus came and touched them and said: "Arise, and do not be afraid." When they opened their eyes, they saw only Jesus; Elijah and Moses were now gone. Here we get an exhortation of the thrill and importance and benefit of engaging two precious senses, to keep our sole attention on Jesus.

The writer of Proverbs 4:20 brings further emphasis and clarity: "My son, give attention to My Words; incline your ear to My sayings; let them not depart from before your eyes; keep them in the midst of your heart; for they are life unto those who find them, and health unto their flesh." Like Peter, we so often need repeated trials before we learn and establish a truth in our hearts. Out on the lake one day in a ravishing storm, Jesus came to the boat, walking on the water. Impulsive Peter laid his staring eyes upon Jesus, prayed for a favor, a blessing, heard the gentle invitation "Come" and did very well walking on the water until he allowed his eye to fall from Jesus onto the storm, which filled him with fear and a drowning situation. Oh, to keep our eye on Jesus that we might "see His glory and grace," on that One who tells us in Isaiah 43:1: "I created you, oh Jacob. I formed you, oh Israel. Do not fear for I have redeemed you. You are mine. I call you by name, so that when you pass through the water I will be with you, and when you go through the rivers they shall not overflow you. When you walk through the fire you shall not be burned, nor shall the flame scorch you. For I am the Lord your God, the Holy One of Israel, your Savior."

What a day that will be when we see Jesus face to face on the other side of our resurrection, and see Him sitting on the Throne of Judgment, and hear Him say: "Enter in and inherit the kingdom prepared for you from the foundation of the world, My good and faithful servant."

March 11

"The changeless Christ" Hebrews 13:8

> "I know not what the day may bring-
> Tomorrow waits unknown;
> But this I know, the changeless Christ,
> My Lord, is on the throne." Anonymous

And this I know, that when I stood at the foot of that cross with child-like faith, confessed my sin from a truly repentant heart, and was bathed in the blood of Jesus flowing from His side—this I know—that cross became a bridge over the deep gulf that afore existed between me and that throne room, and into the presence of a never changing God (Matthew 3:6), and His unchanging Son, "Jesus Christ, the same yesterday, today, and forever." Hebrews 13:8

I love that confidence-building, security-endowed phrase "the changeless Christ," Who is the same today as before the day of creation. What a truth to let linger in our hearts and meander through our minds daily when we search the scriptures in our times of joy, and with hearts of thanks and praise, and find we are listening to, and conversing with, the same God, the same Jesus as David or the sons of Korah, or Peter, James and John, or the many old testament saints whose inner man was literally exploding with ecstasy. Or, on the other hand, when trials, temptations and tribulations are so heavy upon us, and divert our course of life, we suddenly find ourselves walking side by side with Abraham, Jacob, Samuel, Hannah, Ruth, Elijah or Elisha, King David, Daniel, or the three Hebrew children, King Jehosophat, Jeremiah, or the four lepers, and brother Paul, and again we find we are rescued, encouraged, edified, set free by the same God that they were in their life experiences. Oh, what a wonderful comfort to know a "changeless Christ," One Who never experiences a need, totally complete, even as cultures and times change. How severely all things in my life have changed since 1926, so changed that it is unbelievable in every facet of life imaginable. Why? Because I needed change to be able to claim the "changeless Christ" as my Lord and Savior.

Has Jesus revealed Himself so clearly in the scriptures to you, that you have discovered, too, that Jesus is a "changeless Christ," sitting in control on your heart's throne today?

From Matthew 22:42 we hear Jesus asking some Pharisees: "What do you think about the Christ?"—a very personal question we all need to face and then dig into our heart for an honest answer. Is He just a Sunday morning acquaintance to you, or seven-day-a-week Lord of your life in spirit, soul, body, finances, and your relationships?

Oh, to remember that this "changeless Christ" has already "been there and done that"!! Next time when things turn against you, remember Hebrews 4:15: "For we do not have a High Priest Who cannot sympathize with our weaknesses, but was in all points tempted as we are, yet without sin."

"The grass withers, the flower fades, but the Word of the Lord endures forever." Isaiah 40:8. The Word and the "changeless Christ" are synonymous. John 1:1, 14.

From one whose testimony of the "changeless Christ" never changes.

March 12

"...and on this rock I will build My church..." Matthew 16:18.

Jesus and His little brood were huddled together and suddenly, out of the clear blue sky, Jesus asked them: "who do you say that I am?" The same question each of us truly born-again believers must face and answer and respond to. Bold, impatient Peter, whose name means "rock," fired back a God-inspired answer "You are the Christ, the Son of the living God." Vs. 16. "And I also say to you...Peter... on this rock I will build My church, and the gates of Hades shall not prevail against it." The foundational rock is the heart-felt testimony: "You are the Christ, the Son of the living God." The true church of Jesus Christ has been built on that testimony all over the world. But not without conflict!

In my lifetime of days in the world of agriculture, I have seen both blessing and cursing in the handling of rocks. In the days of old, while manning the horse-drawn plow, to strike a rock could be as thrilling as riding a bronco or a bull in the rodeo. Before the invention of the tractor-pulled rock picker, displacing rocks from a field was tiring, hard, tedious work. And the rock that got missed and was picked up by the combine header sometimes took hours of repair work to replace or straighten damaged parts. Rocks are impenetrable, the analogy Jesus used against Hades, a church whose breastplate of righteousness is the sacrificed, cleansing blood of Jesus.

But what a blessing for the early pioneers, whose outbuildings were set on carefully placed, leveled rocks since cement was costly and rather scarce. Heavy, immovable rocks laid across a river-bed made a dam to divert water into a ditch to carry it to irrigated acres miles away. And, oh yes, it was a large rock out in the Iowa pasture where my mate, then a little girl, would sit hourly as she "practiced" to become a missionary and preached to the cows whom I can imagine lay there half asleep on a sunny afternoon, chewing their cuds, like some of us in church, half asleep, chewing our gum.

On that first Easter morning, the stone, a huge rock we farmers would call it, had sealed the tomb's door, placed there by the Roman enemy. What an illustration of Christ's claim: "The gates of Hades shall not prevail..." as an angel sat there before the tomb's open door—the stone removed and Jesus gone. The Rock of Gibraltar could have been moved as easily, since angels, God's ministering spirits, impregnated with, and conveyors of God's almighty power, will always prevail.

When we Christians sing a favorite hymn "Rock of Ages," I wonder if the author was inspired by Psalm 94:22: "But the Lord is my defense; and my God is the rock of my refuge." Or, thinking of our human weakness without Jesus, "The rock badgers are a feeble folk, yet they make their homes in the crags." Proverbs 30:26. And we sing: "Rock of ages cleft for me, Let me hide myself in thee, Let the water and the blood, From Thy wounded side which flowed, Be of sin the double cure, Save from wrath and make me pure."

March 13

"What must I do to be saved?" Acts 16:25

Good morning to friends of Abiding Savior and whoever may read this devotional, well described by an old cliché: "nothing more than one beggar telling another beggar where to find food." Early this morning this beggar went to God in prayer and in the Word and found some bread for the hungry little boy inside of me, and would now share a morsel of what I found.

I see some bait; really a subtle invitation, in Malachi 3:10, where God promises the giver of tithes and offerings of material goods: "I will open the windows of Heaven and pour out a blessing you cannot contain." And likewise with the one who will invest tithes and offerings of his time and talent will God bless the inner man. I know this from experience as I have pursued the daily radio broadcast, and have watched Him redeem the time throughout the remainder of the day.

In Acts 16:25, we find a beautiful illustration of this, where we find Paul and Silas chained in jail, but even late at night working overtime to invest their time and talent in behalf of unsaved people, and the Lord opened the windows of Heaven in the midst of an earthquake and intense fear and confusion, and poured out an abundant blessing not only for Paul and Silas, but more importantly for the jailer and his family—an unexpected blessing upon some beggars needing bread.

From Acts 16:25 we read: "At midnight, Paul and Silas were praying and singing hymns, and the prisoners were listening to them." Suddenly, from the heart of a fearful beggar comes the sweet, sweet question; "What must I do to be saved?" And Paul answered; "Believe on the Lord Jesus Christ and you will be saved, you and your household."

The windows of Heaven were opened wide, and out poured the greatest blessing known to man, all because of the powerful influence, the Spirit-filled influence of two faithful men willing and able to give of themselves in worship, even at a midnight hour, in a place of total darkness. Praise God that "Your compassions never fail; they are new (fresh) every morning; great is Your faithfulness." Lamentations 3:23.

March 14

"Do not fear nor be dismayed...for the battle is not yours, but God's." II Chronicles 20:15

My personal faith in Hebrews 4:12; "For the Word of God is living and powerful, and sharper than any two-edged sword...a disclaimer of the thoughts and intents of the heart" has made II Chronicles 20:15 a real "escape route" many times in my life, applied with child-like faith in times of various trials. So it worked for King Jehosophat and his people, "that Word that endures to all generations." Psalm 100:5a.

As often happens, this Word from II Chronicles 20 came to my acute attention about three weeks prior to my first really needing to apply it, one day when I suffered a severe financial setback on the ranch. I literally dissected those first thirty verses with a fine-tooth comb, hungering for help as I sensed the Lord not only comforting me with like fellowship of a troubled people, but teaching me some principals I could sink my teeth deep into for days and needs ahead.

Like King Jehosophat and his Godly people, we are surrounded constantly by enemy forces as pilgrims walking across this planet on our way to a promised land for eternity. "Satan is god of this world and prince of the air above." John 14:30, Ephesians 2:2.

The king's first reaction upon hearing that the people of Ammon Moab, and Seir have come to battle against him, was fear, quickly overcome by prayer and fasting. "For God has not given us a spirit of fear, but of love, power, and a sound mind." II Timothy 1:7. I learned how to apply Jesus' teaching of the Lord's Prayer, that we open and close it with praise. "Lord God of our fathers, are You not God in Heaven, and do You not rule over all kingdoms...and in Your hand is there not power and might?" Vs. 6. And then went on to praise God for past blessings ever since Abraham. From his heart of prayer and supplication, the king humbly confessed: "we have no power against this enemy, and we don't know what to do, but our eyes are upon You!" How good I felt to be able to empathize and verbalize with that man of God! My real victory and security came with his when I heard, like the king and his people, from a prophet raised up in their midst "Do not fear 'nor be dismayed...for the battle is not yours, but God's". Think of that! Not my battle, but God's because I am His child...the bright light at the end of the tunnel.

A heavy load fell from my back, and I heard him continue: "...go down against them; you will not need to fight...Position yourselves, stand still, and see the salvation of the Lord Who is with you." Vs. 16-17.

As I listened to, and walked with the king, Vs. 22 caught my eye as another helpful Godly principal with a promise: "NOW, when they began to sing and praise, the Lord set ambushes against the people of Moab, Ammon, and Mt. Seir, and they were defeated." Praise triggered the heart and arm of God, so that when God's people came over a certain hill, there lay the self-destroyed bodies to the last man.

March 15

"I call heaven and earth as witnesses today against you, that I have set before you life and death, blessing and cursing; therefore, choose life, that both you and your descendants may live." Deuteronomy 30:19. (NKJ)

This is a true story of a small, Midwestern congregation, a matter of life or death. The church was having MILD financial problems. They acted decisively, and at the annual meeting, members of the congregation voted to take care of "our own". They stopped ministering to the community so they could minister just to their members only.

The following year they had SERIOUS financial problems. At the annual meeting, they voted to take care of "our own". That year they stopped serving inactive members of the congregation so they could focus on active members only.

The next year, they had OVERWHELMING financial problems. They passed a resolution at the annual meeting to take care of "our own". They stopped helping those who did not attend the annual meeting so they could more fully help only those who did attend.

The following year, they had CATASTROPHIC financial problems. They passed two resolutions at the annual meeting. The first was to take care of "our own." The second was to close the church.

Slow learners!

Jesus, in Luke 6:38, said: "Give, and it will be given to you, good measure, pressed down, shaken together, and running over will be put into your bosom. For with the same measure that you use, it will be measured back to you."

From Mark 14:3 we read of Jesus going to Simon's home. His first visit to Bethany, where Mary, Martha, and Lazarus had blessed Jesus so often. From a most tender, perhaps heavy heart, wanting to shower bountiful love upon Jesus, Mary brought "an alabaster flask of very costly oil and poured it on His head" Vs. 3. "But there were some who were indignant among themselves and said, 'Why was this fragrant oil wasted? For it might have been sold for more than three hundred denarii and given to the poor.' And they criticized her sharply. But Jesus said in her defense: 'Let her alone. Why do you trouble her? She has done a good work for Me... She has come beforehand to anoint My body for burial.'" Vs 6, 8

That testimony is still being heralded today as a work that pleased Jesus, a complete surrender of time, talent, and treasure. May our testimony be like Mary's as we share our time, talent, and treasure for every good work that pleases Jesus.

"I have been young, and now am old; yet have not seen the righteous forsaken, nor his descendants begging bread. He is ever merciful, and lends; and His descendants are blessed". Psalm 37:25-26.

March 16

"For to me, to live is Christ; to die is gain" Philippians 1:21

After my brother's death at age 37 in Moorhead, MN, his almamater college art department painted a huge mural on a large wall in his honor, an alumnus who had gone into a local business, and who had done very well in his support of the college's financial needs and student activities, having lived those past sixteen years only a couple blocks off campus, rubbing shoulders daily with the teachers and administrators who would now miss him greatly. He was overly zealous for life and extremely active in most facets of life from showing horses to political prowess in his state and metropolitan area. Therefore, the artists depicted a portrayal of a human life at its very best on this earth, life in both the secular and spiritual worlds, a fair resume of his short life. Only praise and honor rang out freely from the artwork, without any opposition.

Many years later, a couple of college students in that same area painted a mural outside their dormitory room, a mural which showed a school of fish all swimming in the same direction except for one single fish heading the opposite way, that fish intended to depict the age-old symbol for Christ. Printed on the picture were the Words: "Go against the flow." To me, it said: "follow Jesus," who said: "If any would come after me, let him deny himself..." The natural flow is that "me-first" syndrome, and not "deny yourself" University officials ordered the two students to paint over it lest the mural might offend the non-Christians on campus. I wonder how long it will be before road signs like "Jesus Saves" will be illegal because they are offensive, a spiritual warfare, to the non-Christian?

As I think of the years elapsed between that mural of the mid-1960's and the one of today, I get a real feel of the spiritual deterioration of our great nation, not willing today to go against the flow of unsaved society. "They think it strange that you do not run with them in the same flood of dissipation, speaking evil of you." 1 Peter 4:4. It takes conviction, boldness, confidence, and courage to march to the drumbeat that Jesus marched to, because when we walk with our hand in His hand, we will be out of step with the influential world around us. "For all that is in the world—the lust of the flesh, the lust of the eye, and the pride of life—is not of the Father, but is of the world." John 2:16.

"He who is not with Me is against Me, and He who does not gather with Me scatters abroad." Matthew 12:30.

My testimony this day lines up with Paul's: "For to me to live is Christ; to die is gain." Philippians 1:21.

March 17

"You are not your own...for you were bought for a price..." I Cor. 6:20

Every western rancher owns a brand with which he marks his calves in the springtime, born, usually of a mother with that same brand on her hip or rib, right or left. No two rancher's brands are alike, each registered at the state capital office of Marks and Brands.

It's made up of letters, numbers, bars, slashes, quarter circles, etc., burned into a young calf's hide. There is nothing a rancher is more proud of on the whole ranch than his brand, often engraved on his belt buckle, on his saddle, on a wall in his barn, on his license plate, or on a plaque hanging over the farmstead entrance, or with a hundred other brands on a wall in a popular meeting place in town.

One of my fondest memories of boyhood days was when all the neighbors would gather at one ranch after another and help each other—the singed hair smell, the mournful cry of mother and calf: the wrangler on horseback roping the calf's legs, and us eager boys holding the calf down while the brand was placed appropriately. As the animal grows, so does the brand, covering the whole hip or rib of a mature animal. The brand denotes possession, its only purpose, especially in the early days of large, unfenced community pastures.

In Acts 9, I see Jesus, riding on His steed through the heavens, lasso the very heals of Saul and bring him to the ground where He claimed him for his very own, and Saul quickly surrendered, and before it was over, was branded in the inner man by the cross of Calvary, marked for life as "a man in Christ Jesus so that all things became new, old things passed away." 2 Corinthians 5:17. Jesus could claim Saul because He had purposely paid the price for him at Calvary, and now took possession of his spirit, soul and body, his entire life, and the gifts of time, talent, and treasure, branded by His mark of ownership, the cross.

Now, to saved Paul, Jesus could lay claim according to 1 Corinthians 6: 19-20: "Do you not know that your body is the temple of the Holy Spirit Who is in you, whom you have from God, and you are not your own? For you were bought at a price; therefore, glorify God in your body and in your spirit, which are God's."

"...knowing that you were not redeemed with corruptible things like silver or gold...but with the precious blood of Christ, as of a lamb without blemish and without spot." I Peter I: 18-19.

Oh to be wrestled down and branded on the inner man with that cross which bridges forever that deep gulf between every man and God at birth so that now the "branded" one has free access to the throne room, "my dwelling place...abiding under the shadow of the Almighty," (Psalm 91) his name now registered in the book of "Marks and Brands"—the Lamb's Book of Life, lying open on the altar, and can now sing with the hymn writer: "when the roll is called up yonder, I'll be there."

I trust we will see each other there, branded with the cross of Calvary.

March 18

"...now abide faith, hope, love...the greatest of these is love." I Corinthians 13:13.

Etched solidly into the rocky side of Mt. Rushmore are the faces of four of my favorite presidents of the U.S. The work took many years of planning, faithfulness, patience, perseverance and hard work to complete. It was done with impeccable detail, and will undoubtedly last to the end of the ages. My first viewing, years ago, made a deep impression on my mind that frequently returns as I study S.D. license plates, brochures, and from a rambling mind that stops by Mt. Rushmore from time to time.

"My son, give attention to My Words...keep them in the midst of your heart..." Proverbs 4:20-21. In other words, etch My Word solidly into your heart—hard work that takes daily faithfulness, discipline, patience, perseverance, and detail, "truth that endures to all generations." Psalm 100:5.

Romans 8:29 tells us clearly that God's purpose in our calling is "to be conformed to the image of Jesus"—Jesus, who is synonymous with love, around which all of a truly born-again person's life must evolve as growth turns into maturity in a Christian's walk—"the greatest...is love;" the toughest tousle I have had to contend with in my personal walk.

As I prayed one day for Divine help in my love walk, Mt. Rushmore flashed before my eyes. I got the message, and with that, I Corinthians 13, the "love chapter", and Galatians 5:22, the fruit of the Spirit. I cannot dig deep into those two scriptures without heavy conviction, guilt, condemnation and failure running rampant in my inner man; especially those first eight verses of I Corinthians 13. Then came an idea: spend quality and quantity time daily in prayer, face the issue and memorize these scriptures so they may become DEEPLY ETCHED into the recesses of my inner man, fully available for the Holy Spirit to bring them up like a saved message on the computer, and suddenly reap the blessing intended from Psalm 119:11: "Your Word have I hidden in my heart that I might not sin against You." I am reminded daily, in answer to my prayer for Divine help, and with gradually a bit of deliverance I know will take a lifetime to perfect, that "love suffers long and is kind; love does not envy; love does not parade itself, is not puffed up; does not behave rudely, does not seek its own, is not provoked, thinks no evil; does not rejoice in iniquity, but rejoices in the truth; bears all things, believes all things, hopes all things, endures all things. Love never fails." Vs. 4-8. May my heart be another Mt. Rushmore for my inner man's blessing.

I challenge you to join with me in this spiritual, scriptural exercise, and you will find your marriage blessed, your physical health, your emotional health, all your relationships, and a heap of brand new hope, love, joy, peace, and security will come to you, a pilgrim passing through to the eternal promised land just ahead.

"Praise God from whom all blessings flow."—"The greatest of these is love."

March 19

"I have prayed for you, Simon." Luke 22:32

The rising of the sun of this new day has brought with it brilliant light for the physical world like as Jesus did when He arose from the grave that Easter morning, a light unto the dark world all men are born into spiritually, so that the testimony of the Psalmist may truly be: "Weeping may endure for a night, but joy comes in the morning." Psalm 30:5

Early this morning, as I ate some manna from above and drank some living water from God's Word, I found it to be my light for today's trip in the spirit world: "A lamp unto my feet and a light unto my path." From Psalm 91:1, I found praise to the Lord for all His wonderful attributes: "You are my refuge, Jesus, for in You I find my provision and my protection for today, myself fenced in and the enemy out, for in Your bosom I hide today. You are my fortress, my rock of Gibraltar that I can hide behind in this day of spiritual warfare. You are my shield going out ahead of me to absorb the deadly, poisonous darts of my enemies. You are my Savior Who died for my sin on a cross on Calvary where Your body was broken and Your side pierced, resurrected with new life, giving me that same hope. You are my Lord in Whom I trust with all my heart, and lean not on my own understanding, but I acknowledge You in all my ways, and I know You will direct my paths You are my God, my creator Whom I worship, with no other gods before You."

I remember the days of WWII in Europe where the enemy had planted so-called "land mines," miniature bombs buried cleverly in known roadsides, just under the surface of the ground, to be set off by the pressure of a man's foot or of a vehicle that left some men dead and others without limbs. I remember hearing of a gadget called a "mine detector" which could reach out ahead like a man's cane and indicate trouble and avoid disaster, for some eternal disaster and for others temporary. Such is God's Word: "A lamp unto my feet, a light unto my path", a spiritual mine detector that shows man how to avoid, how to overcome, how to detonate without disaster the wiles of the Devil that Peter speaks of in I Peter 1:8: "Be sober, be vigilant, because your adversary, the Devil, walks about like a roaring lion, seeking whom he may devour." And Jesus, in John 10:10: "The thief comes but for to kill, steal and destroy, but I have come to give life, and to give it abundantly."

I find Jesus in Luke 22:32 our perfect mine detector where He said to Peter: "I have prayed for you Simon, Satan has asked to sift you as wheat, but I have prayed for you, Simon; that your faith fail not."

Little do we know the blessing of praise we owe Jesus for constantly interceding for us at His Father's right hand in Heaven. Even before Satan had attacked Simon, Omni-Jesus headed him off by His plea to the Father to send out angels and ministering spirits to protect Simon and prepare him for an onslaught. Oh mighty Jesus, "the same yesterday, today and forever," that You plead our causes against our enemies today, that You detonate their mines, and expose their devious devices of destruction, so that we might continually know, and walk in the love, joy, peace, hope and security we all crave, and that You intend for Your free people.

"God frustrates the devices of the crafty so that their hands cannot carry out their plans." Job 5:12.

March 20

"Thus says the Lord of hosts: consider your ways." Haggai 1:4, 7

The unbecoming, cold, parsonage, one of the early-day homes of that western, pioneer town, needed to be laid aside and replaced. The days following WWII, on the heels of the depression of the 1930's, was a prosperous time financially for most people in that agricultural area. The five young "elders" of the church board voted unanimously for a new parsonage, while the five older "stewards" voted unanimously against a new parsonage. The congregation voted two to one in favor, and the parsonage was built. Haggai 1:4-5 speaks loud and clear to me as I rehearse the debate: "Is it time for you yourselves to dwell in your paneled houses, and this temple to lie in ruins?" Now therefore, says the Lord of hosts: "Consider your ways." Each of the five stewards, older and wealthy men, had just completed brand new homes for themselves or a marvelously remodeled home. I've heard the Lord loud and clear during the furious debate: "...Consider your ways!!" "Go up to the mountain and bring wood and build the house, that I might take pleasure in it and be glorified." Says the Lord. Vs. 8

When I receive a letter in the mail from, Life, a ministry of James and Betty Robison of Ft. Worth, TX., wherein I see pictures of little black boys and girls in Africa drinking water from a slough alongside domestic animals, and I hear their plea for money to help dig a fresh-water well, I have a propulsion: "Consider your ways." I review my checking account and PTL for my own abundance of clear drinking water, a staple of life we Americans take for granted.

That day when Jesus stood by and watched the poor widow give all she had, sacrificially, out of a heart of love, I wonder how many of the others He was tempted to remind "Consider your ways" as they lay only their tithe, perhaps, on the same altar. What about the 90%? Her sacrifice is recorded to this day in God's Word as a memorial to her, while none of the others are remembered.

Paul counsels us like this from II Corinthians 9:6-8 for those of us who sincerely stop and "consider our ways." "But this I say: "He who sows sparingly will also reap sparingly, and he who sows bountifully will also reap bountifully." (Good health? Sound marriage? An abundance of hope, love, joy peace, and security? Daily work and sound finances?) "So, let each one give as he purposes in his heart, not grudgingly or of necessity; for God loves a cheerful giver. And God is able to make all grace abound toward you, that you, always having all sufficiency in all things, have an abundance for every good work."

I hear Jesus speaking to me: "Consider your ways."

March 21

"If you would have asked Him, He would have given you living water." Jesus, John 4:10:

It is difficult to believe that today's large, beautiful Lake Lillian in Minnesota, just north of town, could have been completely dry for a time in the 1930's, so that crops could be planted on its lake bottom. But, that is not unusual for bodies of water fed only by snow and rain runoff. They are only surface deep, like the bones in Ezekiel 37, human bones dispersed in a very dry valley, "Son of man, can these bones live?" Vs. 3. Some must have wondered about Lake Lillian: "will it ever fill up again? Is it dry forever?" Because Israel's faith had faded to be only surface deep, "They indeed say: our bones are dry, our hope is lost, and we ourselves are cut off.'" Dried up! God said to Ezekiel: "Prophecy to these bones...oh dry bones, hear the Word of the Lord" Vs. 4, "life unto those who find them (God's Words) and health unto their flesh." Proverbs 4:23. It may as well have been Moses speaking to them "I have set before you life and death, therefore, choose life that both you and your descendants might live": Deuteronomy 30:19. The bones rattled, sinews and flesh covered them, and air filled their lungs. Vs. 7-8. They rose up alive!!!

Quite different was the well my uncle drilled in 1912, and cased with tile. After the homestead days were ended, the water became stagnant, the pump dormant for sixty-five years. Like the Dead Sea in Israel—no outlet, no movement of the water below sea level. Dead!! It's there, stopped, thick with salt so that no aquatic beings can live in it. That can and does happen to one of us who takes in a volume of God's Word, love, and grace without letting it flow into a ministry to needy people, keeping the good news to himself, unwilling to share his time, talent, and treasure. Jesus, in Matthew 28:19: "Go therefore and make disciples...baptizing them...teaching them..."

The best of all in my lifetime of observation is illustrated by the artesian well my dad discovered on his farmstead in 1926. It was soft, clean, tasty, fresh spring water running freely to this very day. In John 4, we read of Jesus and His meeting with the woman of Samaria by Jacob's well. Jesus, "living water" He called Himself, said to her: "The water that I shall give him will become in him a fountain of water, springing up unto everlasting life." "The grass withers, the flower fades, but the Word of the Lord endures forever" Isaiah 40:8. I see here the River of Grace whose source is the heart of God, flowing through Jesus, therein securing its real power, and as it flows by, I see the Holy Spirit sifting off, minute by minute, just enough grace for the "now." "My grace is sufficient for you, for My strength is made perfect in your weakness." God to Paul in II Corinthians 12:9.

Our Christian faith and walk may be only surface deep, and then dry up. Or, it can be deep enough, but become stagnant because of neglect, attention and exercise. Or, our faith and walk can flow daily from an under-girded River of Grace, fountain of living water, a blessing to us, to our God, and to those around us as we share, and: "He shall be like a tree planted by the rivers of water, That brings forth its fruit in its season, whose leaf also shall not wither, And whatever he does shall prosper." Psalm 1:8.

March 22

"...there is great gulf fixed..." Luke 16:26

    I can just picture the pompous, gloating, prideful, rich man who had no need, his false god, financial wealth and stature, satisfying the old nature flesh. I can just see him step over, or kick aside, the beggar "laid by his gate" as he wallowed in that "me-first syndrome." "The beggar has made his own nest, now let him lay in it"—a hard-hearted, unsympathetic remark I have heard more than once in like situations—a poor man needing a rich man's help. "The rich man died and was buried." Vs. 22. "And being in torments in Hades...he cried out...'have mercy on me...for I am tormented in this flame.'" The voice from heaven: "...between us and you there is a great gulf fixed, so that those who want to pass from here to you cannot, nor can those from there pass to us." What finality, a heart-wrenching scene I see here: the Jesus of Heaven, the Jesus of mercy and compassion, "cannot pass from here to you, nor can you pass to Me." Impossible!! No way out! The door of the ark has been shut. "...but now you are tormented." Vs. 25.

    Our God of love and mercy, full of compassion, one day arranged for a bridge to cross over that "dead man's gulch" "because of His mercies, I am not consumed because His compassions never fail... great is Your faithfulness." Lamentations 3:22-23. His love, His power, was manifested that day when Jesus, on His way to Calvary, said to any man who has an ear to hear: "Whoever desires to come after Me, let him deny himself: and take up his cross and follow Me." Mark 8:34. The rich man failed to deny himself and follow, but let his pride lead him to eternal destruction. At that moment, on that trip to Calvary, Christ was on His way to build a bridge that would transcend the great gulf. He was ready to be nailed to a cross that Good Friday, and feel the disastrous pain of sin for His first time as God reached down and poured the cup of sin upon Jesus, every man's sin since Adam and Eve. As His body was broken, they pierced His side and out flowed that pure, clean, innocent, sinless blood to bathe clean of sin every person who would humbly fall, with child-like faith, at the foot of that cross with confession of sin from a truly repent heart. He is now qualified to meet His God of Heaven face to face. That cross has now become the bridge over the gulf: and freed man is ushered into the very throne room of God. His name is written in the Lamb's book of life and God whispers into his ear from Isaiah 1:18; "Come now, let us reason together: though your sins be as scarlet, they shall be white as snow; though they are red like crimson, they shall be as wool."

How wonderful to know that for the child of God the gulf has been bridged so that on that final day His Word to His child will not be "the gulf is fixed," but rather: "Come, you blessed of my Father, inherit the kingdom prepared for you..." as He ushers His sheep into heaven. Matthew 25:34.

PTL that there is no power in Heaven, on earth, or below the earth, that can destroy the bridge Jesus has built for us to the throne room, the cross!! "Greater is He that is in me than he that is in the world." I John 4:4.

From one who loves to skip freely over that bridge daily.

March 23

Lord's Word, my GPS!

While traveling on a certain route through Houston, TX last spring, I was both amazed and amused with my first experience with satellite GPS, coming from a gadget sitting on the dash of the vehicle. The intended trip had been entered into the devise, and soon a lady's voice was naming the street to follow, reporting the mileage to the first stoplight, and eventually the right or left exit. Her counsel was accurate almost to the foot on maneuvers. Amazing!!

But then my friend, well acquainted with several routes to the airport, rebuked her direction and made a turn to suit his fancy. Instantly, without argument, the lady jumped over to "our" route and began direction thereon. And a second time our driver switched courses and again she tagged along, and took up her scheduling for us. Comical!!

Isn't that just like us? Isn't that just like God? Our Lord has a path we should follow and we jump track on Him. Do we not pray, in fact: "Lord, anoint me this day to trust You with all my heart, lean not unto my own understanding, acknowledge You in all my ways and trust You to direct my paths." Proverbs 3:5-6. And then let our flesh get in the way?

At the start of a severe snowstorm on the wide open prairies of Southern Sask., my father-in-law would secure his path to the barn and outbuildings, by tying a rope to the door knob of the house and also the barn door, lest he would follow the storm and perish. Lest this happen to us, blinded and disoriented in the storms of life, our Lord anchors us to Psalm 119:105 by faith: "My Word is a lamp unto your feet, a light unto your path." Let not yourself become disoriented and perish!!

Some days when I veer from Proverbs 3:5-6 and walk down the path of worry and fear, I hear Him out of His Word: "Do not fear or be dismayed for the battle is not yours, but God's" II Chronicles 20:15. And from Philippians 4:5-6: "Be anxious for nothing, but in all things, by prayer and supplication, with thanksgiving, let your requests be made to God and the peace of God, which passes all understanding, will guard your hearts and minds through Christ Jesus." We worry sometimes because we have chosen, like my driver in Houston, to take another route. Can I venture out on my own? But, like the lady's voice, God switches over "by prayer and supplication, make your requests known...", God each time changing courses as we choose, but continually in charge, directing, even without our permission.

In spite of my pride and carelessness, or recklessness, or stiff-neckedness, I can empathize with Psalmist David who also sometimes maneuvered onto another path, but then could testify after confession from a repentant heart: "I waited patiently for the Lord, And He inclined to me, And heard my cry. He also brought me up out of a horrible pit, Out of the miry clay, And set my feet upon a rock, And established my steps." Psalm 49:2. That rock is Jesus!

March 24

"I will return and take you unto Myself" Jesus, John 14:2

I sat at a funeral the other day and heard the familiar scripture John 14:1 read once again: "Let not your heart be troubled...in my

Father's house are many mansions...and I go to prepare a place for you; and if I go to prepare a place for you, I will come again and take you unto Myself, that where I am, there you may be also." As I sat there, I thought of the anxious, mixed-up, discouraged, curious disciples He had just spoken to: "Simon Peter said, 'Master, where are You going?' And Jesus replied, 'You cannot go with Me now; but you will follow Me later'...Thomas said, 'We haven't any idea where You are going, so how can we know the way?'" John 13:16-17

Then I thought of the coming celebration of Memorial Day, and a similar wondering crowd I once was part of. On a cold, wintry morning in 1941, thirteen men of various ages stood on the railway platform in my home town in Montana, meager personals in hand, and with them a large crowd including the High School band. Those men, our first WWII inductees, were answering the call of the conscription act of 1939, facing a dismal day when Hitler was running unchallenged over Europe, freely and victoriously, hanging a dark cloud even over America.

The parents, wives, sweethearts, sons and daughters and neighbors and friends gathered there to see them off, surely wondering: "How many of them may never come back," as tears flowed freely. "Where will they be sent to, and for how long?"

The big, unknown answer to "how long" reminds me of the same plight the disciples experienced: "Where will You go? How long will it be? And will You return?" Fortunately, all thirteen returned four years later, one with an amputated limb. There was a welcome home just like every truly born-again person is going to enjoy when "I will return and take you unto Myself." Jesus, John 14:2.

Every Memorial Day for sixty-one years now I remember my high school classmate and close friend whose body laid on Belgium soil after the Battle of the Bulge—not even a burial, his bones now smothered beneath foliage and blown dirt—known only to God. Lonely parents? A forgotten son? Unappreciated? Disrespected? Never a flower to decorate his grave, never a single family or friend's visit. In a military cemetery in France are number of grave markers with inscribed Words: "A soldier of the great war: known unto God."

Like the psalmist, we cry out: "Will the Lord cast off forever? And will He be favorable no more?...Has God forgotten to be gracious? Has He, in anger, shut up His tender mercies?" Psalm 77:9

No! No! But rather: "I will extol You, oh Lord, for You have lifted me up. You have not made my enemies to rejoice over me... You have brought my soul up from the grave, and kept me alive..." Psalm 30:1-3

America's inherent freedom won on the earthy battlefields is synonymous with man's spiritual freedom won at Calvary. Both cost dearly!!!

March 25

"Beloved, do not believe every spirit, but test the spirits, whether they are of God, because many false prophets have gone out into the world." John 4:1

I learned a valuable lesson many years ago as a young Christian when a zealous group of end-time prophets published and preached that the day of locusts, prophesied for end times, is upon Israel now, and swarming out of control. Visitors to Israel proved that false, and I learned to test the spirits.

Reminds me of some areas I have visited in America's South where buildings must be constructed to withstand termites, overly destructive to wood structures, costing millions of dollars of damage as they literally devour and consequently devalue a wooden home. Hearts and minds, too, insensitive to the Holy Spirit living within, allow "termites" to enter through the flesh of the old nature. Let us define "termites" working within our hearts for what they really are: sin, the world, and Satan, bent on destroying us eternally. They come in under the calloused cover of a carnal mind, a mind set not on things above, but on this earth. Termites are today coming into some people's souls because of the teaching they are sitting under, while on the other hand, many people are building brick homes for the little boy or girl on the inside of the clay body to live in by sitting under Godly teaching, and putting on the full armor as they daily search the principals and promises of God's Word. "My son, give attention to My Words; incline your ear to My sayings; let them not depart from before your eyes; keep them in the midst of your heart; for they are life to those who find them, and health to their flesh." Proverbs 4:20-23. "Put on the whole armor of God, that you may be able to stand against the wiles of the devil." Ephesians 6:11.

In Old Testament prophesy, Daniel I, we find four young Hebrew men now in Babylon captivity, whose heritage had built over them a brick house to keep out devouring, destructive termites in a day of severe trial. "Daniel purposed in his heart that he would not defile himself with the portion of the king's delicacies..." Daniel 1:8. Three of the Hebrew boys' names were: Shadrach, Meshach, and Abednego. "As for these four young men, God gave them knowledge and skill in all literature and wisdom..." Vs. 17. Now, King Nebuchadnezzar made an image of gold, so that when a herald cried aloud, when the people heard the sound of instruments in symphony, they should fall down and worship the gold image. And whosoever would not, shall be cast into the midst of a fiery furnace stoked up seven times hotter than usual, hot enough to kill the attendants. The three Hebrews refused, were brought to the furnace, and threatened. But the brick house built over the little boy on the inside (their faith in and obedience to the God of Heaven only), kept out the devouring, killing termites of doubt and unbelief, and that ugly "me-first syndrome." The brick house on the scene? "Our God whom we serve is able to deliver us from the fiery, burning furnace and He will deliver us from your hand, O King. But if not, let it be known to you, O King, that we do not serve your gods, nor will we worship the gold image which you have set up." Daniel 3:17-18. The power of their verbal testimony, their brick house, stood, as we read from 3:25: The king: "Look...I see four men loose, walking in the midst of the fire, and they are not hurt, and the form of the fourth is like the Son of God."

March 26

Servant or Slave?

As a teenager, I spent two summers as a hired hand for a farmer neighbor who paid well, was extremely disciplined on his daily regime; his wife very generous with meals, and the lodging clean and decent. Our day began early in the dairy barn, but it also ended at precisely six p.m. without fail. I was then free to mount my saddle horse and ride two miles to my home for the evening. I felt like a servant to my employer.

Jacob, endowed with a heavy, dark spirit of deception, lies, greed, and fear was born a slave to sin like we all are from our mother's womb—"dead in trespass and sin" Ephesians 2:1. His taskmaster drove Jacob to deceive blinded Isaac, father of twins Jacob and Esau, and literally stole his twin brother's birthright, plus his father's blessing belonging to Isaac. At his evil mother's suggestion and prodding, Jacob left home to avoid his brother's threat to kill him. He prevailed upon Uncle Laban and spent the next twenty years working for another deceiver who could match his wits. Can't you just see Jacob's taskmaster, Satan; grinning from ear to ear as he played havoc with that young life?

One day after twenty years, we read: "Then the Lord said to Jacob, 'Return to the land of your fathers and to your kindred and I will be with you.' " Genesis 31:3. "But what about my brother Esau who wanted to kill me?" Jacob must have wondered. Here is where I believe the life and prayers of Grandfather Abraham together with father Isaac, surely must have secured Jacob's future.

In obedience to God, Jacob rounded up his two wives, their families, and material goods, and sent them on ahead, on two different routes, lest brother Esau should destroy them both, since Jacob had received word: "We came to your brother Esau and he is coming to meet you, and four hundred men are with him." Wow!! "So Jacob was greatly afraid and distressed." Genesis 30:7. After sending his two families on ahead, "Jacob was left alone, and a Man wrestled with him until the breaking of day." Genesis 32:24. Wrestling all night, I suspect convicted Jacob confessed his sin from a truly repentant heart looking for complete freedom from God. His conscience clear, now forgiven, he confessed: "I have seen God face to face, and my life is preserved." No longer slave to sin but servant to God, who went ahead, touched angry, revengeful Esau's heart and removed the stone therein, and blessed him with a heart of warm flesh. Ezekiel 36:26. When the twin brothers met: "Esau ran to meet him and embraced him, and fell on his neck and kissed him, and they wept." Genesis 33:4

Born into slavery because of inherent sin; set free by redemption, grace, unto servanthood!! From one who has "come face to face with God and my life is preserved"...preserved for eternity!

March 27

"...Mary has chosen that good part." Luke 10:42

Brothers Pete and Henry, my Hollander grain farming neighbors, loved to fish. It was not uncommon to see their jeep descend from their home atop a range of hills onto the alkali flat below and onto a well worn trail, and for hours sit on the bank of the Poplar River and draw in one fish after another from the free-flowing water. The River's source is many miles to the north in Sask., Canada, a river that was dammed a few years ago near the Canadian border to run through turbines to make electrical power for South Sask. The excess water flows over a spillway and on down to Montana, to finally run into the Missouri River.

There is another river called the River of Grace whose source is the heart of God. I see Jesus' heart as the dam the River of Grace must run into, a dam called Calvary which, like a turbine, translates the water into power for salvation of man's soul. That in turn releases an overflow for continual potential human blessing here on earth. The river runs lazily into every truly born-again heart where the Holy Spirit is standing by, like a fisherman on a river bank, sifting off just enough grace for today, no more, and no less. The River of Grace flows on and empties into another that runs forever, "a fountain of water springing up into eternal life." John 4:14. Like the Poplar River, full of fish ready for plucking, is the River of Grace, full of hope, love, joy, peace, and security, satisfying the inner man.

I have sometimes envied the "spare time" my neighbors enjoyed so many hours of their lives sitting out in the warm, sunny, quiet day beside the sound of the rippling waters full of life, ready for their appetite's satisfaction.

In Luke 10 we find Mary, analogous to my bachelor brothers, and her sister Martha, analogous to me, envying her sister's freedom of ample spare time. One day Jesus stopped by to see Mary and Martha, a "River of Grace" was He, and there we find Mary sitting at His feet to hear His Word. Vs. 39. She had her line all baited, sitting on the river bank, casting, and finding wonderful food, satisfaction for the hungry little girl inside of her. She sat there watching gems of truth fill her hungry heart. But Martha, so often analogous to me, too busy to fish, envied her sister sitting so quietly by, resting, listening to the ripple of a soul-satisfying river of love flowing from the heart of Jesus. "Martha was distracted with much serving, and she approached Him and said: 'Lord, do You not care that my sister has left me to serve alone?'" Vs. 40. Like many of us, Martha let her busyness steal away her balmy summer time of life, and soon finds the river frozen over for a long season, her day past, and no goodies to fill the inner man's needs. How many of us short-sighted Christians miss the blessing: Jesus at hand. And then we hear Jesus: "Mary has chosen the good part, which will not be taken away from her." Vs. 42.

When I visualize Mary that day in Bethany, or my bachelor brothers sitting on the river bank, I see the beautiful picture of Psalm 23:2-3: "He makes me to lie down in green pastures; He leads me beside the still waters. He RESTORES MY SOUL..." That's grace!!! (Emphasis mine).

From one who is enjoying His grace today.

March 28

"For by grace you have been saved through faith..." Eph. 2:8-9

The twenty-year old rancher's son in Montana, a man of God, was offered an opportunity to buy a neighbor's herd of cows and rent his pasture. A banker financed the project at 9% interest. All went well as he steadily increased his herd numbers, built facilities, dug a well, and erected some fences. Then came the days of uncontrolled inflation and those perilous high rates of interest, his floating rate rising to 15%. Simultaneously, calf prices took a dive and eastern Montana entered into a long drought, therefore, neither grass nor hay. One day the banker called his loan because of delinquent payments, leaving the young man, now age 30, with thousands of dollars he could not pay after complete foreclosure. He had two choices: bankruptcy or adequate time to repay from another income. The banker agreed to refrain from charging any future interest if the principal could be secured eventually. By twelve years later, bankruptcy and its stigma avoided, the loan was satisfied.

In II Kings 4, we find a widow also with two choices immediately following her husband's death. The creditors forced her mortgage to be satisfied, and her only equity was her two sons, which they would take. Give up the boys' bankruptcy, or earn enough to pay the debt. She went to the man of God, Elisha, for counsel. The prophet questioned her: "Tell me, what do you have in your house?" Vs. 2. And she answered: "Your maidservant has nothing...but a jar of oil." Then Elisha said: "Go, borrow vessels...from all your neighbors-empty vessels; not just a few...shut the door behind you and your sons; then pour the oil into all those vessels, and set aside the full ones." Vs. 4. When every vessel was full, Elisha said: "Go, sell the oil and pay your debt; and you and your sons live on the remainder." Vs. 7, "For with God nothing will be impossible" Luke 1:37. "My God shall supply all your needs according to His riches in glory in Christ Jesus." Phil. 4:19.

Everyone of us fell into spiritual bankruptcy in the Garden of Eden, a debt no man could pay. And the familiar refrain comes to mind: "I owed a debt I could not pay, He paid a debt He did not owe." Our "creditor", God, had two choices: leave mankind die by the law of works or live by the blessing of grace. He chose grace, which demands a blood sacrifice, pure, clean, innocent, sinless blood that only the Trinity possessed. The Incarnate, Jesus, came from heaven, the second person of the Trinity, as a human baby, born in Bethlehem of Judea, and walked eventually to Calvary, outside Jerusalem, and gave His body and His blood in payment for every man's sin, that man might avoid bankruptcy, a certain eternal death.

Indebted man's part to play is found in Rom. 10:9, 13: "...if you confess with your mouth the Lord Jesus, and believe in your heart that God has raised Him from the dead, you will be saved...for whosoever calls upon the name of the Lord shall be saved."

From one now free of debt, and etched across his heart: "PAID IN FULL."

March 29

"...And He shall direct your paths..." Proverbs 3:6

Every springtime as I see these S.D. farmers busy in their fields, my mind goes back to springtime eight hundred miles west to Montana, and in particular the trails, the dirt and gravel roads and the paved road beside our farmstead. Every road has a specific purpose, going east, west, north, and south. Before my boys came into the picture, I hired men unfamiliar with our terrain and needed me to "direct their paths" like I need God to "direct my paths" in my spiritual walk.

One morning I directed a young man to a point ten miles south. I warned him that when he would come to a crossroad, "don't turn right or left but continue straight ahead." He came to the crossroad, turned right, traveled miles, realized his mistake, lost an hour, and came back to the intersection, turned south, and continued on his way to point "B".

Another missed his detour cue I had given him, crossed a narrow bridge and put the disc to eternal rest.

In God's Word, both Old and New Testament, we find a certain road had a specific purpose to illustrate a simple truth for people even down to today.

In Acts 9 we read of how naughty Saul was cast to the ground three miles from Damascus, was blinded, humbled, and surrendered to Jesus. After three years of "seminary training", now Paul, became perhaps the greatest evangelist of all time out in the Gentile world, his influence in Europe becoming our salvation as the good news of the gospel he preached skipped across the Atlantic to America. "And He shall direct our paths."

On Easter Sunday two of Jesus' followers were walking on the road to Emmaus. They were talking of Jesus' death, when suddenly Jesus Himself came along and joined them. But they didn't recognize Him. As He listened, momentarily He asked: "What are you so concerned about?" After a lengthy discussion from them about all the weekend's mysterious happenings, Jesus reminded them of much prophesy now being fulfilled. But they did not catch on until at the evening meal's table they saw on His body evidence enough to open their eyes that He was Jesus. Then He quickly disappeared.

"I will direct their paths" is a considerful blessing for success in a young farmer on his way to a field, a sinner on his way to salvation, or a man on the road to understanding the mystery surrounding Christ's crucifixion and resurrection.

March 30

"He touched me, and made me whole." The Gaithers

One of my favorite, most exciting boyhood games on the Montana farmstead was "hide and go seek." A number of boys would gather in our yard with several buildings to hide behind or inside. The goal was always just inside the wide west barn door, and a "goal tender" was like a hockey goalie, to not let anyone get by him and touch the goal and score. Most of us wanted to be a runner rather than tender, so that when it looked like the tender had reached out far enough, a runner could beat him to the goal, the object of the game.

Jesus makes a good goal tender when it comes to salvation, as He is One who strays from the goal from east to west, from pole to pole, looking for a lost sheep while the other ninety nine run safely to the goal, the throne room of God, to enjoy His Refuge. In Acts 9 we find unregenerated Saul a runner on the road to Damascus, having hidden behind heritage, tradition, incomplete doctrine, and was touched by the Goal Tender, Jesus, and brought to his knees with a repentant heart. "Suddenly, a brilliant light from heaven shown down upon him. He fell to the ground and heard a voice 'Paul, Paul, why are you persecuting Me?' 'Who are you, Sir?' Paul asked. 'I am

Jesus, the One you are persecuting! Get up...go into the city...and wait for direction.'" Paul was "tagged" for eternity.

I remember the time in my young life on the road called "the glitter of this world," having hidden behind unforgiven inherent sin, and the "GOAL TENDER" brought me to confession and repentance, and put me on the "road of life." I first heard as I knelt with child-like faith at the foot of the cross with a truly repentant heart: "Your sins are removed from you as far as east is from the west." Psalm 103:12. Then I heard from Jesus: "If any would come after Me, let him deny himself, take up his cross, and follow Me." Matthew 16:24.

PTL for Jesus, the goal tender, for "whosoever will" I hear God speaking: "Come now, let us reason together: though your sins be like scarlet they shall be white as snow. Though they are red like crimson, they shall be like wool." Isaiah 1: 18.

From one who can now sing with Bill Gaither; "He touched me, O He touched me, and O the joy that floods my soul; Something happened, and now I know, He touched me, and made me whole."

March 31

"Count it all joy...trials." James 1:2

Oh for the many ways of handling trials I've seen in my lifetime—my classmate who picked up his typewriter in the middle of a test and pounded his desk with it, the neighbor lady who had watched her life fall completely apart, and she went out behind the barn and shook her fist at God with a spirit of blame. Or the lady who showed her broken glass on her cell phone, and declared: "Look what Satan did to me." Or the farmer who tore up his implement by dropping into a washout with uncontrolled speed and blamed Satan, giving praise, honor, and glory to that one hungry for attention! Or my friend who suddenly lost his only son in a vicious vehicle accident and then could kindly praise God for those twenty years which many have been "cheated" out of.

Many people have trouble recognizing the difference between a trial organized by God for a blessing and a Satanic blast intended to "steal, kill, and destroy" like we hear from John 10:10, without considering the second half of that verse where Jesus promises: "but I have come to give life, and to give it abundantly."

We are living today in a time of much "criminal mischief", not a trial but a Satanic bluff, lie temptation called scam. Dishonest evil doers playing on the naivety and innocence, especially of older people.

Jesus, God's own Son, even tempted and left us a perfect pattern for overcoming without injury when He was tempted by the god of this world. He simply said: "It is written: and then quoted God's Word, and the devil left.

Paul writes in I Corinthians 10:13: "The trial you are going through is one that is common to man; but God is faithful, Who will not allow you to be tried beyond what you are able to stand; but will make a way of escape, that you might be able to bear it."

I am blessed to follow the trial Hannah of I Samuel endured gallantly for many years. She played "second fiddle" to her husband's other wife, Peninnah, who was able to birth one child after another while Hannah's womb was sealed to pregnancy. All she wanted was a baby boy, for which she prayed without ceasing while bearing the taunts and teasing of her counterpart. God also needed and wanted a son to become a prophet in that day of history. One day when she finally prayed the prayer God was waiting for, her womb was opened and she bore a son. Yes, when she prayed God's will: "If You will give me a male child I will return him back to You at weaning time." She "made a deal" with God, her trial was ended, she could "count it all joy," and God made a prophet out of her son Samuel. From her lips flowed much praise: "My heart rejoices in the Lord My horn is exalted in the Lord." I Samuel 2:1 And this is the rest of the story: the Lord blessed Hannah with five more children.

"Count it all joy when you fall into diverse trials, knowing that the trying of your faith works patience..." James 1:2

April 1

"For if you forgive men their trespasses, your heavenly Father will also forgive you." Matt. 6:14

Almost every day at our house one of us asks the other: "What shall we have for breakfast or for dinner today?" a meal to satisfy and nourish the old clay frame we live in. Quite often one will say: "Shall we try this dish we haven't had for some time?" And so I thought this morning of Matt. 6:14 when I began preparing a good meal for the inner man, a delicacy we may not have tasted for awhile, a good meal for the soul living inside this well-fed outer man, where Jesus said: "For if you forgive men their trespasses, your heavenly Father will also forgive you. But if you do not forgive men their trespasses, neither will your Father forgive your trespasses." This ought to be a portion we feed our inner man every day, but oh how frequently we need to be reminded. It's so good and nourishing for the soul, but very often neglected one day after another as we try to live on chips and grudges. How many times have we "parroted" with a congregation from the Lord's Prayer: "Forgive us our trespasses as we forgive those who trespass against us" without one conscious thought of what we just prayed, our thoughts on the roast at home, the football or baseball game already in play, or the round of golf awaiting us. Do we really want God to answer that flippant phrase of the Lord's Prayer like we carelessly prayed it, when we have not forgiven, but rather pray with a grudge in our heart or a chip on our shoulder? I believe that God answers that prayer, too, just like we pray it from a heart He sees so clearly. Jesus forgives and forgets each sin we confess from a repentant heart, having paid for that sin on Calvary.

Many years ago I had legitimate occasion, I thought, to forever break a relationship that had been good, just over a business dealing involving greed where I felt cheated. My first impulse was to break that relationship. But Matthew 6:14 gripped my heart in the midst of that trial, and I truly forgave from the heart. Now, the forgetting part! No, I haven't forgotten as is evident by this testimony, but the memory that does sometimes surface has no twinge of anger, bitterness, unforgiveness, or anxiety at all. I believe that's what it means to "forget," a big victory in a Christian man's walk. He is sometimes reminded of that beautiful victory, and is encouraged.

I hear Jesus this morning saying to the adulterous woman in John 8:11: "Go and sin no more."

April 2

"It is finished..." Jesus, Matthew 27.

Don't we all have times in our lives that are especially meaningful? Two afternoons in my life are especially significant: the afternoon I met Jesus at the cross at Calvary, Good Friday afternoon, and the afternoon Alice and I met at the Bible Camp in the Rocky Mountains of western Montana. Jesus gave me a full measure of faith, hope, love, joy, peace, and security in the inner man for the now and for eternity, and Alice the same for our remaining days together in the flesh on this earth; unforgettable blessings were both afternoons.

I came face to face with Jesus Friday afternoon in Matthew 27, where I heard the testimony of how His Roman enemies spat on Him, struck Him on the head, mocked Him, and compelled Him to bear His heavy, wooden cross on a severely fatigued, weakened body. They gave Him sour wine to quench His thirst, but He refused it. With large spikes and a heavy hammer they nailed His wrists and feet to the cross. Then one of the enemy guards standing by, saw an earthquake and with the supernatural darkness all around, feared greatly, saying: "Truly, this was the Son of God." I heard Him say: "It is finished," and He gave up His spirit.

As I learned that His sacrifice was for me personally, a sinner of sinners, headed for hell for eternity, conviction came upon me, and from a truly repentant heart, I confessed my sin, was bathed in the pure, clean, innocent, sinless blood that poured from His side, was set free with the assuring promise: "Though your sin be as scarlet, it shall be white as snow. Though your sins be crimson red, they shall be like wool." Isaiah 1:18. For "as far as east is from the west, so far has He removed our transgressions from us." Psalm 103:12.

The more recent, second afternoon blessed both of us to find that our faith walk, with Jesus at the center; was identical. We also spent three hours sharing our testimonies, our backgrounds, our former marriages, our loneliness, and finally, our telephone numbers. After a few months, and huge phone bills, we accepted each other in a human marriage like we had accepted Jesus in a spiritual marriage, one until "death do us part", and the other for eternity, since "God so loved the world that He gave His only begotten Son, that whosoever believes in Him shall not perish, but shall have everlasting life." John 3:16

<u>April 3</u>

"The joy that was set before Him."

Because of the high wind, the fruit tree out in the orchard blew over, and the keeper of the orchard gathered up the fruit and tossed the tree into a fire. I see an analogy here at dusk that Good Friday afternoon: Jesus' cross was laid over, His work done, the cross empty, and now He could begin to gather up the fruit, His saved people, giving proper perspective and meaning to Hebrews 12:2: "...Who for the joy that was set before Him, He endured the cross." Immediately, His people of the Old Testament saints, captives waiting for the promised Messiah with childlike faith, were released from captivity, and on their way to Heaven. Their sin, which also had to be covered by His sacrifice on the cross ahead, like yours and mine, had literally been rolled ahead to this moment, rolled ahead one year at a time as an earthly priest took the blood of a lamb into the Holy of Holies and sprinkled it over the Mercy Seat behind a heavy curtain no other man could enter. "The joy that was set before Him," His fruit are all the saints who will one day worship Him and fellowship with Him for eternity

"The steps of a good man are ordered by the Lord, and in his ways does the Lord find His delight." Psalm 37:23. Jesus finds His delight in every surrendered soul. How could that "tree" at Calvary possibly be a fruit-bearing tree? I believe John 25:4 tells the miracle very well: "As the branch cannot bear fruit of itself unless it abides in the vine, neither can you unless you abide in Me" Jesus intimates here that for you and me to be fruitful, and therefore fruit unto His glory like He was fruitful, He is allowing His life to flow through us. Fruitfulness is my being in close fellowship with Him through prayer, worship and His Word. We feast on and drink of the "Living Water," like the woman by the well in John 4, who was convinced that she wanted and needed. Fruitful life is like my neighbor's flowing spring water out in his pasture. It flows 24 hours per day and gives life to his cow herd that drinks of that water like the Word of God flows daily through man's soul..."Life unto those who find it and health unto their flesh..." Proverbs 4:23. His life flowing through us gives us opportunity to invest our time, talent, and treasure in ministries that bear fruit, "first in Jerusalem, then in Judea and Samaria, and to the uttermost parts of the earth." Matthew 28:19.

My fruit-bearing friend, you and I are "that joy that was set before Him as He endured the cross." We are branches of a Vine whose roots reach deep into God's heart, from which flows the River of Grace, flowing into each redeemed heart where the Holy Spirit stands by and literally sifts off just enough grace for today.

April 4

"Trust in the Lord...lean not unto your own understanding..." Proverbs 3:5.

An Easter reflection: "...they came to the tomb when the sun had risen. And they said among themselves: 'Who will roll away the stone from the tomb's door for us?' ...they looked up and saw the stone had been rolled away." Mark 16:24

A needless concern over a prospective difficulty, a huge "rock", we farmers would call it—hard, heavy, clumsy, perhaps sunken a bit into the soil. The young effeminate, perhaps ladies of small stature in my imagination, saw a problem unlikely for them to handle physically. "Who will roll away the stone for us?" They didn't indicate prayer as one way out, but rather seemed anxious about enough human strength, "leaning unto their own understanding." They seemed to walk in unnecessary anxiety, worry, and groundless fear—"When they looked up, they saw the stone had been rolled away," and here we may gain some practical admonition for ourselves, guilty of the same, when we rely on our own human strength...

"In today's bright sunlight basking,
Leave tomorrow's cares alone—
Spoil not present joys by asking:
"Who will roll away the stone?"
Oft, before we've faced the trial
We have come with joy to own,
Angels from Heaven descended
And rolled away the stone." Anon

I was half way to my attorney's office to make the down payment on a half section of land, and "What if I lose this down payment?" flashed through my mind, and literally forced me to turn around, return home, and give up an opportunity that proved to be a major mistake as time went on. "Lean not unto your own understanding." "Why are you fearful, oh you of little faith?" Jesus, Matthew 8:26.

The Marys and I contrast severely in faith with what we see of three Jewish boys in Babylon captivity when their faith in God far surmounted even a touch of their "own understanding." Old testament faith builders they knew by heart from their young synagogue days came into full play to "trust the Lord with all your heart" when they were standing before the fiery furnace, stoked up seven times hotter than usual, threatened to be their doom unless they bowed down to the King's false god. Their bold, confident testimony, arising out of their obedience to go "remove the stone" between their life and death. "We know our God is able...we know our God is willing...but, if not, we will not serve your gods, nor will we worship the gold image..." Daniel 3:17-18. Jesus rescued them in the midst of the fire!

Their verbal confession of their faith in God thrust Jesus, the fourth man, into the furnace for their deliverance, so that not even a hair was singed, "their stone rolled away."

My God has removed the stone in my life in times of loneliness, when stocked with a bondage, a financial crisis, a broken relationship, and twice a physically terminal illness.

If God doesn't "remove the stone" as He did for the Marys, He will find a way for us around it as with Meshach, Shadrach, and Abednego.

His name is Jesus in either case!!

April 5

"He is not here...He is risen." Matthew 28:5

Joyce proudly beckoned to us, "Come, look at my peony." There it was, a healthy, green, prosperous plant like a peony should be. Years ago the peony had been planted alongside the graveled driveway, which recently was paved. Over the time, shingles had been piled on top of it; two kinds of fill for a base for the pavement; and then a real heavy, thick application of tar. The tiny peony had been forgotten about until one day recently when the pavement developed a noticeable bulge, and within only a few days, the bulge cracked wide open and out popped that healthy peony, having undoubtedly struggled for life, was buried, but now resurrected. At its original sprouting, she had often applied TLC. Now, once again, TLC as it is resurrected.

When I saw the plant and heard the story, I thought of Mary Magdalene. Her inner being as a young "sprout" was heavily covered with seven demons, a young lady struggling for survival. Jesus cast them out, and from that day, her spirit now resurrected, she ministered to Jesus with TLC, "provided...for Him from their substance." Mark 8:20.

Then Jesus was crucified on a cross, died, and was buried in a tomb. The tomb's door was secured by a large rock and Roman guards. But, like the peony, Jesus was not to be bound by anything, and was resurrected on the third day. "...as the first day of the week began to dawn, Mary Magdalene and the other Mary came to the tomb." Matthew. 27:1. They came with spices and anointing oil in their hand to minister final rites, since the Sabbath celebration, beginning Friday eve, had cut them short of time. Like Joyce with the peony plant, Jesus and Mary had fellowshipped in a spirit of love and TLC. So this resurrection was of special significance when

Mary found her Savior not dead after all, but alive. She heard, "He is not here for He is risen...go quickly and tell His disciples that He is risen from the dead...so, they ran with...great joy...to bring His disciples Word." Matthew 28:5-8.

So it was with Joyce when she eagerly invited us with great joy to come see the resurrected peony.

That must have been the tenor of Job's heart also, when he refused to lose his faith as his trials wore on; "I know that my Redeemer lives, and He shall stand at last on the earth. And after my skin is destroyed, this I know, that in my flesh I shall see God...How my heart yearns within me." Job 19:25-27.

From one who has been resurrected once (Ephesians 2:1), and now am joyfully waiting for the second one at Christ's coming in the clouds. I Thessalonians 4:16.

April 6

"Be still and know that I am God." Psalm 46:10

Have you ever been accused of talking too much? I have, and rightfully so, because when I talk too much, I am not listening at all. "The wise old owl, he sat on an oak. The more he saw, the less he spoke. The less he spoke, the more he heard. Why aren't we all like that wise old bird?" Oh, how those talk show hosts and their guests are so nerve-wrecking and difficult to stay tuned to, where there is zero consideration for one another, and it ends up in a "pell mell" confusion and competition. It is a disgusting display of rudeness that defeats any probability of productiveness.

How do you feel when talking to someone and it's very evident he is not listening? I feel let down, discouraged and even humiliated and embarrassed. Perhaps it's a friend who is just bursting at the seams, trying to break in with a profound thought all conjured up while you are speaking. Or, it can be he just isn't interested in your topic and doesn't want to hear what you have to say.

Does God get equal time in your prayer life? Could it be that the way I talk to God is a one-sided conversation dominated by me, who loves to talk too much? For most of us, giving God equal time is very difficult for two reasons. One, we are in a hurry to get done. Second, we are impatient, not well adapted or well prepared to just wait and listen. I have an acquaintance or two like that, so slow and deliberate, I wonder if they are going to respond, so I just pick up again and go on talking. Here is a wonderful time to know scripture, and even more so, to have it memorized. God speaks to us through His Word as we read it or allow Him to draw it from our experience or our memory bank by the working of His love in our minds and hearts.

When prayer is at its best, we wait in silence for God's voice to us, and we find our time is spent in a much more productive manner. God loves a listening ear just as much as we do.

I hear God saying to us this morning the Words of Proverbs 4:20: "My son, give attention to my Words; incline your ear unto my sayings; let them not depart from before your eyes; keep them in the midst of your heart, for they are life unto those who find them, and health unto their flesh."

April 7

"I sought the Lord, and He heard me." Psalm 34:4

At noontime, my mouth spewed (without thinking) a word that I could see immediately hurt one whom I loved in my presence, and immediately I sensed a heavy cloud hovering over both of us, and I deeply regretted my wallowing in darkness, coming out of the flesh, the world, or Satan, but once more soon purposely wrapped my soul around I John 1:9: "If we confess our sin, God is faithful and just to forgive our sins, and to cleanse us of all unrighteousness." Then I heard the Lord whisper into my ears from Isaiah 1:18: "Though your sin be as scarlet it shall be like wool." And from John 3:17: "God did not send His Son into the world to condemn the world, but that the world might be saved through Him." And from Romans 8:1: "There is therefore no condemnation to them who are in Christ Jesus, to them who walk not after the flesh, but after the Spirit.'

The next time I pondered my naughty word, I praised God for Luke 4:18: Jesus speaking: "The spirit of the Lord is upon Me, for I have been anointed to preach good news to the poor, to open the eyes of the blind, to heal the broken-hearted, to set the captive free set free them that are bruised." There is my deliverance! I looked around and saw the sun coming up in the eastern sky and a refreshing experience from my boyhood days in "Big Sky Country" and it overcame me, and I felt set free as a bird in the sky above. I recalled the loud, wonderful sound of the train whistle every Saturday morning, originating seven and a half miles away, but just bellowing down that valley I lived in, and with it a spirit of power, life, enthusiasm, zeal, and freedom that I cannot describe, hovered over me. David sang it so eloquently in I Chronicles 29:11: "Blessed are You, Lord God, Father of Israel forever and ever. Yours is the greatness, the power, the glory, the victory, and the majesty; for all that is in Heaven and in earth is Yours. Yours is the Kingdom and You are exalted over all."

That train whistle I heard so clearly and which so impressed my heart reminds me of how big, powerful, and majestic our God must have sounded when twice He bellowed across the Universe: "This is My Beloved Son in whom I am well pleased." once at His coming out of the River Jordan and His baptism, Matthew 3:17 and again at the Mt. of Transfiguration, while Jesus shone dazzling white, center of attention. Matt 17:5.

With a heart of thanksgiving and lips of praise, I turned to familiar verses of Psalm 34 and bathed the little boy inside of me in the comfort of several messages to this now free, jubilant heart. Ps. 34:4: "I sought the Lord and He heard me, and delivered me from all my fears." Vs. 6-8: "This poor man cried out, and the Lord heard him and saved him out of all his troubles. The angel of the Lord encamps all around them that fear, and delivers them." Vs. 17-18: "The righteous cries out and the Lord hears and delivers them out of all their troubles. The Lord is near to those who have a broken heart, and saves such as have a contrite spirit." And verse 22: "The Lord redeems the soul of His servants, and none of them that trust Him shall be condemned."

My friend, enjoy your Omni-Sovereign, forgiving God today... He is just waiting to bless you like He has blessed me in my plight!

April 8

"Life unto those who find it..." Prov. 4:21

    Good morning friends who, like me, are constantly and naturally looking for life and health to just go on, to never wane but just go on strong. Those of us who have come this morning for a morsel of food and a drink that will guarantee life and health for the inner man not only for now but for eternity have come to the right place as we share God's Word, a Word I would begin with from Proverbs 4:20-21, "My son, pay attention to what I say; listen closely to my Words. Do not let them out of your sight, keep them within your heart; for they are life to those who find them and health to a man's whole body." The table has been set and the invitation sent out too: "Let us then approach the throne of grace with confidence, so that we may receive mercy and find grace to help us in our time of need." Hebrews 4:16.
    The inner man is hungry, empty, and destitute, and along comes Jesus with maybe only a fish or two, a verse or two to share, but it is just enough. How many times I have filled my tummy more than full at a Thanksgiving dinner and foolishly jested: "I won't have to eat again until Christmas," only to find at bedtime or sooner a hunger for food, which is normal and healthy. And so it is food for the inner man, a large meal at 11:00 on Sunday morning but by bedtime a longing for more prayer, more devotional time, more worship time that will satisfy one more hunger pang of the inner man.
    Peter was inspired to write about all this in I Peter 5:10 where we read: "And the God of all grace, who called you to His eternal glory in Christ...will Himself restore you and make you strong, firm and steadfast." To believe we totally are debt free is not easy. But oh what joy when we can see our farm mortgage paid off, or our home debt paid in full, or the business on Main Street, and rejoice at the burning of the mortgage on the school or the church.
    But sometimes so different for the inner man's rejoicing as partial belief or unbelief takes hold. It's just too simple, we reason. It just cannot be that easy. We surely must have to do something, our old nature wanting to be involved, wanting to work his way to God like all faiths teach their people, except Christianity, religions where

they work hard to reach up to God, but in Christianity our faith tells us God came down to us in the flesh of Jesus. The other day at a Bible study a man asked: "What does it mean to be set free?" in the context of Galatians. I answered: "Accepting Jesus and Calvary sets us free from sin, death, and the power of the Devil, justified of our sin, present, past and future; free from eternal death of the inner man in a place called Hell; and by standing on the Word 'free' from the power of the Devil to destroy us."

To believe that we are totally free without doubting a bit is seldom easy. To wholly accept grace is anti-natural and difficult, but entirely possible on the other hand, as we endorse with child like faith I John 1:9; "If we confess our sins, God is faithful and just and will forgive us our sins and purify us from all unrighteousness." It is the power to turn us around 180 degrees and walk away from a besetting sin, bathed in the blood of Jesus as we come to His pierced side with child like faith. God's Word and Jesus says: "The truth shall set you free."

April 9

"A spring of water...unto eternal life." John 4:14

There is an old adage: "You can take the boy from the farm, but you cannot take the farm from the boy." My mind, even now eight hundred miles away and several years passed, is constantly roaming those hills and valleys, looking over the familiar grain fields, driving the old highways and byways and forever sensing the immense freedom I enjoyed seventy three years of my life on the prairies of Montana.

A Word from the book, Song of Solomon, captures my fancy this morning, and I took off again for my Montana ranch and the surrounding neighborhood. It is a verse I see as a good metaphor for a spiritual lesson for us today. The verse reads from chapter 4:12b "you are a spring enclosed, a sealed fountain." I see this metaphor 'spring fountain' as having reference to the inner man's life of a truly born again believer, a spring definitely shut up, a secret spring enclosed, sealed fountain is its reality.

Such it was in Solomon's day in the Mideast when sometimes a spring was covered over by a building which no one could enter except a select one who knew the secret entrance. It reminds me of the artesian well of my early childhood. It poured out super soft water that served neighbors who had come to haul it away for their Monday morning clothes washing in the day before water softeners had been invented.

Is there anything more refreshing than a drink of cold spring water on a hot day, water coming from far below the surface? The human spirit is like that artesian well, a source of living water that needs to be tapped, a spring enclosed, a sealed fountain one that even the owner cannot describe to a neighbor because it is housed deep down inside a clay frame. Only Jesus has the key to unlock the door. Only Jesus knows the secret that lies there, the built in image of God all men are created to be.

The spring itself may be hidden, but what a blessing, how refreshing to all humanity when that little secret is exposed by Jesus as the gift of faith is exercised and the born-dead are raised up, and the spring is opened to flow freely to the entire world. I can picture this morning that beautiful watering of many Angus cows in my neighbor's pasture lined up around that huge circular tank to drink of a spring so forceful out there in the hillside that it fills a two inch pipe the year round, "for they (Words) are life to those who find them and health to a man's whole body." Proverbs 4:23

Let those of us to whom Jesus is real rejoice this morning that He reached down and miraculously tapped a source within us that can bring life, refreshment, encouragement, and edification to a thirsty people around us, the real commission He left us with. The water that flows is from Jesus, who said in John 4:14: "but whoever drinks the water I give him will never thirst. Indeed, the water I give him will become in him a spring of water welling up to eternal life."

April 10

"The sheep of His pasture..." Psalm 100:3

This morning I came to the Lord with an exceptionally thankful heart for His blessing to me in spirit, soul, body, finances, and my relationships with other people I am experiencing in my marriage, with countless people at Abiding Savior, and out in other tangents of this community. In my ecstasy, Ps. 100, which I recently memorized, began flowing through my mind, and I recognized it as the voice of God speaking to me, in the same tenor He spoke to the psalmist centuries ago. While slowly and deliberately rehearsing the Psalm, I was especially attracted to verse three, where it says: "Know that the Lord, He is God; it was He Who made us, and not we ourselves. We are His people, the sheep of His pasture." Two beautiful pictures came to my mind: one in answer to the cloning fiasco the Christian world faces with disdain today, where the Word plainly states: "It is He Who has made us, and not we ourselves." It is the Potter Who puts our clay bodies together. Jeremiah 18:1-4. So, why, now in the brilliance of our times, should we make an effort to so-call "make ourselves?" God's Word is truth, and God always says what He means and means what He says, like we also read so clearly in Isaiah 43:1: "I created you, oh Jacob." And from Jeremiah 1:5: "I knew you before you were conceived."

The second picture developed with: "We are His people, the sheep of His pasture", coupled with Vs. 4: "Enter His gates with thanksgiving and His courts with praise." Here my mind went instantly back to my boyhood days of the 1930's when we had on our Montana ranch a small flock of sheep, which I can well remember would show up in a long parade in the dusk of the evening, and slowly enter their compound for the night to rest. They would enter through an open gate and into their courtyard to sleep in peace, sheltered from the coyote predator, their bellies full, their thirst satisfied with clean water, a memory I cherish to recall, because while attending to them, it also put a pleasant sense of security and peace in my own heart, even to now, these sixty some years later, as I recall those evenings, and can imagine those sheep after another day of "lying down in green pastures and walking beside still waters", they would enter the gates with thanksgiving in their hearts and into the courtyard with praise as they bleated a word to their lamb proudly displayed by their side, protected one more day and one more night. I can imagine myself as a Christian, a sheep of His pasture with those kinds of blessings closing out the day with verse 5: "For the

Lord is good; His mercy is everlasting, and His truth endures to all generations."

My friend, spend a time today in quietness before the Lord when your inner man would rise up and sing a song of praise for the Lord's faithfulness to the "sheep of His pasture." You will be richly and abundantly blessed!

April 11

"This night your soul will be required..." Luke 12:20

In my day of living and walking amongst the people of Montana, I have seen more than one rancher, a cowboy at heart, go out on horseback for his last roundup of cows and calves. The heart's desire of those cowboys is that they might die with hat and boots on, and a lariat rope in their hand. They love that freedom of the wide-open spaces. The Big Sky that proudly shows off every sunrise and sunset, that "home on the range where the deer and the antelope play", is an undeniable allure of freedom all around. I knew just such one, a neighbor who was stricken with a heart attack as he roped a steer, his last one, and only minutes later died with hat and boots on, and a lariat rope in his hand on his way to eternity in Heaven or Hell, depending on a single choice he had made before that fateful morning. Each and every one of us will face our last roundup. The time will come when we will find we cannot go on any longer on this earth. All mankind faces a last meal, a last heartbeat, a last kiss, a last ride, a last thought, a last breath, which may come quickly to the young, and agonizingly slow to the elder folk.

Believe me, friend, God's Word tells us that the real "me" and the real "you" is not the clay we see with our eyes, but the invisible inner being, the spirit part of us, since Genesis 1:27 tells us: "God created man in His own image", not visible clay He gave each of us to live in here on earth, but invisible beings; and like Himself, like Jesus, like the Holy Spirit, never to die, but to live forever in Heaven or Hell.

Malachi 3:6 says: "I am God, and I change not" Hebrews 13:8 says: "Jesus Christ, the same yesterday, today, and forever."

I fear the eternal fate of many of those ranchers and cowboys who have misused their freedom, and are living, under the old proverbial: "eat, drink, and be merry, for tomorrow you may die." One such man told me that he was not going to choose either Heaven or Hell, but to remain in his grave forever, totally ignorant of the above testimony of God's plan for everyone. The Bible tells of a man who was like many of my rancher-cowboy friends, materially successful, but spiritually bankrupt. Jesus called him a fool because he had placed more attention and importance on the present life than on the future eternal one, and had more concern for the outer man than the inner.

I am so thankful that there is a bank in Heaven where we can make investments, where "moth and rust corrupt not", but where we can invest our faith, time, talent, and treasure, and draw big dividends earth's economy knows nothing about.

April 12

"Encourage one another." Paul

On April 12, 1945, Vice President Harry Truman, was quickly thrust into the White House as President of the U.S., having been second man for less than ninety days. I remember how inadequate he felt, and humbly said so. But, his mother, who boasted that Harry could plant corn in straighter rows than anyone else in Missouri, encouraged him, as did many others, friends and politicians, as they stepped forth with their good counsel from their experience in Washington. He needed that encouragement, and prospered well because of it.

In Deut. 3, Moses was now relieved of his leadership of the Israelites at God's command, and Joshua was to become leader and take them across the Jordan River and into the Promised Land. God knew Joshua's trembling heart, and said to Moses in Vs. 28: "Command Joshua, and encourage him and strengthen him." Encouragement dispels fear.

Many of us have experienced the truth that a word of encouragement can make the difference of giving up or going on. After eight years of drought during the years of the depression, in 1937, my neighbor begged his banker to foreclose on his farm and clear his name so he could move on, totally devastated and without hope. "I will not," said the banker, "I don't want your farm: Go back and try one more year." Rains came in 1938, ending the period of drought, and the depression turned to prosperity during WWII, enabling that farmer to sell out in 1948 and retire with dignity, worth enough to take him and his wife to their final days. He needed that banker's word of encouragement.

An anonymous writer puts it this way: "The human spirit can gain new hope from an encouraging word." Not long after my daily radio broadcast began in 1975, the enemy plagued me with guilt, condemnation, and fear of failure; that no one was listening, but everyone laughing. Discouraged, and on the verge of giving in to the negatives, I almost quit. One evening, my mate came home from a meeting with other ladies and could hardly wait to tell me. "Jane told me tonight to tell you that today's message was meant 'just for me.'" That simple word of encouragement at just the right time spurred me on, and I have never been tempted to worry or quit since... That bit of encouragement has lasted for years.

An old cliché: "To ease another's burden, help to carry it." On that day two thousand years ago when Jesus walked through those hot, narrow streets of Jerusalem, stripes being carved into His back, perspiration running from His body like a river, a crown of ugly thorns placed on His bleeding head, and carrying His heavy, wooden cross over His shoulder, faint and physically weak, it says in Matt. 27:32, "Now, as they came out, they found a man of Cyrene, Simon by name. Him they compelled to bear His cross." How I would like to have been drafted for that privilege, honor and responsibility to encourage my Savior and Lord in such a simple but significant way for that hour.

But, the source of the greatest encouragement of all is where King David found it when he and his army returned home from battle and found their city of Ziklag burned to the ground and their wives and daughters taken captive. "David and the men with him lifted up their voices and wept until they had no more power to weep...David strengthened himself in the Lord, his God." I Samuel

30. I suspect it was prayer and the Word of God that he fed his weeping soul with. "Weeping may endure for a night, but joy comes in the morning." David, Ps. 30:15

April 13

"Call upon Me and I will answer..." Jeremiah 33:3

This morning as I went to prayer, the thought came to me: "How wonderful that when I come to the throne of God to thank Him, praise Him, visit with Him, reason with Him, and plead with Him, I have His full attention immediately, no waiting in line, no busy signal, nor recording machine, no voice that says "our office hours are eight to five weekdays, closed on weekends." No female voice asks me my name as I try to reach the Chief Executive. No, friends, if all six billion people on earth this morning should pray at the same time to the God of Heaven, it would make no difference, but God's ear and His full attention would be as if only one of us were knocking at His door. I don't understand all this because I'm living, contained in such a box here on earth, severely short of mental capacity to see the real bigness of our Omni, sovereign God. How thankful I am that God is not boxed in, confined, or handicapped in any respect, but all-knowing, everywhere present, with power over all other forces. Jesus was one day in the same box we are in when He was here on earth in His physical body. He could be in only one place at a time, doing only one thing at a time, hearing only one person at a time. That's why He said in John 16:7: "Nevertheless, I tell you the truth, it is for your advantage that I go away, for if I do not go away, the Helper (the Holy Spirit) will not come to you; but if I depart I will send Him to you." PTL that only fifty days after His ascension, Pentecost Day, God the Father and Jesus the Son poured out their very Spirit upon the earth with Divine power from pole to pole, and from east to west, just as if Jesus Himself was still here.

I hope that what I've shared so far has encouraged someone like as we see from Acts 18:27 where we read of Apollos who shared with other believers, and it says: "Apollos greatly helped those who had believed through grace." Every fall on the Montana ranch I heard and saw huge flocks of geese migrating south from northern Canada, always flying in a v-formation, honking at one another, a sort of melancholy experience for me as I knew winter was approaching, and many friends going south with the geese. Geese travel in formation so that the flapping wings of one makes an encouraging draft, a help for the one following, like a big eighteen-wheeler does for a cyclist. Their honking must be their encouragement for one another, perhaps the unfolding or suggesting of plans ahead for the next feeding station, or open pond. We also need "honkers" who will fly in formation with us and encourage us to keep on keeping on.

Is there someone in your formation to whom you might give encouragement to with a compliment, a phone call, an invitation to dine together, or to share God's Word at a Bible Study, or as a comfort to a hurting person? Someone has said: "When you encourage someone, both of your loads will be lighter."

April 14

"You believe in God, believe also in Me" John 14:1

Good morning to everyone, each of you a treasure in my heart and a great big jewel in the heart of God and of Jesus. I say a treasure to me because I want to spend eternity with every one of you sharing with me this morning. So, consequently I take seriously this opportunity to share "the old old story of Jesus and His love"; and to share John 14:6 where Jesus said of Himself: "I am the Way, the Truth, and the Life, no man comes to the Father but my Me." I say that each one of you, too, are a jewel in the eye of the Father who created you, who has protected you, who knew you before conception, and has a plan for your life, a plan He has shown so clearly put forth in John 3:16-17: "For God so loved the world that He gave His only begotten Son, that whosoever believes in Him shall not perish, but have everlasting life. For God did not send His Son into the world to condemn the world, but that the world might be saved through Him."

But I am a bit disturbed this morning because twice this past week I discovered 58 and 60 year old men who have listened to the

Word of God preached and taught over radio, TV and from the pulpit but are still bypassing Jesus as their only way to salvation, and their only way to Heaven. Neither would settle for the alternative, which is Hell, but neither heart has been eternally touched by the love of Jesus and His work of salvation on Calvary. As I have mingled with Lutherans and Catholics up in Montana, I have found so many who believe God, but shun the Name of Jesus and the Person of Jesus. Jesus reacted to this in John 14:1: "You believe in God, believe also, in Me", a plea from Him to settle a troubled heart. And then only five verses later: "I am the Way, the Truth, and the Life; no man comes to the Father but by Me." When we receive and accept that Word with child-like faith peace comes in like a flood.

An anonymous writer puts it this way:
"If you should wake some dreadful day
Before His throne, and hear Him say:
I am the Way you did not take,
Although I died once for your sake;
I am the Truth you did not heed;
You were so sure you had no need;
I am the Light you did not see—
Now, darkness for eternity!
You cannot say, "I did not know"
He plainly wrote and told you so.
And if you would not read His Word???
That Word still stands, "Thus sayeth the Lord!"

April 15

"Allow the little children to come unto Me" Matthew 19:14

One of the most pleasant experiences out on the highways, streets, and by-ways is to come upon a stopped school bus with all those blinking, warning lights, and then see the little ones unload with arms full of clothes and books, and "stuff", usually hitting the pavement on a run as they joyfully, playfully saunter toward their home. Oh, for the soulish warmth of that word "home", the earthly one here and the heavenly one when we will one day fall into the arms of Jesus, and into the presence of our Father-home at last.

> I empathize today with an unknown poet:
> "Someday the bell will sound,
> Someday my heart will bound
> As with a shout that school is out
> And, lessons done, I homeward run."

In the springtime when we head for Montana, back to the land, people, and rural culture where I was born and lived for more than seventy years, it's "back home" to, where I grew up, was educated, married, and blessed with a large family. I then pursued a ranching vocation for fifty three years, coming home to a heritage that brought me into a full U.S. citizenship, now for a short while my home, "the land of the free and the home of the brave." It was there I was first exposed to Jesus as a very young boy, and that longing for a citizenship for eternity in heaven. John 3:16, my first memorized verse of scripture, became a living, accepted reality at an early age: "For God so loved the world that He gave His only begotten Son, that whosoever believes on Him shall not perish, but have everlasting life." And then came II Cor. 5:17: "If any man be in Christ Jesus, he is a brand new creation, old things passed away, all things become new." Near the front door of our home on the ranch hung a plaque: "My home is where I hang my heart." The old west I grew up in, full of young, roaming men on horseback, so carefree and unsettled in their lives, used to claim: "My home is where I hang my hat", very often the home of a hospitable homesteader. It is good for us to have a home on either end of our trip to Montana, but, oh how much better to look upward along the way and sense the warmth of that one our Lord has prepared for us in heaven. John 14:2. When someone asked Jesus where His earthly home was, He replied: "The birds of the air have a nest, the fox has a hole to call home, but the Son of Man has nowhere to lay His head." Oh how free of earthly things was Jesus when His Father called Him home, nothing to leave behind, back to His real home from which He came to us in the flesh. It was a reunion His heart longed for like the little children unloaded from the school bus. All so that you and I might have that same hope on the other side of the grave, and we move into that new mysterious realm with our glorified bodies and sinless hearts.

This morning, we are all aliens and pilgrims "headed home" with like joy and gladness of a little child after school, like we enjoy coming and going to Montana.

Won't it be exciting when "The roll is called up yonder" and you and I can answer "present, Lord?" Home at last!!

"For to me, to live is Christ, to die is gain" Paul, Phil. 1:21

April 16

"Do this in remembrance of Me" Luke 22:19

On that pleasantly warm spring day when I walked through my hog confinement barn just to "check on things," I noticed a day-old baby piglet lying by himself, away from the litter gathered under the heat lamp. I picked him up, shook him a bit to awaken him, but saw no life and felt no heartbeat. I assumed he must be dead and tossed him toward "baby pig cemetery" for late-burial. Sometime later when I heard an anxious piglet looking for a mother, and saw him running around in the sunshine, I remembered the "dead" piglet, now evidently resurrected, the least of my expectancy.

Likewise, in the scriptures, we find in John 2:29, Jesus speaking to the bargaining Jews he had just removed from the temple for desecrating the house of the Lord: "Destroy this temple, and in three days I will raise it up." Preposterous, if He was speaking of their house of worship which took them forty-six years to build! But Jesus was speaking of another temple—the temple of the Holy Spirit, His body. "Therefore, when He had risen from the dead. His disciples remembered this saying, and believed the scriptures and the Word which Jesus had said." Vs. 22.

About this same time, two men were walking together on the road to Emmaus, John 24:13, talking about the death and burial of this Man, Jesus, of angels who had said that He was alive when the Marys had come to the tomb early that morning, and now suddenly this man, unexpected, unnoticed, unidentified, walking alongside them. But, while walking together, He had opened the scriptures to them, "and their eyes were opened and they knew Him." They remembered the prophecies when Jesus opened the Word of God to them. "Thy Word is Truth." John 17:17. "...keep them (My Words) in the midst of your heart, for they are life and health..." Prov. 4:23. (Parenthesis mine.)

At every Holy Communion service, we share His body and blood "In remembrance of Me," of His death and resurrection, and our faith and hope are renewed because in life and in death Christ is our hope. Those who live only for this life are to be pitied, without hope. "For to me, to live is Christ, and to die is gain." Paul, Phil. 1:21.

Let us remember that there must first be a death to the old self before a resurrection of "the new man in Christ Jesus." II Cor. 5:17.

Some of us need a severe jolt like the little piglet on the way to the cemetery, or like Paul on the way to Damascus in order to resurrect the dead unto life, the greatest miracle of all.

April 17

The antique old bridge...

When I received in the mail a copy of last week's hometown paper from Montana, I saw on the front page a picture of an old-time steel bridge hanging in mid-air, suspended with heavy cables and a crane. The narrow, locally famous "Tande" bridge, built almost a hundred years ago for horse and buggy days, and for Model T and Model A Ford cars have served their purpose of helping farmers and ranchers cross the Poplar River on their way to the county seat. The old steel bridge we cherished so much in the early days has literally been pulled up from its thick concrete foundation, from its first roots, on its way now to the museum grounds three miles away. As I studied the picture with a bit of nostalgia, going back to my early beginnings, I thought of how this illustrates the present-day taking up of many of our basic foundations, traditions, and principals of America and of the Christian church; also nostalgia, dangling them arrogantly in mid-air before our faces, nowadays hearing and seeing only a skeleton of the firm foundation, one no longer supporting the inherited virtues I knew as a child. Humanists and New Agers are today boldly tearing down the structure, leaving it dangle in midair. Destroyed is the biblical structure of our Universe and life in this Universe; our Judeo-Christian judicial system; man's origin; the Godly marriage covenant; Satan and his fall and its effect on humanity; destruction of a free democratic government structure making mockery out of Christianity, and laughing at the idea of a Godly, chosen people on a pilgrimage to a place called Heaven on the other side of the grave.

One of two scriptural bulwarks of strength we have in our arsenal to fight against those evil forces is found in Ephesians 6:12-18, armor for the front side only as we face them head-on, but no armor for the back side. You and I can daily dress ourselves with child-like faith with the full armor of God and stand like a David against a Goliath. The second bulwark of strength is a Word for a nation as well as an individual, a nation like America who will hear God from I Chronicles 7:14: "If my people which are called by My name will humble themselves and pray and turn from their wicked ways, I will hear them from Heaven, I will forgive their sin, and I will heal their land."

"Praise God from whom all blessings flow,
Praise Him all creatures here below
Praise Him above, all you Heavenly host;
Praise Father, Son, and Holy Ghost."

April 18

"...I am the resurrection and the life..." John 11:28

When Jesus came knocking at my mind's door through the voice of my son-in-law Greg, on Main Street that brilliant, sunny April morning in 1977, my son Lee had already been deceased about an hour and forty-five minutes. Three hundred miles away, on a two-lane highway engulfed in dense fog, he met his instant death when a huge, heavy, logging truck blindly wandered into his lane on a curve and ran over the little LUV pickup Lee was driving.

When I delivered the sad news to my mate, Lois, only minutes later, her first response was: "Lee is alright!" meaning that he was truly born-again, and now in Heaven with Jesus. We had watched him surrender his life to Jesus at an altar only ten months earlier. His testimony to friends and high school classmates was simple, but bold, and confident: "I can hardly wait to get to Heaven." He believed Jesus from John 14:2: "In my Father's house are many mansions...I go to prepare a place for you. And if I go, I will come again and receive you to Myself, that where I am, there you may be also." He believed Jesus from John 11:25: "I am the resurrection and the life."

As I put all this together today from memory, I see a real analogy of Martha and Mary at Lazarus' death from John 11.

When Jesus came to Bethany after several days delay, Martha, with mixed emotions, said to Jesus: "Lord, if You had been here, my brother would not have died (a scolding mixed with faith). But even now, I know that whatever you ask of God He will give you." John 11:22. Jesus said to her: "I am the resurrection and the life...and whoever lives and believes in Me shall never die." Do you believe this? Lee believed that truth.

Because of his faith in Jesus, Lazarus' inner man was taken out of the grave he was born into, his first resurrection of two "I will extol You, oh Lord, for You have lifted me up...You have brought my soul up from out of the grave, and have kept me alive, that I should not fall into the pit..." David, Ps. 30:1, 3. And now Lazarus' second resurrection, a physical one we who believe will all experience, a resurrection from an earthen grave unto eternal life.

Because Jesus has risen from the dead, He is now authority in both life and death of the inner man.

Seminary professor, Walter Bauman, learning of his soon eminent death from cancer, saw Jesus work in his life like this: "I have bet my living, and now am called to bet my dying, that Jesus will have the last word." "For I know that my Redeemer lives,...this I know, that in my flesh I shall see God...and my eyes shall behold... how my heart yearns within me!" Job 19:25-27

We mourned Lee's demise, so young, but how easy to let him go when we knew how his faith complimented Job's testimony.

<u>April 19</u>

"Be anxious for nothing..." Philippians 4:6

What a sunken feeling hit my stomach when the news of my son's losing his home in Montana by fire came to my ear by phone. It caused me to reflect about my days out there on the prairies from whence I have accumulated both mountaintop experiences like births, weddings, lifetime friendships, bountiful harvests, and countless sunrises and sunsets in the Big Sky Country. Then there were those in the valley below: death, drought, hailstorms, gossip, and the "dirty thirties", all beyond my control. We can dig into the biographies of anyone who has lived a long life, be it on earth today or from the scriptures going back centuries, most lives have been lived with a mixture of valley and mountaintop experiences.

Even Jesus, ejected from the very womb of heaven itself when He came to us here on earth in the flesh, knew and lived both mountaintop and valley experiences. It is just part of our earthly trek as pilgrims crossing a land on our way to heaven if we are truly born again in the inner man, having truly accepted Jesus with child-like faith, and His work on that cross on Calvary as a personal blessing of grace, having accepted that Jesus Who made it crystal clear in John 14:6: "I am the Way, the Truth, and the Life; no man comes unto the Father but by Me." "For God so loved the world that He gave His only begotten Son, that whosoever believes on Him, shall not perish, but have everlasting life." John 3:16.

Oh, that sunken feeling!! From Matt. 22, we read that Peter walked on the water in the midst of a stormy sea, at the bidding of Jesus. It says: "He saw the boisterous wind", and took his eye off from Jesus and sank into the waves. Why did Peter both walk and sink in the same sea? Fear grabbed him the moment he took his eyes off Jesus and onto the wind and wave. On my way to an attorney's office, with down payment in my hand, fear grabbed me as I was about to go into debt on 320 acres of cropland. I turned around in the middle of the road, went back home, and to this day regret the blessing I lost as a very young man whose eye stayed on the negative of fear rather than on Jesus, the positive. We need to discover, like Peter, we are safe in the presence and arms of Jesus in any experience.

That afternoon when the news of the fire arrived, Alice and I went to prayer at once, and from what I've gathered, our prayer has been beautifully answered as people have reached out with all kinds of blessings for the family, including a furnished home, free of charge. "Thank you, Lord, you've made a valley experience into a mountaintop one as usual, in that community of good people."

I see here once again that large picture that hung on our living room wall, where an arm is extended with a large open hand in which a little boy is peacefully settled, even while dark, heavy, storm clouds are hanging overhead, and a violent, turbulent ocean of water below, secure in the extended hand of Jesus with child-like faith. It is a tribute to life as against abortion.

Then will hope, love, joy, peace, and security replace that feeling of fear!

April 20

"In the shadow of Your wings..." Ps. 57:1

This morning, my mind ambled back out to Montana where I know many bird hunters are scouring the brush for grouse, sage hens, the ducks on the pond, and most prized of all, the multi-colored Chinese rooster. I never did keep hunters off of my land, but did have a gentleman's agreement for no pheasant hunting in or about our shelter belt, simply because we wanted some of those charming, colorful birds to parade later in the winter around our home, and into the farmstead, where I would feed them a real treat when the air is cold, all other nature is dormant, and the ground is covered with snow. And then, too, I wanted to preserve some seed for next year's hatch. How many times I laughed at my son-in-law and other ardent hunters who would drive up our driveway only to be interrupted, or even stopped, by perhaps a dozen beautiful roosters strutting proudly, heads erect, enjoying their refuge. They seemed to know that they had this safe place during hunting season.

Almost every morning I praise the Lord as I begin my day from Psalm 91:1-2: "He who dwells in the secret place of the Most High shall abide under the shadow of the Almighty. I will say of the Lord: You are my Refuge, my Fortress, my God, in Him will I trust."

It gives me personally a special blessing of hope, love, joy, peace, and security when I see Jesus as my refuge in times of trouble and in good times, as like a game refuge that is all fenced as a special place for birds and all wildlife to find protection from hunters, an acreage with lots of water and grass, with "no hunting" signs posted. This morning I dipped into Ps. 57, one it is believed David wrote while fleeing from King Saul, who was tenaciously hunting down David with his heart full of jealousy, which had hatred with one intent in mind: to kill the little shepherd boy whom Samuel had anointed to be king when Saul would pass out of the picture. Jealous Saul could not wait, so took things in his own hands as powerful king to hunt David and destroy him. The eleven verses of Ps. 57 are David's plea to God for safety from his enemy, a place of refuge. From verse 1..."In the shadow of Your wings I will make my refuge until these calamities have passed by."

Let that be our testimony for today as we "trust in the Lord with all our heart, and lean not unto our own understanding, but acknowledge Him in all our ways, and He will direct our paths." Prov. 3:5-6.

April 21

"God made Him Who knew no sin to be sin for us". II Cor. 5:21

My paternal pioneer family found the native grass on the Montana prairies tall enough to touch the stirrups of a saddle atop a cowboy's steed on that March day of 1901. You see, only the buffalo, evidently in slight numbers, and the deer and the antelope had grazed those prairies. No domesticated animal, the horse, cow or sheep had ever inhabited that nomadic, unsettled land. What a blessing for the homesteader on the one hand, and yet a dreadful curse on the other hand. It was abundant grazing for the livestock, but at the same time an abundant dry tinder to feed a lightning ignited fire, along with usually a strong wind. Many young pioneer's families, possessions, hopes, and dreams were wiped out in only minutes of time. That was the worst scenario. But the best scenario came for those who had "backfired." Before the huge, wind driven prairie fire arrived, to protect their human bodies and even maybe a saddle horse, oxen, or milk cow, they would purposely set fire to an acreage behind them that would naturally stop the big fire on the way

THEY WOULD STAND ON GROUND WHERE A FIRE HAS ALREADY BURNED!!

What a post-season Easter thought, the reality of our standing on ground where the wrath of God, a fire, has already purposely burned.

"All have sinned and fall short of the glory of God." Rom. 3:23, enough to draw the fire of the wrath of God; for Rom. 6:23 says: "The wages of sin is death..." meaning consumed because of alienation from God. But the gift of God is eternal life. That gift is for those only who have accepted Christ as their "backfire" on God's wrath. They believe with child-like faith in the crucifixion and resurrection of Jesus Christ, a supernatural "backfire".

John 3:16 says: "For God so loved the world that He gave His only begotten Son, that whosoever believes on Him shall not perish, but have eternal life." Can you see here how God's love became a "backfire" for us who see Him as also a God of justice with His sacrifice? Those who believe on Christ and His work on Calvary have prepared themselves "ahead of the fire" for a safe haven when God's wrath comes upon unsaved humanity at the white throne judgment. Rev. 20:15 says: "Anyone not found written in the Book of life was cast into the lake of fire." No time left to create a "backfire."

PTL that we who have aligned with Jesus don't have to "wait out" the flames of the fire of God's wrath, "for the battle is not yours but God's." II Chronicles 20:15

From a pioneer's son who will escape the fires of Hell because of the love of God, the grace of our Lord Jesus Christ, and the communion and fellowship of the Holy Spirit. Amen.

April 22

"Except for the grace of God, there go I." Livingstone

    Last week I spent a couple hours with officers of the sheriff's department at a meeting regarding Christian ministries at the new jail just completed. An under-sheriff offered us a tour of the new facilities-a basement and three stories above. As we made almost any move from entering an elevator to passing through a gate, our guide had to push a button, speak into an intercom and then see the gate open. We walked right into the inmates quarters, and I thought: "Lord, how I appreciate my freedom", as I saw those bunks, as many as sixty four in one room, all huddled together, never a breath of fresh air and no sight of daylight; their quarters for sleeping, eating, exercising, and entertainment all in one; some men in solitary confinement on third floor. But, oh the eerie sound of those heavy, clanging, metal doors that open and shut only as a lady in the central electronic system wills. It was depressing, even though very nice comfortable and new, the thought of no freedom to roam the hills and valleys I've known all my life, or the streets and avenues of our cities. I wondered: "Why are most of them here?" And then concluded: because they are already, by and large, prisoners and servants of an evil force that compels and propels them day and night, so that even on the outside from whence they came, they are prisoners. The real person inside that clay body has never experienced freedom from the driving forces of flesh, the world, and the devil; every one of us is born with sin-our old nature. We find that it has been that way down through the ages, and certainly in the writings of both old and new testaments. From inside those prison gates, I thought like missionary David Livingstone once when he saw an inebriated man wobbling down a London street: "Except for the grace of God, there go I."

    Billy Graham once illustrated the bondage of sin and the freedom from it like this:

> "Johnny went with his sister, Mary, to visit their grandparents on the farm. Grandmother had a pet duck she was very

fond of. One day, as Johnny was playing, he aimed his slingshot at the duck, and the bird toppled over, kicked a few times, and died. Johnny was frightened; grabbed the duck, ran into the woods, dug a hole, and secretly buried the duck; so he thought! That evening it was Mary's turn to do the supper dishes. But, Mary turned to Johnny and said: "You do the dishes tonight." "No", he said, "This is your night. I am going outside to play." Mary said: "I saw you kill that duck. If you don't do exactly what I tell you to, I'll tell Grandma what you did. It was her prize duck." "All right," said Johnny, "I'll do the dishes:" The same next time: "Johnny, remember the duck," At last, Johnny went to his grandmother, stood around, twisted his ear, bit his nails, and finally said: "Grandma," and she interrupted: "I wondered how long you were going to take this bondage of Mary's, two weeks now already, waiting for you to come."

Our Heavenly Father is also waiting for us to come to Him and confess our sin, repent of it and say; "God, here I am. Forgive me. I want to be free, and have a fresh start. I want a new beginning, a new birth, and to be Yours from now on."

My friend, have you been set free from the bondage you were born into, a prison only Jesus can bail you out of?

April 23

"And the two shall become one flesh." Eph. 5:31

One day I discovered Song of Solomon 2:15, and I've tripped over that simple little verse time and again from one angle after another, where we read: "Catch us the foxes, the little foxes that spoil the vines, for our vines have tender grapes." Can you imagine my shock one warm, sunny, spring morning when I came out to the lambing compound on the Montana ranch and found a whole den of baby foxes running and playing amongst the mothers and lambs? "Where did they come from" I wondered? "Where is the real villain, the mother?" They looked so innocent, but give them a few weeks!

Ever since I came to be part of this unusually peaceful congregation at Abiding Savior nine years ago, a blessing I have never known before, I have prayed faithfully: "Lord, if anyone comes to this church this morning, including me, with a little fox in his heart, on his shoulder, in his hip pocket, or on his mind that would eat away at the precious vines of tender grapes in this unusually peaceful gathering of God's people, let it not enter, but destroy it at the doorway." It was Abraham Lincoln who walked miles one evening to correct an innocent little thing: a penny or two he had found was his mistake and cheated a housewife out of just a little thing, but now one hundred sixty years or so later, still being talked about and read in his biography. The widow's mite was the least of all that was laid on the altar that day, but the only gift Jesus praised and recorded 2000 years ago, still being read today from God's Word, a little thing that made its way into the greatest publication of all time, the Bible, God's Word.

We sometimes wonder why this chef or that chef puts out food that tastes super good. It's the little details that make the difference, like as with my mother's cooking. How many marriages have failed because the spouses, one or the other, or both, have failed to pay attention to the little things that can make or break a marriage? Sometime ago, I sat in the presence of a couple married many years where the wife said: "He never tells me he loves me, nor praises my dress or appearance." She was starving for only a little hug once in a while, or a compliment which she well deserved, a word of encouragement and affection, little gems that would bless her tender little heart and help seal that marriage. Just little things, but oh so big to her just once in a while: a hug, a kiss, a compliment, and an "I love you". In his defense, the husband's ears burning with embarrassment, he said: "I told you on our wedding day that I loved you. If I change my mind, I'll let you know," a pledge coming from a macho, stoic front.

During my time of being a lonely widower, I constantly rehearsed the little things of my forty six year-old marriage: the wide open arms at homecoming from the day's work, the warm heart sitting next to me in the gym, in the church pew, in the front seat of the car, or at the dining room table. And then the many weeks together at the

Rocky Mountain Bible Camp. And the almost daily notes of communication left by either of us on the dining room table. So many thousands of little things linking two spirits together, discovering how my deceased spouse had truly become a part of me because of the little things we shared along the way. "And the two shall become one flesh." Eph.5:31.

April 24

"Come now, let us reason together; though your sin is as scarlet, it shall be white as snow. Though your sin be as crimson red, it shall be like wool" Isaiah 1:18.

"You will cast our sins into the depths of the sea." Micah 7:19.
"As far as the east is from the west, so far has He removed our transgressions from us." Ps. 103:12.
The kind of inner man freedom we know and experience from those three assurances of forgiven sin coming from a truly repentant heart reminds me of a few cows once inadvertently held in captivity for several days without water or feed on a western ranch. The roundup was over, the branding done, the vaccinations completed, the corral out on the open range, far from the rancher's farmstead, was emptied and the happy, satisfied rancher carelessly left the scene and drove home.

I said "carelessly" because he never secured the gate panel either open or shut. The cows later came back into the corral and accidentally pushed the gate shut. They became captives, imprisoned, shut away from the world of grass and water. Days later, while checking his herd, the rancher found the near disaster and freed the cows.

Captivity like that is what sin is in an unbeliever with a deep void, with dark days of fear, hungry for love, joy, peace, and security, thirsty for the "living water" as Jesus portrays Himself to the woman by the well in John 4. Man, captive unto the point of death, until a redeemer comes along and sets him free, opening the door to a wide open world of freedom from sin, death, guilt and condemnation. "The Spirit of the Lord is upon Me, because I have been anointed to preach good news to the poor, to heal the broken-hearted, to set the captives free, to restore sight to the blind, and to set free them that are bruised." Luke 4:18.

An old man had served almost a lifetime in prison. Late one afternoon, he was released, his time served, let out of prison with only the clothes on his back and a few personals in a paper sack. Full of fear, unsaved, discouraged, hopeless, helpless and depressed, he assessed his future as the evening darkened. The prison was built on a hill on the south side of town and on the north side was a river with a bridge over it. Satan spoke to him of a peaceful way out of such fear and despair—suicide at the bridge.

Heading north, he faintly began to hear music, and the further he walked, the music became louder. His soul began to lighten and respond with a ray of hope. Soon he came to an open door of a little old church. He stopped on the sidewalk, listened carefully to the gospel songs, and then noted an empty pew in the back of the church. He went in and sat down, soaked up the music, heard a salvation message that he thought was zeroed in on him only.

He soon found himself on his knees at the altar, tears running down his cheeks, confessing his sin from a truly repentant heart. He asked Jesus to come into his life and was freed from suicide, sin, eternal death and the power of the Devil. He had heard the truth in song and Word and was blessed with salvation. He was hungry now for the food of the Word and thirsty for a drink of "living water".

"You shall know the truth, and the truth shall set you free." John 8:32.

"I will extol You, oh Lord, for You have lifted me up; You have not made my enemies to rejoice over me. I cried unto You, and You have healed me. You have brought my soul up from out of the grave, and kept me alive so that I shall not fall into the pit..." Ps. 30:1-3.

My, friend, can you sing that song of praise with David this morning?

April 25

At our house during our devotional time of prayer and praise, Job 5:12 has become an everyday must which declares: "God frustrates the devices of the crafty before their hands can carry out their plans, "We use that truth to praise and thank God for His protection, giving Him 100 % credit as He uses our FBI, CIA, police, sheriffs on the ground at a precise time and place to foil the enemy in this day of spiritual warfare against America and Israel. Our jails and prisons are full of the "would-be" bombers like the Christmas undercover bomber of a couple years ago. Can't you just see that suicide bomber frantically burning his fingers and his undies without success? Can't you just see the four men flying from Britain to cities in America while authorities on both sides of the Atlantic worked together to down the plane into the ocean or return to London? Frustrated by the eye of God now spending time in British custody. On and on goes the true testimonies of God's frustration activity as it protects America day and night since 9/11.

"I will bless the Lord at all times; His praise shall continually be on my lips..." Psalm 34. Oh that every truly born again Christian in America would remember Job 5:12 and its power everyday at prayer time.

What I have written in behalf of America, can be well illustrated by the day I drove past my pasture full of sheep and in the northeast corner a coyote, undoubtedly hungry, his salivary glands acting up, until one gun shot put him down and out of commission.

In II Chronicles 20 we see again how God frustrated this enemy in behalf of King Jehosophat and the inhabitants of Judah and Jerusalem. Three armies were standing by like coyotes after a flock of sheep, to swallow them up in combat. Fasting and prayer immediately expelled their fear and brought the God of Heaven into the picture. "Oh Lord God of our fathers, are You not God in Heaven, and do You not rule overall the kingdoms of the nations, and in Your hand is there not power and might, so that no one is able to with stand you?" vs. 6. Thus says the Lord: "Do not fear nor be dismayed, for the battle is not yours but God's." Vs. 15 "...go down by the river, stand still, and see the salvation of the Lord...Believe in the Lord Your God and you shall be established; believe the prophets and you shall prosper...(King Jehosophat)...now when they began to sing and praise...the Lord set ambushes against the people of Seir, Ammon, and Moab...So when Judah came overlooking the wilderness, they looked toward the multitude and there were their dead bodies fallen to the earth. Not one had escaped."

PTL that God has been "frustrating the devises of the crafty..." for centuries, down to this day, protecting His people of Israel and America!

April 26

"I am the Vine, you are the branches." John 15:15

Have you ever imagined yourself as a branch on a tree, just "hanging in there", attached to a tree trunk? That's how Jesus describes His family members in John 15:5: "I am the vine you are the branches." I like that plural, since, like as with a tree, we huddle together and are much more useful than one by one. I marvel at all the names we followers of Jesus are called: branch, sheep, little children, disciples, lost coins, a bride, sons, and friends. After a severe windstorm our sidewalk is littered with pieces of dead, brittle, broken off branches, and think of John 15:6. "If anyone does not abide in Me, he is cast out as a branch and is withered; and they gather them and throw them into the fire, and they are burned." Some branches even attached to Christ are dead!

I look up into the tree and see more dead, dry branches without even leaves-life gone, useless, ready to break off or be cut off and thrown into a garbage bag or a fireplace. Am I, or are you, a dead branch? Or rather a choir loft the songbirds perch on; or a race track for squirrels to run on; or a shady place for monkeys to spend an afternoon floating around on. Out on the open prairies of Montana we so appreciate shelter belts, branches galore to break the northwest winds. Branches-the delight of adventuresome boys and girls as they climb amongst them, once in a while falling as the branch gives way. Branches good protection during a severe hailstorm. So branches serve a myriad of purposes.

When we look at what was a beautiful, live, green tree only a few weeks ago, now so dead looking, no color—only dry sticks ejecting from it, we could become depressed but for the fact it is dormant only for a season, the life-giving sap having gone into the root for storage but to revive again in the spring. So it is with us, that hope when our clay body becomes lifeless, we need not become depressed because we know we will be resurrected again with new life that will last forever, glorified bodies housing a saved soul in Heaven.

We believers in Jesus are thought of as branches on a special tree, a fruit-bearing tree, a tree whose heavy trunk bears many branches bowed with fruit at harvest time, the strong vine anchored with a densely populated root system, reaching down into water and nutrients—down into the River of Grace, whose source is the heart of God, giving life to the vine and the branches.

Every branch that stays attached and draws life from the vine bears fruit, the special tree not showing off just pretty leaves for their beauty, but fruit that gives life, and sustains for the consumer. And when a tree is chopped down, it is the trunk, not the branches, that is used to make lumber to build with. Jesus, our tree trunk we "branches" are attached to, was used likewise when He was cut down physically on that cross. He immediately was resurrected and ascended back to Heaven with the good news for us He left behind: "Let not your heart be troubled...In My Father's house are many mansions...I go to prepare (build) a place for you...I will come again and take you to Myself, that where I am, there you may be also." John 14:1-3.

Oh, to be the blessing described in Ps. 1:3: "He shall be like a tree planted by the rivers of water, that brings forth its fruit in its season, whose leaf shall not wither, and whatever he does shall prosper."

Fellow "branch", go out today, a branch pouring out love, joy, peace, and security to a needy person, the tasty fruit of the "tree of Life", now ready to be pruned, to bear more fruit. John 15:2.

April 27

"His praise will continually be in my mouth." Psalm 32:1

When the news came to me that my lifelong friend and neighbor Fred was stricken with an incurable disease, and only a short time to live, I phoned him and enjoyed an hour or so of his usual cheer and positive demeanor. He immediately set the stage for Paul's testimony from Philippians 1:21: "For to me, to live is Christ, and to die is gain." I detected complete absence of any self-pity, but rather from Psalm 100:1: "Let us make a joyful sound unto the Lord all you people. Serve Him with gladness; come before His presence with singing." As he joyfully poured out his testimony in a lively word of truth, I stood by with Psalm 32:1 rushing in from my memory: "I will bless the Lord at all times; His praise shall continually be on my lips...come, let us magnify the Lord, let us exalt His name together."

The highlight of the evening for us was Fred's assurance not only of his own salvation but also of his family's as he soon leaves them behind. His exciting testimony here may be summed up in Acts 16 where Paul and Silas were chained to a prison floor and an earthquake unloosed them and all the inmates for an escape. The jailer awakened, saw the chains loosed, assumed the inmates there in the midnight darkness had escaped. His unnecessary attempt at suicide was thwarted by Paul's assurance that all was well for the jailer who then fell before Paul, was immediately saved both physically and spiritually, and Paul assured him: "Both you and your household" as Paul showed them the way: "Believe on the Lord Jesus Christ and you will be saved, you and your household."

Fred and his family had heard likewise from Romans 10:9 "If you mouth the Lord Jesus and believe in your heart that God has raised Him from the dead, you will be saved."

"What a day that will be when my Jesus I shall see", and can declare with Job from 19:25: "For I know that my Redeemer lives, and He shall stand at last on the earth; and after my skin is destroyed this I know, that in my flesh I shall see God."

"Because of the Lord's mercies we are not consumed, because His compassions fail not. They are new every morning. Great is Your faithfulness." Lamentations 3:23-24

April 28

Another Nebuchadnezzar?

A strange, yet wonderful thought came to me the morning of Dec. 14 as I watched the beautiful news of Saddam's surrender, and saw the almost animal-like man dragged out of a mice and rat infested hole in the ground, and saw them searching him for lice in his beard and long hair, a beaten down and bedraggled old man. What a legacy to leave historians, his family, his nation, and more seriously, the God of Heaven. As I viewed those first few glimpses, I thought: here is a man worth eight billion a year ago, super powerful in his own right, wallowing in unbridled pride, now brought down to where a former king of Biblical days in that same area found himself—King Nebuchadnezzar who found glory in making a golden image of himself, like Saddam had done, and then a mandate that all should bow down to him and worship him. Those who refused, like the three Hebrew children, would be thrown into a fiery furnace to destruction. His legacy reads like this from Dan. 5:20: "But when his heart and mind were hardened in pride, God removed him from his royal throne and took away his glory, and he was chased out of his palace into the fields. His thoughts and feelings became those of an animal, and he lived among the wild donkeys; he ate grass like the cows and his body was wet with the dew of Heaven, until at last he knew that the most High overrules the kingdoms of men, and that He appoints anyone He desires to reign over them." The king later had a real change of heart.

Then that morning I turned from Satan's defeated foes to God's people and nations walking in victory and freedom. The most hated little nation of Israel that no despot has been able to push into the ocean because the powerful Omni hand of God rests upon her, and God will keep His Abrahamic covenant with her until Jesus returns to earth. I thought of Saul, a super evil man Jesus spoke to on the road to Damascus and out of him made a great evangelist, a reminder for us to pray for Saddam, since his life was spared for some reason, that he still has time to surrender to Jesus like many wicked men have even on death row. What a glow of light that could be to the Arab world!

I hear God saying to us this morning from Prov. 3:5-6: "Trust in the Lord with all your heart and lean not unto your own understanding. Acknowledge Him in all your ways, and He will direct your paths." That was America 228 years ago when our constitution and Bill of Rights were shaped out of God-fearing statesmen. We

PTL this morning for our God of Heaven, confidently into this New Year, praising Him from our hearts like King David when he took time to inventory the great and powerful blessing God had showered upon Israel, preparing to build the temple. "Blessed are You, Lord God, our Father forever and ever. Yours, oh Lord, is the greatness, the power, the glory, the victory, and the majesty; oh Lord, and you are exalted as head over all. Both riches and honor come from You, and You reign over all. In Your hand is power and might; in Your hand it is to make great, and to give strength to all. Now therefore, our God, we thank You, and praise Your glorious name." I Chron. 29:11-13.

April 29

Draw today from His vast supply!

A certain woman cried out to Prophet Elisha: "'...my husband is dead...And the creditor is coming to take my two sons to be his slaves.' Elisha said to her: 'What shall I do for you? What do you have in the house?'...'your maidservant has nothing in the house but a jar of oil. Go borrow vessels...from all your neighbors, empty vessels...not just a few'" Then she was instructed to pour her jar of oil into those vessels, and set aside the full ones, one at a time. All the vessels miraculously filled, and Elisha said to her: "Go, sell the oil and pay the debt; and you and your sons live on the rest." II Kings 4.

As I pondered this beautiful faith builder, this never-ending supply coming out of faith and obedience, I thought of Phil. 4:19: "My God shall supply all your needs according to His riches in glory in Christ Jesus." I saw those big steel bins I once had full of grain on the Montana ranch, and I saw, too, a tiny mouse we sometimes found just inside the bin door when we unloaded the bin. I see myself as that tiny little mouse as I size up God's unlimited daily blessing and provision for me. I see myself like that mouse, sitting in a warm, cozy place, devouring the tiny kernels of grace sufficient for me, one kernel at a time trickling down from such a vast supply. I am surely as amazed and overwhelmed as the mouse when he stands back and takes inventory of the millions of kernels, far more than he needs, and far more than he can consume in a lifetime. And let us not forget, the mouse had absolutely nothing to do with this vast supply—its growth, harvest, or storage. It's all free! Inside that metal door is the mouse's salvation, complete safety from a cat, a fox, a hawk, or an eagle.

Such blessing do we truly born-again believers enjoy in the family of God, shut away from sin, death, and Satan's deadly power when we put on the full armor our Lord has given us, impenetrable, covering like a steel bin covers the mouse. "I Myself will help you, declares the Lord," Jesus speaking to each of us as we survey His vast supply of grace He has stored up for us, both for today and into eternity. I hear Him say: "I created you, gave you life, sacrificed My body and blood in your place for your sin. I have redeemed you, you are Mine, I call you by name..." Isaiah 43:1-2. "I left My glory in Heaven to become man in the flesh for you. You need much, and I have more than you can consume. Bring your empty vessel, your woes, wants, and needs, and I will instruct the Holy Spirit to draw off daily just enough from the River of Grace that runs from My heart to yours, a never-ending supply trickling down daily." Jesus speaking. "The thief has come but for to kill, steal, and destroy; but I have come to give life, and to give it abundantly." John 10:10.

PTL, little mouse, for "Every good gift and every perfect gift is from above, and comes down from the Father of lights, with Whom there is no variation or shadow of turning." James 1:17.

Draw today from His vast supply, my brother and sister in the Lord.

April 30

Rescue the perishing!

How would you personally relish the statement Paul made to the Jews, God's so-called "chosen people" in Romans 2:24: "The name of God is blasphemed among the Gentiles because of you?" Or, "the lost world around you sees you, a professed believer in Christ, blaspheming the Person and Name of God by your thoughts, words, and deeds." One TV ad I see daily, purposed to warn the public, shows a man digging in another man's garbage by the curb, and finding a cache. He tucks it under his jacket and goes on down the street with only one thought in mind: to fraudulently use that social security number, or that bank account number, or that credit card number which is that person's identity. Beginning now, your honest name and reputation could be blasphemed any moment ahead. That's the same business our flesh, the world around us, and Satan are in with God's name when we believers foolishly fall for the bait of temptation to sin. The moment we are truly born-again, that old hard, stony heart we are all born with is exchanged for a soft, warm heart, and He gives us authority and privilege to use His name as a citizen in His Kingdom, a family member. How proud I am to use the name "America" to go out with as I mix with people of other lands.

I think here, however, of my own days right after WWII when I fell away from my earlier close walk with Jesus, and my mouth spewed out filthy Words, and taking the name of the Lord in vain. I remember the spirit of greed I portrayed in my neighborhood as I tried to build an empire at any cost. I remember the severe cost of the "me-first syndrome" in my relationships in my family, my church, and my community, blaspheming the name and person of Jesus I pretentiously professed Sunday morning in church. Because of ignorance, pride, arrogance, and sensuality, I blasphemed without shame that One spoken of in Phil. 2:9-10: "Therefore, God has highly exalted Him, and has given Him the name which is above every name, that at the name of Jesus every knee should bow, and every tongue confess that Jesus Christ is Lord."

I once knew a dad who always said to his son as he was leaving the home for an evening with friends on Main Street: "Don't forget your name is..." How proud I have been when my sons and daughters names were mentioned in the local paper with honor and respect; and how ashamed when I once saw a son's prank on Halloween night on main street listed as "criminal mischief" in the local paper, an inscription that hurt the son, I well remember, even more than me when he saw it in black and white. What a gamble our Lord took when He accepted us weak, perverse sinners into His Kingdom, and then instructed us to "go out in My name". But we don't catch Jesus by surprise nor off guard, for He says in Ps. 37:23: "The steps of a good man are ordered by the Lord, and in his ways does He find His delight; though he fall, he shall not be utterly destroyed, for the hand of the Lord will uphold him." God's grace was sufficient for a Jew named Saul, and it is sufficient for a saved Gentile like you or me when we fall.

May 1

"My son, give attention to My Words..." Prov. 4:20

"Your radio message last Monday really hit home for me!" A listener in Montana shared with me. "Oh, what was it about?" I asked. "Well, to be honest, I just cannot remember exactly now." "Wasn't Pastor's message this morning really something?" "I wasn't there, but tell me, what was so good about it?" "I can't remember exactly, but it surely fed me and blessed my soul."

After years of saying these same things myself, and hearing others with the same problem, I realized that much of the food our inner man takes in is just like the food our physical takes in: we receive it, we swallow it, we digest it, and our inner organs break it down and miraculously assimilate every nutrient to the exact place in our body that needs the protein, minerals, vitamins, or carbohydrates for our good health and life. Can you tell me exactly what you ate for dinner yesterday? Most of us cannot, but it doesn't make any difference because the multi-blessings are miraculously and mysteriously at work anyway. Likewise, with our inner man we feed on from God's Word as it is read, taught, or preached, and the goodies we find a blessing that supernaturally, at the will of the Holy Spirit, takes it in through the inner man's ear, chews on it in meditation, digests an intended personal message just for me, and stashes the nutrients away in the heart for growth and maturity to take place. From Prov. 4:20: "My son, give attention to My Word; incline your ear to My sayings; let them not depart from before your eyes; keep them in the midst of your heart; for they are life unto those who find them, and health to their flesh." Did you notice: "keep them in the midst of your heart (even memorize), for they are life and health."

Peter, in Acts 3:19, preaching in Solomon's Portico, illustrates what a good ration of God's Word is able to do for the inner man, a manna from above: "Repent therefore, and be converted, that your sins may be blotted out, so that times of refreshing may come from the presence of the Lord." Confession and repentance refreshes the soul.

In I Samuel 16 we find Samuel anointing David to eventually become King of Israel after King Saul's demise, a time that spanned thirteen years of waiting. Upon hearing of the anointing, King Saul became distressed, actually jealous and fearful, and in vs. 14: "But the Spirit of the Lord departed from Saul, and a distressing spirit from the Lord troubled him. Saul says: 'provide me now a man who can play a harp well and bring him to me'" Vs. 17. Saul needed a refreshing of his spirit, and he looked to the man of God in his midst, David. And so it was that whenever the spirit from God left Saul that David would take a harp and play it with his hand. "Then Saul would become refreshed and well, and the distressing spirit would depart from him." Vs. 16:23. Even David, the refresher, needed refreshing one day himself. Coming home from the war front to the city of Ziklag, David found the city destroyed from fire, and the women of Ziklag, wives and daughters, taken captive. "Then David and the people who were with him lifted up their voices and wept, until they had no more power to weep." I Sam 30:4. "But David strengthened himself in the Lord His God." Vs. 6. (God's Word): "Life unto those who find it, and health unto their flesh." A healthy ration of God's Word and a big drink of that Living Water, lifts up and refreshes the soul as we daily give Him our attention, our ear, our eye, and our heart, and serve Him with our gifts of time talent, and treasure.

May 2

"It ain't over 'til it's over," Yogi Berra.

"It ain't over 'til it's over", a slogan I've used and heard many times, coined originally by Yogi Berra, a N.Y. Yankee's baseball player a few decades ago, meaning a baseball game, until the last whistle is blown. That surely must be what goes through the mind of a bareback or bull rider at the rodeo when the chute gate opens and he must endure eight grueling seconds of spurring, bucking, twisting, bouncing, and hanging on for dear life, waiting for the whistle, determined with clenched teeth: "It ain't over 'til it's over." How refreshing to find healing in the presence of Jesus for a young married couple on the verge of divorce, and to pleasantly discover: "It ain't over 'til it's over," and the marriage lasts "until death do us part."

We find in John 11 that Lazarus was sick and his sisters, Martha and Mary, had sent for Jesus to come and heal him. But Jesus remained where he was for a couple more days before heading for Bethany, where, in the meantime, Lazarus had died. For sisters, Mary and Martha, it was all over. So Lazarus, wrapped in grave clothes, his funeral over, his body placed in a tomb with a rock over its top, was gone into eternity for sure. Four days later, Jesus and His disciples came to Bethany, where both sisters chastened Him for being so late that He let Lazarus die; that if only He had hustled a bit, the brother may not have died. But Jesus answered: "Your brother will live again." In their grief, they had developed a negative mind-set that it was all over for Lazarus. Jesus asked: "Where have you laid him?" They showed Him the tomb and He said: "Remove the stone!" Still they interjected: "It has been four days now, and his body has a stench", manifesting again that mind-set that it was all over for Lazarus. Jesus replied: "Did I not say to you that if you would believe, you would see the glory of God?" They removed the stone, their actions revealing: "Maybe it isn't over yet." Jesus stood before the tomb and shouted: "Lazarus, come out". And Lazarus came wiggling his way out of the tomb, and Mary and Martha discovered that in the presence of Jesus, "It ain't over till it's over."

But Jesus looked at them (disciples) and said: "with men this is impossible, but with God all things are possible." Matthew 19:26

"The steps of a good man are ordered by the Lord, and in his ways does God find His delight" even unto the resurrection, purposed and planned by God for that "good man."

Sometimes it takes a lot of faith to believe "It ain't over 'til it's over."

May 3

An untainted offering.

On that day when international TV displayed all day long that skinny, lame Holstein cow reported to have the "mad cow" disease every rancher should fear, my mind went back to livestock sales rings where I sometimes watched "cancer-eye" cows come through for sale, so gross to look at that it almost caused me to vomit. Some meat packing buyer would bid and buy the beast for a pittance and transport her on for processing into hamburger, the head, of course, eliminated. I often asked myself "Why would a rancher bring such a spectacle into town, with ugly cancer evident?" Or like as with the skinny Holstein wobbling about, a confessed suspect of "mad-cow" disease, so repulsive to the public eye.

I opened my Bible to two portions that came to mind regarding God's perspective on such a matter of the offering coming to Him as a part of worship, coming maimed. At the institution of the first Passover when God would send the death plague on all of Egypt to destroy the oldest of the family, as well as in the stable, we read this from Exodus 12:3: "..Every man shall take for himself a lamb...a lamb for a household...your lamb shall be without blemish...from the sheep or the goats." That blood from untainted, normal, as perfect-as-possible animal God would honor and protect that household from death, as He saw the head of the house sprinkle blood on the gatepost and on the lentil. And from Malachi 1:7: "You offer defiled food on my altar...when you offer the blind as a sacrifice, is it not evil? And when you offer the lame and sick, is it not evil? I have no pleasure in you', says the Lord of hosts, 'nor will I accept an offering from your hands.'". I call it tainted money laid on the altar when it comes from the sale of liquor, drugs, gambling, pornography, or any fraudulent business dealings.

I watched my son year after year donate a weaned calf to a nearby boy's ranch, and was proud and elated to see him always try to pick his best steer calf before sending the others off to market. On the contrary, I saw others with rented state farmland, turn in their poorest quality of their harvested crop, regardless of the tract of land, deeded or rented, it was grown on. Usually the lowest protein, the lightest test weight, the poorest quality, since only bushels of grain were required, no other eye watching over them than the eye of God. Now I come to the guiltiest of all—myself. I sometimes sit in a worship service Sunday after Sunday at Abiding Savior and find my heart and mind constantly drifting off into other facets of life while my offering of worship. My heart is pretentious, inattentive, disobedient, at times rebellious, lacking attention to that which God desires most-heart worship, untainted, unblemished. The noon lunch, the afternoon football game, the evening social hour, the bank account, the cranky neighbor, the snow covered ramp and sidewalk at home, the son or daughter far away, the needed shopping close by, or the squalling baby in the back pew.

My friend...are you feeling convicted and guilty yet? I could go on and list more, but it is like this: "At the heart of worship is worship from the heart."

May 4

"The ax head fell into the water." II Kings 6.

Have you ever been all set to do something and a key component failed you? Such was the case with the sons of the prophets around Prophet Elisha in II Kings 6 when they made a move to cut down trees and make beams to build a larger dwelling place by the Jordan River. "But, as one was cutting down a tree, the iron ax head fell into the water....and the man of God (Elisha) said: "Where did it fall?" And he showed Elisha the place. So he cut off a stick and threw it in there, and he made the iron float and said: "Pick it up for yourself. So he reached out his hand and took it." That stick became a magnet to the ax head like Jesus is when we cry unto Him: "Master, have mercy on me" and He pulls us up out of the depths and takes us into His proffered hand. A mother of five sons in Billings, Montana prayed faithfully and confidently for years for their salvation, but to no avail in her lifetime. Five years after her death, all five sons were truly born-again, plucked out of the sea of death, and their inner man salvaged for eternity. Her unfailing faith in prayer to the living

God, her sons' creator, was the magnet that drew them to Jesus, like Elisha's stick drew the ax head back to its rightful owner. Millions of men, women, and children, feeling an empty void from birth, have found the Cross, Christ, and Calvary their magnet to bring them into the hope, love, joy, peace, and security every man craves, and is found only in coming to Christ by way of the new birth, and brought from death into life, and into fellowship with the Holy, Righteous God of Heaven.

In I Kings 18-19, we find Prophet Elijah enjoying a mountain top experience, having proven to the false prophets of Baal that the God of Heaven had the real, genuine, legitimate power, while their gods had no power to bring fire down from above. However, in his hour of seeming success, the power of God definitely on his side, Elijah saw something thwart his plans, Queen Jezebel, who, when she heard of the purposed disaster against her prophets, sent Word to Elijah: "...your life as the life of one of these by tomorrow about this time" vs. 19:2. Like the fallen, cut off ax head, Elijah needed a magnet to attach himself to for restoration. That magnet proved to be God, a "still, small, voice" Vs. 12, Who took him under His wing, restored his faith, and put him to work on his return to the wilderness of Damascus. 19:15.

"The steps of a good man are ordered by the Lord, and in his ways does He find His delight; though he fall, he shall not be utterly destroyed, for the hand of the Lord will uphold him." Psalm 37:23-24.

May 5

"Therefore, if your enemy hungers, feed him....For in so doing you will heap coals of fire on his head." Romans 12:20.

Sixty-one years ago, this first week of May was commemorated VE Day—"Victory in Europe"—the end of WWll, a war that actually sprouted when WWI ended in 1918, and a war that claimed thousands upon thousands of American lives on European soil. Very costly!! The victors of WWI left Germany disastrously crippled physically, economically, militarily, and psychologically, a breeding ground for revenge which Adolph Hitler capitalized on and promised Germany a way for coming back, to bring them up off from their knees. Twenty one years after WWI, and only seven years after Hitler's election as dictator of Germany, seven years of unimaginable economic prosperity, and military buildup, they were on their way to revenge and to become the world's dominant race. In post-World War I, Christian America and her allies failed to heed the Word of the Lord found in Matthew 5:44: "Love your enemies, bless those that curse you, do good to those that hate you, and pray for those who spitefully use you and persecute you." "If your enemy hungers, feed him..."

What a price we paid for our lack of love, but what a lesson we learned!!!

Immediately after WWII, the same enemy brought to her knees again, America launched the Marshall Plan, which gave millions upon millions of financial aid to rebuild and restore both Germany and Japan. They both came back quickly, fell into the family of nations respectably, flourished in every facet of life, kept the peace, and became friends of our country almost overnight. "For if you forgive men their trespasses, your heavenly Father will also forgive you." Matthew 6:14.

I see an analogy here: that when man unconditionally surrenders to Jesus, like the Axis powers of 1945 surrendered, the warfare ends, Satan is defeated, and the Lord offers us a special "Marshall plan" as He becomes our refuge, our fortress, our shield in front of us, our Lord we trust and acknowledge to direct our paths, and we reap the blessing of Luke 6:38: "Give and it will be given to you, good measure, pressed down, shaken together, and running over shall men give into your bosom. For with the same measure that you use, it will be measured back to you." And the best blessing is yet to come: eternal life in heaven, and no more war, no more tears, pain, sorrow, death, or anguish—born an enemy of God, but now unconditionally surrendered, forgiven. "For by grace are you saved, through faith, not of yourselves; it is a gift of God, not of works, lest anyone should boast" Ephesians 2:8-9.

"Our God is a faithful and just God." I John 1:9.

The victory is won—it is time to celebrate and commemorate!!

May 6

"Germany Surrenders"

I remember well that morning in May 1945: the joyous headlines around the world: "GERMANY SURRENDERS." Colossians 2:15 is that same good news for the inner man of the truly born-again when Jesus left His clay body on that Cross, and descended into the bowels of the earth: "He overcame powers and principalities, and made an open show of them, and triumphed over them in the victory He had had on the Cross." "SATAN SURRENDERS." "Truly this was the Son of God." Matthew 27:54. The battle between Jesus and Satan now over, so a saved man's death is now over because of Christ's shed blood on Calvary and His resurrection. Satan has unconditionally surrendered his claim to a child of God. So, when my surrender to Jesus is complete because of my child-like faith in Him, His work on Calvary, and in His resurrection, the Holy Spirit moves in and sets up housekeeping with my inner man. He seals my saved soul forever. II Corinthians 1:22, Ephesians 4:30. The wars in Iraq and Afghanistan have never ended with a real surrender, nor with an authority from both sides signing a final peace, guaranteeing cessation of hostilities like we have seen in most other wars in our nation's history. Consequently, endless war! This reminds me of a person who has said "yes" to Jesus on Sunday evening at the altar and then goes out on Monday morning without a repentant heart, engaging in the same old lifestyle-no true surrender, but only an assumption.

Jesus Himself sets us a perfect example, since He lived a totally surrendered life: "I came down from Heaven, not to do My own will, but the will of Him Who sent Me." John 6:38. Christ spoke those Words as a flesh-and-blood man: "The Word made flesh". John 1:14. He came to earth to live as a human being, a "High Priest Who can sympathize with our weaknesses, in all parts tempted as we are, yet without sin." Hebrews 4:15. Like us, He had a will, manifested in the Garden of Gethsemane: "Not MY will, but Thine be done."

Paul, put down by the power of Jesus on the road to Damascus, surrendered his life and obediently asked: "Lord, what will You have me to do?" Completely surrendered, he became the greatest evangelist of all time, a man who up to that time, hated Jesus and His followers. Abraham, in the land of Ur, obedient to God's call on his life, headed for the Promised Land. Genesis 32:24. Peter, James, and John left their fishing nets and obediently surrendered their lives to Jesus from that day on. Mark 1:16, 19. The man on the cross, in his twelfth hour of life, surrendered to Jesus, and that day was found in Paradise with Him. It's an unconditional surrender like the Allies of WWII demanded and received of the Nazis in May 1945.

Have you unconditionally surrendered your soul, your vocation, your resources, time, talent, and treasure, your social life, your position, your pride, and that "me-first" syndrome to Jesus, that One Who makes it very clear in John 14:6: "I am the Way, the Truth, and the Life, and no man comes to the Father except by Me"? Surrendered to that One Whom "God has highly exalted, and has given Him the Name which is above every name, that at the Name of Jesus, every knee shall bow, and every tongue confess that Jesus Christ is Lord." Philippians 2:9-10. Like a downed, knocked out boxer in the ring, the countdown on the time may be too short to rise up, and the match is over. The verdict "surrendered to the Champion!"

May 7

"You must be born again." Jesus, John 3:3

Early one morning as soon as I finished GGN over KGGM radio in Scobey, Montana, my phone rang and the male voice asked me immediately, "When are you going to get off from John 3:16 and on with something else?" I was stunned and speechless since only twenty four hours earlier a listener called and told me how my message had blessed him and encouraged me to keep on keeping on. I read recently of a pastor likewise challenged as to why he keeps on preaching John 3:3 "You must be born again." The pastor responded, "Because you must be born again—Jesus said so."

Shortly after coming to Abiding Savior Free Lutheran Church here in Sioux Falls, my pastor, Michael Brandt, gave me some simple, but excellent counsel. He had asked me to teach a Bible class and I accepted the assignment. A few days later I confided with him that I was having trouble deciding on a subject. He gave good sound advice and said, "Teach on something you know something about." So I teach and preach on salvation, including, of course, justification, sanctification, and glorification. I leave most of the history, details of the end times to men like Hal Lindsay who has spent a lifetime there, and much of the book of Revelation to its students. I believe Jesus would say, "You must first of all be born again to really satisfy the vacuum within, the soul, to feed the hungry inner man.

After dark one night a Jewish religious leader named Nicodemus came for an interview with Jesus. "Sir, he said, we all know that God sent You to teach us. Your miracles are proof enough of this. Jesus replied: that with all the earnestness I possess, I tell you this: unless you are born again you cannot enter the kingdom of God." Nicodemus replied, "How can an old man go back into His mother's womb and be born again?"

Mystery of mysteries until we hear from Genesis 1:26: "Let us make man in our own image" (God speaking). Hence, man was created to be a spirit being, unlike any of His other creatures with man to purposely be born onto this earth with the potential of housing God Himself in his clay body. "Know you not that your body is a temple of the Holy Spirit?" I Corinthians 6:19

But that inner man is born dead, alienated from God because of trespasses and sins we are all naturally born with, called the old nature. "But you He made alive, who were dead in trespasses and sins." Ephesians 2:1. Then grace enters into the equation when God sent His son Jesus to be that perfect sacrifice for sin, the only sacrifice that would satisfy God—the perfect, clean, innocent sinless blood of Jesus carried out on a cross of Calvary that Good Friday afternoon.

Paul sums it up like this in Ephesians 2:4: "...but God who is rich in mercy, because of His great love with which He loved us, even when we were dead in trespasses, made us alive together with Christ (by grace you have been saved) and raised us up together, and made us sit together in the heavenly places in Christ Jesus—for by grace you have been saved through faith in Christ Jesus, not of yourselves, it is a gift of God, not of works, lest anyone shall boast."

"To every man has been dealt the gift of faith," Romans 12:3. When the Holy Spirit brings us to a place where we can exercise that gift and accept Jesus as our Savior and Lord of our life, we are truly born again, as we believe in His resurrection of Easter morning.

"If any man be in Christ Jesus, he is a new creation, old things passed away, all things become new." II Corinthians 5:17

May 8

"Remember me..." Joseph, Genesis 10:15

Otis and Molly lived on a farm about forty miles from town in Montana during the 1930's. One day Otis loaded wheat into his 1928 Chevy truck, helped Molly into the vehicle and headed for town, where she was to busy herself with needed shopping while Otis would unload the grain at an elevator. His truck unloaded, Otis headed for home. Upon arrival and Molly was nowhere to be found: "Well, I declare, I must have left Molly in town." Have you ever been left out, forgotten, not included?

I have heard many times a speaker on a platform thank and praise specially deserving people, only to forget one. Or a newspaper article listing names of pertinent distinction, and miss one. Or an obituary where one family member is omitted. Or a list of honor students, and one inadvertently unlisted. How demoralizing to be left out!

The thief on the cross cried out "...Lord, remember me..." And to the repentant sinner I hear Jesus: "Today will you be with Me in Paradise." Included! "In My Father's house are many mansions. I go to prepare a place for you...I will return and take you unto Myself, that where I am there you may be also." Included! John 14:1.

Except for Jesus, young Cyrus could have been left out of Heaven forever. Although his parents were Christians, he didn't have much use for the Bible, but much more interested in Shakespeare and history. He became a respected lawyer, and at age 36, a friend came into his office and confronted him about his lack of faith in Christ, a conversation which led him to salvation, truly born-again. Realizing that he knew nothing about the Bible, Cyrus determined to know and appreciate God's Word more than anything else. Thirty years later, in 1909, the Scofield Reference Bible was published, completing the great work of Cyrus Ingerson Scofield. "I will never leave you nor forsake you." Included!

In Genesis 40 we find innocent Joseph locked up in a prison where later we find also Pharaoh's butler and baker each of whom had a dream one night, which Joseph interpreted for them by inspiration of God, declaring that both of them would be freed in three days. To the butler, Joseph asked a favor after having spent eleven years there. "Remember me...make mention of me to Pharaoh and get me out of this house." And in Vs. 23: "Yet the butler did not remember Joseph, but forgot him." And Joseph served another two years in prison. Days of blessing followed, and Joseph would experience Jeremiah 29:11: "I know the thoughts I think toward you, thoughts of peace, not of evil; I give you a future, I give you a hope...I will be found by you, says the Lord, and I will bring you back from your captivity." Now included!

"Thank You, Lord, for having remembered me, included me, set me free that Good Friday afternoon."

May 9

"For to me, to live is Christ, to die is gain" Philippians 1:21

The huge, jagged pieces of ice, hailstones, came down with force out of the thunderous clouds above, beating grain crops into the ground, pounding out windows, destroying roofs, and damaging siding. The rancher watched and worried—he had a young colt and a mare out on the open range, unprotected. Surely the colt will die! After the storm, he took inventory of the damages and found the colt unscathed, but the mother's flesh torn open and bleeding. She had instinctively protected her baby regardless of the torture to herself. What love, mercy, compassion, and faithfulness.

The apostle Paul risked his life like that mare on behalf of others of his day. He was stoned and left for dead. He was mobbed, whipped, and imprisoned, shipwrecked, and beaten many times with lashes and rods. Why? PTL he was thinking ahead to you and me of the Gentile world, like innocent, defenseless colts, thinking in terms of eternal fire versus eternal life, so he gladly undertook the risk. He was willing to give his life, if necessary, to take the gospel of good news, the gospel of truth, to an unsaved world. "For to me to live is Christ, to die is gain," Phil. 1:21, was his testimony.

When I come to the foot of the cross at Calvary with child-like faith, I see Jesus as that same kind of protector, as He literally stands above me with outstretched arms, the crown of thorns on His brow drawing blood; the nails in His hands and feet drawing blood; the blood flowing from His flesh-pierced side; and the awful welts on His back, oozing blood from His flesh when the lashes had cut deeply into His back. And there I kneel beneath the vicious storms of life under His full protection—the belt of truth, the breastplate of righteousness, my feet shod with the gospel of peace, the helmet of salvation to protect my mind, the Word of God, my sword of the Lord in one hand, and shield of faith in the other, out in front where He absorbs all the poisonous, deadly, darts of the enemy coming my way. Eph. 6:14-17.

"I will say of the Lord, He is my refuge, and my fortress; my God, in Him will I trust—He shall cover me with His feathers, and under His wings I shall take refuge." Ps. 91:2, 4.

May 10

"Seek Him with your whole heart." Psalm 119:2

On the Montana ranch before electricity became a reality for us, the old kerosene lantern we carried in our hand was a "lamp unto my feet, a light unto my path" as we walked the farmstead, doing chores in the evening time, especially the long nights of winter. Psalm 119:105 says exactly of God's Word...a beautiful description I enjoy in my personal daily walk with Jesus, and being able to keep in step with His Word..."a lamp, a light." As a G.I. in WWII, I had a practical taste of keeping "in step" as we marched in cadence to our leader's chant. In front of me marched a young Mexican boy in unbelievably perfect rhythm, the best in our battalion. On my left was a big, clumsy, overgrown "clod" whom I felt sorry for, never, never in time. The right foot always came down on a "left" chant and the left on a "right foot" chant. Since coming to Sioux Falls and leaving the daily exercise of farm and ranch works, I find it necessary to walk several days of the week. These warm days of walking the streets are a special delight: hearing the songs of birds, smelling the fragrant flowers and the barbecued meats, studying the people I visit with, watching the traffic, and the backhoes at work on another basement, the manicured lawns and shrubs getting T.L.C., all makes me feel good, edified, uplifted and encouraged. Discipline, sweat, energy—yes—but it is well worth it.

Psalm 119:1 speaks of another walk just as necessary for our health; a blessing and an exercise for the little boy or girl inside our clay frame which we dare not neglect. Read Psalm 119:1-16 today and you will be blessed. Good exercise for the inner man on this journey across the stage of life here on earth, where we can take the easy route and depend on others for our light and growth, our exercise, speed read a verse or chapter of scripture to ease the conscience and call it "devotions", or make a real purposed, disciplined effort to get close to God by way of prayer and the Word. Why not seek Him today and walk in perfect cadence as verse 2 suggests: "seek Him with your whole heart", and I hear Him promise: "I will hear and answer you, and show you great and mighty things you do not know". Jeremiah 33:3

May 11

"...life was the light of men." John 1:4

"For what is your life? Is it even a vapor that appears for a little time then vanishes away." James 4:14

Life is like the wick of a kerosene lantern, full of fuel, glowing with a bright, yellow-colored light, and suddenly the teenager breaks the globe of the lantern and the wind blows out the flickering light. Many of us see only one life to contend with on this earth, but there really are two: the heartbeat that keeps our clay body functioning, called life, and the little boy or girl inside called the inner man, that God-like part of us, our soul, the little spirit being that lasts forever, unlike the life that keeps the clay body going and the heart beating. I saw this vividly early one April morning when Word came to me that my twenty-year old son had been killed when a huge logging truck ran over his little pickup under a heavy covering of fog. When the shocking news came to me, the Lord immediately gave me a vision of the demolished body, and above the trauma I saw him patiently lingering for a moment, very sober, but with a peaceful countenance as the noise and the dust settled down upon the scene, his clay body lingering in the wreckage and his inner man lifted up, quickly disappearing into the heavens — "A vapor that appears for a little time and then vanishes away."

When the lantern's globe broke into pieces, the light went out; and likewise when the demolished clay body fell silent, that visible went out. When the lantern globe was replaced, the protected light shone again; and when my son's clay body is resurrected from the grave with a glorified body, life will show again, the temple replaced, never to be extinguished: life in the flesh so fleeting; life in the spirit eternal.

"And the Lord God formed man of the dust of the ground, and breathed into his nostrils the breath of life; and man became a living being." Gen. 2:7. "The days of our lives are seventy years...for it is soon cut off and we fly away." Ps. 90:10.

The inner man, born dead in trespass and sin, cries out for life to fill the void within, a needed mended relationship with the Holy, Righteous, God of Heaven. Along comes Jesus: "In Him was life, and the life was the Light of men." John 1:4. The extinguished wick lights again and the resurrected clay rises up to house the eternal flame within.

May 12

"The hand that rocks the cradle rules the world," an old adage complimentary to mother... "the hand that rocks the cradle..." a truth that history proves so well.

As I recall mothers of my boyhood days, divorce was seldom, always a word of shame. And "stay-at-home moms" was almost universal. I have in hand a picture of my eighth grade class of forty-five pupils, taken in 1939, wherein not one came from a divorced parent, and only one from a "working mom", a widowed mother with a large, young family. It was the mother who stayed by and held the family and home together, the one always at home when school dismissed and little John and Jane came home to the smell of fresh baking. When a "mischievous" dad came back home, it was tolerant mom who kept the marriage intact, and the "home fires burning."

A typical testimony of a pre-WWII South Dakota mother goes like this: a widowed woman left with eight young children, each of whom recall:

> "Mom used her water well to store our milk, cream and butter from the cows. She used a wood stove to cook the meals and bake the bread. She was seldom seen in town, so she stored large supplies of flour, sugar, coffee, and the staples for the long, cold, snowy winter and plugged roads. On the opening day of school her children proudly walked the mile and a half with brand new shirts and skirts mom had sewed. When bored with "cabin fever," mom heated up several rocks, and placed them under heavy quilts, hitched the team of horses to a sled, and off to the neighbors for an evening of fun for all."

Daughter Frances claims "that her mother never lost her temper, but loved us equally with praise for any good thing we could do to help out. She cherished each of our eventual marriages, and loved us to the very end."

"Who can find a virtuous wife? For her worth is far above rubies. The heart of her husband safely trusts her...she does him good, not evil, all the days of her life." Proverbs 31:10-12.

A Godly mother and wife is worth her weight in gold to her family, her church, her community, and to the whole world.

We love our mothers!!

May 13

"The hand that rocks the cradle rules the nation."

As I look back on my boyhood days of the 1920's and 30's, I remember my mother and all her peers as the toughest people in the world, toughest in spirit, soul, and body. I saw them as God's greatest gift to humanity, with the greatest responsibility of all people, to be a steward of God's "loan" for a season, a caretaker of His beautiful creation, a life He not only created but also died for on that cross at Calvary, a child destined by God for eternal life for the inner being after a short sojourn here on earth.

An anonymous writer puts it like this: "Of all the earthly things God gives, there's one above all others: It's the precious, priceless gift of loving Christian mothers."

Mary, Jesus' mother, was surely one of these as she stood by that Good Friday afternoon at Calvary. I can imagine how that her mind went back only about thirty-three years when the angel delivered the good news to her that she was favored and honored to become the mother of God's Son, and His name would be called Jesus, the Savior to be for all mankind.

Before assisted living, nursing homes, Medicare, and Social Security, I remember how son's and daughter's families took Grandpa and Grandma into their homes in their final years. Jesus, too, had such love and respect for His now elderly mother we find in John 19:23: "When Jesus saw His mother, and the disciple whom He loved standing by, He said to His mother, 'Woman, behold your Son!' Then He said to the disciple: 'Behold your mother'. And from that hour that disciple took her to his own home." How tangible was Jesus' love for His mother and friend. John 19.

History tells us of many mothers "who have rocked the cradle" and made America a bastion of strength. Susannah Wesley spent an hour each day praying for her eleven children. She believed that God answers prayers raised up to Him with a fervent heart. Then she would take each child aside privately every week to share God's Word and spiritual truth. The fruit of her vineyard were sons

Charles and John, whom God used in a beautiful way to bless not only America, but nations around the world.

I cherish the heart-felt testimony of my favorite American president — Abraham Lincoln: "God bless my mother, all I am or hope to be I owe to her." I can say Amen and Amen to that confession.

On this special day, let us thank God for the precious mothers who have molded our hearts.

"Her children rise up and call her blessed..." Proverbs 31:28

May 14

"Let us therefore come boldly to the throne of grace to obtain mercy and to find grace to help in time of need." Hebrews 6:14

Job feared God and shunned evil...Job would rise up early in the morning and offer burnt offerings according to the number of them (his sons and daughters) For Job said: "It may be that my sons have sinned and cursed God in their hearts; thus Job did regularly." "In God's sight...that man was blameless, upright, and one who fears God and shuns evil." Verse 1:8 From this I gather that God is pleased and blessed by a parent who prays daily for his family.

These two portions of scripture put faith, hope, boldness, and confidence in our hearts at our home every morning and evening when we pray for our families, now totaling 40 sons and daughters, their mates, grandchildren and great-grandchildren. We are daily mindful of the truth that we cannot see their hearts and therefore their relationship with God which is either negative or positive since there is no in between.

We are mindful of the truth that there is no grandfather clause, so that each one is totally responsible for his own decision. "... if you confess with your mouth the Lord Jesus and believe in your heart that God raised Him from the dead, you will be saved." Rom. 10:9. "For I am not ashamed of the gospel of Christ for it is the power of God to salvation for everyone who believes." Rom. 1: 16 "For by grace are you saved through faith, not of yourselves, it is the gift of God, not of works..." Eph. 2:8. After all, God has far greater interest in our family members than we have...greater quantity and quality of love, since it was He who created them and gave His life through Jesus to redeem them and bless with the truly born-again experience He truly lays on our hearts. John 3:3, 7: "You must be born again" Our sons and daughters and the fruit of their vines are a short term, a wonderful blessing, a gift, a loan, as like Samuel was to Hannah in I Sam. 1, a wonderful testimony of how every parent's heart ought to be when he prays and then can stand assured on I John 4:14: "And we have seen and testify that the Father has sent the Son as Savior of the world." Oh that we would remember that they are just a gift like Hannah seemed to know, a gift we dedicate and consecrate back to Him.

I have been so blessed as I have spent much time meditating on Hannah, a young bride who could not conceive, so that in verse 10 we read "She was in bitterness of soul, and prayed to the Lord, and wept in anguish... then she made a vow and said, 'if You not forget Your maidservant, but will give her a male child, then I will give him to the Lord all the days of his life.' So it came to pass in the process of time that Hannah conceived and bore a son...Samuel..." "Now when she had weaned him, she took him up with her...to the house of the Lord in Shiloh. 'For this child I prayed and the Lord has granted my petition...Therefore I have also lent him to the Lord; as long as he lives he shall be consecrated to the Lord. So they worshipped the Lord there.' And Hannah prayed...'my heart rejoices in the Lord; my strength is exalted in the Lord. I smile at my enemies because I rejoice in Your salvation.'" Vs. 2:1

When we conclude our daily prayer for our family, we have the same love, joy, peace, and security in our hearts as Hannah had, giving them to Him for His ultimate glory, standing on Matt. 19:26: "With God all things are possible."

May 15

The dawn of a new day.

Out of habit, I awaken very early in the morning the year round. I love daybreak this time of year, especially because at that early hour I hear some birds chirping and chattering and others singing melodiously outside my window. I see faint light beginning to overcome the darkness of the night. All of nature seems to be awakening. On the farm I would hear the rooster crow, see the deer at crack of dawn amble away from the river out into the hills and valleys. Many mornings emerged with heavy dew on the grass, waiting for the baler, and on the wheat leaves, waiting for weed spray, an ideal situation. Coming from the barnyard, a hungry lamb bleating or a bawling, restless calf coaxing his mother out to pasture. Regardless of yesterday's trials, every dawn of a new day fills my whole being with fresh hope and renewed faith. My friend, Lyder, out in Big Sky Country, walked the streets at daylight for his daily exercise, and while walking sometimes awakened others with his rather boisterous tenor voice singing out old familiar hymns.

I have often wondered what trip on earth could be more exciting than the morning when the two Marys headed for the tomb with spices to anoint the body of Jesus, a chore the dusk of Good Friday denied them when their Sabbath day began. And now they found the huge, heavy rock, rolled away and a young man sitting by: "Do not be alarmed: He is risen: He is not here." Heaviness and a dark cloud hovered over the ladies, and life looked lost and bleak to His disciples who were hiding away in fear and sorrow, behind them a dark, dark night with no hope. But then, like rays of the sun of a new day, very dim at first, turned bright and penetrated the darkness so that it vanished. At His death that Friday before, His Spirit left the clay body and descended into the bowels of the earth where: "He overcame powers and principalities, and made an open show of them; and triumphed over them with the victory He had just had on the Cross." Colossians 2:15. And now this morning, by the power of God, His inner man was again injected into a brand new glorified body, and He arose to face a brand new day, having overcome death, man's last enemy. Jesus, the Spirit-Being, was set free. "Now, the Lord is the Spirit, and where the Spirit of the Lord is, there is liberty." I Corinthians 3:17.

The devil may be trying to hold back the dawn of a new day, a new day of freedom for you this very hour, trying to hold you in bondage, captive, bound in grave clothes of sickness, addiction, poverty. Or some crippling sin—a huge, heavy rock that needs to be rolled away, and a new day of healing and deliverance on hand. "Weeping may endure for a night, but joy comes in the morning." David sang that out early one morning in Psalm 30:5. Two thousand years ago Jesus walked out of the tomb at the dawn of a new day to take care of our every need in spirit, soul, body, finances, and relationships.

May 16

"Greater love has no man..." John 15:13

How blessed we are with the genuine spirit of love we see the caretakers shower upon the helpless occupants of the Alzheimer wing of a local rest home. We see noisy, unruly elders, blind ones, deaf ones, wheel-chair ones, second childhood ones, lovers, singers, complainers, cranky ones, loveable ones, and obnoxious ones. Upon each one, regardless, we see hugs poured out constantly, extreme patience, and understanding, gentle voices and personalities, and we marvel at the manifestation of such love for the often unlovable. It's good therapy for me to soak up, as I look on and see myself as either the patient or the caretaker.

On this sixtieth anniversary of "D-Day 1944" we see on TV many of those brave teenagers of yesteryear, now in their eighties, emotionally broken as they recite that day's life on the shores of Normandy and Omaha beaches of France. Can you imagine the fear and dread of facing well fortified weapons as they sat out in the water like clay pigeons? And now today the survivors gaze upon the thousands of crosses of the buddies that fell that day the English Channel flowed with blood-stained ripples. I personally cannot help but love them who loved America and their fellow man down to this generation enough to offer their clay body as a sacrifice to preserve America's freedom from the evils of Fascism of that time in history.

I share these testimonies as real evidence of what I read in I John 4:1-2, 11: "Beloved, let us love one another, for love is of God, and everyone who loves is born of God and knows God. He who does not love is not of God, for God is love...Beloved, if God so loved us, we also ought to love one another." Sometimes when I preach or teach from this text, I feel checked in my spirit. Am I living what I know is truth, and what is expected of a child of God? Our testimony bears out our real inner man's life—real, tested, love, or fake, imitation love.

A little four-year old son brought his parents to tears and repentance one day as he innocently showed love from the heart in a physically unpleasant sight at times—his grandfather—the story from an anonymous author.

"The frail old man went to live with his daughter-in-law, and four-year old grandson. The old man's hands trembled, his eyesight was blurred, and his step faltered. The family ate together at the table. But the elderly grandfather's shaking hands and failing sight made eating difficult. Peas rolled off from his spoon onto the floor. When he grasped his glass, milk spilled on the tablecloth. The son and daughter-in-law became irritated with the mess. 'We must do something about Grandfather' said the son. 'I've had enough of this spilled milk, noisy eating, and food on the floor.' So, the husband and wife set a table in the corner. There, Grandfather ate alone while the rest of the family enjoyed dinner. Since Grandfather had broken a dish or two, his food was served in a wooden bowl. When the family glanced in Grandfather's direction sometimes he had a tear in his eye as he sat alone. Still, the only words the couple had for him were sharp admonitions when he dropped a fork or spilled food. The four-year-old watched in silence. One evening before supper, the father noticed his son playing with a piece of wood on the floor. He asked the boy sweetly: 'What are you making?' Just as sweetly, the boy responded: 'Oh, I am making a little bowl for you and Mama to eat your food in when I grow up.' He smiled and went back to work. The words so struck the parents that they were speechless. Then tears started to stream down their cheeks. Though no word was spoken, they knew what had to be done. That evening, the husband took Grandfather's hand and gently led him back to the family table. For the remainder of his days he ate every meal with the family. And for some strange reason, neither husband nor wife seemed to care any longer when a fork was dropped, milk spilled, or the tablecloth soiled."

"Out of the mouth of babes and infants You have ordained strength." Psalm 8:2.

May 17

"Try Me and prove Me..." Malachi 3:10

Since the truth of God's Word intrigues me and challenges me daily, I find pleasure and just plain fun giving it opportunity to test me as I live it out, not in theory, but in real life. It creates a good testimony for my personal growth and for sharing with others. One morning recently, I awakened early and prayed: "Lord, anoint me heavily this day to trust You with all my heart and lean not unto my own understanding; to acknowledge You in all my ways, and to trust that You will direct my paths like You have promised" in Proverbs 3:5-6. He didn't wait long to test me and my sincerity of faith.

Recently, while mowing the lawn, I thought I was back in Montana in my childhood...an unbearable stench welled up in my nostrils, and engaged my memory bank once again. The culprit? A large metal garbage can whose lid was missing, full of water and five bags of bird feed we had stored away in "safe keeping." But, no pigs!!

So now what do I do in this sophisticated, city neighborhood? I carried the water out to the curb and then brilliantly devised a plan for the bird seed: use my pickup box for a bird feeder, scattering the soaked, smelly grain on the floor to dry; and "presto", the birds would pick it up eventually! But my oh my, what a stench hovered over our neighborhood the next morning. Only one recourse—the landfill, fourteen miles away, for immediate disposal. Then came Proverbs 3:5-6 into play. Heading west on 57th, common sense, "my own understanding" started to play with my mind. Fourteen miles? Ten dollars to get in? Perhaps another ten dollars for no tarp cover? "Lord, remember that deserted, isolated, out of the way trail that is not even close to a dwelling or a farmstead? I have an idea: sweep that little dab of garbage off into the tall grass and watch the big, hungry birds devour it in short time. But if this "common sense" way is not Your way, tell me plainly since my conscience pricks me."

The isolated, deserted trail showed up with five vehicles on it within a quarter of a mile. I got the message and headed joyfully for the landfill many miles away. "But now, Lord, go ahead of me and do a mighty work in the minds of the landfill attendants, that this "small load" may not cost ten dollars, nor the tarp penalty another ten dollars." Upon arrival, I heard her voice: "Good morning", opened my door, poured on my best charm, and a true, hard luck story, and she suddenly said: "Get going—no charge—just get rid of that smelly, spoiled bird feed." Rejoicing, I went on my way. "Thank you, Lord, for keeping my devisive mind honorable, and for saving me perhaps twenty dollars. But what about the twenty dollars, Lord?" Only twenty four hours later I mingled with a friend who needed some financial help. "What goes around comes around." And I keep hearing Him say: "Try Me and prove Me...and see if I will not open the windows of Heaven and pour you out a blessing you cannot contain." Malachi 3:10

May you have a little fun-time with the Lord today, too.

May 18

"I am the resurrection and the life." John 11:28

Jesus came knocking at my mind's door through the voice of my son-in-law, Greg, on the main street on a brilliant, sunny April morning in 1977.

Greg told me that my son Lee had been killed in a traffic accident. Three hundred miles away, on a two lane highway engulfed in dense fog, he met his instant death when a huge logging truck blindly wandered into his lane on a curve, and ran over the little pickup truck he was driving.

When I delivered the sad news to my wife, Lois, her first response was: "Lee is alright", meaning that he was truly born again, and was now in heaven with Jesus. We had watched him surrender his life to Jesus at an altar only ten months earlier.

His testimony to friends and high school classmates was simple but bold, and confidant: "I can hardly wait to get to heaven." He believed Jesus from John 14:2: "In My Father's house are many mansions...I go to prepare a place for you. And if I go...I will come again and receive you to Myself, that where I am, there you may be also." He believed Jesus from John 11:25: "I am the resurrection and the life."

As I put this together from memory, I see a real analogy of Martha and Mary at Lazarus' death from John 11. When Jesus came to Bethany after several days of delay, Martha, with mixed emotions, said to Jesus: "Lord, if You had been here, my brother would not have died." A scolding mixed with faith. "But even now, whatever You ask of God He will give You." Jesus said to her: "I am the resurrection and the Life; and whoever lives and believes in Me shall never die. Do you believe this?"

Lee believed that truth because of his faith in Jesus. At his death, Lazarus' inner man was taken out of the grave he was born into, his first resurrection of two. David said in Psalm 30:1, 3: "I will extol you, of Lord, for You have lifted me up...You have brought my soul up from the grave..."

May 19

"I am the resurrection and the life..." John 1:25.

What fun it was for a couple of curious young boys on that Montana ranch when, in the springtime, my brother and I would quietly peek through a knot-hole into the room where a number of "setting hens" were expecting their hatch after sitting on their eggs to keep them constantly warm, turning them once every so often, waiting patiently for the twenty-one day incubation period to end. We sometimes saw a mother hen off the nest, feeding or drinking, and we would quietly sneak in and very often see a cracked egg shell, or a tiny hole in one, sometimes a wet little "peeper" struggling beside a broken, open shell, in the straw nest. You see, that "fertilized" egg produced a baby chick, which at twenty-one days was growing and expanding so fast, putting pressure on the shell, bursting it open...a new life inside. Some eggs, however, failed to produce.

What an analogy for the person who accepts Jesus' invitation to believe on Him, and His work at Calvary, where a new life inside bursts forth, uncontained, and is easily manifested as a "brand new creation, old things passed away, all things become new" for the inner being inside the clay body, the spirit part of us. Then, like a proud hen parading the yard with her brood, the "resurrected" from the grave we all are born into, a grave that cannot hold the new creation, now burst open with new life, the angels of heaven rejoicing. Psalm 30:1-3.

Would my brother and I ever foolishly think of trying to put the eggshell together again and chuck the little chick back into it? No, never, because we were so elated to see the new life. Likewise, none of us would think of wishing the return of a saved, departed one. Now in the arms of Jesus, having burst out of this old clay body, a nice nest for incubation, on the pilgrimage to Heaven, on the way to a new glorified body on the day when those who "sleep in Christ" will be called out of the earthen grave.

"What a day that will be when my Jesus I shall see." The cracked shell, the open grave, now bringing forth new life which shall never end. PTL.

From one who would sing with gusto: "Great is Thy faithfulness, oh Lord, unto me."

May 20

"... the Spirit of Truth dwell with you, and will be in you." John 14:17.

As a young boy and teenager, one of my favorite memories that has stayed with me from our every Sunday worship service in the old Lutheran church in my hometown was seeing the long queue of gowned adult choir members filing down the center aisle to open the service, always singing out so harmoniously: "Holy, holy, holy, Lord God Almighty...God in three persons, blessed Trinity! Casting down their golden crowns around the glassy sea." It was exciting, encouraging, and refreshing to a young boy like me back in the "dirty thirties" when we were literally surrounded with desolate, barren prairies in those days of severe drought and economic depression. But, as they sang "Blessed Trinity" I never really connected that as praise to Father, Son, and Holy Ghost because there was so little teaching and appreciation on the Holy Ghost of the Trinity. Emphasis encircled Christ's birth and life up to Calvary, and including special emphasis on His crucifixion and resurrection, a mention of Pentecost once a year and not much special importance put on the Holy Spirit.

In Old Testament times, the Holy Spirit came upon certain men as God willed and needed. But in New Testament times, on Pentecost Day, after Christ's ascension, He was literally poured out to cover every square inch of the earth, available to every man "to convict the world of sin, and of righteousness, and of judgment." John 16:8. Jesus said of Him: "You know Him, for He dwells with you, and will be in you." He dwells with us as a Paraclete, one who walks beside; and when we say "yes" to Jesus He enters into our inner being and makes understandable 1 Corinthians 6:19: "Do you not know that your body is the temple of the Holy Spirit Who is in you...?" So, I see Him tucked away in my body, myself impregnated, He being attached to my inner spirit being like as a Siamese twin, ready every moment to sift off just enough grace from the River of Grace flowing from the heart of God into us, like quenching my thirst from a mountain stream, sufficient for the moment, for the hour, for the day, and for eternity. He is a busy Being as He "lifts us up together, to make us sit together in the heavenly places in Christ Jesus," our intercessor Who gives our prayers an extra lift. Ephesians 2:6. He is to our inner man as intimate as our mate is to the physical, outer man—a wonderful companion!

I have purposely memorized Psalm 119:11: "Your Word I have hidden in my heart, that I might not sin against You," and what a tool to put down the enemy as the Holy Spirit figuratively blows a whistle, waves a flag, and awakens, warns my inner man in time of impending temptation.

"May the love of God, the grace of our Lord Jesus Christ, and the communion and fellowship of the Holy Spirit be and abide with us all, both for now and for eternity."

May 21

Bluff, deception or a lie?

"The old mare has finally come up for sale," a neighbor heard of the horse he had coveted for years. So he went to the owner across the way and emphatically said: "Be honest with me now, is there anything wrong that you know of with this horse I have had my eye on for years?" The owner hesitated a bit as though he were in deep thought, and then answered: "Well, she doesn't look too good." The prospective buyer acknowledged that and assured him that lots of oats in her feed box would take care of that. The exchange of money and horse was made, and away went the happy buyer leading his horse home. Back he came about an hour later, a bit angry and irate, and said to the neighbor: "This horse is blind." The neighbor answered: "Well, I told you that she doesn't look too good."

You see, it is possible to tell a lie while making a true statement: "She doesn't look too good." It is done by using words that have a double meaning like "look," or by making incomplete statements that leave an erroneous impression or presumption. I once bought a used combine from a neighbor who knew the water circulation system was malfunctioning on a hot afternoon out in the harvest field, so he delivered the machine very early on a cool morning. Deception?

In Genesis 29 we find a whirlwind of a deception. Jacob fell in love with Rachel and made a deal with Uncle Laban to have her for his wife after seven years of serving her father on the farm. "So Jacob served for seven years for Rachel...Then Jacob said to Laban: 'Give me my wife.' In the evening, Laban took his older daughter, Leah, heavily veiled into Jacob, and he innocently, naively, accepted her." Verse 25...in the morning: "What is this you have done to me? Was it not for Rachel that I served you? Why then have you deceived me?" You see, in Laban's culture it could not be that the younger daughter could marry before the older, but Laban never explained that to Jacob before the deal was made, so that Jacob had to work another seven years for Rachel.

I once learned myself, the hard way, the wrong of the convenience of deception which cost me a sizable dollar and a night's sleep. That was the night I searched God's Word with a truly repentant heart and heard the Lord speak loud and clear from Proverbs 8:13: "The fear of the Lord is to hate evil; pride and arrogance and the evil way, and the perverse mouth I hate." That Word penetrated my repentant heart and set me free to this very day.

Instead of stretching or bending the truth, or erecting a cover-up, (deception), let us heed the Words of scripture for what it really is: "Do not lie to one another." Colossians 3:9.

May 22

A friend loves at all times.

"You'll never know, Dale, how many times I have defended you," this remark coming from a friend who listens daily to Gospel Good News on radio out in Montana, and who enjoys the freedom of mixing with both believers and nonbelievers in Jesus, He is one of the most successful men I have known in all facets of life, a positive man of tremendous character, a contemporary of more than fifty years, and a very dear friend who commands enormous respect in any crowd, and is bold enough to courteously stand by my absent side when slander, ridicule, persecution and bashing of my name and stand for Jesus as it permeates the community. Jesus and I have "enemies" in that Big Sky Country as well as many friends; and while we are daily walking hand in hand, I hear Him loud and clear: "Love your enemies; bless them that curse you; do good to them that hate you; and pray for those who spitefully use you, and persecute you," Matthew 5:44. Thank and praise God daily for loyal friends! "A man who has friends must himself be friendly." Proverbs 18:24.

Lois, my best friend for forty-six years of marriage, partially immobile from stroke damage her last twenty-one months, once looked at me through those pretty, tear filled eyes when we were "reasoning together," and sobbingly said; "You sure are an encourager," the most treasured compliment I have ever received, never to forget as I befriended my needy best friend. The sister-in-law at the Alzheimers ward seemingly has no short term memory, but she apparently enjoys the moments of love and friendship we share with her regularly, because while we are with her she knows we love her, since she responds in a beautiful way,

For several months before her cancer-ridden friend died, Lois sat by her bedside, pouring over the Psalms, most often to an apparent sleeper, but whose spirit evidently soaked it up because sometimes she would ask, "Would you read that verse over again?" "What a friend we have in Jesus, all our sins and griefs to bear...weak and heavy laden, take it to the Lord in prayer:"

Ruth, a foreigner from Moab, a young widow now living with her mother-in-law Naomi in Judah during a day of '"tough times" even a shortage of food in their household; found a friend, a real testimony of the old cliché; "A friend in need is a friend indeed!" "And Naomi had a kinsman...Boaz." Ruth 2:1. Boaz owned fields of grain, and befriended Ruth for being so kind and considerate to her mother-in-law, and in verse 12, "The Lord repay your work, and a full reward be given you by the Lord God of Israel, under whose wings you have come for refuge." A friend to friend, "Boaz commanded his young men, saying 'let her glean even among the sheaves, and do not reproach her. Also, let some grain fall purposely for her; leave it that she may glean, and do not reproach her:'" verses 15-16. "A friend in need is a friend indeed!"

What a living testimony of the prophetic Word Jesus gives to us in Luke 6:38; "Give, and it shall be given to you, full measure, pressed down, shaken together, running over shall men give into your bosom; for as you mete it out, it shall be meted back to you,"

"A friend loves at all times, and a brother is born for adversity." Proverbs 17:17

May 23

"Abide in Me." Jesus, John 15:7

    Are you sitting by this morning with a listening ear? I can just see our Heavenly Father sitting by twenty-four hours a day with a "listening ear" as He waits for His sons and daughters to "call in," give Him a "ring," so to speak, waiting for our conversation with Him, be it praise or petition. He speaks to us very dearly in His Word, the Bible, and most often encourages us to speak, to respond, and to keep up our end of the two-way communication—He, by His Word, and we by our prayers. "Call upon Me, and I will answer you, and show you great and mighty things you do not know." Jeremiah 33:3. God has power and authority, and when coupled with our power and authority in prayer "shows us great and mighty things we do not know." What a powerful, productive partnership! I've noticed in the several court cases, trials, that are now smoldering here in America, that when the judge speaks, either in a soft, gentle voice, or in a scolding, harsh voice, he speaks with absolute authority, and has the complete respect and attention of both the defense and prosecuting attorneys, and of the jury when he instructs them. He knows his authority, and speaks with authority which usually blesses the scenario. Likewise, has God delegated authority to us believers in prayer, encouraging us to come out boldly and confidently standing on solid ground, God's Word tucked away in our hearts.

    We are reminded of another most important, necessary principal in Psalm 66:18: "If I regard iniquity in my heart, the Lord will not hear" The best antidote? "Thy Word have I hidden in my heart that sin not." Psalm 119:18:"My Words abide in you." Remember how God turned His back on Jesus that dark Good Friday afternoon? God cannot and will not face sin with an open eye or an open ear.

    A neighbor in Montana double-crossed me in a land transaction, and immediately I found in my heart a high wall erected between us as shock overcame my usual demeanor. I was tested and tried Gods Word "abiding" in me rose up quickly, clearly, decisively and convicted me. "For if you forgive men their trespasses, your Heavenly Father will also forgive you: but if you do not forgive men their trespasses, neither will your Father forgive your trespasses." Matthew 6:14-15. That puts a proud, stiff-necked, angry hurt man of God between a rock and a hard spot. God's authority written here, coupled with my authority as a prayer warrior, set me free, set my neighbor free and mended fences quickly in my heart, a repair job that lasted until the day he passed into eternity.

"Therefore, come boldly before the throne of grace to obtain mercy and to find grace to help in time of need." Hebrews 4:16

May 24

And the symphony played on!

Good morning friends, whom I trust are ready to meet this brand new day, the little child to romp and play, the teenager to wonder, dream, and plan, the young adult perhaps coming into marriage, and then to pursue a vocation for those many years of financial responsibility, and finally retire and slip into those senior years which are beautiful and long-lasting for some, while short and testy for others. As I write, it may all seem so simple, planned, and orchestrated, but is it really for each one of us personally—this journey of life across a rugged terrain and through a wilderness where we try to find meaning and sensibility in it all? It's about like I experienced last weekend as I observed the busyness of Pickerel Lake from my chair on the deck, sitting under a shade tree. I saw a life-like panorama that reminded me of a grand symphony when I saw and heard almost every kind of performance imaginable, each playing a key part in the symphony—the jet skis flying through the waters at high speeds and great noise; dramatically twisting, turning, and maneuvering over high waves for a thrill; and then, in sudden contrast, a decrescendo, the quiet pontoon boat loaded with spectators enjoying a gentle, peaceful ride, waving to us on shore. Then, suddenly, out of the clear blue a loud crescendo, the engine of a small boat towing a water skier or a couple of rafts loaded with screaming boys and girls as they tried to stay on board. Then comes a canoe slicing the waters quietly and slowly, an oarsman physically propelling it along the shoreline with not a sound but yet part of the scenario. Then, occasionally at dawn or late evening or even into the night, the trolling vessel, barely moving, its electric motor hardly stirring the water, and fishing lines baited for northerns or walleyes. Finally, here comes the quiet grand finale, the little paddle boat, and a young blond lady propelling it along the shoreline, her legs moving energetically up and down, a marvelous decrescendo. The whole theatrical I watched; like all of nature, is a grand symphony conducted by God Himself, we must admit, since He put the lake there, created the vessels and the fish to inhabit, and the people to enjoy it.

One day, in I Kings 19:11, Elijah, hiding in a cave, witnessed a similar symphony as he stood at the entrance of a cave, wallowing in self-pity, trying to escape from wicked, angry, Queen Jezebel. "And behold, the Lord passed by, and a great and mighty wind... but the Lord was not in the wind; and after the wind, an earthquake, but the Lord was not in the earthquake; and after the earthquake, a fire, but the Lord was not in the fire; and after the fire, a still, small voice." A symphony of strong, noisy, wind, sneaked upon by a quiet earthquake, followed by a hot, crackling fire, closing with a still, small voice-from crescendo to decrescendo and then could he hear the still voice of God encouraging him and exhorting him—"Be still and know that I am God; I will be exalted in the nations, I will be exalted in the earth." Ps. 46:10.

It seems to me that all of nature, God's creation, coupled with trials in our lives, is a grand symphony conducted by our great Creator, and purposed for our blessing.

And the symphony is free!!

"Ho, everyone who thirsts,
Come to the waters,
And you who have no money,
Come, buy and eat...
And let your soul delight itself in abundance," Isaiah 55:1-2.

May 25

"Train up a child in the way he should go..." Proverbs 22:6.

My mentor in the insurance business I once pursued as a young man and I were driving toward a potential client one warm, sunny afternoon in late May. Suddenly, the man remembered his son's high school graduation just ahead, and big tears ran down his cheeks when it dawned on him: "My son is graduating and I don't even know him." He had spent those eighteen years becoming a millionaire in the financial world while becoming a pauper in his fatherhood role. Regret and shame! Sixty five hundred unredeemable days now gone, the most precious, heartwarming opportunity slipped away forever for that middle-aged dad.

On the other hand, I rubbed shoulders with a most versatile man I've ever known: a smart athlete, a talented musician, experienced from childhood as an expert hunter, fisherman, and trapper, and with a keen aptitude for the business world. His vocation gave him ample opportunity with his sons on the baseball diamond, time on the river bank and out in the brush, hills, and valleys, as well as almost daily a "music concert" in the home. Time to share his interests, his enthusiasm, and his fun time, his coaching with his children, all of whom are now a wonderful testimony of their blessed childhood, citizens with character, manifesting honor to their parents and glory to God.

"Behold, children are a heritage from the Lord, the fruit of the womb is a reward...Happy is the man who has his quiver full of them; they shall not be ashamed, but shall speak with their enemies in the gate." Psalm 127:3-5.

Children, whether our own or ones we mentor or disciple are our lasting legacy...a loan from God Who expects us to be good stewards, an investment we will never regret nor tire of.

How wonderful, refreshing, and uplifting, and encouraging to spend time in the narthex at Abiding Savior and see many little ones crowding the big room. Some are in parent's arms, some in baskets, some running loose, others hand in hand with Mom or Dad. What a treat to walk by the busy nursery and see those excited, lively little ones being helped by dedicated men and women. And to hear the cries of some during the service in the sanctuary. Such a church will be long lived!

"I have been young, and now am old; yet I have not seen the righteous forsaken, nor his descendants begging bread..." Psalm 37:25-26.

May 26

Life has many deadlines.

The fifteen minute radio broadcast message comes to me so easily some mornings, a definite direction, a certain point to emphasize, while other mornings it is like pulling teeth. But in either case, there is the pressure of meeting a specific time deadline to fit perfectly into radio format many miles away. DEADLINES!! How many high-school or college students struggle with deadlines...a set date and hour an assignment must be completed and turned in, often without a grace period. The contract for the purchase of a home, business, or farmland, calls for a deadline date for the down payment, or severe consequences. Long lines of people at the courthouse at tax time, trying to meet the deadline without penalty, usually under pressure because they purposely procrastinated. We are all confronted with deadlines. Bills must be paid, licenses renewed, tax returns filed; and yes, even the hour our wedding is set for!

Is anyone foolish enough to try to escape that one certain deadline every person is destined for...death of the clay body, thrusting the inner man into an eternity of either Heaven or Hell? "It is appointed for man, once to die, but after this the judgement" Hebrews 9:27.

Jesus speaks of two men in Luke 16, both of whom have met their deadlines of life on this earth. What a fitting place for Psalm 90:12: "So teach us to number our days that we may gain a heart of wisdom." "Lord, make me to know my end, and what is the measure of my days, that I may know how frail I am." Psalm 39:4. Lazarus, a pauper, a beggar, "desiring to be fed with the crumbs which fell from the rich man's table," died and was carried by an angel into the bosom of Abraham, known as God's best friend on earth one day, but now a resident of Heaven. "The rich man died and was buried," ending up in a place of torment. Hades, pitifully separated by an impassable gulf between Abraham and himself. Oh, that he might have considered his ways, and buried that me first syndrome, and had "gained a heart of wisdom" in his day on earth, "that I may know how frail I am." That final deadline can often be a missed, coveted opportunity, as we see here when salvation is at stake... Heaven or Hell for eternity, blessing or cursing, light or darkness, eternal freedom or eternal bondage.

Only a few days ago, a man retired, he and his wife perhaps looking forward to years of travel and a life without the pressures of workday deadlines. Only two days later, she was driving alone and was killed in an accident. Like many others, she met her final deadline quickly and unexpectedly. Like the auctioneer would cry out: "All in, all done." So final! Even now, as I write, a phone call...a young man killed in a cycle accident only a short time ago. His appointment with God, his deadline, now a realty! "For what is your life? It is even a vapor that appears for a little time and then vanishes away." James 4:14.

You and I were born to come to that final deadline just like Jesus did: the clay body to an earthen grave, while the inner man leaves the clay, waiting for the resurrection that will reunite the inner man with a glorified body.

May the Lord bless and prepare you today for that final deadline just ahead.

May 27

Unflattered monkeys.

Oh how I shudder when I hear on TV the strong political movement toward forced teaching of evolution in our public schools. But I am not the only one who shudders about evolution. Let us see what those who remained monkeys think about those who supposedly evolved from monkey hood to become human beings. Let your heart be lightened by this bit of nonsense I recently read, where even the monkeys aren't flattered by the thought of evolution.

Three monkeys sat in a coconut tree,
Talking of things that are said to be,
Said one of them: "Listen you two...
There's a certain rumor that can't be true
That man descended from OUR noble race;
The very idea; it's a sad disgrace!
No monkey ever deserted his wife,
Starved her baby, and ruined her life.
And you've never known a mother monk
To leave her babies with others to bunk
'Til they hardly know who their mother is.
No, monks don't stoop to such low biz.
And another thing you will never see:
A monk put a fence around his coconut tree,
And let the coconuts go to waste...
Keeping other monks from having a taste.
Why...if I put a fence around my tree
Hunger would make you steal from me
Another thing a monk would not do
Go out at night and get on a stew;
Or use a gun, a club, a knife
To take some other monkey's life
If man descended, the ornery cuss
Brothers, he didn't descend from us."

But maybe there is something to this idea of evolution proposed by Darwin. Maybe people did descend from lower animals. You know, church folks are often stubborn as mules about church work; sly as a fox in their business deals; busy as bees in spreading gossip; blind as a bat to the world's needs; quiet as a mouse in spreading the gospel; but have eyes like a hawk in seeing the mote in a brother's eye. They are eager as a beaver about a bazaar or barbecue, but lazy as a dog about a prayer meeting; mean as snakes when they don't get their way; but gentle as a lamb when they need the pastor's aid; noisy as crows for the church to advance, but slow as snails in visiting the unchurched. Many are owls on Saturday night, but bed bugs on Sunday morning, slippery as eels on Sunday night, and scarce as hen's teeth during a revival.

This is a tongue-in-cheek article of many years ago, submitted by L.C. Spencer of Iowa. I couldn't top this, so thought I would share it with you. No offense to anyone, please!

May 28

Commencement time.

I remember May 28, 1943 and the evening when thirty-seven of us were awarded our diplomas from Scobey High School, the end of one facet of life and the commencing of the next. Most of the boys had either volunteered for service in the military or were waiting the draft to send them into WWII. That evening was the last time I saw two of them, as one was killed in Italy and the other in the Battle of the Bulge in Belgium only months later. Some went immediately on to a college or university, some back to the family farm as a career. Some went into marriage, while others fell into the regular work force. There was no unemployment in those fast-moving, exciting days after Pearl Harbor Day.

As my graduation and commencement were exciting to me, so it must have been for Peter and brother Andrew we read of from Matthew 4:18 where the commencement speaker, Jesus, came along with the invitation: "Jesus, walking along the sea of Galilee saw two brothers, Simon, called Peter, and Andrew, his brother casting a net into the sea for they were fishermen. They immediately left their nets and followed Him." What a graduation from a secular vocation of catching fish to a spiritual vocation of "fishing" for human souls, a commencement which eventually Jesus used to birth the church we know, love, and appreciate today, having added ten more disciples.

In Acts 9 we read of another graduation commencement when Saul (Paul), a prominent destroyer of the "Jesus Way", was supernaturally put to the ground, graduated from a purpose of destruction to become perhaps the greatest evangelist of all times.

May 29

"...be strong in the Lord..." Eph. 6:10

During the last political campaign, I heard much of how our troops in Iraq are fighting without full armor. Be that truth or political jargon I do not know, but I do know that some warriors in God's army on earth today are "fighting" either out of ignorance or out of poor discipline, without the blessing of the full armor Paul laid out for us in Ephesians 6.

Each morning, like the Roman soldier going out to battle, we dress up our inner man by childlike faith in the breastplate of righteousness ...the shed blood of Jesus, impenetrable, so that "No weapon formed against me this day shall prosper." Isaiah 54:17. "When the enemy comes in like a flood, the Spirit of the Lord will raise up a standard against him. Isaiah 59:19. Each morning, we put the shoes of peace on our feet so that wherever we walk this day we will carry with us the Prince of Peace, and hear Him counsel us: "Love your enemies; bless them that curse you; do good to them that hate you; and pray for them that spitefully use you and persecute you." Matthew 5:14. "If it is possible, as much as depends on you, live peaceably with all men." Romans 12:18.

Each morning, we put on the helmet of salvation to protect our minds from the flesh, the world, and the devil, lest they use our minds for a workshop or a playground like the man of the unsaved world lives in. "Be not conformed to this world, but be you transformed by the renewing of your mind, that you may prove what is the good, perfect, and acceptable will of God" Romans 12:2. "That we may be conformed to the image of His Son." Romans 8:29.

Each morning, we take in our hand the "sword of the Spirit," — God's Word, so that, like Jesus tempted in the wilderness, we may overcome with a simple truth..."It is written," and recite God's Word as a weapon to defend us from falling into sin.

Each morning, we take in our other hand the "shield of faith" which covers us from the top of our head to the tip of our toes as protection from the deadly, fiery, poisonous darts of the enemy bent on "killing, stealing, and destroying." John 10:10. Our assurance of faith is found in Colossians 2:15, where, as our creed declares, "He descended into the bowels of the earth and overcame powers and principalities, made an open show of them, and triumphed over them in the victory of the cross." Satan's wings clipped of his power in the life of the redeemed.

Each morning, we hear the call to prayer from 1 Timothy 2:1: "Therefore, I exhort first of all that supplications, prayers, and intercessions, and giving of thanks be made for all men; for kings, and for all who are in authority, that we may lead a quiet and peaceable life in godliness and reverence..."

We find that in God's divine full armor there are no glitches like we see in Goliath's secular armor. I Samuel 17:49. I feel so safe all dressed up in that armor. How about you, my beloved?

May 30

How ashamed and grieved was my teen-age son who engaged in Halloween frolics in our home town to the extent of disturbing the safety and peace of ordinary citizens. The city police arrested him that evening and that was bad enough. But worse yet was the next Thursday when the weekly local newspaper came out and listed his name in the court docket as guilty of "criminal mischief". His pride in his ordinary good conduct and character was shattered over the conviction "criminal", and guilt and condemnation took their place. To him, his name and the family name were important, but now tainted by his foolish actions. That was an experience he regretted. But, only a year or two later, he accepted Jesus at a public gathering, and that marred name was written in the Lamb's Book of Life, and only a few months before his final demise. His name is now etched on a footstone in the family plot west of town. Now when I see his name there on Memorial Day, I seldom recall the Halloween incident, but rather that evening when his name became written in Heaven, a name now that will last forever with honor, forgiven.

"A wise son makes a glad father, but a foolish son is the grief of his mother." Proverbs 10:1.

"He who walks with integrity walks securely, but he who perverts his ways will become known" Proverbs 10:9

"A good name is to be chosen rather than great riches." Proverbs 22:6

On this Memorial Day in the U.S., perhaps every cemetery will be visited, and flowers and crosses and veterans standards will be placed on thousands of graves. And then the tombstones and footstones with names etched into them, indicating the place of rest for one gone into eternity. In my hometown cemetery are hundreds of names I recognize, having lived there all my life. They tell me a story, a biography of life. The compassionate pioneer doctor, the popular school administrator, the community-minded banker, the hardy pioneer farmer and rancher, the teenager killed in a vehicle accident because of liquor, the mother of a large family, all of whom were a blessing to humanity, and then the father of another who "lived it up" foolishly. Some names remind me of Jesus and His people, while others remind me of excessive pride, greed, arrogance, instability, drunkenness, broken marriages, illicit business dealings, and mockery of the God of Heaven Who will not be mocked. Galatians 6:7.

What do people hear or think of when they hear my name or your name? That name is etched in people's minds and hearts, so important that it bears influence on other lives even when seen engraved on a tombstone in the days ahead.

We cannot beat the system, because our reputation and relationships, good or bad, are forever tied to our name, and memories of that name will linger forever.

From a tomb near old Jerusalem on Easter morning, God proudly raised up an obedient Son, "exalted above all others, and given a name which is above every name..." Philippians 2:9.

HIS NAME IS JESUS!!!

May 31

Are you one this morning, fellow believers in Jesus, who would say to God: "Come now, let us reason together?"

Early this morning many scenes of the desperation of life in today's America flashed before my eyes like as on a TV screen:

a boatload of Haitians running toward Florida's shoreline, school bombings, hostages being held, snipers on the loose, plane crashes, kidnappings, starving people, 4,000 young mothers aborting daily in America, and terrorist threats. On and on goes the list and perhaps many hurting people are asking and wondering: "Is God unfair? If there is really a God in the Heavens above like Christendom describes and Christians nail their eternal fate on, where is He in all this, and why allow such suffering?" they ask. This thought mingles through the minds of all people.

Last year we stayed a few days in the home of a couple in Sweden; very kind, super hospitality, over enthused about treating us royally, but with hearts set severely and adamantly against God whom they accused of taking their only two children by death while others of us have several children living normally. I can still see those piercing eyes from that father as he questioned us and challenged us like a defense attorney because of our faith in God.

This morning I turned to Acts 12 where King Herod killed the Apostle James outright, without a second thought, an act Herod saw pleased the Jewish leaders. Then he arrested and jailed Peter, and while awaiting the Passover to end, and in answer to much prayer, God sent an angel to the jail to awaken Peter at night, to unlock his chains and tell him to dress and follow the angel. Lights that only Peter and the angel could see by, an automatic door opener, and an unlocked steel gate all made for Peter's release and escape to his friends praying for him across town. I wonder if James' family may have questioned God's fairness when he was executed and Peter miraculously set free. "Is God unfair?"

It's true that life often seems unfair and it will be until Jesus returns and sets up His thousand-year reign, all because of the blight sin has put on all of God's creation.

What a day that will be when Jesus returns and the lamb and the lion will lay side-by-side, and the earth will know perfect peace. In the meantime, "we will trust the Lord with all our heart and lean not upon our own understanding; but will acknowledge Him in all our ways and He will direct our paths." Proverbs 3:5-6

June 1

"Three in one."

Little did I realize in 1936 when I was ten years old and seeing the Ft. Peck dam in eastern Montana being built that some fifty years later the Lord would use the lake behind the dam to show me by illustration as I gazed upon it, a good lesson on the work of the Trinity—Father, Son, and Holy Spirit. The dam is built on the Missouri River and backs up water for about 300 miles, its main resource of supply coming from the snow of the Rockies where three rivers converge into the Missouri. The Trinity is a mystery—Three in One; inseparable, yet each participant designed for a specific purpose

As I gazed upon that huge lake one day, I imagined that vast body of water as the power of God behind a tremendous blessing. But to be a blessing, that contained body of water must be monitored into enclosed turbines that would make electricity. And here I picture Jesus of the Trinity as the real blessing of grace, as God's power poured through Him on Calvary to turn the wheels of salvation. But the electrical power is useless until the power lines or underground cable carry the electricity out to the towns and farmsteads where transformers necessarily reduce it to safe usage. This is the imaginary work of the Holy Spirit, a work of coming directly into His home, man's clay body, to give power for light and healing and deliverance, for conviction of sin and of righteousness as He keeps a tender conscience sensitive to God's Word, the good news of salvation. Like the Trinity changes for better the life inside of man, so does electricity make for better life of the outer man.

As the Trinity, God the Father, God the Son, and God the Holy Spirit are one, so is man-a clay body, a soul, and a spirit all in one. "Now may the God of peace Himself sanctify you completely; and may your whole spirit, soul, and body be preserved blameless at the coming of the Lord." II Thes. 5:23.

June 2

"Forgive and you shall be forgiven..." Matthew 6:12

The telephone rang in my barn on a severely cold, stormy February day, and the man and the message on the other end was the worst phone experience I've ever had. He angrily cursed me and threatened me in a vile display of uncontrolled temper. My heart was broken, heavy with guilt and condemnation. He was an ungodly, self-centered neighbor about seven miles distant, who had unfenced haystacks out on the prairies, almost covered with snow banks, and my horses, four of them, had walked over their pasture fence on hard snow banks and found their way to his hay, about three miles from the pasture.

I apologized and corrected the unfortunate situation immediately. One spring evening about four months later, not having seen him since, I passed by his field, and I noticed that he had lost a wheel from his implement, so I stopped to help him, not knowing what kind of reception I might receive. I gambled between more tongue lashing or a spirit of forgiveness and our usual friendship we had always known before. PTL, he received me graciously, and our relationship grew better than ever. I thanked and praised God for setting up that opportunity for me to bless that man and mend fences.

A human relationship trial like this makes Matthew 5:44-45 ever so precious. A principal right from the heart of Jesus: "Love your enemies; bless those who curse you; do good to those who hate you; pray for those who use you spitefully and persecute you." "For if you forgive men their trespasses, your heavenly Father will also forgive you. But if you do not forgive men their trespasses, neither will your heavenly Father forgive you." Matthew 6:14-15. "Keep your heart with all diligence, for out of it flow the issues of life." Proverbs 20:23. "He who despises his neighbor sins..." Proverbs 24:21a. "If you really fulfill the royal law according to the Scripture, 'You shall love your neighbor as yourself,' you do well."

I was seated with the mourners at his funeral ten years later.

Is your ugly neighbor precious to you?

June 3

"Sport's" keen ear.

Early this morning, my farmer-rancher son in Montana called me because he knew I would give him a careful listening ear to a problem he had, trusting my years of experience, and expecting some sound counsel as he carefully listened. Both of us listened carefully, and in a few minutes both were blessed. About that same time, the phone rang again, and a local friend encouraged us to turn to channel 30 and listen to one of our favorite men of God on earth today—Dr. Hagee of San Antonio, Texas, a very sound proclaimer of the best good news afloat today—Jesus, Calvary, the cross, and the resurrection. We listened and were blessed.

My friend, are you a good listener? Have you paid attention so far?

I remember well my childhood days of standing by Highway 13 and waiting for the school bus to pick up my brother and me for school seven miles away. We were intrigued how that every morning, rain or shine, cold or hot, fall, winter, or spring, intrigued by the keen, sensitive ear of our friend "Sport", the ranch dog who accompanied us every morning and met us every evening. We watched him, his ears up, and his attention on one thing—listening at that precise moment when he would arise from his usual perch on the pavement to meet the bus on the south hill about a quarter mile away. Long before we could hear the coming bus, Sport's keen ear heard it, and not only heard as he listened, but recognized the bus' familiar "voice". Sport was never fooled, since any other truck or vehicle could come down that hill but its muffler or engine sound never deterred his ear or attention from that CERTAIN ONE he listened for. We learned to trust old Sport and take our cue from him. If he didn't move when our human ears could hear an oncoming vehicle, we knew it was not the bus. Sport listened intently, and would respond to only one voice out there on the prairie.

We believers can learn a valuable lesson: "Be careful of the voice you listen to, since there are many out there in person, in print, and on TV and radio." Take this cue from Proverbs 4:20: "My son, give attention to My Word; incline your ear to my sayings; let them not depart from before your eyes; keep them in the midst of your heart, for they are life unto those who find them and health unto their flesh. Keep your heart with all diligence, for out of it flow the issues of life." This sounds like the voice of God—listen carefully!

June 4

"A lamp unto my feet, a light unto my path..." Ps. 119:105

Good morning, friends, with whom I would share a gem of truth from God's Word—the Bible, a blessing for today's walk across the stage of life right here on earth for us pilgrims sojourning in a foreign land on our way to Heaven.

Every time I hear of another suicide, especially a teenager, I always feel badly that someone, somehow, could have seen inside that desperately hurting soul, and could have shared Jesus, the giver and sustainer of life and real purpose in life with that young, empty-hearted boy or girl. I always wonder what makes a person scrap his sense of self-preservation, a God-given virtue for self destruction. It's on the way to try and fill that void, that empty spot we are all born with, that desperation must take place, and the enemy takes them by the hand and lures them into a "quick fix" called suicide. My life could have been, and perhaps would have been, one of such desperation in an effort to fill that void had it not been for the Jesus I found early in life at my Mother's knee, a good Sunday School, and in those pleasant boyhood hours of searching the Psalms and the Gospels in the quietness of that old haymow on the ranch, and then the blessing of that Gideon New Testament I literally lived in during my G.I. days of WWII.

Proverbs 4:20 says: "My son, give attention to My Words; incline your ear to My sayings; let them not depart from before your eyes; keep them in the midst of your heart; for they are life unto those who find them, and health unto their flesh."

Friend, I believe with all my heart that is where it is found—life and health for spirit, soul, body, relationships, and finances—giving attention to God's Word "A lamp unto my feet. A light unto my path..." Psalm 119:105.

All this amounts to trying to fill the vacuum, the empty spot inside God created us all with for the purpose to fill it with faith in Christ, the cross and the resurrection so that He might enjoy the company of the saints in Heaven forever. He would draw us unto repentance and forgiveness and righteousness, out of the tomb we are born into and back into a right relationship with Him who created us in His own image, the only creature He created with a soul like His, and for one purpose only: to spend eternity with Him.

PTL—the truth has been revealed to us and we can walk in that wonderful privilege today!

June 5

Worthy because he paid the price.

Early in the past century, my Dad placed a fence-line between his land and his neighbor, as did all pioneers of that homestead day. What he or they actually used as their basis for establishing of that fence I do not know, except that the U.S. government had already surveyed the land, and had driven into the ground a permanent steel rod on the comer of each section (640 acres), and placed a cap on top of the rod with that land's particular description inscribed, a very systematic and accurate work that all men honored. It was an official signia of solid proof of "address," so to speak. Some seventy years later, as I drove down a county road one morning, I found my brand new neighbor out in the middle of the road with a magnet of a kind trying to find that metallic government rod so that he could prove to me that the earlier established fence was taking a rod of land from him, about an acre. He never proved his point, so the fence remains as established.

Like my neighbor, Christians need to know their full possession as truly born-again people. So, when I hear some such person profess and confess before God: "Oh Lord, I am not worthy to come before You this morning, since I am and have been such a terrible sinner, and a no good person" and on and on goes the degrading lingo, amounting to a flat denial of what Christ's Crucifixion and resurrection, His broken body and shed blood, have done, and that is to make us worthy as soon as we accept Jesus as our Savior and make Him Lord of our life. He died for our sins to make us worthy to be called "Sons and daughters of God", expecting us then to be thankful and sing praise to Him like David sang in Psalm 30: "I will extol You, oh Lord, for you have lifted me up; You have not made my enemies to rejoice over me...You have brought my soul up from out of the grave, and you have kept me alive so I shall not go down to the pit." God loves a heart of thanksgiving and praise, a heart full of joy and a positive attitude.

In our old nature, we are certainly not worthy, but, "If any man be in Christ Jesus he is a brand new creation, old things passed away and all things become new." II Corinthians 5:17. Now worthy because we have found our way to the throne room where we find our name written in the Lamb's Book of Life, forever forgiven.

Christ is truly our cornerstone we build from, and claim with child-like faith every blessing we have been made worthy of both for now and for eternity, because of His sacrifice at Calvary where we, too, were crucified when we accepted Him as our Savior. Galatians 2:20.

June 6

Called to serve my country—1944.

I, Dale Manternach, think of myself as one of the most blessed of all GIs in the armed services of WWII days. I came home without a blemish on my life, while two of my classmates of 1943 died for their country—Wyman Jones in Italy, and Ormond Paus, Jr. in the Battle of the Bulge, where his bones still lay. Almost a half million peers of mine across America gave the ultimate sacrifice. Thousands more came home with nerves destroyed, like my friend, Vernon Vanderpan. Some had deaf ears and some blinded eyes. Others came home with appendages missing like Ben Danelson and Clifford I. Hanson, both of whom returned with leg amputations, and went on to marry, raise a family, and succeed beautifully in their lifework.

On D-Day, June 6, 1944, I began my basic infantry training in Camp Roberts, Calif., while my life-long friend, Alvin Rustebakke, faced Normandy Beach, France that same day, and was wounded, while about 3,500 sacrificed their all in the blood stained water of the English Channel while trying to scale the steep embankment against the enemy fire from above. Henry Schauer, a natural sharpshooter, of the Silver Star community, faced hours of Nazi fire out alone in the open range, claiming seventeen German lives to earn the Congressional Medal of Honor. I was still far behind the front line in Germany.

I claim that the greatest blessing for me came the same day Germany surrendered. My outfit had hustled for three weeks to catch up to General Patton and his troops. One day at noontime we came to within a mile of Pilsen, Czechoslovakia and were ordered to sit there all afternoon, waiting for instructions. At six o'clock that evening, the war ended, and our unit was never engaged.

I was drafted as an eighteen-year old, and inducted into the army in Utah, and then sent to Camp Roberts, Calif. for the seventeen weeks of basic training. After a furlough when we finished basic, we gathered at Camp Chaffee, Arkansas, to pack up for overseas duty. On my nineteenth birthday, Feb. 3, 1945, seven thousand of us boarded an Italian luxury liner and arrived safely at Le Havre, France eighteen days later. We were with the 16th Armored Division. The Le Havre harbor was destroyed for docking by American bombers, so that we had to ferry onto French soil. The Allied armies were moving quickly across the Rhine River and on toward Berlin. They had no time to take in the German POWS that were falling by the thousands, so, our unit rode the 40x8 rail cars to the front lines for a short season to help. On the day of President Roosevelt's death in April, we were returning for our equipment and the long trip across France and Germany to reach the front lines at Pilsen!

While the men who fought so long and hard, so deserving, left for home, we stayed on until November 1945 to take care of thousands of displaced civilians. They came from all over Eastern Germany in horse-drawn wagons with only the clothes on their back, and no food, bedding, or even kitchen utensils. I saw men reach full length of their arm into the GI garbage disposal to find a solid piece of food to feed their family.

Our unit headed for home in late fall, celebrating Thanksgiving 1945 on board ship, another long trip across the Atlantic. As we passed by the "lady", the Statue of Liberty, in the N.Y. harbor, I was sobered, I remember, when I thought of the possibility many tears of joy the fighting men must have shed as they readied to meet their wives, sweethearts, children, or parents, and once again set foot on "the land of the free and the home of the brave."

I went on to Camp McCoy, Wis., and was discharged December 1, 1945. I've lived sixty-three years now since that time as a proud American, ever so thankful for our veterans of both the Pacific and European theatres of operation in WWII. They are leaving us now at the rate of fifteen hundred men per day, laid to rest, and many of them on their way to eternal peace.

June 7

"Rejoice always. Pray without ceasing." II Thessalonians 5:16, 17.

Every day for many years, a mother of five sons in Billings, MT, prayed for their salvation and the infilling of the Holy Spirit. She died without having seen any success in her praying, prayer time she had prevailed in with child-like faith. Five years later, all of her sons were saved, her prayers answered. Oh how this testimony has blessed me, encouraged me, and has put joy, peace, love, and security in my heart as I pray for my offspring whose hearts I cannot read, nor see any evident fruit in that life. But, Philippians 4:6-7 says: "Be not anxious for anything, but by prayer and supplication, with thanksgiving, let your requests be made known unto God, and the peace of God which passes all understanding will keep your heart and mind in Christ Jesus." Supplication means persistent begging, and "with thanksgiving" for what you know He has already done in your past, including your own miracle of salvation, a tremendous faith builder.

The Word of God that established my faith in rock along this line is found in Jesus' parable of Luke 11, where He tells of a man who went to his friend's house at midnight and asked for some bread to feed his unexpected, late arriving visitor. "Do not trouble me; the door is now shut...I cannot rise and give to you." verse 7. Finally, verse 8, Jesus speaking: "I say to you, though he will not rise and give him out of friendship, yet, because of his persistence he will arise and give as many as he needs." If a friend, operating in the flesh, filled with that "me-first syndrome" can be moved like this man, think of how much more our God of agape love will listen and be overly generous concerning our needs when we prevail in prayer. "Ask and it shall be given you; seek and you shall find; knock and it shall be opened unto you." verse 10.

Bernice, my neighbor lying in a hospital bed in Billings, MT said "no" when I suggested we should pray for her recovery. "God is too busy to bother with someone like me." She didn't want to bother God. Another claims that she never prays more than once for the same issue, lest she weary God with her repeated requests. These two women bring to mind Luke 18, another parable, telling of a persistent widow who came to a certain judge every day, saying: "Avenge me of my adversary." She implied: "Hurry with this case I have entrusted to you. Settle this estate. I have great need." A plea He had heard so frequently over and over again, that He condescended, and in verse 5: "...because this widow troubles me, I will avenge her, lest by her continual coming she weary me." And then Jesus' explanation in verse 7: "And shall not God avenge His own elect who cry out day and night to Him, though He bears long with them."

"Rejoice always. Pray without ceasing" II Thessalonians. 5:16, 17.

"Now, this is the confidence we have in Him, that if we ask anything according to His will, He hears us; and if we know that He hears us, whatever we ask, we know that we have the petitions we asked of Him." I John 5:14-15.

June 8

"Cleansed by the blood of the lamb."

When St. Helen erupted in Washington state in the summer of 1979, the westerly prevailing wind carried the sediment of the explosion as far as twelve hundred miles eastward, and the air in eastern Montana was filled with fine, fine dust. We farmers were warned not to run our tractors in the field because the air filter could not take out much of the fine particles and consequently would ruin the engine. Vehicle, tractor, combine, and baler engines come from the factory with replaceable, built-in oil and air filters to sift out harmful particles and protect the life of the engine, purifying the air that is breathed and capturing the fine particles of wear within the engine.

All around us in our pilgrimage of life here on earth are the old-nature flesh, the world, and Satanic forces all of for which God has built into our inner man a filter to check them from destroying our lives for now and for eternity, a filter to cleanse us from sins that would deter us from His kingdom. "Do you not know that the unrighteous will not inherit the kingdom of God? Do not be deceived. Neither fornicators, nor idolaters, nor adulterers, nor homosexuals nor sodomites, nor thieves, nor covetous, nor drunkards, nor revilers, nor extortionists shall inherit the kingdom of God." I Corinthians 6:9-10. And then the filter we find in verse 11: "And such WERE some of you. But you WERE washed...sanctified...justified in the name of the Lord, and by the Spirit of our God." What a filter we find in verse 11!! The inner man now washed in the pure, clean, innocent, sinless blood of Jesus as he kneels at the foot of the cross with child-like faith and with confession on his lips coming from a repentant heart, sanctified, set apart from the world, and justified: "just as if I had not sinned," totally forgiven, "though my sin be as scarlet, now white as snow." Isaiah 1:18.

So, within each of us who are truly born-again, lives the Holy Spirit, our filter who convicts us of our sin, directs us to confession, and empowers us for real, genuine repentance, so that we are not a broken down engine parked on the sidelines, but a living testimony of what God can do with a Living Word like we find in Luke 4:18, Jesus speaking: "The Spirit of the Lord is upon Me, for I have been anointed to preach the gospel to the poor, to heal the broken hearted, to preach deliverance to the captives, and recovery of sight to the blind, to set free them that are bruised..."

"If we confess our sin, God is faithful and just to forgive our sin, and to CLEANSE us from all unrighteousness." 1 John 1:9. When the Holy Spirit, the inner man's filter is in place, He will sift out the destructive particles and extend that life unto eternity.

June 9

"Trust and obey..."

"Trust and obey for there's no other way" may have been my theme song in May 1944 when I entered the induction center on my way into the Army. My first morning I went to breakfast, leaving my bed unmade like I had always done at home. But in the Army, this was a "no-no" and I spent the remainder of my time there on K.P. three times a day. I learned quickly to "trust and obey" because lack of obedience prompts severe punishment.

On the other hand, after a three-week furlough later in the season, I fell into another long line of inductees at Camp Chaffee, Ark. where I experienced a blessing for obedience rather than a curse for disobedience. The officer asked me: "Have you had a furlough yet?" I answered: "Yes, sir," and he called a sergeant and told him to take me to the train station and buy me a ticket for another three-week leave, only because I was the only one in that whole line so far who had told the truth. I went home and spent Christmas with friends and family while my disobedient, deceitful buddies prepared for our shipment overseas, maybe having learned: "Trust and obey for there's no other way; since a lie just doesn't pay."

From I Samuel 13:8 we find King Saul also had to learn the high cost of disobedience. One day he faced the prospect of fighting a huge, well-equipped Philistine army, and fear overcame him because of his few frightened and untrained followers he had to work with. Samuel had promised to come and help him prepare, but while waiting for Samuel to offer a sacrifice in this desperate situation before going to battle, King Saul became impatient and illegally and disobediently offered the sacrifice himself, even though he knew God had reserved that chore for the priests, and only the priests, not the Kings. It was a costly mistake we find in verse 13-14: "Now if you will fear and worship the Lord and listen to his commandments, and not rebel against the Lord...then all will be well. But, if you rebel against the Lord's commandments, and refuse to listen to Him, then His hand will be as heavy upon you as upon your ancestors." From that point on, Saul's life was a sad, downhill journey.

In our day, disobedience to II Corinthians 6:14 has brought one of the most disastrous, downhill journeys to marriage and business partnerships to many innocent, but disobedient people. Paul, speaking to a believer: "Do not be unequally yoked together with unbelievers. For what fellowship has lawlessness with righteousness? What communion has light with darkness?" "No man can serve two masters...he will be loyal to one and despise the other" Luke 16:13.

June 10

"I will dwell in the secret place of the Most High." Psalm 91:1

As a curious young boy out in the rural prairies. I made some observations of the birds of the air and the animal creatures of the earth that could speak well a lesson to us Christians today. When I ran across a nice, neat, small hole in the ground, I knew it was a gopher's place to live. Likewise, the large, hard, mud nest under the bridge, a swallow's home; a cave in the side-hill, a coyote's hideout; a hollow in the tall dry grass in the summer, or in a snow bank in the winter, a rabbit's burrow; a large hole with a huge mound of dirt beside it, a badger's resting place; the geese, ducks, mink, and muskrat enjoying the ponds, lakes and rivers; the hard, solid, large dome-shaped mounds, the home of millions of ants. For our best testimony as believers, however, the super-patient, nocturnal owl crouched in a tree top; "The wise old owl, he sat in an oak; the more he saw, the less he spoke; the less he spoke, the more he heard." Why aren't we all like that wise old bird?

The throne room of God is home for the spirit part of me, the real me, to dwell in even now while I am planted on this earth, where my clay body is the temple for my spirit to live in, David: "I will DWELL in the secret place of the Most High, and ABIDE under the shadow of the Almighty. And I will say of the Lord, 'You are my refuge, my fortress, my God in whom I will trust.'" Psalm 91:1-2.

My faith here, coupled with the power of the Holy Spirit to lift me up into God's immediate presence, especially at prayer time.

When the call came upon Gideon to lead his people out against their enemy, the Midianites, Gideon responded: "Oh, my Lord, how can I save Israel? Indeed, my clan is the weakest in Manassah, and I am least in my father's house." Judges 6:15. But God prevailed on that weak, introverted young man whom He had purposely placed at the winepress; and now for a specific purpose, but not in Gideon's power or strength, but "surely I will be with you, and you shall defeat the Midianites as one man..." Then sending Gideon out with only three hundred men, with trumpets, jars, and candles against thousands of Midianites, the Midianites were defeated by this man dwelling in a certain place, at a certain time, for a special purpose— God directed.

My friend, are you "created in the image of God, housed in a clay body, sanctified before your birth, and anointed by God,"? Are you satisfied where God has placed you to best serve Him with an obedient, thankful heart, a unique person in a unique ministry?

June 11

"Mary has chosen that good part." Luke 10:42

How blessed are those of us who have a good balance between service and devotion in that part of our daily devotion, worship, and walk with Jesus. In Luke 10, we find Jesus arriving at the home of sisters Mary and Martha of Bethany. Martha opened the door and welcomed Jesus into their home, and then turned to the kitchen to prepare "goodies" for the flesh, to prepare tasty food. "She had a sister who sat at His feet and heard His Word." Mary invited Him to be seated in the most comfortable chair and fell on her knees before Him to just listen and satisfy the little girl inside of her, her spirit being. She could wait for the "social hour" later on. Like Martha, some of us are doers, while others, like Mary, are more devotional type. The circuit riders of the early days down to the evangelists of today, the pastors, preachers, and teachers are servers—as they span the universe on horseback, bus, van, TV, radio, satellite, airplane—

always serving as they share the Word of God with hungering souls. I think here of John Wesley, Billy Sunday, D.L. Moody, David Livingstone, Billy Graham, and David Wilkerson. Like Mary, some of us are more quiet-like devoters, meditators, writers, researchers, scholars, and much of their works handed to us on the shelves of a Christian book store. Augustine in such a classic as "Confessions," Charles Spurgeon, Oswald Chambers, Max Lucado, C.S. Lewis, and a host of others, sharing behind the scenes. What a blessing when spiritual service and devotional and reflection flow through the Christian's life in balance—lots of time early in the day for God's Word and prayer to be shared generously throughout the day as opportunity presents itself with family, co-workers, service people, street people, incarcerated ones, shut-ins, nursing home occupants, neighbors and social friends. Mary, at Jesus' feet, soaking up His teaching, "has chosen the one thing that would never be taken away." Luke 10:42. Martha got so wrapped up in service like many of us in our churches these days—all good, but missing so often the most important thing of all—intimate fellowship with Jesus. We see in Matthew 7 the ultimate importance of keeping works and devotion in balance, where Jesus said; "Not everyone who says to Me 'Lord, Lord', shall enter the kingdom of Heaven...many will say to Me...'Lord, Lord, have we not prophesied in Your Name, cast out demons in Your Name, and done many wonders in Your Name.?' Then, I will declare to them 'I never knew you'; depart from Me..."

God's Word keeps the scales balanced as we learn to lean on the Lord and share the three precious gifts of time, talent, and treasure in proper perspective with our brothers and sisters around us... Marthas and Marys in balance.

June 12

"A tree is known by its fruit." Matthew 12:33

While in Montana, I sat on a bench alongside the "main street" of "Pioneer Town" at the museum grounds, and beside me sat a Canadian gentleman about my age, a total stranger to me until we discovered a mutual friend we had both known over the years. I liked the man at first sight—an outgoing personality, a twinkle in the eye, and a cheerful countenance. But I soon heard cursing and vulgarity flowing from his mouth, even the name of the Lord in vain. I knew right away that there was a need for Jesus in his life because I know from personal experience and from the testimony of many others, that the first noticeable change about a truly born-again person is the cleansing of the tongue. It just seems to be automatic, and the scriptures bear this out in Luke 6:45: "A good man, out of the good treasure of his heart brings forth good; and an evil man, out of the evil treasure of his heart brings forth evil..., For out of the abundance of the heart his mouth speaks." We can judge no man as to his relationship to Jesus because we cannot see into his heart, but we can and do see the fruit he bears—good or evil.

That man's family came by and interrupted our conversation, but as I rehearse it in my mind, the thought comes to me, a rather startling thought- -"What if we each had to pay for our sins in order to bridge that gap between us and our God of heaven Who alone holds eternity in His hand for both the good fruit bearer and the evil? Wouldn't most of us procrastinate until it is too late?" "It is a fearful thing to fall into the hands of the living God." Hebrews 10:31. Yes, one day God is going to call every person out of his grave, and Jesus will separate the sheep from the goats, the sheep into Heaven, and the goats to eternal destruction. Matthew 25:31-34, 46. Our physical death would suddenly creep upon us, and we would pass into eternity without the forgiveness of sins because the required penalty was not paid in time. But oh how wonderful, to know that the penalty, has already been paid two thousand years ago, and our acceptance of Jesus' work on that cross, a total surrender of self on our part, confession of sin from a truly repentant heart made possible as the Holy Spirit convicts and moves us to accept that free gift which sets us free from sin, death, and the power of the devil. I am not speaking to one single person this morning who wants to die and be sent to Hell, but I may be speaking to some, who have not yet taken care of this most important issue of life. I visited the cemetery west of town and saw some tomb stones and foot markers, including my own, not yet dated, whereby we have taken care of the clay, but what about the little fellow inside, who will never die, but will leave the clay body and end up in either Heaven or Hell, depending on a single choice made here and now? John 3:16 tells it all in one little nutshell: "For God so loved the world that He gave His only begotten Son, that whosoever believes in Him shall not perish, but inherit everlasting life."

June 13

"God inhabits the praises of His people" Psalm 22:3.

Good news, because I want to be a part of that which God inhabits—a righteous, holy, sovereign God.

Psalm 150, only six verses, entitled: "Let all things praise the Lord." Good news laid out for us like I learned in elementary school about journalistic writing of news, that it must answer: "where, when, who, what and why." Psalm 150, a beautifully written, exciting, moving, thrilling expression of praise, answers these same questions.

Where to praise?—"In the sanctuary...in His firmament." Vs. 1. My heart is God's sanctuary on this earth, and wherever I take up space on this earth today is a proper place for praise? His firmament with no boundaries, no limits.

Why praise?—"For His mighty acts and His excellent greatness." Vs. 2. "It is by the power of God that men are brought unto salvation", and therefore the greatest of all miracles is to remove man's stony heart he is born with and replace it with a heart of flesh. Ezekiel 36:26. Out of His greatness He has created and sustained the universe and all its blessings: the light we see with, the air we breathe, the sweet-smelling fragrance after a rain, the songs we hear, the food we taste, the controlled temperature and humidity we exist in and feel with our flesh.

How to praise?—"Praise Him with the trumpet (loudly); praise Him with the lute and harp (quietly, gently, softly); praise Him with the timbrel and dance" (enthusiastically, rhythmically, boldly, actively, and even unexpectedly)... in many ways, diverse times, and in unusual situations and circumstanced, praise Him."

Who should praise?—"Let everything that has breath praise the Lord." Vs. 6. Every living creature, even the playful lambs at evening time, the lazy deer lying on a sunny hillside, the bird perched in the shade of a tree, or on a playful wing in a gentle breeze. Even the multi-colored flowers for a season, or the blossoms on a head of wheat in the passing from seedtime to harvest—praise the Lord!

One morning I drove by my neighbor's farmstead and noticed water overflowing his stock tank in the corral, and running down over the gravel road I was traveling on. Praise is like that, the overflow of a fresh, joyful heart, not self-centered, but running all over that man's domain.

Genuine praise is all summed up in the doxology we so often sing: "Praise God from Whom all blessings flow, praise Him all creatures here below; praise Him above ye heavenly host, praise Father, Son, and Holy Ghost."

June 14

"Cast your cares upon Him." I Peter 5:7

"I tired, Grandpa" came invariably from the voice of my two-year old grandson as we readied ourselves to leave the barn or the machine shop and head for the dining room table for dinner. That simply meant "Carry me and my toys." It worked every time for him. At the lake in Minnesota, however, "I tired, Grandpa" resulted in a different approach to his plight. His other Grandpa got down on his knees and invited Gregory to do likewise, and they crawled up the steep bank away from the lake, toward the trailer house. A different approach from that Grandpa, but the same result—their arriving back home, safe and sound, ready for a good meal.

As I reflect on these two differing testimonies, I think of Jesus' functioning on the one hand and the Holy Spirit on the other—both with a same heart, as with the two Grandpas, to ascertain the exact same result—to alleviate the pressure like that on the little boy's mind and heart, analogous to that of our pre-salvation days. From James 5:6-7 we read of Jesus: "Therefore humble yourselves under the mighty hand of God, that He may exalt you in due time, casting all your cares upon Him, for He cares for you." The Holy Spirit prodded me to do likewise one day on a busy street; when I saw a little elderly lady burdened down with grocery bags in each hand. I pulled to the curb and invited her to cast her burden into my vehicle and I would take her to her home. Jesus lifts our burdens when we call upon Him in prayer for help, be it for salvation, loneliness, sickness, a broken relationship, financial trouble, or in need of an extra measure on love, joy, peace or security.

Jesus and the Holy Spirit, of one like mind, like two Grandpas, because they are each an integral part of the Trinity, being one, yet two entities—the Holy Spirit lifting us up, directing, encouraging us to focus on our Savior, who alone can save us for eternity. Jesus, in John 14:6: "I am the way, the truth, and the life; no man comes unto the Father but by Me." That same Jesus delegates power to the Holy Spirit who, now since Pentecost Day, inhabits the entire earth invisibly, but for the same exact purpose—to bring lost man, burdened down with sin, unto salvation.

"Jesus. I tired, carry me." So He picks me up with my toys, and I hear Him say: "Cast your cares upon Me, for I care for you."

"Holy Spirit I tired, carry me." So we see the obvious coming alongside as Jesus explains in John 14:16-17: "I will pray the Father, and He will give you another Helper, that He may abide with you... you know Him for He dwells with you (walks beside you), and will be in you." Parenthesis mine.

I am a little man on earth this morning who sees Jesus and the Holy Spirit waiting to lift me and my burden when I call upon Them with a proper heart. "Call upon Me and I will answer you, and show you great and mighty things you do not know." Jeremiah 33:3.

June 15

"...to be conformed to the image of His Son..." Romans 8:29.

Is there anything more complimentary to a dad than to hear someone say: "Your son is surely a chip off the ol' block"? We've seen it with pastors, ranchers, music men, lawyers, politicians, basketball and football coaches, golfers out on the green, hunters, and fishermen and, oh, yes, the calf ropers in the cowboy world, all decked out with hat, boots, and a classy rope, like dad on top of a well-trained quarter horse.

To be qualified as a "chip off the ol' block" requires a certain intimacy, a DNA that matches even the world of botany, where an evergreen chip is no match for a cedar, or birch. It requires a father-son relationship as so evident with Jesus and His Father, perfect DNA...concerned with pure, clean, innocent, sinless blood running through Jesus' physical arteries here on earth to humbly manifest not only His love for humanity, but also His Father's. "For God so loved the world that He gave His only begotten Son, that whosoever believes in Him shall not perish, but have everlasting life." John 3:16.

The "Chip off the ol' Block", full of agape love like His Father, had an identical feel for sacrifice, a sacrifice of body and blood that would satisfy His Father in paying for the sins of humankind by His death on a cross at Calvary.

Paul alludes to this "chip" in Ephesians 5:1-3: "Therefore be imitators of God as dear children. And walk in love, as Christ also has loved us and given Himself for us, an offering and sacrifice to God for a sweet-smelling aroma."

Thinking of myself as a sacrifice "chip", I hear Jesus from Matthew 16:24: "If anyone desires to come after Me, let him deny himself, and take up his cross and follow Me." Get rid of that "me-first syndrome", nail your rotten old flesh to a cross by child-like faith and follow Jesus to Calvary, and lay down that inherent sin from a truly repentant heart, to reap the love, joy, peace, hope, and security His forgiveness yields.

Oh to be that "chip" "...a brand new creature, old things passed away..." I Corinthians 5:17. To be that "chip" filled with the fruit of the Spirit: "love, joy, peace, patience, kindness, goodness, faithfulness, gentleness, and self control" Galatians 5:22-23.

From a "chip" looking forward to an eternity with the "Block" I came from.

June 16

"What father gives his son a stone for breed?" Matthew 7:9

    On this Father's Day, would we not have to admit that we dads have a tough act to follow, having celebrated Mother's Day only a month ago? God took care of this, however, when He created male and female and the family, and endowed moms and dads with complimentary gifts and virtues rather than competitive ones. They first enter into marriage, and then together make and mold their children into Godly citizens. It all begins with Ephesians 5 where God clearly exhorts: "Husbands, love your wives just as Christ loved the church and gave Himself for it...so husbands ought to love their wives as their own bodies....And to wives...submit to your own husbands as unto the Lord, for the husband is head of the wife as also Christ is head of the church..." God endowed husbands with a generous Godly ability to love their female mate, and also did He endow wives with a special Godly ability to respond.

    The factor that keeps the knot securely tied and the nest unruffled is prayer, which ushers in the love, joy, peace, and security that only God can bring. In Matt 7:9-10 Jesus asks: "What man is there among you who, if his son asks for bread, will give him a stone? Or, if he asks for a fish, will he give him a serpent?"

    Six-year old Brandon decided one Saturday morning to bake pancakes for his parents. He found a big bowl and spoon, pulled a chair to the counter, opened the cupboard, and pulled out the heavy flour canister, spilling it on the floor. He scooped some of the flour into the bowl with his hands, mixed in most of a cup of milk, and added some sugar, leaving a floury trail on the floor, which by now had a few tracks from the kitten, too. Brandon was covered with flour and frustrated. He wanted this to be something special for mom and dad, but was getting worse by the minute. He didn't know whether to put it in the oven or on top of the stove, not knowing how to operate either.

    Suddenly, he saw his kitten licking from the bowl of mix and reached to push her away and knocked the eggs to the floor. Frantically, he tried to clean up this terrible mess, getting his pajamas white and sticky. Just then he saw dad standing at the door, and big tears welled up in his eyes. All he had wanted to do was good, but then this mess. He waited for a scolding or maybe even a spanking, but his father just watched. Then, walking through the mess, dad picked up his crying son, hugged him, and loved him, while his own pajamas became messy in the ordeal.

That's how God deals with us in a sticky marriage, or an insulting friend, a work we hate, or a health problem. Sometimes we just stand there in tears, and that's when God picks us up and loves us and forgives us even though our mess gets all over Him. So, let's just keep on making pancakes!! God's grace is sufficient.

"He (Job) would rise up early in the morning and offer burnt offerings according to the number of them (his ten children)." For Job said: "It may be that my sons have sinned and cursed God in their hearts. Thus did Job regularly." Job 1:5.

Dad, can you do any less for your son or daughter?

June 17

"Jesus saves."

As we travel the interstates on our way to Montana, we see large billboards outside the larger cities, and on them so many familiar names: John Deere, Ford, Chevrolet, Levis, J.C. Penneys, Super 8, Ramkota, Country Kitchen, McDonalds, Texaco, and Conoco. On and on goes the list of names we learn to know just because we are Americans, and in many cases having been a tiny part of each name as a consumer in need of something for our very existence and pleasure. They are attractive eye-catchers with an exit number, a street address, and a faith that billboard advertising pays off financially.

Also out there on billboards is the name of Jesus in such expressions as, "I am the Way, the Truth, and the Life." or "Jesus, the Light of the world" with a Biblical address, a name most Americans recognize; the very foundation of our heritage; a name we believers have consumed in our inner man for our very need and pleasure both here and for eternity. No other billboard advertising pays off with such dividends.

Those huge billboards are out there to grab a weary travelers eye and attention like Philippians 2:9-10 did for me one day early in my life when I was traveling through God's Word, looking for an extra measure of love, joy, peace, and security, a weary traveler on my way to satisfying my inner man's need. My acting on that "advertisement" from Philippians 2 was for my inner man like food, bed, clothing, or gasoline satisfies the outer man's need. Paul writes thusly about the person and name of Jesus: "Therefore, God has highly exalted Him and given Him the name that is above every name, that at the name of Jesus every knee should bow, of those in heaven, and of those on earth, and of those under the earth; and that every tongue should confess that Jesus Christ is Lord, to the glory of God the Father."

It was that same person, with the name of Jesus, that set me free from many inner grievances when I heard Him speak very clearly to me from Luke 4:18: "The Spirit of the Lord is upon Me, because I have been anointed to preach good news to the poor, to heal the broken hearted, to set the captives free, to open the eyes of the blind, and to set free them that are bruised." My energized faith then led me into confession and repentance, a forgiving heart, and some real soulish healing and deliverance as Holy Spirit conviction took place, and I now relished "Search me, oh Lord, and know my heart, try me and know my thoughts and reveal to me any wicked thing standing between us..." Psalm 139:23.

Believe me, friend, it is the name of Jesus that is the key that unlocks the door of our captivity to sin on this earth so that we can walk into heaven one day through the door that same key unlocked for us at Calvary when the "veil was rent from top to bottom" that Good Friday afternoon.

The hymn writer puts it this way:

"His name is Wonderful. His name is Wonderful,
His name is Wonderful, Jesus, my Lord;
He is the mighty King, Master of everything,
His name is Wonderful, Jesus, my Lord.
He's the great Shepherd, the Rock of all ages,

Almighty God is He;
Bow down before Him, love and adore Him,
His name is Wonderful, Jesus, my Lord."
A billboard reader—a Jesus lover!

June 18

"...and be sure your sin will find you out." Numbers 32:23.

It must have bothered my tender conscience to continually, constantly break the law simply because I do not like being hemmed in by a seat belt. But, one day I heard a gentle reminder as I backed off my ramp: "You can be sure your sin will find you out." I knew where the quiet voice came from, along with instantly one more quick reminder; "Your Word have I hidden in my heart that I sin not." Psalm 119:11. Wow! ...A gentle scolding I needed as a regular, purposed breaker of the seat belt law! I immediately had a vision of something perhaps ahead out on the roadway that I would rather escape. It worked! I haven't broken that law since that gentle reminder which I give the Holy Spirit living within me full credit for.

I wonder: did not that same Holy Spirit touch the tender spot of Ananias and Sapphira's conscience with such a gentle reminder regarding deception and lying? Did they not hear: "...and be sure your sin will find you out."?

We read from Acts 5:1: "but a certain man named Ananias with Sapphira his wife sold a possession. And he kept back part of the proceeds, his wife also being aware of it, and brought certain part and laid it at the apostle's feet." They had seen Barnabas sell his land and bring all the money and laid it at the apostle's feet. Vs. 4:36. They had all agreed in that congregation to sell their possessions and bring in the proceeds to a common collection, for distribution to the poor who had need. Vs.4:34-35.

Who wouldn't want to be in on the glory? And who would know my complete story? They must have connived.

So, Peter, filled with the Holy Spirit's nudging, asked: "Why have you conceived this thing in your heart? You have not lied to man but to God." Vs. 5:5. "You can be sure your sin will find you out." "Then Ananias fell down and breathed his last." Vs. 5.

What a cost for a sin he had lived carelessly with like the seat belt law I, too, was knowingly careless with.

Sapphira appeared three hours later, a known accomplice, and was also tested by Peter, and "fell down at his feet and breathed her last." Vs.1.

"So, let each one give as he purposes in his heart, not grudgingly or of a necessity, for God loves a cheerful giver." II Corinthians 9:7. And with it an honest heart.

What's in your giving heart today? Pride or humility?

May you be blessed today by these testimonies.

June 19

"Give not as a grudging obligation..." II Corinthians 9:5

Katie Rowland was only 16 years old when she died in a tragic car accident. She wanted to help change the world and make it a better place for everyone. The kindhearted teenager was often moved to tears when she saw the needs of the poor around the world. She always wanted to give, but her family did not always have the means. One day later, as her mother Carrie was walking with her five-year old daughter, little Kristy looked down and saw a penny. Kristy immediately said, "Mommy, this penny is from heaven. Katie gave it to us. She wants us to collect pennies to help the children." She was thinking of the $4,800 cost for a water well in Africa, where many little black boys and girls are sharing a slough of water with livestock, only to die young from diseases.

Pennies are the most insignificant coin we carry. Most people ignore them, but that day Kristy saw the eternal value of one penny. God spoke to her through this "penny from heaven" because of what her sister's tender heart had taught her.

One night at church, mother Carrie had a vision of kneeling in front of a garden where she planted pennies instead of seeds. Then those pennies began to sprout into dollars. It was then that Carrie and Kristy began asking others if they would honor Katie's memory by giving their pennies, helping to raise enough money to drill a water well. That's 480,000 pennies! Within two years, the Rowland family presented a check for $7,650 to Life Outreach to help drill water wells!

Instead of drowning in the grief of losing Katie, they rose up to honor her memory by saving lives with their pennies. Carrie shared: "I know Katie is rejoicing in heaven over this."

The widow of Zarephath we read of in I Kings 17 experienced similar blessing, twofold, when she, too, unselfishly, sacrificially spent her means to bless Elijah, God's man of the hour. God had planted Elijah beside the Brook of Cherith, from which he drank for a season, and ate bread and meat the ravens brought to him daily. "And the brook dried up....no rain in the land..." Vs. 6-7. God spoke to Elijah; "Arise, go to Zarephath...I have a widow there to provide for you." Vs. 9. At the gate to the city was the widow gathering sticks for fire for her and her son's last meal, because their oil and flour were all gone. Times were so bleak that they were prepared to die. He asked her for a portion of both scarce commodities, water and bread. Then the test of her love and obedience in her destitute life. "Please bring me a little water that I may drink." Vs. 10 "...make me a small cake first, and bring it to me...then make for yourself and your son." Vs. 13. Then, to encourage her and strengthen her faith: "For thus says the Lord God...'the bin shall not be used up, nor the jar of oil run dry until the day the Lord sends rain...'" Vs. 14

"The flour was not used up...nor the oil run dry..." Vs. 16.

"Give, and it shall be given unto you, full measure, pressed down, shaken together, running over shall men give into your bosom." Luke 6:38

June 20

"Israel has sinned...stolen...deceived..." Josh. 7:11

The temptation, or maybe I should say the habit, was too severe to escape. The pastor was very highly respected, and very successful from the chore of the pulpit to tending to the needy in his flock. He was a very pleasant man of God in all his relationships. He was the proper age, and had much valuable experience and wisdom and talent as an administrator. Consequently, when the synod needed a candidate for bishop, he was the favored one of all the applicants, pretty much of a shew-in. At dinner time one day at the Synod's Bible camp, the outgoing bishop casually stood by as people selected their food, buffet style. Every single item had a price on it; nothing free, food or drinks. As the outgoing bishop stood there, he saw the candidate deliberately cover up several patties of butter so the cashier could not see them. The old bishop pulled him aside, and on the spot, removed his name from the big promotion on ground of dishonesty and deceit, which no Godly man ought to practice, and especially the top leader.

What a price to pay because of an old nature out of control, in need of sanctification and deliverance.

"The fear of the Lord is to hate evil. Pride and arrogance and the evil way; and the perverse mouth I hate." God: Prov. 8:13.

Seven times of marching around the city of Jericho, and the city fell into Israel's hands as God had promised and empowered the walls to fall. God had told them: "Don't take any loot, for everything is to be destroyed...all the silver and gold and bronze and iron must be brought into the treasury." Josh. 6:19. "But there was sin among the Israelis...for Achan took some loot for himself; and the Lord was very angry with the entire nation of Israel."

"You can be sure your sin will find you out." Numbers 32:23.

Can't you just see God looking down from heaven into Achan's heart as his hand slyly stole from the Lord's treasury? Israel's very next battle was against the small city of Ai, and the Israelites were soundly defeated. Vs. 4. The Lord said to Joshua: "...Israel has sinned...taken loot I said was not to be taken...have lied about it... and hidden it..."

Deliberate, unconfessed sin removes God's protective hand from a person and from a nation so the enemy has free-wheeling.

"If my people which are called by My name will humble themselves and pray and seek My face and turn from their wicked ways, I will hear them from heaven, I will forgive their sin, and I will heal their land." II Chron. 7:14.

"Thy Word have I hidden in my heart that I sin not." Psalm 119: 11.

Whether it's a stolen patty of butter or wealth taken from God's treasury, it's sin, an abomination in God's sight, as He looks at the heart of the sinner.

The antidote, reconciliation, a healing balm is found in I John 1:9: "If we confess our sin, God is faithful and just to forgive our sin, and to cleanse us from all unrighteousness."

June 21

The sword of the Lord: "It is written."

"Something is killing four or five of your chickens every night" said my neighbor on the phone at the Rocky Mountain Bible Camp I was enjoying 500 miles away from home. One hundred and fifty chickens almost ready for the frying pan or the deep freeze, now in trouble!! Upon arriving home a day or two later, I gathered a few traps, set them carefully in the "right" spot, baited them generously with the remains of last night's kill and went to bed with peace in my heart-a job well done! The next morning, four or five more dead chickens and all traps still intact, my determination toughened, my scheme changed each evening, but the same reward every morning.

My temper bristled, my two hairs stood on end, and I finally desperately placed several traps in a circle, tied an almost whole dead suspended chicken in their midst, just high enough to make the enemy, a suspected raccoon, jump and surely land in a trap. Very clever, well done, thorough job!! The next morning, more dead chickens, the bait consumed, and all traps intact.

I gave up; having learned a good lesson—raccoons must have headlights at night like my vehicles. In Matthew 4:3 my Bible says of Satan, a trapper trying to catch Jesus: The tempter came to Him, (baited Him with a rock), and Jesus escaped the trap with "It is written," and quoted God's appropriate Word. In verse 5, again the devil set a second trap. "Then the Devil took Him up and set Him on a pinnacle," (baited Him), and Jesus escaped the second trap with a second quote of memorized scripture. "It is written"...And in verse 8, a third trap: "The Devil took Him to a high mountain, (baited Him) with showing Jesus all the kingdoms of the world and their glory," and offered Jesus all that in exchange for his worship. Jesus escaped the trap with a third quote from God's Word: "It is written," and in verse 11, "The Devil left Him." The Devil gave up.

I learned a good lesson as I was no match for the nocturnal raccoon, Satan was no match for Jesus, who knew how to thrust the "sword of the Lord" (Ephesians 6:17) into Satan's heart and destroy his evil strategies plotted to cause sinless Jesus to fall. Believe me; I've had much greater success fighting Satan with memorized scripture than fighting raccoons with metal and flesh. Try the "It is written" sword today and you will be successful like Jesus was in escaping the enemy's traps when tempted with "the lust of the eye, the lust of the flesh, or the pride of life" 1 John 2:16.

June 22

"Lord, I believe; help my unbelief." Mark 9:24

A great multitude had gathered around the disciples when Jesus came along. He asked the scribes what the discussion was all about. Then a father in the crowd answered: "Teacher, I brought You my son, who has a mute spirit" Vs. 17. They ushered the agonizing, tormented boy to Jesus and the boy manifested the truth about himself with another attack. Jesus said to the pleading, trusting, Father: "If you can believe, all things are possible to him who believes." Immediately the boy's father cried out and said with tears: "Lord, I believe, help my unbelief."

That honest father spoke out my testimony of many times under such duress, a gray area between total faith on one end of the totem pole and total fear (unbelief) on the other.

For weeks a most important, significant meeting of the congregation was planned and the date announced. The business at hand required unequivocally a quorum to be present to make or defect a call for our next senior pastor. The man had already candidated and was now waiting for our response. When I heard the word "quorum" I developed a dark, negative cloud over my head as my ordinary faith turned to fear for various reasons. I had never seen a quorum present previously. A number of other negatives poured over my soul as I wanted ever so badly to see this meeting speak its immediate answer and settle things for everyone's benefit.

As I heard the Lord from Jeremiah 33:3: "Call upon Me and I will answer you, and show you great and mighty things you have not known." I could only reply "Yes, Lord, I believe, but help my unbelief." A terrible plight for a deacon to confess!

The meeting was scheduled for 7 PM Sunday evening, and upon arriving with another couple at 6:45 to pray for the conduct of the meeting, we found ourselves on an empty ramp outside, and alone in a dark narthex on the inside. And, we wondered...???? "Just as I thought" came to my puny faith as we sauntered off to the prayer room.

"Why are you fearful, O you of little faith" Jesus chastised the disciples in the great tempest at sea, their boat filling with water, while in the very physical presence of Jesus, the disciples saying, "Lord we are perishing!" "He arose, rebuked the winds and the sea and there was great calm...and the men marveled." Mark 8:23-27.

I came to the sanctuary door at exactly 7 PM and the room was almost full! I immediately mentally calculated "far more than a quorum." Yes, even on a still, warm Sunday evening, so inviting to be on a lake, on a golf course, or just enjoying a time of rest on the deck at home.

My eyes filled with tears of joy as, convicted, I began to confess my sin of unbelief from a truly repentant heart. The cloud overhead disappeared and I found my usual self full of quality hope, love, joy, peace, and security, as I am sure the sick boy's father experienced at his son's deliverance.

When will I learn: "Do not fear nor be dismayed, for the battle is not yours but God's." II Chronicles 20:15. "...casting your cares upon Him, for He cares for you." I Peter 5:17.

"Let not your heart be troubled...you believe in God, believe also in Me..." Jesus speaking, John 14:1

June 23

"The poor you will always have with you..." Matthew 26:11.

We find that food was scarce for the poor people when Naomi brought her daughter-in-law, Ruth, home with her from the land of

Moab, both of them widows. But God blessed young Ruth when she went out into the field of Boaz to pick up any spilled, shelled, or non-gleaned kernels of barley. "And when she rose up to glean, Boaz commanded his young men, saying, 'So let her glean even among the sheaves, and do not reproach her. Also, let grain from the bundles fall purposely for her...that she may glean; and do not rebuke her.' So, she gleaned in the field until evening, and it was about an ephah (bushel) of barley." Ruth 2:15-17.

"Pure and undefiled religion before God...is this: to visit widows and orphans in their trouble..." James 1:27.

We see here a testimony of Christianity in action! Boaz had a heart for the poor, especially the widows. What a heyday Ruth could have enjoyed at threshing time in our Midwest before the days of combining, when every floor of the old hayracks hauling bundles of oats from the field to the threshing machine was covered thick with shelled kernels and kernels from the bundle landing on the floor. Many shovels full were thrown into the machine at evening time.

I remember when my uncle, during the drought and depression years of the 1930's in Montana, would very often ask his wife to cook a hot-dish to take to some large, poor, hungry family in my hometown, And quite often to a dormitory where farmer's high school students bunked during the week days to go to school before buses came on the scene. You see, he was the county undersheriff, earning $150 per month. Theirs was sacrificial giving since they had their own family to provide for, too.

"So, let each one give as he purposes in his heart, not grudgingly or of necessity, for God loves a cheerful giver." II Corinthians 9:7

During those same days the family doctor often was called out twenty miles or more on a winter day when only a horse and sleigh could get through the snow. He went faithfully, often times knowing there would be no pay, just to save a life or comfort a suffering human.

Every life we touch like that as Christians experiences God's love, compassion, and mercy, some unto their very survival, both for now and for eternity.

"...assuredly, I say to you, inasmuch as you did it to one of the least of those, My brethren, you did it to Me." Jesus, Matthew 25:40.

June 24

"So He opened not His mouth." Isaiah 53:7

Early one spring morning, as I was exiting the John Deere Implement store in my hometown, a contentious neighbor proceeded to enter. From an ugly heart, darts literally showing from his eyes, and a mouthful of venomous poison, he angrily said to me "Why don't you practice what you preach?" He had listened to my radio message that morning wherein I dealt with "love your neighbor as yourself" I tried desperately hard to remember a time I had had trouble with him, but failed. However, as I quickly recalled the many others he had had trouble with, all good people, I immediately jumped on the offense and made a simple, sarcastic, unkind statement I immediately regretted. Conviction came heavily upon me, and I took it to the Lord in prayer as I headed for home. I remember so well the Lord ministering to me when I passed through the "five-mile" bridge south of town. With a truly repentant heart, I heard the Lord loud and clear in my spirit from Isaiah 53:7: "He (Jesus) was oppressed and afflicted, yet He opened not His mouth. He was led as a lamb to the slaughter, and as a sheep before its shearers is silent, so He opened not His mouth." "I got the message, Lord!!" I said quietly. Then I rehearsed His heavy affliction compared to my puny one.

My pride stirred my temper while in His humbleness: "He has borne our griefs; carried our sorrows...was smitten by God and afflicted...wounded for our transgressions, bruised for our iniquities; and by His stripes we are healed...laid on Him the iniquity of us all... oppressed...afflicted...led to the slaughter as a sheep...Yet He opened not His mouth." Isaiah 53:4-7. Shame came heavily upon me as I had arrogantly defended myself with a naughty tongue.

And from Matthew 26, regarding His day of crucifixion: "He has spoken blasphemy...He is deserving of death. Then they spat in His face and beat Him; and others struck Him with the palms of their hands...But again he (Peter) denied with an oath: 'I do not know the Man!' (His third lie of denial). And while He was being accused...He answered nothing. 'Do You not hear how many things they testify against You?' And He answered him not one Word. They stripped Him and put a scarlet robe on Him. They twisted a crown of thorns and put it on His head...they mocked Him, saying: 'Hail, King of the Jews.'" Then they spat on Him, and took the reed and struck Him on the head. And they nailed Him to a cross."

"Life and death are in the power of the tongue; they that love it shall eat of its fruit." Proverbs 18:21. We speak negative words that kill, and we eat of that fruit, a curse. We speak Godly, positive words that produce life and we are blessed in our relationships.

Oh, that my heart and my testimony could be like as Jesus': "Father, forgive them, for they know not what they do." Luke 23:34.

"Be still and know that I am God." Psalms 46:10.

June 25

"If My people which are called by My name will humble themselves, pray, and seek My face, and turn from their wicked ways, then I will hear from Heaven, forgive their sins, and heal their land." 11 Chronicles 7:14.

What a wonderful direction from the heart of God! I see here a mixture of four principals and three promises to save our nation now so deluged. "If My people." the Christians, God inviting and expecting them to take up their cause of our nation's troubles today, a trouble that needs healing and protection from both inside and outside our borders.

If My people, the Christians, "will humble themselves," see and confess their hopelessness and helplessness by admitting the spiritual warfare is too big for us to cope with. We praise God daily for His Word from Job 5:12, our greatest security: "God frustrates the devices of the crafty before their hands can carry out their plans." Many of them are jailed today.

If My people, the Christians, "will pray." "Call upon Me and I will answer you, and show you great and mighty things you do not know." Jeremiah 33:3. "Pray without ceasing" I Thessalonians 5:17. "The fervent prayer of a righteous man avails much." James 5:16.

"My son, give attention to My Word; incline your ear unto My sayings; let them not depart from before your eyes; keep them in the midst of your heart, for they are life unto those who find them, and health unto their flesh." Proverbs 4:20-23; Psalm 119:105.

If My people, the Christians, "will turn from their wicked ways," confess their sins, repent and turn around 180 degrees, and walk away in the opposite direction. "Except you repent, you shall... perish". Jesus, Luke 13:3, 5. When proud, haughty, belligerent Jonah repented and preached to the city of Nineveh, there was great revival. "Not by might, not by power, but by My Spirit, says the Lord of hosts." Zechariah 4:6.

Then the three promises. "I will hear from heaven," "Now this is the confidence that we have in Him: that if we ask anything according to His will, He hears us..." I John 5:14.

"I will forgive their sins." "If we confess our sins, God is faithful and just to forgive our sins, and to cleanse us from all unrighteousness." I John 1:9. "As far as east is from the west, so far has He removed our transgressions from us." Psalm 103:12. Let us be encouraged that when lone Nehemiah, Amos, and Daniel each confessed the sin of their nation, Israel, and God responded with forgiveness. We Americans today need to recite to Him the sins from Hollywood to Broadway, and all the little hamlets between, the sins of pornography, immorality, abortion, same-sex marriage, gambling, lust, greed, pride, and a long list of other ungodliness.

"I will heal their land." King Jehosophat and the people of Judah in II Chronicles 20 were threatened by three enemy armies. The people went to prayer and fasting, encouraged by a prophetic Word: "Do not fear nor be dismayed, for the battle is not yours but God's." "Position yourselves, stand still, and you will see the salvation of the Lord." "Now, when they began to sing and praise, the Lord set ambushes against the enemy, and they were destroyed to the last man."

"God bless America, land that I love..."

June 26

"...Who Himself bore our sins in His own body on the tree..." I Peter 2:24.

It was a quiet, peaceful morning when I rode my horse down the lane leading to the river bottom pasture. I looked up and there it was, that lone tree, miles away on the riverbank. It was a tree nature had planted there long before my day. That tree, not overly beautiful to look at, is gnarled a bit, having withstood many harsh storms. It was the only one in sight for miles either north or south, a tree you wouldn't travel very far to observe, but one that every summer was doing its job of providing shade on a hot July afternoon for a cow and her calf, or a colt and his mother, and a bird haven for nests on its branches. That tree is a beautiful illustration of the old adage: "Bloom where you are planted." You see, I've put my eyes on that tree hundreds of times without its even knowing or seeing me, has done its job, has served its purpose, and has been an ever so silent blessing without ever being recognized for it until maybe this day. Oh, to be a quiet blessing like that lovely, humble tree, planted by God Himself, a refuge, a landmark.

That morning, as I rode along, I began to think of the one tree in all of history that had the honor of being the cross our Jesus was crucified on at Calvary. Was it a lone tree on the bank of the Jordan, gnarled and leaning, or was it a tall, stately tree selected from the forests of Lebanon? Its significance was not meant to be firewood, a haven for birds, or shade for man or beast, but to stand straight and strong, and erect, selected to perform the most important chore in the history of mankind, chosen to hold upright for a few hours the most important Man in all of history, the Man named Jesus, a perfect sacrifice that would satisfy God Himself as the One called the Lamb of God. Little did that tree know that its ultimate chore, its final work, would be to become that bridge that the believer with childlike faith would use to walk across the deep ravine every person is born with between himself and God. It would carry saved man into the entrance of the very throne room where David declared in Psalm 91:1: "I will dwell in the secret place of the Most High, and abide under the shadow of the Almighty. I will say of the Lord 'You are my Refuge, my Fortress.'" From one who praises God daily for that tree where Jesus bore my sins in His body.

June 27

"Trust in the Lord with all your heart" Prov. 3:5.

One day, years ago, when my mate, Lois, and I were meditating together from Matthew 14 where it says in verse 22: "Jesus made His disciples get into the boat and go before Him to the other side..." we saw a revelation of truth here; ourselves individually and personally spoken to. We heard Him from Jeremiah 1:5: "I knew you before you were conceived; I sanctified you before you were born; I ordained you." Jesus put us in that boat when we were created, started us out from a certain dock, and headed us toward the other side — to the far shoreline where our trip would end much too far away to be visible today.

Early in our individual voyages our boats came together one day and for a season, floating lazily and quietly in the calm waters where we made a choice to tie them together with a cable called marriage. Verse 24 tells us, "The boat was now in the middle of the sea, tossed by the waves, for the wind was contrary." Our calmed sea soon turned to rough waves as we rode up and down together through the tragic death of her oldest brother our first year out, followed by the loss of our own first son at birth, and soon thereafter my only brother's shocking death at age 37.

The stress of agricultural problems coupled with the upbringing of six children caused the waves some severe ups and downs until that day in 1975 when Jesus appeared on the waters in His fullness, and our eyes opened to see Him in new dimensions.

Verse 25 says: "...the disciples saw Him walking on the sea..." Good news!! Verse 32 says: "And when they (Peter and Jesus) got into the boat the wind ceased," Oh to see Jesus afresh, His full Person, His absolute truth, His unlimited power, His fabulous glory came into our boats with us, and to hear Him say: "Seek ye first the kingdom of God and His righteousness and all these things will be added unto you. "I have been anointed to preach good news to the poor, to heal the broken hearted, to set the captives free, to restore sight to the blind, and to set free them that are bruised."

Did you ever wonder about the rest of their voyage? Were there more storms now with Jesus in the boat, or perfect calm? My wife and I discovered almost immediately more severe storms than ever before, but help unlimited to go through the waves when we lost a twenty year old son so quickly then suffered eight years in a row of severe drought and grasshoppers, our relationship with the old heritage and tradition bound church, and consequently financial troubles that only the Lord in the boat with us could help us through. He proved: "I will never leave you nor forsake you", as we saw our life's work vanishing; we heard Him from II Chronicles 20:15: "Do not fear or be dismayed for the battle is not yours but God's."

My mate developed severe vascular problems, and after ten years we could see the far shoreline one morning where she would soon fall into the arms of Jesus for eternity. Our marriage vow: "Until death do we part" became real, our cable severed, and back to sea I went alone, only, to find another boat, also severed from her mate by death, and again we chose to tie our two boats together knowing full well the beckoning of the same shoreline just ahead, though invisible for now.

The Man in the boats with us had comforted us in our lonely hours: "I know the thought I think toward you, thoughts of peace not of evil, plans to give you a hope and a future." Jeremiah 29:11.

We thank God for the dock He sent us out from, for His eye on us all the way, and for His promise at the far shoreline. His Word is steadfast!

June 28

"I know the thoughts I think toward you...of a future and of hope." Jeremiah 29:11

There we were, without realizing it, investing our time in one of the two most significant afternoons in our life's history. It was noontime, the opening day of Hungry Horse Bible Camp on the west edge of Glacier Park in Montana, when two widowed, lonely-hearted people met in the dining room. Since "old jiggers" cannot stand upright for long, we sat up to a table where we faced each other and poured out our hearts for the next four hours. Alice had been a Lutheran pastor's wife, now widowed for six years, and I a farmer-rancher now widowed four years. She and Arnold had spent their lifetimes in Minnesota and Iowa parishes, plus a pleasurable time in a Mexico mission program, while I had spent my seventy-three years in a single farmstead in eastern Montana. We soon found we had an identical faith walk with the Lord, and in God's Word. Background and other similarities also surfaced that afternoon when we exchanged telephone numbers and other amenities the remainder of camp. The rest is history, and we both PTL for that significant afternoon.

The other most significant afternoon, even more significant, in our life's history, is called Good Friday, when we came face to face with Jesus, our emancipator. Once again, where lonely hearts met, a vacuum that needed filling, not only for the now, but for eternity. He shares His testimony with us from Matthew 27:31: "And when they had mocked Him...and led Him away to be crucified...to Golgotha... gave Him sour wine to drink...then they crucified Him and divided His garments, casting lots for them. And then they put on His head a crown of thorns, and above Him the accusation written against Him: "THIS IS JESUS, THE KING OF THE JEWS." And about the ninth hour (three o'clock) Jesus cried out with a loud voice, saying...'My God, my God, why have You forsaken Me?'" The cupful of all of humanity's sin had been poured over His head by His Father, and His body was broken and a short season of separation had come upon Him, perhaps the loneliest time of His entire earthly walk. "And Jesus cried out again with a loud voice, and yielded up His spirit." They pierced His side, and out flowed that pure, clean, innocent, sinless blood intended to be a bath for the inner man of him who would surrender to Jesus as his Lord and Savior.

"Now when evening had come, a rich man...named Joseph... asked for His body...and laid it in his new tomb, hewn out of rock, and he rolled a large stone against the door of the tomb and departed."

PTL for those two most significant afternoons: one of which brought two lonely hearts together for freedom in the flesh, and one which made it possible to come to Jesus to set us free in the spirit both for now and for eternity.

I had seen Jeremiah 33:3 come into full play: "Call upon Me and I will answer you; and I will show you great and mighty things you did not know."

June 29

"The great exchange."

In my ramblings this morning through various publications searching for an idea for today's broadcast, I saw a familiar sight I have seen many times in the old courthouse back home and in the bank across the street, and at the attorney's office next door. It's a little rectangular gadget with a handle sticking up from it to grasp, and when all is said and done, stamped before your very eyes on a contract are the Word(s): "PAID" Or sometimes, "PAID IN FULL", and dated.

What a satisfaction to know that which has been hanging overhead as a long time obligation, or even an annual tax fee, is now "paid in full" and the endorsement is handed to the payer to joyfully file away as a receipt. Done deal!! Likewise, when the hour comes that anyone of us will come to the foot of that cross at Calvary with childlike faith and confess our sins from a repentant heart, we walk away with a life's certificate engraved by the hand of God, an eternal guarantee on which is literally printed "PAID IN FULL", written on our heart because, like the county treasurer, the banker, or the attorney, Jesus has authority to declare that truth because He was there alone when all of every man's sins, yours and mine included, were laid upon Him that Good Friday afternoon on that cross at Calvary. He paid the ransom fee with His body and blood. Done deal!!! And here are His "PAID IN FULL" endorsements:

PSALM 103:12 "As far as the east is from the west, so far has He removed our transgressions from us."

MICAH 7:19 "You shall cast all our sins into the depths of the sea."

ISAIAH 55:7 "For He will abundantly pardon."

JEREMIAH 31:34 "For I will forgive their iniquity, and their sin I will remember no more."

PSALM 130:4 "But there is forgiveness with You, that You may be feared."

HEBREWS 10:17 "Their sins and their lawless deeds I will remember no more."

COLOSSIANS 2:13 "And you, being dead in your trespasses, He has made us alive together with Him, having forgiven you all trespasses."

I JOHN 1:9 "If we confess our sins, He is faithful and just to forgive us our sins, and to cleanse us from all unrighteousness."

ISAIAH 1:18 "Though your sins are like scarlet, they shall be white as snow; though they are red like crimson, they shall be like wool."

It's called the "great exchange"— His blood for my sin!

June 30

"Little things Count."

Good morning friends with whom I love to share Jesus, sometimes in a powerful testimony and sometimes in just "small stuff" that shows up in our daily trek across the stage of life. This morning I am still baffled by the story of the rescue of nine miners in Pennsylvania, trapped 240 feet underground. A miracle indeed, because many prayer warriors prayed: "Cast all of your cares upon Him, for He cares for you." 1 Peter 5:7. The most impossible task of drilling that six foot hole at exactly the proper spot in a mile-long run to pipe warm air to the trapped men was no small task, but a miracle.

To the casual observer taking only a glimpse of TV news, this may have seemed like every day news, "small stuff" but to the miners and their families it was a matter of life and death.

From II Kings 6, I read this morning of an analogy, "small stuff" to most, but big to one man in particular. We find several young seminarians felling trees to build a new seminary and, in the process, one lost his ax-head as it plunged into a river. It had been a borrowed ax. The young lad cried out to prophet Elijah for help to retrieve the ax-head. Elijah tossed a stick into the water at the exact spot and retrieved the ax-head, a "small stuff" thing to all the boys but one, the one who lost it in the river.

This miracle illustrates a simple but profound truth: God cares about the "small stuff in your life and mine: lost ax-heads, lost coins, lost keys, lost files, lost contact lenses, accidentally tossed into the garbage can, the little things that cause frustration, anxiety, confusion, and worry in our daily walk. But our small worries mean everything to Him Who daily invites us to "come boldly before the throne of grace to receive mercy and to find grace to help in time of need," Heb. 4:16, and "to cast all our cares (big or small) upon Him because He cares for us." I Peter 5:7.

May the Lord's blessing rest upon you this day!

July 1

"A bruised reed…smoldering wick" Isaiah 42:3

As a very young, curious boy on that Montana ranch, I never could understand why tall, green, heavy-looking stocks, called reeds in the big slough on our meadow were so flimsy. So easy to bend, so shallow rooted that even a strong wind or a duck perching on them would lay them over, shallow-rooted because they stood in water and never had to suffer drought and go down deep for a drink like the old oak tree. The reed grew up spoiled like the young lad I knew back in the thirties, the one with a new, open roadster car while all the others of us walked, rode on horseback, or rode a bicycle. But at age 42, still single, having squandered a nice estate like the prodigal son, fallen into drugs, alcohol and homosexuality, he was shipped back home in a box for a burial in the local cemetery. Shallow roots—broken reed!!

Then one day I learned some real good news about a weak reed when I read a prophecy about Jesus from Isaiah 42:3, "A bruised reed He will not break, and a smoldering wick He will not snuff out." What is weaker than a bruised reed or a smoldering wick?

I remember the many wives of our community before electricity came to the farms and ranches and the kerosene lamp, a necessary everyday farmstead fixture, how they tended the wick, held by metal jaws, the wick, soaked in kerosene, but in its burning became frayed and "dirty" and needed occasional trimming with a scissors to bring forth a bright light again. "A smoldering wick" has a tiny spark within it, but it is almost smothered, so frail a baby could blow it out! Weak things, bruised reeds, smoldering wicks. Many of us are like that, like the starling bird, scared by every passerby; or like a frightened flock of sheep at the sight of a coyote out there on the open range, all huddled tightly together as one.

One day in my Christian walk I saw myself as a bruised reed when Jesus spoke to me from Luke 4:18, where He said in part: "I have been anointed…to set free those that are bruised." I had noticed how these bruises were a primary cause of a smoldering spark in my life, as against a bright flame I desired. Unforgiveness and grudges!! I sat down that very hour and made a long list of people's names who had bruised, hurt the inner me over the years, and then I spoke to each one forgiveness from my heart, even to those deceased, a list including teachers, friends, neighbors, brothers, parents, law officers, preachers, etc., who had bruised this shallow rooted, easily toppled reed. Jesus kept His Word and this bruised reed was set free from all that heaviness, and the smoldering wick turned into a zealous, hungry, thirsty man of God, willing now to share generously of the time, talent, and treasure He has generously given me. Are we not all a "bruised reed and a smoldering wick" until He sets us free?

July 2

"A smith, the mighty man is he…" a poem.

In my early days, there was a blacksmith shop in thousands of hamlets across America in the days when mold-board plowing was the predominant way of tilling the soil, preparing it for seeding. I was fascinated to watch the blacksmith take a red hot plow lay out of his stoked-up forge with a pair of tongs, and place it across an anvil and pound with a large mallet on the red hot edge, and make the lay as sharp as a new one again. As I write, I remember a phrase of a poem we learned in lower grade school: "The smith, a mighty man is he...," usually a large, powerful person. At times I also watched him bend and twist a red hot iron into a pattern to suit someone's special need on the farm.

So it was in Jeremiah 18, a potter working with clay, and in verse 3: "Then I went down to the potter's house, and there he was, making something at the wheel." But it didn't turn out as he planned, so he did it over again. "'Oh house of Israel, can I not do with you as this potter?' says the Lord, 'Look, as the clay is in the potter's hand, so are you in My hand, O house of Israel.'"

"Before I formed you in the womb, I knew you; before you were born, I sanctified you. I ordained you..." Jeremiah 1:5.

"I created you, oh Jacob, I formed you Oh Israel; fear not, for I have redeemed you; I have called you by your name; you are Mine..." Isaiah 43:1.

From one whom the Lord has been forging with fire like the blacksmith, and forming like the potter with clay in his fingers throughout a lifetime of trials and tribulations, purposely being conformed to the image of His Son. Romans 8:29.

July 3

"...given a name that is above every name...the name of Jesus..." Phil. 2:9-11

"What's in a name?" A question human nature has contended with since Adam and Eve, two names humanity will never forget. I met a young man recently whose name is Robert Boothe. I couldn't resist: "Any connection with John Wilkes Boothe, Lincoln's assassin?" "Yes" he said, "a very distant cousin; and, ironically, my maternal grandmother was a distant relative of Lincoln." How exciting for this history lover for just a moment to be part of our nation's most tragic story, Boothe and Lincoln, two names etched deeply into the heart of America's history.

Prov. 10:7 says: "The memory of the righteous is blessed, but the name of the wicked will rot." And Eccl. 7:11: "A good name is better than precious ointment..." And from Song of Solomon 1:3: "Your name is ointment poured forth." Our name is a tag we cannot get away from once the birth certificate is recorded and established at the Baptismal font. Like the little baby himself, that name grows into something big, too, as it makes a choice at the fork of the road... down the left to infamy, or to the right to honor and virtue.

I had a classmate in school days who liked booze mixed with writing "bad checks," until he was one day imprisoned and that stigma upon his name at his release drove him to suicide. Another classmate became a CPA, part of an accounting firm in Los Angeles. One day he was selected auditor for MGM in Hollywood. His personality and integrity, along with other wholesome values, later ushered him to Comptroller of MGM, and with it multi-millions of dollars of salary. To this day, he reaps the highest respect wherever he goes.

Most of us along life's way have been miffed because our name was misspelled, or inadvertently left out, overlooked, or unfairly played second fiddle to someone else's name. We love recognition and praise at times. A dad whose teenage daughter was killed in a snowstorm accident on her way back to college after Christmas, begged me to eulogize, lift up her name one morning on the radio broadcast, a very deserving name, a top scholar, a very decent young lady, with excellent character, personality, and beauty. Another dad saw eulogy differently, a dad of two top scholars, both valedictorians, very clean and decent boys with excellent citizenship records. His comment to me one day: "If their horn is to be blown, it will have to be by someone but me." He felt that if they earned some bragging and recognition with their lives, the world around them would see it and lift them up by name.

Prov. 18:10 describes the most powerful and precious name of all, Jesus, as a "strong tower, and the righteous runs into it and is safe." In Matt. 1:21: "She will bring forth a Son, and you shall call

His name Jesus, for He will save His people from their sins." "Jesus, the only name under heaven by which man can be saved."

Let us praise the name of Jesus, soon to return to earth, and carry His bride home in His everlasting arms; and then one day He will open the Lamb's Book of Life and find our name when the "roll is called up yonder."

From one who loves to sing, "His name is Wonderful..."

July 4

"I have been anointed...to set at liberty those in bondage..." Jesus – Luke 4:18, Isaiah 61:1

Liberty!...the trademark of America, the gist of an annual celebration on Independence Day, July 4. The passion of millions ably felt in the heart of patriot Nathan Hale; "Give me liberty or give me death."

"Oh give me a home where the buffalo roam," a physical analogy of my heritage. Growing up on the wide open spaces of Montana, the Big Sky where the "deer and the antelope play...where the skies are not cloudy all day." I grew up tasting of liberty in spirit, soul, and body, living up the theme of the old popular song: "Don't fence me in."

From history I find that the theme of liberty came from Europe to America in 1620 when the pilgrims, one hundred and one men, women, and children, Christian people seeking freedom of worship, worship without bondage. Their first winter cost them half of their population as they struggled to survive and to fulfill God's plan to plant the Rock named Jesus; and make a model of true liberty for the world to see, to envy, to settle, and establish the greatest government ever under a sound constitution and Bill of Rights. It took courage and the Revolutionary War to break loose from England. Their pioneer spirit then drove them West to claim land, to build towns and establish businesses, churches, schools, homes, county borders, and community centers. That's liberty! That's freedom that we heirs are enjoying down to this very hour.

The few numbers and other resources they had on hand to fight that war, "not by might, not by power, but by My Spirit says the Lord," reminds me of God's call on His servant, Gideon. In order to prove to Gideon that God was to get the credit for victory in his battle against thousands of well supplied, well armed Midianites, He convinced Gideon to cut his army of 30,000 men to 300 men, and equip them with jars, candles, and trumpets only. They went out very evident in God's power, stood strong against many odds and defeated the affluent enemy. Gideon and his troops could now revel in an Independence Day, their "July 4th" celebration.

That struggle to secure the signing of the Declaration of Independence was not free, but costly in human lives, as has been the cost of the many wars fought since, to preserve that precious blessing.

Two thousand years ago, our Declaration of Independence for the inner man's eternal security was not free either, but very costly, since "God so loved the world that He gave His only begotten Son, that whosoever believes on Him shall not perish, but have everlasting life." John 3:16. That Man Who declared in John 14:6 "I am the Way, the Truth, and the Life; no one comes to the Father but by Me" gave His body and shed His pure, clean, innocent, sinless blood for us, sacrificed His all, and "paid a debt He did not owe, a debt I could not pay." We rejoice in the spiritual freedom we enjoy because of our faith in the sin canceled by Jesus death on the cross at Calvary.

So, let us "stand fast, therefore, in the liberty by which Christ has made us free, and do not be entangled again with a yoke of bondage." Galatians 5:1.

July 5

"...for the Lord sustained me" Psalm 3:5

Just moments ago I saw dazzling white, pure, clean, beautifully pressed wedding gowns on TV advertising, and the sight birthed this morning's sharing tied with word receivers, whom I trust have had a good nights sleep, a genuine rest and can now share with David this early hour of a brand new day from Psalm 3:5: "I lay down and slept, I awakened for the Lord sustained me." What a beautiful testimony David could bring from a heart of thanksgiving and praise from his lips even while fleeing from his son, Absalom, who was in hot pursuit. Have you ever raised up your voice with thanks and praise that he built into each of us the need, desire and capability to sleep so that our bodies and minds may rest for a short season, and then rise up refreshed and ready for another day, even during a stormy trial?

And oh the blessing of another "sleep" Paul speaks of in I Thessalonians 4:14; "God will bring with Jesus those who have fallen asleep in Him." So, we have two "sleeps" both meant for rest, one for now for the body on its way to an earthen grave, and one for the soul, in Jesus, in Heaven. When Jesus literally whispers in our ear, "Today you will be with Me in Paradise" that saved soul does not hibernate, become dormant, not insensitive to its surroundings as it leaves its earthly home, the clay body. The soul of that saved one, having fallen asleep in Jesus, goes immediately to the throne of God, praising Jesus day and night for His bathing them clean of sin in His shed blood on Calvary. Here will we truly experience and enjoy and appreciate more than ever the blessed freedom our redemption has brought us. The clay body rests in an earthen grave under six feet of dirt covered with grass, resting, waiting for the hour of its resurrection and a new glorified body. Oh what a coveted experience!!

And now let me speak to you procrastinators and gamblers with your eternity, you who are dragging your feet regarding the most important decision in life. Your trip may end suddenly, even today, and your time to be washed clean of sin in the blood of Jesus at the foot of His cross where you must come with child-like faith will be gone forever. Only those washed in His blood are made right with God, sin forgiven, and ready for the wedding feast prepared in Heaven for all saints. Jesus said in John 14:6, "I am the Way, the Truth and the Life; no one comes to the Father but by Me." The sleep Paul speaks of in I Thessalonians is the final night of rest which none of us can escape, and which will usher us individually into one of two places for eternity, into Heaven or Hell, depending who we last went to bed with: Jesus or Satan. Oh happy are they who die clutching the hand of Jesus, now resting from their labors and awaiting their eternal rewards.

My friend, are you ready for the wedding gown and the coming marriage when the Groom comes back to take His bride home?

July 6

Be an encourager!

This morning as I went to prayer the thought came to me how wonderful that when I come to the throne of God to praise Him, visit with Him, plead with Him, to accept His visitation from Hebrews 4:16:"Therefore come boldly before the throne of grace to receive mercy and to obtain grace to help in time of need." I have His full attention immediately; no waiting in line, no busy signal, no answering machine, no voice that says: "our office hours are 8 to 5 weekdays, closed on weekends;" no female voice asks my name while on my way to the chief executive.

I do not understand all of this because I am living or contained in such a box here on earth, severely short of mental capacity to see the real bigness of our creator. But oh how thankful I am that God is omniscient, "all knowing, everywhere present, and with power over all other forces." Jesus was one day in the same box we are in when He was here on earth in the physical body, Son of God, and Son of Man. He could be in only one place at a time, doing only one thing at a time, hearing only one person at a time. That is why he said this in John 16:7, 13a, 14a: "Nevertheless, I tell you the truth. It is to your advantage that I go away, for if I do not go away, the Helper (the Holy Spirit) will not come to you; but if I depart I will send Him to you; He will guide you into all truth. He will bring glory to me by taking from what is mine and making it known to you."

Praise the Lord that after 50 days past His ascension, at the birth of Pentecost Day, God the Father and Jesus the Son poured out their very selves upon the earth with power of Heavenly force from pole to pole, from east to west, just as if Jesus were Himself here physically.

Oh how many believers are living on cheese and crackers today, when a luxurious meal is set before them in their prayer fellowship with God since that veil was torn from top to bottom that Good Friday afternoon, opening the throne of God to every saint personally, to capture the beauty, power, and strength of Psalm 91:1: "He who dwells in the secret place of the Most High shall abide under the shadow of the Almighty."

My neighbor lady, Bernice, said "no" when I stood by her bedside with her husband and suggested we join our hearts in prayer. She reasoned that God is too busy to be bothered by one like her. But oh, how mistaken when we consider Isaiah 43:1: "I created you, oh Jacob, I formed you, oh Israel; do not fear for I have redeemed you; you are mine; I call you by name."

July 7

"Get thee behind me, Satan"

It was 4:00 o'clock in the morning and my whole being came suddenly to life, and with that, far too early awakening. It was an attack from the enemy, a spiritual warfare in the form of regrets of the past, guilt and condemnation, a bit of fear, and plenty of discouragement that entered my being. At such time the options are plenty: fight it with carnal weapons like denial and self-justification, but it will be to no avail since Paul tells us in 2nd Corinthians 10:3-4: "For though we live in the world, we do not wage war as the world does. The weapons we fight with are not the weapons of the world. On the contrary, they have divine power to demolish strongholds."

Little David faced the giant, Goliath, "I come to you in the Name of the Lord of hosts...this day the Lord will deliver you into my hand..." Gideon faced thousands of Midianites with only 300 men, jars, candles, and trumpets and faith in the mighty Word of God's promises. Joshua and the Israelites took down twenty-nine enemy nations in the power of God only, as they saw cities with high walls around them fall into their hands.

The "breaking news" that came to me at 4:00 o'clock in the morning was what I remember Jesus doing with the experience He had one day with the same enemy and the lesson that He teaches to us from the Gospel of Matthew, Chapter 4. Three times He quoted appropriate O.T. Scriptures from memory and completely overcame Satan. In verse 11 it says: "Then the Devil left Him, and angels came and attended Him."

As I floundered, tossed, and tumbled in my bed, trying to pray, I was reminded of that part of the full armor of Ephesians 6 where we take in one hand the "sword of the Lord" (God's Word), the very same sword Jesus thrust so victoriously and left us an example. 2 Chronicles 20:15b-17 came to my mind: "Do not be afraid or discouraged because of this vast army. For the battle is not yours but God's. Tomorrow march down against them... Take up your positions; stand firm and see the deliverance the Lord will give you."

As I was further plagued by the bygone days of regret, even days of that 'me first syndrome', I reminded the enemy: "If any be in Christ Jesus by a brand new creation, old things passed away, all things become new." "If we confess our sins, He is faithful and just and will forgive us our sins and purify us from all unrighteousness." 1 John 1:9.

What I had just experienced is aptly explained by Jesus Himself in John 8:31-32 "To the Jews that had believed Him, Jesus said, 'If you hold to my teaching, you are really my disciples. Then you will know the truth, and the truth will set you free.'"

July 8

"...I will show you great and mighty things you do not know"

If there be one thing that "bugs" me today, it is when I hear from Washington D.C. a severe warning that we must expect another act of terrorism any moment now. We do not know where it will strike, who will perpetrate it, not even the nature of the impact. So I ask myself, like millions of Americans; "What can I do about it, or what shall I do?" And then I go on living and the bomb that was expected at Times Square on New Year's Eve, or the stadium packed with 70,000 football fans, or the bridge, or the dam, or the nuclear tank, remain untouched. Praise the Lord!! The real reason I hate such announcements that have no real momentary evidence is it negates my daily prayer and the prayers of others of the remnant who are praying in full faith that God's hand is able and willing to cover our nation, especially when we are personally daily confessing the sins of our nation from repentant hearts like as the remnant of Israel's day when enemies faced them on all sides, and God heard their plea for help and forgave them and restored them back to His full grace.

II Chronicles 7:14 is as sound as brass to hang our hat of faith on this morning: "If my people who are called by my name, will humble themselves and pray and seek My face and turn from their wicked ways, then will I hear from heaven, and will forgive their sin, and will heal their land." II Chronicles 20:15b is a sound rock to hide behind as the Rock of Gibraltar. "Do not be afraid or discouraged because of this vast army. For the battle is not yours, but God's." Jeremiah 33:3 is so sure that we can hang our life on it: "Call to Me and I will answer you and tell you great and unsearchable things you do not know." God's Omni eye is the only eye that can see into the devious, ungodly, wicked hearts of men bent on our destruction, and the only One with power to divert their plans, depending on the constant, incessant, deliberate, disciplined, everyday prayers of the saints wherever they reside.

Just this morning I read from II Kings 19:19: "Now, O Lord our God, deliver us from his hand, so that all the kingdoms on earth may know that you alone, O Lord, are God." Here we find a leader like our President in deep trouble, King Hezekiah of Judah, having received a threatening letter from a neighboring enemy, King Sennacharib of Assyria, who was serving papers of war now on Jerusalem after having conquered many other cities. He was a feared enemy like our terrorist enemies all over the world, so near with modern technology and nuclear power that our two oceans are no longer a safe deterrent.

In II Kings 19:10-12 we find the enemy king even mocking God much like today's believers in Allah are doing, and he said; "Do not let the god you depend on deceive you when he says, 'Jerusalem will not be handed over to the King of Assyria. Surely you have heard what the kings of Assyria have done to all the countries, destroying them completely. And will you be delivered? Did the gods of the nations that were destroyed by my forefathers deliver thee?'" I love verse 14 where King Hezekiah went immediately up to the temple and spread the letter before the Lord.

July 9

"My grace is sufficient for you." II Corinthians 12:9

Jesus said in John 4:14, as He was ministering to the Samaritan woman by Jacob's well "...whosoever drinks of the water that I shall give him will never thirst. But the water that I shall give him will become in him a fountain of water springing up into everlasting life." Beneath the physical earth there seems to be everywhere a body of water that humanity can tap into by digging a well, a wonderful blessing that God created man, beasts, and plants to need for their very survival. In John 4 Jesus sets aside Jacob's well to reveal a better water to quench a different thirst. I think here of the wonderful River of Grace as an unlimited ocean of water whose source is the heart of God, and whose compelling force is Jesus, a river that flows freely into the heart of God, and whose compelling force is Jesus, a river that flows freely into the heart of every believer as a "fountain of living water, springing up into everlasting life," regulated daily by the Holy Spirit Who has attached Himself to the believer's inner man, and doles out, sifts off, taps into the flow with just enough grace for today. "My grace is sufficient for you." II Corinthians 12:9.

I think of the artesian well my family was blessed with on the Montana ranch. In 1926 my dad was drilling for a water well for both livestock and family to survive on, and the water started to flow freely, even to this day. From the well, the water was first piped into a large barrel from which we drew by the pail full for household use. An overflow pipe from the barrel to a large wooden tank supplied a steady flow for the livestock, and the overflow from that tank out onto a hillside where wildlife could drink and grass could flourish.

I've often thought: what a blessing to our household, to our domestic herds and flocks, to wildlife that needed water in the drought years of the 1930's, and the laundry ladies that were blessed in the day before water softeners. No end to the blessing!

Jesus, the Living Word of God, is like that artesian well, with a source of life flowing out of the cross, the crucifixion and the resurrection; life for the inner man that never runs dry, but freely flows daily with blessing to each of us personally—salvation, deliverance, and healing, a blessing to all of nature all around us, and to the people in our community and in our church we share Him with at no cost. Proverbs 4:20 says it all in a nutshell: "My son, give attention to my Words, incline your ear to My savings; let them not depart from before your eyes; keep them in the midst of your heart, for they are life to all who find them, and health to their flesh."

No life can survive without water, and no life can stay healthy without clean water. Jesus is that drink of clean water for the inner man. How wonderful that we do not need a pump to get the water of life out of the well, since our works are not needed nor necessary, but the flow just keeps nurturing us as we sit by with child-like faith, drink of the water, eat of the food that satisfies the inner man's hunger, and bathe in the blood that cleanses from all sin. I John 1:9 says: "If we confess our sin, God is faithful and just to forgive our sin and cleanse us from all unrighteousness."

July 10

"Because of your mercies I am not consumed..." Lamentations 3:2

Recently, when I considered one of my favorite Old Testament verses from Isaiah 43, I was reminded of June 1953 out on the ranch in Montana when some differing parts of our small county were rained upon every day of that month. The skies would darken, the thunder crash, and the lightning flash, and down would pour another inch or two of rain. And then the sun would suddenly appear in a clear sky; the air and the grass and the earth so refreshed, and the little rivulets of water running toward lower ground in the fields and pastures. By the first day of July, the Poplar River running through the country was not affordable, and my neighbor, crossing the river on horseback, just hung onto the saddle as the horse swam to safety on the far bank. Isaiah 43:2 says: "When you pass through the waters I will be with you, and through the rivers, they shall not overflow you..." God divided and banked up the waters of the Red Sea, dried the river bottom instantly, and the three million Israelites "passed through the waters," their only escape from their pursuing enemy, God with them. "Through the rivers, they shall not overflow you."

When I have passed through the flooding waters of my life, trials in time of drought, grasshoppers, economic hardship, widower-hood, death of a loved one unexpectedly, loneliness, conviction, and a host of other "waters," I've sensed the presence of my Redeemer at my side as I prayed and searched the Word with a fine-toothed comb, and found His real reason to help me, like as with the Israelites: "I created you...I redeemed you, you are Mine, I call you by name..." verse 1. "Because of Your mercies I am not consumed; Your compassions never fail; they are new every morning. Great is your faithfulness!" Lamentations 3:22-23

Is your life in the midst of a flood this morning, a place in life you seem to have no control over? "Do not fear nor be dismayed because of this multitude for the battle is not yours but God's." II Chronicles 20:15.

Like the grass after the rain you and I can become a shining testimony of His protection, His provision, and His keeping power, our refuge, our fortress, as we experience a new and full measure of love, joy, peace and security bolstering our inner man, simply because we have energized our gift of faith in God and His Word.

July 11

"How Firm a Foundation" a favorite hymn.

As usual, I began the day with a Word of praise to God this morning, reading from Psalms 89:15-16 LBV. "The Heavens are Yours, the Word, everything, for You created them all. You created north and south. Mount Tabor and Mt. Hermon rejoice to be signed by Your name as their Maker. Strong is Your arm. Strong is Your hand. Your right hand is lifted high in glorious strength. Your throne is founded on two strong pillars; the one is justice and the other righteousness. Mercy and truth walk before You and Your attendants.

Blessed are those who hear the joyful blast of the trumpet, for they shall walk in the light of Your presence."

Did you ever notice that almost everything in life has a foundation, be it a building, a business, a religion, a government, a vocation we pursue, and even the home we are born into, where our basic foundation in most issues of life—our physique, our traits or personality and character, our political and philosophical views, our educational opportunities, our social graces, and many more influences that build our foundation for life?

One of my most melancholy moments of life shows up when I drive past a nice shelterbelt on the farmstead, planted maybe seventy-five or one hundred years ago, and as I look carefully, the concrete foundation of a young couple's dream home, nestled behind the trees, a home now gone, but the evidence still remaining, the foundations, not only of their house, but the outbuilding's foundations the young couple built their future on.

Psalms 89:14 says: "Righteousness and justice are the foundations of God's throne," and then the psalmist adds; "Love and truth go before Your face." Love and truth are about like the Siamese twin girls we saw last fall on TV who were born with their heads joined, inseparable until the surgeon's knife cut them apart. So it is with truth and love, inseparable in God's mind.

All this for a specific blessing to a lost man we see in Vs 15: "Blessed are the people who know the joyful sound." In living this out in real life, I see this like the actions of a fireplace, where burning paper and wood have heated up the incinerator like God's Word does when conviction of sin burns hot in a sinner's bosom, and from all the dancing flame and the crackling sounds comes the desired warmth, as the heat pours out into the room. Truth and love, hand in hand! Without love accompanying truth, truth is just a constant consuming fire, as sin without Jesus is a consuming fire. But with Jesus in the midst of the flame the consuming fire becomes comforting warmth for the inner man as forgiveness pours forth from the heart of God, so we can declare with the Psalmist: "Righteousness and justice are the foundation of Your throne." Doesn't it feel good, warming, and settling inside, to know you are forgiven by Mom or Dad, or when God says from psalms 103:12: "As far as east is from the west, so far have I removed their sins from them." I know of a young man who has a pet toy he spends all his spare time with, really a false god to attraction of his heart, day and night, weekdays and weekends, summer or winter. Like a family member, the toy goes along everywhere. When my mate and I thought of the irony of this, I asked her: "Would you leave your God home when you go on vacation, be it a short or a long time?" False gods, false foundations, can become as precious to the old nature as does the God of Heaven to the new nature when a man is truly born-again.

I stand with the old hymn writer this morning: "How firm a foundation, ye saints of the Lord, is laid for your faith in His excellent Word."

July 12

A bridge or a fence?

This morning I take the liberty to send your way an exact copy of an article I found in "The Bible Friend." Some of us walking in unforgiveness, with a chip on our shoulder or a grudge on our heart over a festering or broken relationship, will find a blessing in building bridges rather than fences in a strained relationship with a mate, a son or daughter, a neighbor, friend or a banker who has said "no." May the Lord bless as we share.

"Once upon a time two brothers who lived on adjoining farms fell into conflict. It was the first serious rift in forty years of farming side by side, sharing machinery, and trading labor and goods as needed without a hitch. Then the long collaboration fell apart. It began with a small misunderstanding and grew into a major difference and finally, it exploded into an exchange of bitter words, followed by weeks of silence.

One morning there was a knock on John's door. He opened it to find a man with a carpenter's toolbox. "I'm looking for a few days' work," he said. "Perhaps you would have a few small jobs here and there that I could help with. Could I help you?" "Yes", said the older brother, "I do have a job for you. Look across the creek at that farm. That's my neighbor, in fact, my brother, younger than me.

Last week there was a meadow between us, and he took his bulldozer to the river levee and now there is a river between us. Well, he may have done this to spite me, but I will go him one better. See that pile of lumber by the barn? I want you to build a fence, an eight-foot high fence, so I won't have to see his place nor his face anymore." The carpenter said: "I think I understand the situation. Show me the nails and post-hole digger, and I'll be able to do a job that pleases you."

The older brother had to go to town, so he helped the carpenter get the materials ready, and then he was off for the day. The carpenter worked hard that day measuring, sawing, and nailing. About sunset, when the farmer returned, the carpenter had just finished his job. The farmer's eyes opened wide, his jaw dropped. There was no fence there at all. It was a bridge, a bridge stretching from one side of the creek to the other. A fine piece of work, handrails and all, and the neighbor, a younger brother, coming across with hand outstretched. "You are quite a fellow to build a bridge after all I have said and done," he said to his brother. They turned to see the carpenter hoist his toolbox to his shoulder. "No, wait" said the older brother, "because I have lots of other projects for you." "I'd love to stay on" the carpenter said, "but I have many more bridges to build."

Reminds me of a more important bridge that Jesus built. I was born alienated from God by a deep gulf greater than our own Grand Canyon because of inherent sin. I was born with my hand clasped in the hand of God's enemy, on the wrong side of the gulf that I could not cross over without a miracle.

Now can we sing with David as we walk forgiven into the throne room: "I will dwell in the secret place of the Most High and abide under the shadow of the Almighty. I will say of the Lord: 'You are my Refuge and my Fortress'..." Psalm 91:1-2.

Praise the Lord for that bridge that brought two enemy brothers together again – Jesus and me!!

July 13

My favorite bird – the eagle!

How exciting is my worship time early in the morning when Psalm 103:5 occasionally ambles out of my memory bank to meditate once more on the "king of the skies," the eagle, the very epitome of size, strength, patience, instinct, beauty, and freedom. I envy the eagle!! Psalm 103:5 says of God in a Word of praise: "He fills my mouth with good things so that my youth is renewed like the eagle's." Maybe it is just an old man's dream of the days of his youth returning! I think of two things God fills our mouth with for our good and blessing—good food for the keeping of our clay body, and then God's Word we share with one another for the keeping of the inner man: "Life unto those who find them, (God's Word) and health unto their flesh." Proverbs 4:22.

As I have driven through the Rockies of Western Montana, my imagination pictures the luxurious life of the eagle, sometimes floating to the right or left; and I imagine the beauty before his eyes as he reaches the summit and rests for a season. Here I picture myself as a Christian, one day a mountain top experience, a time of victory, and the next a deep down valley experience, a trial in life. These I realize to be my real luscious feeding, for growth and maturity is in the valley.

From the summit we see springs of living water flowing quietly down the gorges cut into the soil. That is delicious to the taste buds of an eagle, a deer, an antelope, a person, or a bear, but Jesus tells us of a better, far more lasting water in John 4:13-14, a good, satisfying drink for the little boy or girl inside our clay frame. "Whosoever drinks of this water will thirst again, but whoever drinks of the water I shall give him will never thirst. But the water I shall give him will become in him a fountain of water springing up into everlasting life." We see the pine trees, the evergreens, standing so stately, pointing upward like a man of God looking to and reaching for heaven, his eternal home, the summit.

We see other eagles soaring so freely, companions to fellowship with in either the valley or on the summit, one big family joined together with a common child-like faith in God's Word, our manna from above that sets men free as they eat, digest, and assimilate the goodies to spirit, soul, and body.

Like as with our eagle's keen eye, we see and sense a full meal wherever we look. Like as a rabbit, a gopher, or a mouse is to the eagle, so are our books of Law, Psalm, Proverbs, Prophecies, and the gospels to the child of God, satisfying his hunger.

On the days of severe storm, heavy black clouds, rain, and hail, and wind, the eagle flies to even beyond the summit, above the clouds and into the ever present sun to soar for hours, the same escape we have in the ever present Son to soar for hours, the same escape we have in severe storms of the heart. It's Jesus, the Son of God, just above the heavy black clouds where we may soar freely in the Spirit, and praise Him from Lamentations 3:23: "Because of Your mercies, I am not consumed, because Your compassions never fail, they are new every morning."

Friend, may you soar today as freely as an eagle in the Rockies!!

July 14

"Shorty" Zach, perched in a tree!

Being short of stature can be a very frustrating thing at times, but rewarding at other times, like as with Zachaeus, who planned ahead of time to perch in a tree so that he could see Jesus go by on a certain road. Jesus looked up, saw old Zach, and invited him to come down and take him to his home where a wonderful transformation would take place in a sinner's heart—confession, repentance, and true salvation.

Zacchaeus came down from his lofty physical perch in a tree, matched beautifully by his coming down from his high spiritual perch, from a lofty, proud, arrogant, greedy, dishonest, wealthy tax collector to a humble, contrite disciple of Jesus, "sins of scarlet now white like snow, the sins of crimson red like wool." Isaiah 1:18

This morning I stretched my reach just a bit farther than possible to retrieve the round oatmeal box from a pantry shelf, an experience common to us short of stature, very often seen carrying around a ladder, a footstool, or on the ranch, a five gallon pail turned upside down. As I later rehearsed this frustrating drama in real life, I thought, now this is just what every man, woman, or child in every religion around the world is doing, except Christianity. Millions are reaching up in the inner man, stretching farther than they can reach to come to God for their eternal salvation, to fill that void inside. But to no avail, as they count beads, crawl on their knees, go through rituals, invest their time, talent, and treasure in false hopes, pray to false gods, and gather to worship around a false book, false doctrine, heritage, and tradition. They remain as frustrated as I am when I try to unscrew a light bulb I can't quite reach on tiptoes. On the other hand, Jesus, the central figure of Christianity, relieved us Christians of that frustration when He came down to earth that night in Bethlehem in human flesh. He literally came down to earth from that same Heaven we all want to attain, and, because of His invitation of Matthew 16:24, "deny yourself, take up your cross and follow me." We know He will carry us home to that place He Himself has gone back to, to prepare a room for each of us who have followed him to Calvary, laid down our life, and are now waiting for the trumpet blast and the call of Jesus to "arise," come with Me and be there when "the roll is called up yonder."

Short or tall, we cannot reach heaven by works, for "I am the Way, the Truth, and the Life; no one comes to the Father but by Me." Jesus, John 14:6.

The short and the tall, Jesus raises up to heaven, for "by grace are you saved through faith, not of works, lest anyone should boast." Ephesians 2:8-9.

<u>July 15</u>

"Victory belongs to the Substitute."

Have you ever said or thought, "I wouldn't trade places with him or her?" Or say, "Margarine is a poor substitute for real butter." Or, "Coach, why don't you try to substitute from the bench?" Reminds me of the good old day when the mail order catalogues, Montgomery Ward and Sears Roebuck, were household names across our nation, long before the wholesalers or the big multi-retailers of today. I remember the testimony of one such man of the dirty thirties, living in the boonies where the mailbox was his best friend. He noticed at the bottom of the order from the statement: "If we do not have the article you ordered in stock, may we substitute?" The first time he wrote "yes" they sent him something that was worth double the price of the article he had ordered. The company explained, "We are sorry we do not have the article in stock which you ordered. We are sending something better at our expense." After that, the man said he always printed out more boldly the word "yes" at the bottom of the order blank. He knew he would not be disappointed with the substitution.

Oh, yes, you've guessed what I am coming with. I like that last statement of his testimony, "I knew I would not be disappointed with the substitution." When I read from Isaiah 53, the prophecy later fulfilled to the letter, and find that Jesus, "bore my griefs, carried my sorrows, was stricken for my sin, bruised for my iniquity," I cannot but turn my eyes upon Him, seated this morning at the throne of God, interceding for me. And then enter His gates with thanksgiving and His courts with praise for taking my place, for being my substitute on that cross. Never will I be disappointed. Even my reflection back to Old Testament times when a lamb, a bullock, or a bird were a substitute after a fashion, for the time being, like the man who ordered a product out of stock, and they substituted with something better at "Company expense." As with Jesus, a much better, one-time sacrifice that covered all of humanity from the beginning to the end, a sacrifice that cost the CEO and company, God Himself, a lot more than the previous created substitute.

Are you satisfied this morning to let Jesus, your Substitute on Calvary, be the big "God" in your life today, or have you substituted a lesser god: family, vocation, recreation, money, power, or position, to fill that void inside of you, that emptiness that God purposely created you with to bring your attention, your heart, back to Him by way of the Substitute? He purposely sent His son Jesus, Who confidently and boldly declares in John 14:6, "I am the Way, the Truth, and the Life, no man comes to the Father but by Me." The Psalmist, in chapter 31:14 challenges us, "All you who put your trust in the Lord, be strong and brave." In other words, "Trust in the Lord with all your heart, and lean not unto your own understanding, but acknowledge Him in all your ways, and He will direct your paths." Proverbs 3:5-6.

July 16

"The name of the Lord is a strong tower; the righteous runs into it, and is safe." Proverbs 18:10.

I see here a tall watchtower like we see along a coastline, a brilliantly lighted tower in the center of a courtyard, around which is a very high wall no man can scale, pass through, nor dig under. That wall has only one door, plainly visible to those who hear the call from the tower. Milling around the outer perimeter day after day, a lifetime for most, are the billions of people on earth looking for something or someone to fill an empty void inside, a void caused by lost men being out of relationship with the righteous, Holy God of Heaven, alienated from his Creator.

Those nearest there are closest to the light, like as we Americans with our Christian heritage. The further out ones soon fade into total darkness, like a deer passing through a lighted farmstead and on into the night. Some nations far out are in total darkness because the light hasn't reached out that far yet. It is very noticeable that every so often the door opens and a joyful saint enters the courtyard with thanksgiving in his heart and with praise on his lips, having heard the watchman's call, and having seen the beckoning arm: "Behold, I stand at the door and knock; if any man hears My voice and opens the door I will come in to him and dine with him and he with Me." Revelations 3:20. The call is clear and the response is positive. It is no wonder that in spite of the light and the call and the beckoning arm, that so many blindly pass day after day by the door, since Jesus Himself said: "Only a few will enter therein." The prophet Isaiah, looking forward to that eternal hour and its blessing in chapter 65:19 tells us: "The sound of weeping and crying will be heard no more." But the saint has found in Jesus, the strong Tower, his Refuge, his Fortress, his Shield, his Savior, his Lord, his One and only God – The Way, the Truth, and the Life. There is no more weeping, no broken friendships, no poverty, famine, peril persecution, slander, pain, death, nor bereavement. No more fear, now taken over by love, joy, peace, and security. No more trials, tribulations, temptations, nor storms, but now a sunlight that never dims nor sets behind the horizon, a drink of water from the River of Grace flowing out of the heart of God, never to run dry. No more "grass that withers nor flower that fades." But rather, the "weeping willow," now a palm branch, victory, and weeping eyes now turned into bright pearls of eternal joy and bliss.

"What a day that will be when my Jesus I shall see,
And I look upon His Face – the One Who saved me by His grace.
When He takes me by the hand, and leads me through the Promised Land,
What a day, what a glorious day that will be."

July 17

"Oh death, where is your sting?" I Corinthians 15:55

Early one frigid morning in February 1950, parents Mel and Marian awakened to the tragic news that their twenty-year old son had been killed on a mountain highway near Bozeman, Montana, one of six university students killed as their car left the pavement on a sharp curve, and landed upside down on a railroad track many feet below. The shocking news of that death of such a popular, handsome, top student scholastically, excellent athlete, full of musical talent, and an almost unblemished character, put a heavy cloud over our town that cold wintry day, socked in by snow banks on every side. That day, I saw Philippians 4:6-7 lived out to the fullest in that dad's heart. The scripture says: "Be anxious for nothing, but in all things, by prayer and supplication, with thanksgiving, make your requests be known to God, and the peace of God which passes all understanding shall keep your hearts and minds in Christ Jesus." That Godly dad, from a truly thankful heart, made a public testimony of his faith and thanksgiving when he said, "I have enjoyed my son for twenty years, while others have had no son at all." Harvey was an only son, whose unselfish dad gave back to his Creator with thanksgiving in his heart for a twenty-year cozy relationship, now severed until they meet again in heaven.

In I Samuel 1, we find Hannah so troubled, discouraged, anxious, and worried because she was barren, her womb shut up, and wanting a son more than anything else in life. She did the correct, sensible thing when she continually entered the tabernacle of the Lord and laid out her case before the Lord. "Come now, let us reason together" was the tenor of her prayer and supplication. When Hannah was moved in her spirit to vow that she would "give him back to the Lord all the days of his life," her anxiety and worry miraculously lifted "and her face was no longer sad" Vs. 18. "Be anxious for nothing, but by prayer and supplication..." and her life went on. She then conceived and bore a son, and when weaned at three years of age, she kept her vow, and took that son, now dedicated back to God, and she spoke these words of praise from her joyful heart:

"My heart rejoices in the Lord;
   My strength is exalted in the Lord...
   There is none holy like the Lord, for
   There is none besides You, nor is there
   Any Rock like our God." I Samuel 2:1-2

All He asks and expects is that we pray with supplication from a heart of thanksgiving! Can you face life this morning with a heavy load like Mel and Hannah lived under, and still sing out with David from Psalm 100?

"Make a joyful sound unto the Lord, all you lands,
   Serve Him with gladness,
   Come before His presence with singing."

I hear Him loud and clear from II Chronicles 20:15: "do not fear or be dismayed, for the battle is not yours, but God's."

With Him at our side, let us fight the battle with thanksgiving and praise!

July 18

"The heart of man is desperately wicked, and deceitful above all things." Jeremiah 17:9

In a spirit of heartfelt revenge on a quiet Saturday afternoon, my brother and I took pleasure in destroying a Model T Ford windshield. We had been left home by our dad when he went on a regular Saturday afternoon shopping and socializing trip to town. Hidden from mother's view by a granary, we stood in the middle of our graveled yard and hurled pebbles into the perfect windshield of a vehicle housed in a machine shed open on our side. Inner anger and pouting turned to revenge!! I often wonder how long it took Dad to find that front seat plastered with glass. We never heard from him.

"Why such a heinous act?" one might ask. Only because we were born with "desperately wicked hearts, born without genuine love, love enough to forgive and go on". It was years later, when I had surrendered to Jesus that I would confess that sin from a truly repentant heart and be forgiven, "cleansed from all unrighteousness." I John 1:9

So it was with twin brothers Esau and Jacob found in Genesis 25. Esau was the oldest because of his first birth that day. Being the oldest, Esau was therefore entitled to a special birthright by law and a blessing from his father Isaac (Genesis 25:9). Both boys were born like my brother and I were: "desperately wicked and deceitful," because of inherent sin, "born dead in trespass and sin" Ephesians 2:1. Jacob, born of a naturally deceitful mother, inherited that ugly virtue, and his name means "deceiver." Esau loved the things of the flesh and lived for the glitter of this world. Recognizing this weakness, Jacob and his deceitful mother devised a plot, a plan against Esau, daddy's boy. Vs. 28. That eventually cost him his inheritance and his special fatherly blessing. He sold his soul for a bowl of soup! Upon realizing the trickery, revenge built up in his heart to the point of murder for his brother. Why? He had an untamed heart like Jacob, "desperately wicked, and deceitful above all things." Running for his life, Jacob found welcome refuge with Uncle Laban many miles away.

Here we see a sad dilemma: twin brothers, one with bitter revenge in his heart, the other unrepentant, with fear raging in his heart. "Desperately wicked, deceitful hearts." Jeremiah 39:7.

Twenty years later God entered the picture in a real way, and commanded Jacob to "go back home" and face the music, vs. 31:3. "Take your two families and your flocks and herds and head back", God told Jacob. On the way back, God did for Jacob what he did for me years after my act of revenge, He provided a moment of meeting Jesus face to face and an opportunity to confess his sin from a truly repentant heart, and bring also a blessing unto his brother. At the fork of the River Jabok, Jacob wrestled with a Divine Power all night long, and wouldn't let go until he was set free from his deceitfulness, vs. 3:23. Esau, on his way to meet Jacob with four hundred men, was also touched by the hand of God, causing his heart to melt. When the twins met, after twenty years, they embraced with hearts of forgiveness for one another. "If my people which are called by My name will humble themselves and pray, and seek My face, and turn from their wicked ways, I will Hear them from Heaven, I will forgive their sins, and heal their land." II Chronicles 7:14.

July 19

"Its inhabitants are like grasshoppers." Isaiah 40:22

Years ago, I read from Isaiah 40:22 a rather amusing word: "It is He Who sits above the circle of the earth, and its inhabitants are like grasshoppers." Being like a grasshopper is not very flattering to one who has spent most of his life in "grasshopper land" out on the farm. I have paid attention, studying grasshoppers to get an idea of what the Lord might mean by "seeing earth's inhabitants as grasshoppers." They are extremely destructive, hatching in springtime in grassland beside a crop of wheat that is just emerging from the ground, only to move in swarms, hardly visible, and then blacken a field of green wheat in only hours. They have no direction, flitting about from post to post. They are messy with their excreta, and feel like misguided bullets when they strike a man's face or a windshield or a headlight when full grown. They multiply fast, but are short-lived. They are foolish, slow in the brain, and stupid enough to perch on the combine reel and on into the machine they go. I have seen them so thick in the sky above that they cut off the sun like a cloud, and so thick on a pavement that they make it slippery to drive on. Their primary interest in life is to fill their belly, and then proudly display themselves as some beauty to look at. The only worth I ever see in a grasshopper is to become a lush meal for a turkey out on the range or in the barnyard.

Not a very flattering picture does God see: unstable, flighty, destructive, foolish, proud, short-lived, fleshly, quite often cliquish, with no real purpose in life unless a hungry turkey captures and kills. In our old nature, that must be the picture God sees when He sees us as grasshoppers. Vs. 23 pretty well sums it up: "He brings the princes to nothing; He makes the judges of the earth useless."

As depressing as it may seem, our God "does not leave us nor forsake us" as believers, but gives the prophet a positive note in Isaiah 41:10: "Fear not, for I am with you; be not dismayed, for I am your God. I will strengthen you, yes, I will help you' I will uphold you with My righteous right hand."

The best of all is when Jesus comes on deck in this day of grace from Luke 4:18: "The Spirit of the Lord is upon Me; I have been anointed to preach good news to the poor, to heal the brokenhearted, to set the captives free, to restore sight to the blind, and to set free those who are bruised."

May the Lord bless your flitting about today, fellow "grasshopper inhabitant."

July 20

"Life is but a vapor." James 4:14

On our way home from Grand Forks, ND, where we celebrated with a friend her 100th birthday, I could not help but PTL (Praise the Lord) for her long life on this earth, for a countenance that betrays her age by perhaps forty years, a super healthy body still pretty much free of prescription drugs, a mind as clear as a bell, her senses all working reasonably well, and that same old Swedish charisma I saw in her over 25 years ago. Two years ago she cheerfully and voluntarily handed her car keys to her daughter, but still lives alone, and tends to her apartment herself. Mathilda made my day, and blessed me, her junior by more than two decades.

Then the inevitable happened as we drove toward home when the name of Caleb came swirling out of the Old Testament book of Joshua, and I began to rehearse to myself once again the familiar story of that faithful 85 year old positive man of God, with a testimony much like Mathilda's. Here it is from Joshua 14, beginning with vs. 7: "I was forty years old when Moses, the servant of the Lord, sent me from Kadesh-Barnea to spy out the land. I brought back Word to him as it was in my heart...So Moses swore on that day, saying 'Surely the land on which your foot has trodden shall be your inheritance and your children's forever, because you have wholly followed the Lord my God.' And now, behold, the Lord has kept me alive, as He said, these forty-five years...and now, here I am this day, eighty-five years old. As yet, I am as strong as I was on the day that Moses sent me; just as my strength was then, so now is my strength for war, both for going out and coming in. Now, therefore, give me this mountain of which the Lord spoke in that day; for you heard in that day how Anakim (giants) were there, and that the cities were great and fortified. It may be that the Lord will be with me, and I shall be able to drive them out as the Lord said. And Joshua blessed him, and gave Hebron to Caleb as an inheritance...to this day, because he wholly followed the Lord God of Israel."

I hear our Lord this morning from Deuteronomy 30:19-20: "I call heaven and earth as witnesses today against you, that I have set before you life and death, blessing and cursing; therefore choose life that both you and your descendants may live; that you may love the Lord your God, that you may obey His voice, and that you may cling to Him, for He is your life and the length of your days..."

July 21

"Search me, oh Lord, and know my heart..." Psalm 139:23.

    I once had two ungodly, very proud, greedy neighbors who lived side by side, despising one another for many years. As a teenager, I had occasion to hire out to either of them from time to time in the busy season. Both evidently loved painted buildings and the show business for those driving by to see. I was shocked when I saw the backside of both sets of farmsteads unpainted, and the siding deprecating from the weather.
    As I learned to know myself, the real me, and other people around me later in life, I saw an analogy I'll never forget...the "unpainted" backside. I saw myself like that and many others, the little boy or girl inside looking good on the public side of the heart, but shabby, undecorated on the backside, the hidden side. Serious business according to I Samuel 16:7 "For the Lord does not see as man sees, for man looks at the outward appearance, but the Lord looks at the heart."
    One of my most frequent early-morning prayers is found in Psalm 139:23-24: "Search me, oh Lord, and know my heart; try me and know my thoughts, and see if there is any wicked way within me; and lead me in Thy way everlasting." Almost immediately, one such morning, a friend's face appeared before me while I was waiting on the Lord. And along with the face, Romans 13:8: "Owe no man anything but to love him, for he who loves another has fulfilled the law." Conviction came upon me immediately as I remembered a financial help that friend had blessed me with years ago, and which was very loosely, carelessly handled, not yet repaid, but forgotten. A gentleman's agreement it was as we trusted one another. On top of that conviction came three more from the Word of God: "If I regard iniquity in my heart, He will not hear me." Psalm 66:11. Prayers squelched, and I am between a rock and a hard spot! Now, the ball is in my hand, the choice mine, since I've prayed "search me...both my heart and my mind." Now is my memory bank revealing a truth that a deceitful heart could easily continue to cover up. It was good

looking on the front side of the testimony, but depreciated, unpainted on the back side, that only Omni God could see and reveal.

The second Word of scripture that came to my memory was from Psalm 119:11: "Thy Word have I hidden in my heart, that I sin not." And the third: "Be sure your sin will find you out." Numbers 32:23.

July 22

"The Lord is my refuge and my strength, a very present help in time of trouble." Psalm 46:1

Oh how many elderly people in my circle of acquaintances have literally dug their own graves as they face their loneliness without a mate, their ailing bodies without hope, their lean days ahead without savings, their wayward child with tons of guilt and condemnation weighting them down. Bernice said: "No, God is too busy to be bothered with me and my troubles" as I stood beside her hospital bed, and offered to pray for her recovery. Francis worried herself to a quick death when left alone with all their savings now spent on her husband's lingering bout with cancer. Pete passed away rather suddenly, and his mate never again left her home, even for shopping, until death soon consumed her.

In I Samuel 19 we find a similar, typical, pitiful situation where a man named Barzillai, eighty years old, expecting death any day. His senses of discernment, taste, hearing, and sight all dimmed, forsaken, living in a certain bit of despair, waiting to die and be planted in the family plot at the cemetery. Beginning with verse 34: "How long have I to live?" he asked King David, "...I am today eighty years old...please let your servant turn back again, that I may die in my own city, and be buried by the graves of my father and mother"...the king kissed Barzillai and blessed him, and he returned to his own place." What a sad eulogy. I am thrilled to find in God's Word an antidote for the Barzilla syndrome that is today driving many good people into depression.

From Psalm 103:5: "Bless the Lord, oh my soul, and forget not all His benefits...who satisfies my mouth with good things so that my youth is renewed liked the eagle's." Good food to my mouth that nurtures my body, and good Words from my mouth which sustain the soul. The old eagle's beak has grown to cover his mouth, and is therefore no longer able to pick and pluck food. So, he finds a perch on a rock and waits for death to come. As could be expected, the old starving patriarch is losing weight, becoming thin, his head drooping, no more sparkle in his eyes, nor cackle in his voice. Just hanging in there! So, the young see his deplorable situation, and bring food to him instinctively, and as it piles up before his dimming eyes, his salivary glands begin functioning again, and adrenalin furiously floods his being, and encouraged, he begins to frantically file down his beak against the rock until he can once more pick and pluck food and turn his life around so that "his youth is renewed."

"My son, give attention to My Word...life unto those who find it, and health unto their flesh." Proverbs 4:20:1, 5.

July 23

"God has not given us a spirit of fear, but of love, power, and a sound mind." II Timothy 1:7.

A few days ago I saw the report of an experiment dealing with the high blood pressure problem in people across America today, relative to the effect fear has. A mouse was secured in a cage in a room, and a cat secured in another cage across the room, but in plain sight of the mouse. The experiment went on for several months, and never once did either the cat or mouse get out of their respective cages. The blood pressure of the mouse was tabulated daily, and it was noted to be escalating daily at a noticeable rate, the experiment proving how much effect fear has on blood pressure. If the experiment had lasted indefinitely, the mouse would eventually have died of blood pressure complications, just living in fear of something that never did come to pass. Only when the caretaker ended the experiment and freed the mouse from that dreadful fear did life become normal again. If the mouse could have put his faith in anything but himself, and his negative thoughts and fears and experiences of his old nature and his past; if only he could have seen the picture as it really was (safe as a bug in a rug), but fear and worry stole his joy and with it his health. "Be anxious for nothing, but in all things, by prayer and supplication, with thanksgiving, let your requests be known to God, and the peace of God, which passes all understanding, will be yours in Christ Jesus." Philippians 4:6-7.

As I thought of this plight of fear, I turned to I Samuel 17 and the story of David and giant Goliath; David, a little shepherd boy with a sling and a pebble interceding for a nation bound in fear and despair over the boasting, strutting, and bragging of a Philistine named Goliath, who had literally made the nation of Israel immobile. They were petrified, scared stiff, totally discouraged and demoralized, full of fear, hiding in caves.

So it was with the Israelites hovering together in fear, worrying about the power of the nine foot giant in full armor, a proud spirit, a threatening tongue. In their own power, nothing to do but fear, worry, and wait and let the blood pressure continually rise. Then the Lord came into the picture in the person of little David with no armor, only a sling and a pebble and a testimony of the miraculous power of God. David to Goliath: "You come to me with a sword, with a spear, and with a javelin. But I come to you in the name of the Lord of hosts, the God of the armies of Israel, whom you have defiled." I Samuel 17:45. His shepherding days of taking on a lion and a bear became his confidence and testimony, giving God the praise.

"Do not fear nor be dismayed, for the battle is not yours, but God's." II Chronicles 20:15. "Call upon Me and I will answer you and show you great and mighty things you do not know." Jeremiah 33:3. "Trust in the Lord with all your heart, and lean not unto you own understanding; acknowledge Him in all your ways, and He will direct your paths." Proverbs 3:5-6.

July 24

"My people perish for lack of knowledge." Hosea 4:6

Only ten days after my high school graduation in 1943, I enrolled at the University of Minnesota, 800 miles away – long miles for a Montana farm boy! I was awaiting my eighteenth birthday, my date with Uncle Sam in W.W.II days. Why? To prepare for a vocation; knowledge I would glean from textbooks, the wisdom of instructors, and some on-the-job training. I had an Oriental female neighbor here who came from far away Hong Kong to earn degrees in the medical world. Thousands of students flood our colleges and universities annually from far-off lands to gain knowledge, wisdom, and degrees in this wonderful land of freedom they have all heard about. Secular knowledge and wisdom are so desirous and attainable, but what about an interest in the inner man's needs?

Reading from I Kings 10, we find a woman, driven by the impulse of the inner man, named Queen of Sheba, who reigned over present day Yemen centuries ago. She must have been troubled like every one of us are from our mother's womb, troubled in her soul about truth in life's biggest questions: God, the future, life's purpose, death, and destiny, and had no answers. Sound familiar? You see, in her early lifetime, she was desperate for truth that would set her free in her soul, truth that would satisfy with a sense of peace, that void, that emptiness God has blessed each of us with for a purpose – to be filled with flesh or the Spirit. She heard of the man Solomon, purported as "the wisest man on earth," a blessing God gave him when he asked for it in the days of his youth. One day the Queen set out in a caravan toward Jerusalem, fifteen hundred miles away, a seventy-five day journey. Determined to get to Solomon at any cost, the caravan passed through a hot desert, amidst unmerciful bandits, across lots of barren terrain, short of water, enduring cold nights. Nothing could stop the Queen from filling her hungry soul with wisdom and answers. Oh, that we might all have a testimony like hers for zeal, perseverance, and even sacrifice for that Truth that sets men free.

"She came to prove him with hard questions...and when she was come to Solomon, she communed with him of all that was in her heart." I Kings 10:1. "So Solomon answered all her questions; there was nothing so difficult for the king that he could not explain it to her." (Vs. 3) Imagine the satisfaction, the love, joy, peace, and security that flooded her soul when all her life-long questions were put to rest, one at a time.

"My people are destroyed for lack of knowledge." Hosea 4:6.

"Fools die for lack of wisdom." Proverbs 10:21b

Think of how easy it has been here in America, a nation built on Christian principals and faith in Jesus Christ, to find knowledge that fosters understanding which creates Godly wisdom, Proverbs 8. And yet, millions have passed it by, let it slip away, while basking in the sun of that which will not last, nor answer the eternal quest.

"My grace is sufficient for you…" Grab it, my friend, and take hold!

July 25

"Come."

Did you ever notice on TV that Malabo, Jackson, and others handcuffed are always being driven, pushed ahead, and compelled by the law to command? I see here a lesson for us who are truly born again, set free from out inherent sin – we hear the Lord, now in command, leading us, "Come" over and over again.

Did you ever notice the law: it measures how far man falls short in his old nature he is born with, in his broken relationship with a holy, righteous God? The gospel, grace, however, measures how close, how intimate, we are to that same God. The gospel of grace bridges that void, that chasm, and becomes the bridge that lost man, under the law, crosses over the gulf into the presence of a holy, righteous God. The law says you cannot get close to God, whereas grace says you cannot get away from God. Under the law, man tries to climb up to God by keeping the law, whereas under grace God comes down to earth to meet man right here.

It's: "Come up to Heaven; go down to eternal destruction into Hell." On the western ranch men on saddle horse drive their cattle to the corral, while they lead their sheep, with a trained dog to bring the stragglers. Could that be why Jesus calls us "sheep"? "…the doorkeeper opens and the sheep hear his voice; and he calls his sheep by name and leads them out. And when he brings out his own sheep he goes before them; and the sheep follow him, for they know his voice…I am the good Shepherd, and I know My sheep, and am known by My own." John 10:3-4, 14.

I hear the Good Shepherd this morning:
"Come to Me, your refuge (protector and provider)"
"Come to Me, your fortress (rock of Gibraltar)"
"Come to Me, your shield of faith, and I will absorb the darts of the enemy."

"If any man would come after Me, let him deny himself, take up his cross, and follow Me" – clear to the cross on Calvary where Jesus gave His all, became our Savior, our Lord to follow, our One and Only God; perfect denial of self, bathed in the blood of Jesus.

Still, one more invitation from the precious voice of Jesus in the sweet hour of death, "Come, you blessed of My Father, enter in" – as the gates of Heaven fling open we enter with thanksgiving in our hearts and praise on our lips. While waiting for that glorious day ahead, while still sojourning on this earth, we hear Him say in the final Words of the last chapter: "Surely I am coming quickly!" And we respond: "Amen, even so come, Lord Jesus."

July 26

Availability better than ability!

Good morning to everyone whom the Lord has already tucked away into His bosom for eternity, also to the one whom the Holy Spirit has not yet given up on, in either case, one whom God loves so much that He will go to any extreme of patience to bring the lost into His bosom now while there is still time. "For God so loved the world that He gave His only begotten Son, that whosoever believes on Him shall not perish, but have everlasting life." Friends, that is good news I can back up with my own testimony and that of many others, some in the scriptures, many most unlikely people surrounding Jesus, willing to serve Him.

As I watch the political wrestling match in Washington D.C. these days, I see how all important credentials are in the eyes of a powerful government when it selects people for key posts of service. It takes college degrees, big bucks, and usually a good long service to the party. On and on goes the list for the white-collared people in dress suits. But how different so often with Jesus when He looks over the population for someone to serve Him best here on earth. I am reminded of this from Mark 1:16-20: "...Simon and his brother were fishermen; then Jesus said to them: Come after Me and I will make you fishers of men. He saw James and John, his brother...He called them...and they went after Him." Oh how many farmers, carpenters, clerks, sales people, young and old, rich and poor, and even prisoners who have heard Him call them, and they have followed Him. Even Jesus Himself came from a lowly carpenter's family, born in a manger in a tiny, insignificant town. He chose His followers while walking down a dusty trail alongside a lake, rather than on the sidewalks in front of a divinity school, the scholars of His day. Nor on a trip to a military academy or from a school of political science or homiletics, but rather unkempt fishermen, Peter, Andrew, James, and John. How could He even possibly dream of one day ahead planting His church on earth with such unlikely credentials?? I have noticed that even today and times just past that God has used the unlikely, the likes of Billy Sunday, the baseball player; D.L. Moody the shoe salesman, and Corrie Ten Boom, a WWII POW, all going out with only lay experience with the Word of God and hearts transformed. And what about our own Kirk Flaa, a tire salesman, the POW, and the tire salesman were people anointed of God. And that's what makes the real difference, the real power behind the ministry of each.

At the foot of the cross where repentance takes place and salvation is secured, we are all equal, "the playing field is level." "Hear Me, oh Judah and you inhabitants of Jerusalem...believe in the Lord, your God, and you shall be established, believe His prophets and you shall prosper." II Chronicles 20:20.

July 27

"The name of the Lord is a strong tower and the righteous runs into it and is safe." Proverbs 18:10

On a nice warm, sunny morning while dong some fieldwork, I was rehearsing from memory Proverbs 18:10. Out in the center of a large field, I was turning my tractor for a final round, and a young rabbit darted quickly into my sight, and about that same time, a hawk swooped down out of the sky and rolled the rabbit over. I stopped to watch the scenario. He jumped up and ran again and was once more rolled over. He was headed straight toward a tall, dead weed that would make a haven of safety. I sat in the tractor cab pulling with all my emotional might for the young rabbit, even to yelling "stop under the big weed, and rest, and wait out the ordeal." But instead, he ran quickly by, trying to reach some brush on the far edge of the field. The inevitable happened when another roll or two exhausted the rabbit, and then the death blow and the hawk came down to the ground, put his talon on the rabbit, and enjoyed a nice warm meal.

"The thief has come to kill, steal, and destroy." John 10:10. Like the rabbit, many people are running through life without Jesus, running past a could-be haven of rest. "The name of the Lord is a strong tower." While running, the enemy is rolling them over with sickness, marital problems, financial stress, and addictions. Unless the man comes to Jesus and finds protection in the person and name of Jesus, the enemy will destroy him into eternity.

"Wild Bill" was like that, a very energetic, ambitious, successful grain farmer, but addicted to gambling, booze, and occasional fisticuffs. His long winter months of leisure wrecked havoc against him. Determined to gamble with the "big boys" for big stakes, he set out for Kansas City, a man running from God, refusing the tower where his wife and church were praying for him and his salvation. Arriving in Kansas City, tired and at a late hour, he went to his motel room, satisfied to wait for morning and the "big boys." When he searched for something to read, he found only a Gideon Bible in his room. That Bible became his introduction into the "strong tower," the Name of the Lord. On his knees beside his bed now soaked with tears of conviction, joy, confession, and repentance, "Wild Bill" surrendered. On the morrow, he arose, ate breakfast and headed back for Montana. "a brand new creation, old things passed away, and all things become new." II Corinthians 5:17.

"I will say of the Lord...He is my refuge and my fortress, my God; in Him I will trust." Psalms 91:2.

"I created you, oh Jacob, and I formed you, oh Israel; fear not, for I have redeemed you; I have called you by your name; you are

Mine; so that when you pass through the waters I will be with you, and through the rivers, they shall not overflow you. When you walk through the fires, you shall not be burned, nor shall the flames even scorch you, for I am the Lord your God, the God of Israel, you Savior." Isaiah 43:1-3.

If you need a haven of rest today for your inner being, try Jesus, the strong tower of Proverbs 18:10.

July 28

"...let him deny himself..." Matthew 16:24

As I was enjoying my private, personal time with the Lord this morning, reading from Psalm 119:97-104, and meditating on the message, I suddenly noticed a stark contrast in the using of the Word "I" when I thought of another from Isaiah 14 where we read of Lucifer. One illustrates the power of God to lift up and edify, the obedient one, and the other illustrates God's power to put down and destroy the disobedient. Both stemming from the attitude of the heart, I counted nine "I's" in the Psalm of blessing for the obedient, and five in the destruction of God's enemy Lucifer, whom He cursed. When we lay them side by side, we see the tremendous importance of choice: one unto life, and the other unto death "Life and death are in the power of the tongue, and they that love it shall eat of its fruit." Proverbs 18:21. They that love and confess life with their tongue shall eat of the fruit of life, and they that confess death shall eat of the fruit of death.

"A good man, out of the treasure of his heart, brings forth good, and an evil man, out of the evil of his heart brings forth evil." "For out of the abundance of the heart his mouth speaks." – the psalmist of God and Lucifer of self.

"Keep your heart with all diligence, for out of it flow the issues of life." The humble psalmist sees the power of God in his life through His Word. On the contrary is the heart of a proud egotist, without God, we find in Lucifer in Isaiah 14:12-15.

"How you are fallen from Heaven, O Lucifer, son of the morning! How you are cut down to the ground, you who weakened the nations.

For you have said in your heart: 'I will ascend into Heaven; I will exalt my throne above the stars of God; I will also sit on the mount of the congregation of the farthest sides of the north; I will ascend above the heights of the clouds; I will be like the Most High. Yet, shall be brought down to Sheol, to the lowest depths of the Pit.'"

"Thy Word have I hidden in my heart, that I sin not against You." Psalm 119:11.

Oh, that we might rid ourselves of that "me-first" syndrome!

July 29

My Reachable Jesus!

Good morning to each friend who is literally reaching out with me to touch the "Reachable Jesus" this day, reachable because the Holy Spirit lives in us and about us, reachable as we put our hand in His with child-like faith, and walk another mile across this old earth as a pilgrim headed for a promised land, but traveling on a bumpy road just like Jesus Himself traveled on this same earth. "For we do not have a High Priest Who cannot sympathize with our weaknesses, too, was headed back to the Promised Land where He would prepare a dinner table and a room for every believer." His hand has led—the "Reachable Jesus." And all this because of the bump in the road to Calvary.

My oh my, how they came to Him along the shores of Galilee, and out into the mountains, and on the dusty trails of Canaan to eat of the Bread of Life. Repentant Zacchaeus came to Him from up in a tree for redemption. Nicodemus came at night for counsel, and the woman with the issue of blood came in the crowded street just to touch the hem of His garment for physical healing. Martha and Mary and the two men on the road to Emmaus invited Him into their homes for fellowship—the "Reachable Jesus." Peter walked on the waters with unmatched faith to the "Reachable Jesus," his haven of rest in a storm. Children were placed at His feet, and we hear Him: "Suffer the little children to come unto Me, and forbid them not." Why all this?

Because He was the Living Water offered to the Samaritan woman by the well in John 4, not a mannequin, a statue, nor a stoic priest in an elevated pulpit like I often saw in churches in Norway. He was not to be a dead man's bones lying in an earthen grave, but a resurrected man, a "Reachable Jesus" for now and for eternity, touchable and approachable.

I see this all lived out before our eyes again this morning of another Lenten season and all the Good Friday implications, where we see three crosses on the hill at Calvary: Jesus, a Savior, on the center cross; one thief, a dying sinner on one side, and another thief, now a saint, on the other side. All three crosses on level ground, all men considered criminals but close enough for the repentant thief to reach out to Jesus with a plea: "Remember Me." And then Jesus with a message that would sound like music to his ear: "This day will you be with Me in Paradise."

Have you reached out for the hand of the "Reachable Jesus" for salvation, fellowship, deliverance, or healing? "Behold, I stand at the door and knock; if anyone hears My voice and will open the door, I will come in and sup with him and he with Me." Revelations 3:20.

The "Reachable Jesus" is found in GOD'S Word, HIS LOVE LETTER TO YOU AND TO ME, HIS VOICE BOX, HIS ROADMAP.

July 30

A ladder has its place, but be careful.

A ladder can be very dangerous, even deadly! I once had a homemade, very old ladder, whose wooden rungs were severely weathered, and the nail holes so enlarged that the rungs were wobbly. It laid beside my grain bin year after year until I feared using it, lest a rung should break. A neighbor extended his aluminum ladder to the top of a steel grain bin, only to find himself stranded when the wind blew the ladder down while he was inside the bin. Another climbed up to service an extremely high bin, and while stretching to shut a port on the bin roof, the ladder easily slid on the metal ridge and his fall hurt him severely, effects even unto this day.

That's the way it is with everyone who tries to reach God by climbing up to Him with good works, by keeping the law only, by bypassing Jesus; inevitable shipwreck, pain, and eternal destruction. "The wages of sin is death." Romans 6:23. "For by grace have you been saved through faith, and that not of yourselves; it is the gift of God, not of works, lest anyone should boast." Ephesians 2:8-9. When the ladder fails, it is eternal death.

"The thief has come but for to kill, steal, and destroy, but I have come to give life, and to give it abundantly." Jesus, John 10:10. "I am the Way, the Truth, and the Life; no one comes to the Father but by Me." John 14:6.

How different from all other faiths is Christianity, where God came down from Heaven through His Son Jesus, Who finds us individually, and promises to carry us in His arms back to Heaven for everlasting life. Here I see myself riding an escalator at that time, not a ladder as a means of ascension, solidly in place, no effort on my part; yet quickly and easily do I arrive like the beggar we read of in Luke 17. When he died, "was carried by the angel to Abraham's bosom." The ungodly rich man, clothed in purple and fine linen, fared sumptuously every day "...died and was buried." His false gods, earthly riches, pride, selfishness, greed, and power lifted him up for a short time of pleasure on this earth, but then a deadly fall when his ladder gave way. "Being in torment in Hades, he lifted up his eyes and saw Abraham afar off, and Lazarus in his bosom." "Between us and you there is a deep gulf fixed, so that those who want to pass from here to you cannot, nor can those from there pass to us."

The ladder rung will break; another will blow over in the wind, and carelessness and gamble will send another hard to the ground and destruction. Ladders we try to climb reaching up to false gods are as deadly as a mirage can be on a sultry afternoon on a far off desert. "Therefore humble yourselves...that He may exalt you in due time...be sober, be vigilant, because your adversary, the devil, walks around seeing whom he may devour." I Peter 5:8.

July 31

"The wrath of man does not produce the righteousness of God." James 1:20.

How many marriages, family relationships, social affairs, business dealings, and even sports contests could be so different if wrath (anger, explosive temper) would never emerge in an effort to set someone else straight. It never works because of the Godly principal of James 1:20. How different it would have been for us today had Jesus, as a man, during that Good Friday afternoon been tempted to rail out in self pity, and despair and wrath upon man: "It's because of You vipers that I am put to death on this cross, where your sin causes Me pain, humility, and embarrassment, and even separation from My Father for a season, and beating and shedding of my blood." But think rather of how that Godly love, that agape love we cannot fathom today, but will be part of in Heaven, overcame any such notion of "wrath of man," but rather "peace upon man." "Now the fruit of righteousness is sown in peace by those who make peace." James 3:18. "It is because of Your mercies that we are not consumed, because Your compassions never fail..." Lamentations 3:23. Both testimonies are for the redeemed to stand on securely.

In Matthew 18 Jesus uses a parable to teach us the blessing of laying wrath aside in behalf of the "fruit of righteousness." A certain king called before him those who owed him money, and he made it clear that now is the time to settle accounts. "And when he had begun to settle accounts, one was brought to him who owed him ten thousand talents. But, as he was not able to pay, his master commanded that he be sold, with his wife and children, and all that he had, and that payment be made (wrath). The servant therefore fell down before him saying: "Master, have mercy on me and I will pay you all." Then, "the master of that servant was moved with compassion and released him and forgave the debt." "The fruit of righteousness is sown in peace by those who make peace." James 3:18.

I have a friend who is bearing persecution big time at his work place. I admire how well he is coping with it, even though it hurts right to the core of the heart. He is a Godly man, practicing the good counsel of James 1:19: "Therefore my beloved brethren, let every man be swift to hear, slow to speak, slow to wrath, for the wrath of man does not produce the righteousness of God." But rather, the patient, forgiving heart produces the "fruit of righteousness... peace by those who make peace."

"Love your enemies; bless them that curse you; do good to them that hate you; pray for them that spitefully use you, and for them that persecute you." Jesus, Matthew 5:14.

August 1

Tainted thing...

A lively discussion was aroused in my Junior High Sunday School class out in Montana when I asked if the money that a bar owner in our congregation was "tainted money," acceptable to the Lord as it was deposited in the offering as a worship unto the Lord. A grocer's son argued that it was tainted, since liquor is a destructive, unhealthy drink for the body. The banker's son then reminded the grocer's son that those who over eat food or eat the wrong kind of food also hurt their bodies. Then another chimed in and reminded the banker's son that his dad's money is also tainted since he loans money to both the bar owner and the grocery man, and the interest money must be also tainted. A bit ridiculous, but thought provoking for a few minutes! This all came back to my memory when I read from Ezra 4:1-5, where the descendants of the seventy-year captivity of the Israelites were restoring the temple of the Lord that had been destroyed by King Nebuccadnezzar and his armies. Remnants of the enemy forces came to the rebuilders of the temple and said: "Let us build with you, for we seek our God as you do, and have sacrificed to Him." Ezra 4:1. The King and the heads of the rebuilders rejected the offer because they were found to be Samaritans, a race born out of non-Jews and Israelite women, and now because of that were enemies of the genuine Israelites, "tainted people." They were people who "feared the Lord, yet served their own gods." In today's church we also often find man-made rituals of worship that become more the center of worship than worship of the God of Heaven Himself from a pure, clean, transformed, redeemed heart that knows and loves and fears and worships the God of Heaven, our Creator, our Protector, and our Security for now and for eternity. They "feared the Lord, yet served their own gods."

Any of us, too, may fear the Lord, love Him, and even worship Him, but with "tainted hearts" as we idolize our mates, our family, our vocation, our hobby, our entertainment and recreational world, or a besetting sin we cannot really let go of a kingdom being built on this earth, like the rebuilders of the temple in Jerusalem, are hindered of the Lord's best blessing when they take communion on Sunday morning and by dusk are back at their same old lifestyle of fornication, adultery, drinking and a host of other "no-no's" in God's sight, "tainted believers."

"The Lord does not see as man sees; for man looks at the outward appearance, but the Lord looks at the heart." I Samuel 16:7.

August 2

"...leaning on Jesus' bosom..." John 13:13

On TV I saw the car that had slid on ice over an embankment, unnoticed, but found five days later. The driver, a mother, was dead, and cuddled beside her was her small child, covered with a blanket, and surviving on crackers, severely dehydrated and frost bitten, but still very much alive. This recovery reminded me of a sad, heartbreaking experience when I came upon a lamb's dead mother, the lamb still alive. She had been dead several days, lying out in the hot July sun until disintegration, decay, and the evidence of maggots. Cuddled up against that deteriorating body was her lamb, very gaunt, his coat unbearably offensive to my sense of smell, very weak, but oh so attached and loyal, never giving up to stray away, but ready and willing to perish literally inside his mother's bosom.

Oh, that children of God, to the last one, could be found like that lamb or that small child, cuddled up in the bosom of Jesus, with child-like faith, persevering, trusting God's principals and promises: "My Word...life unto those who find it and health unto their flesh." Proverbs 4:23.

In II Samuel 9 we find King David taking into his bosom one needing love, one cursed from birth, one in need of a refuge like an orphan child or a gaunt lamb needed. Years after King Saul's demise, King David found Saul's grandson Mephibosheth, a cripple from birth, and his heart went out to him. He was son of Jonathan, whom King David loved and with whom he had covenanted in that love. Now, the reality, the pay-off: "Mephibosheth shall eat at my table like one of the king's sons." Vs. 11.

"Now there was leaning on Jesus' bosom one of His disciples whom Jesus loved." John 13:23.

Are you that close to Jesus this morning, my friend? You can be!

August 3

"If my people which are called by My Name, will humble themselves and pray, and seek My face and turn from their wicked ways, I will hear them from Heaven, forgive their sins and heal their land." II Chronicles 7:14.

There it is my friend, in black and white: "humble yourself, pray, feed on the Word and repent," our part, and God's part: "hear, forgive and heal." Here is a proposition from the heart of God that works for both a nation and for a believer.

My sons' home was gutted by fire last fall, leaving the structure and the foundation intact. When I drive across the Dakotas and Montana I see many homesteader's dream house nestled behind a shelterbelt fallen over or leaning severely with the prevailing wind, long ago deserted, now unpainted, windows and doors missing, shingles almost gone, and siding falling off the exterior. A pitiful sight indeed! But, invariably, the cement foundation is as solid as ever. I see America like that today, morally and politically, a house built on a solid foundation over two hundred years ago, leaning with the prevailing wind, gutted of Godly principals by at least half of her people, figuratively seeing the wonderful freedom I knew as a boy, like shingles and siding blowing off the home we live in, America, a bit desecrated. But when I pray for America in the spirit of II Chronicles 7:14, faith and hope sustain me because I know the foundation is as sound as ever, a solid foundation built on Godly principals, a constitution no other nation has known and a Bill of Rights, both of which were put in place by men of God who prayed with integrity in their hearts. When I pray and confess the sin of our nation, as only the Church can do, and hear: "Jesus Christ, the same yesterday, today and forever" from Hebrews 13:8, and then from Malachi 3:6, "I am God; I change not." My Love, joy, peace, and security stay as intact as ever on the foundation they are built on. I hear a note of chastisement coming from a saddened heart when I hear God speak to His people in Haggai 1:5, "...now therefore consider your ways...you looked for much, but indeed it came to little; and when you brought it home, I blew it away. Why, says the Lord of hosts, ... because of My house that is in ruins, while every one of you runs to his own home.."

Have we not dwelled in "panel houses" of personal gratification and illicit freedom, and let the temple of the Lord fall apart as we have aborted babies, and without shame, have seen pornography and casinos and drug dealing as prolific businesses: prayer and other testimonies of the Living God of Heaven legislated out of our society, sexual promiscuity running rampant, along with greed, graft and that "me-first syndrome?"

"The fear of the Lord is to hate evil; pride and arrogance and the evil way, and the perverse mouth I hate." Proverbs 8:13

"Because of Your mercies I am not consumed." Lamentations 3:22

"Consider now from this day forward and from the day this foundation was laid...consider it. Is this the seed still in the barn? As yet, the vine, the fig tree...have not yielded fruit. But from this day forward I will bless you." Haggai 2:18-19

August 4

"God is not mocked." Galatians 6:7

Oh how I crave this morning a gem or two from God's Word called "Good News" to dilute the severity on our minds and hearts of so much of today's secular news. I have not logged the tragic news, but it seems many days in a row of early morning TV covering another kidnapping or outright murder in our nation during the night on one hand and immediately following, a trial of some suspect of an earlier crime on the other hand.

I remember when the enemy struck our nation and a respected man of God spoke up when he saw the tragedy as a wake-up call from God to immoral, ungodly, America. "Wake up and come back to God upon whom this nation's foundation rests." He was laughed at and ridiculed by the press. My Bible says: "Do not be deceived, God is not mocked; for whatever a man sows that will he also reap." Galatians 6:7. And my Bible also says that God is sovereign, an Omni God who has power over all other forces around us, and sometimes gives us personally and nationally a wake-up call to get us back on track.

We hear just such a call in Isa 5:18: "Woe to those who drag their sins behind them like a bullock on a rope. They even mock the Holy One of Israel and dare the Lord to punish them…they say what is right is wrong and what is wrong is right; that black is white and white is black; bitter is sweet and sweet is bitter." {LBV} Because of the truth of this prophecy for today, our America lies under a pall of darkness and sorrow we have never known before, and the Heavens above us are black. How can we entertain ourselves in the evening with fictional scenes on TV that glorify violence, and then be horrified when watching the real thing the next morning?

Even Hollywood asked the same question after 9/11 and postponed releasing films with terrorist themes. But for how long? Perhaps as long as our churches stayed full after 9/11, and then back to the false gods. My Bible says; "God is not mocked." "Do not tempt God." Only God's Word, the sword of the Lord, can safeguard any of us from calling "evil good and good evil." Isaiah 5:20.

August 5

Sustaining scars, either visible on our physical bodies or etched deeply into the soul of the inner man always tell a story of mortal man's trek across the stage of life on this earth.

I remember well that July morning when I was ten or twelve years old, driving a very gentle team of horses on an old "dump rake," the seat three times bigger than I needed, my short legs dangling freely. While turning a corner on the meadow, the rake pole between the houses fell from the ring of the neck yoke, and away went the runaway team, headed for the barn a mile away. I fell under the rake and rolled like a windrow of hay for some time, until one wheel struck a badger hole and tripped the rake tines, leaving me afoot and with a gouge in the flesh of my back, a scar still visible today.

Twice recently, I visited with young people at the Mission in Sioux Falls whose prison time always shows up on their resume for a job, a dreaded scar on their character and on their record. Merle, paralyzed from the hips down, an accident victim as a young boy, the sad scar of a drunken father driving on a public highway. On an on goes the list: boiling water scald burns on the little girl's face, battle scars from the wars, Roe vs. Wade, America's despicable scar, the Holocaust, Germany's heinous scar of WWII days, dishonest CEO's jailed on fraud, Columbine, teenage scars, and the Trade Towers, scars of ugly terrorism.

Even from God's Word, a biography of many men's lives is not without scars on some of our patriarch's bodies and minds and hearts. Most of the scars are a result of carelessness or sin, and are often self-induced. Jacob, Abraham's grandson, was named Jacob because Jacob means "liar, deceiver", and his mother Rebekah fostered and nurtured and encouraged that curse until Jacob literally stole from his elder brother Esau his birthright. Later, he stole Esau's rightful blessing as the eldest from his blind father Isaac, scars of deceit in both cases. Infuriated Esau threatened Jacob's life, forcing him to quickly flee to his Uncle Laban for asylum and a fresh start in life. Twenty years later, God insisted that Jacob return home and to his brother Esau, still harboring a grievous scar in his soul of unforgiveness. Convicted, repentant Jacob, at the fork of the River Jabok. Gen 32:23. "Jacob was left alone and a Man wrestled with him until the breaking of day". Then, "Just as he crossed over Panuel, the sun rose on him and he limped on his hip. The Man had touched the socket of Jacob's hip in the muscle..." Vs. 31:43. What scars—first on his inner man, guilt, fear, and condemnation, then manifested in his outer man with a life-long limp.

"You can be sure your sin will find you out" Num. 32:23, and most often leave a scar even after forgiveness and successful "surgery" on the inner man have taken place.

But, oh, for the blessing of those Divine scars—beautiful, necessary, rewarding, powerful scars in the hands, feet, brow, and the pierced side of our Lord and Savior, Jesus. Purposed scars that remind us of Christ, the Cross, and Calvary, where the power and death of sin were turned into freedom and life everlasting for the truly born-again, having come to Jesus with child-like faith. Consequently, we hear Jesus saying to doubting Thomas' all over the globe: "Reach your finger here and look at My hands, and reach your hand here, and put it into My side. Do not be unbelieving, but believing." John 20:27

Jesus only, like a plastic surgeon, can cover the ugly scars that sin has wrought.

August 6

The lighted cross.

As we drive the rather monotonous plains of the Dakotas on our way to Montana, the flashing lights ahead, presumably a law officer's vehicle, suddenly catch our attention and our minds quickly try to build a scenario. Speeding? Accident? Ambulance? Heart attack? Careless driving? Blinding sun? Injury or death? The monotony is quickly broken; our lethargy quickly broken by flashing lights.

Casual travelers who drive on that gravel road past a friend's home out in the country may be awakened and surprised, their monotony challenged by an unexpected sight: a stately white cross in the center of a neat farmstead, at night all lighted from top to bottom. My friend, Joe, who placed that cross, I am sure, for two reasons: a personal testimony to all the world of that family's faith in Jesus Christ, and then a prayerful hope that someone driving by might catch a glimpse that would register in his mind—a thought, a curiosity that would begin to trigger an unloosing of his God-given gift of faith. Romans 12:3.

As a believer, my heart is edified and encouraged as I drive into that yard because that cross spells life after death, and I feel grateful that just maybe a non-believers attention could one day be drawn to Jesus and the eternal, real meaning of that cross. Oh, yes, a neighbor may drive by many times, but who can predict his trial or mood of the hour, but what even a split-second reaction may mean to that immortal soul. "God works in mysterious ways His wonders to perform."

Out in a neighboring Mennonite community I came from, there the Bible verses like John 3:16 or "Jesus Saves" or "The truth shall set you free," or "I am the Way, the Truth, and the Life," —every so often along those country roads. Occasionally a sinner's eye catches one such message and curiosity is aroused as the Holy Spirit walking beside him woos, begs, pleads, or invites him to "consider his ways." His soul is warmed, and a hunger for more begins to well up inside his bosom as he begins to wonder why someone went to all the effort and bother and time to place that "good news" on a post a few people will see and read.

A little girl in London strayed from her home and became lost. When found by a law officer, she was asked "What is your address?" She didn't know, so he started to drive in a direction she thought she had come from and suddenly a cross showed atop a church, and she burst out: "My home is just below the cross."

Now, what about us as Christians? As we hurry through life, busy, anxious, mixed up a bit at times, on trial, are we not grateful for just any reminder of our Father's love that sent Jesus to that cross at Calvary to redeem us and put that love, joy, peace, and security into our lives that every man craves, and that only Jesus can implement? It matters not whether it be a flashing light, a posted message, a lighted cross, or a choir pouring out its heart into a passer-by heart on a summer evening—just any Holy Spirit oriented way to catch our attention, break the monotony, and arouse our curiosity.

It is a known fact that to know the real meaning of the cross at Calvary, you must know the One who died on that cross.

HIS NAME IS JESUS!!!!

"God forbid that I should boast except in the cross of our Lord Jesus Christ." Galatians 6:14

August 7

"I am Joseph, does my Father still live?" Genesis 42

Relatives can sometimes be tricky like a cousin of mine, or like Joseph, son of Jacob. In May 1944 I rode the train along with a dozen other candidates for military service on our way across Montana to take our physical exam. After standing in line, my turn finally came to step up to the long table and face the men in uniform who were responsible for our processing. A dark, handsome man, with wavy hair, looked at my papers, saw my name, smiled, and immediately asked: "Well, Dale, how is Uncle Bill these days?" And what about Uncle "Whoop?" "And your Dad, Frank, is he still on the farm south of town?" I answered each question with a wondering aire to my personality, and he finally confided: "You don't know who I am, do you?" "No, I don't." "I am your cousin Jim." His mother was my aunt, and cousin Jim was one of the older of thirty-two cousins, and I was one of the younger, so that he had left the community before I knew him. What a pleasant surprise!

So it was with Joseph, son of Jacob. A severe famine and consequent food shortage struck Jacob's Canaan, but Egypt had plenty, and to sell. So Jacob, who "mysteriously" lost son Joseph from his life many years before, sent ten of his remaining sons to Egypt. "So Joseph's ten brothers went down to buy grain in Egypt." Genesis 42:3. Now Joseph, sold by his brothers as a slave into Pharaoh's Egypt as a teen-ager, "... was governor over the land, and it was he who sold to all the people of the land. And Joseph's brothers came and bowed down before him, with their faces to the earth." Vs. 6. "So Joseph recognized his brothers, but they did not recognize him." Vs. 8. After days of bickering and dealing over both food and Joseph's younger brother Benjamin to come on the scene, Joseph, seeing their blindness as to his identity, revealed himself to his brothers. "...make everyone go out from me. So no one stood with him while Joseph made himself known to his brothers...and he wept aloud... and Joseph said to his brothers, 'I am Joseph; does my father still live?' But his brothers could not answer him, for they were dismayed in his presence...I am Joseph, your brother whom you sold into Egypt." What a pleasant surprise!

Jesus, too, had an identity problem. Born a Jew in Israel, a human birth, and in John 1:10: "He was in the world, and the world was made through Him, and the world did not know Him. He came to His own and his own did not know Him." "Come see a man who told me all things that I ever did. Could this be the Christ?" John 4:29. "Who do men say that I, the Son of Man, am? ...some say John the Baptist, some say Elijah...Jeremiah...or one of the prophets. But who do you say that I am? Jesus prevailed with them..." Peter answered and said: "You are the Christ, the Son of the Living God."

May that be each of our testimonies at our coming out of darkness and death and unto life and light. "You are the Christ, the Son of the Living God!"

I know Him, and He knows me.

August 8

Malachi 3:3 says: "He will sit as a refiner and purifier of silver."

As I've studied Daniel 3, I've discovered a beautiful analogy of the heat and the silversmith and the "piece of silver" held over the fire. Three Jewish boys, now in captivity in far off Babylon, under the watchful eye of God while under severe testing, remind one of silver not yet quite perfectly refined. I see the "Silversmith" from heaven holding them in His hand, waiting for their testimony that would prove the purity; ready to see the Master's image in their faces. The pressure raged on, peeling off the final impurity when they confessed to King Nebuchadnezzar: "We know that our God Whom we serve is able, and we know our God is willing to deliver us from the burning, fiery furnace; but if not...we still will not worship the gold image you have set up."

When tossed into the fire, they immediately met Jesus face to face. I can just imagine that He smiled, and I can hear Him say: "Now I see my image in you boys." Untainted faith!!

"For we know that all things work together for good of those who love God, and are called according to His purpose...predestined to be conformed to the image of His Son." Romans 8:28-29.

"I created you, O Jacob...do not fear for I have redeemed you, you are Mine, I call you by name...so when you walk through the fire you shall not be burned, nor shall the flame scorch you, for I am the Lord your God, the Holy One of Israel, Your Savior." Isaiah 43:1-3.

From One who says what He means, and means what He says, Jesus.

August 9

"Stand firm..." Exodus 14:13

Good morning friends whom I know are standing by me in prayer and words of interest and encouragement as I face perhaps the most severe trial of my long life, a potential matter of life or death, cancer.

I cried tears of joy this morning when my big faithful God spoke these Words from Exodus 14:13 to my needy, hungry little boy inside of me: "Stand firm and you will see the deliverance the Lord will bring you today."

Moses and his people faced the Red Sea ahead, and unscaleable mountains, one on either side, a fast-approaching enemy behind them. Just in time, God opened the sea, and saved them, capturing the enemy in the process. I cannot retreat; I cannot go forward normally; this very moment I feel shut in on both sides as I wait for reports. What shall I do now? The Master's Words to me this morning are: "Stand firm." "They that wait upon the Lord shall renew their strength; they shall mount up with the wings of eagles." Isaiah 40:31. When an eagle "mounts up", he rises above the storm, and soars firmly until the storm is over.

The enemy "despair" whispers, "Lie down, give up; let the tail go with the hide." The enemy "cowardice" naps. "Retreat and go the natural man's way, eat, drink, and be merry." "The Christian's walk of faith is too difficult, so give up your principles that don't now work well." The enemy "precipitance" cries out: "Do something. To stand still and wait is sheer idleness."

And yet I hear the voice of God: "Call upon Me; I will answer you and show you great and mighty things you do not know." Jeremiah 33:3.

The enemy "presumption" boasts: "If the sea is before you, jump into it and expect a miracle like Peter expected."

Friend, "Faith" listens not to presumption, despair, cowardice, or precipitancy, all things from the enemy, but Faith hears God say; "Stand firm" like the rock of Gibraltar. "Stand firm" He says to my expectant heart: "I know the thoughts I think toward you, thoughts of peace, not of evil, I give you a future; I give you a hope." Jeremiah 29:11.

One day soon I will hear the command: "Go forward" like waiting Moses heard, and I will again experience a special love, joy, peace, hope and security that only sweet Jesus can give to a longing heart.

"Do not fear nor be dismayed, for the battle is not yours but God's." II Chronicles 20:15

August 10

"...narrow is the gate and difficult is the way which leads to life, and there are few who find it." Matthew 7:14

"For many are called, but few chosen." Matthew 20:16b

One beautiful late afternoon in Montana in the summer of 1937, we Boy Scouts came into town from an outing at Eagle's Nest and were greeted close by with the post ravages of a terrible gasoline fire near the railroad tracks where a delivery truck had been loading from a large tank, and a spark ignited the truck, the fire spreading quickly to the big tank, which swelled and was expected to explode any minute. I admired the guts, bravery, and risk of one older fireman who stood on top of the bulging tank with a water hose, pouring volumes of water over the swelling tank to cool it. That tank stood for many years as a memorial in my mind of that courageous fireman.

Risky? Yes. Foolish? No. He knew that what he was doing would work, and perhaps saved many lives.

We praise the Lord today that apostle Paul also risked his life that you and I of the Gentile world might not burn in Hell for eternity, but escape the ravages of death to live with Jesus in Heaven forever. He put out the fire for a chosen few. Every day he went out he risked stoning and being left for dead. He was mobbed, whipped, imprisoned, three times shipwrecked, and beaten with lashes and rods. Why? His personal testimony of II Tim. 2:10 tells why he risked so much. "I endure all things for the sake of the elect, that they also may obtain the salvation which is in Christ Jesus"…that One Who also risked His all for so few as our opening scriptures reveal… "few who find the way…few chosen."

Like the fireman standing on the bulging tank, or Paul ambling across a wilderness, a continent, our Jesus descended from glorious Heaven, risked His life on Calvary "for the joy that was set before Him"…the truly born again, the few that would choose to walk the straight road and enter the narrow gate.

"Because of love, He came for us.
Because of grace, He died.
Because of hope, He gave His life, a living sacrifice.
Because of Him, we live today.
He freed our souls from sin."
Thank you, Lord, for risking Your life for me!!

August 11

"The Word of the Lord endures forever" Ps. 119:80

Good morning, friends, walking with me this gorgeous morning and another sharing of God's Word which the Psalmist boldly and confidently declares in 119:89: "Forever, oh Lord, Your Word is settled in Heaven." Oh yes, "The grass withers and the flower fades, but the Word of the Lord endures forever." Oh, for the love, joy, peace, and security that the Word, the holy scriptures, God's statutes, His love-letter to humanity, His voice, His roadmap, the Bible, puts into a believer's heart so that his testimony is one with the psalmist's heart: "I rise before the dawn of the morning and cry for help; I hope in Your Words," 119:47. And in Psalm 119:11: "Your Word have I hid in my heart that I might not sin against You." My friend, we need a daily heart searching because of the undermining power of our old nature, the world about us, and Satan himself to determine if our faith is real or imitation. God addressed this in Isaiah 29:13: "These people honor Me with their lips, but have removed their hearts far from Me."

During the time of the prophet Isaiah, many of the people of Israel were merely going through the motions, like many today in their repeated liturgies and masses man has concocted. I spent forty two years in lifeless motions of worship. In Isaiah 1:13 we read; "Bring no more futile sacrifices; incense is an abomination to Me... your new moons and your appointed feasts My soul hates."

David apparently made that very discovery one day, too, about sacrifice and offering being the important part in coming to worship, and in Psalm 40:6-8 recognized his error, as manifested in verse 7: "Behold, I come...in the scroll of the book it is written of me." David, convicted; "My eyes and ears you have opened and I see the futility and emptiness of mere sacrifice and offering unless my heart is in it...unless my heart is pure in motive and my conscience clear, basking in Godly righteousness." "Search me, oh Lord, and know my heart; test me and see if there be any wickedness in me, and lead me in Your way everlasting." Psalm 139:23.

Friend, ponder your motive and enjoy your day with Jesus.

August 12

"For to me, to live is Christ, and to die is gain." Paul, Philippians 1:21

The 18-wheeler hustled down the pavement, my son and I aboard, and suddenly my son, gripping the huge steering wheel, bursting over with joy suddenly exclaimed: "Boy, this is really living!" Bouncing up and down like a ball in the rider's seat, I answered: "If this is living, I've surely missed the mark," since trucking had no appeal to me. "Each to his own" they say of life's choices we make while here.

Having come from a very sheltered home on a Montana farm and ranch where a young boy would automatically fit into the operation while school, church, and high school sports dominated the waking hours, I was shocked to find my buddies in the army so naturally "living it up" in the pleasures of gambling, drinking, carousing, and illicit sex. What a contrast for me who had just come from the University of Minnesota and part of the on-campus fellowship in the Lutheran Student Association, LSA, or the extended Luther League from high school days. Choices! Choices!

And on to vocation, marriage, family, church affiliation, and community service in a nation I love to be a citizen—the good old U.S.A.!

"Life is more than food, and the body is more than clothing... consider the lilies, how they grow: they neither toil nor spin; and yet I say to you, even Solomon in all his glory was not arrayed like one of these."

"For to me, to live is Christ." May speak the testimony of a young man or woman coming from a Godly home, but then the fantasy and glitter of this world comes upon them. Psalm 37:23 tells it well: "The steps of a good man are ordered by the Lord, and in his ways does the Lord find His delight. Though he fall, he shall not be utterly destroyed for the hand of the Lord will uphold him." The prodigal son of Luke 16 I see fitting this category, having come from a proper home to make the complete circuit of falling away and coming back. One day he got his eye on the glitter of this world, took his inheritance, left home, and foolishly squandered all he had down to only the clothes on his back. He took on the lowest job in his culture, in desperation—feeding pigs and coveting their pea pods for his own survival. With a truly repentant heart he found his way back to his father who received him with outstretched arms, a big hug, and a welcome home kiss, a party, a ring on his finger, sandals on his feet, and a robe on his back. "He shall be like a tree planted by living waters, that brings forth its fruit in its season whose leaf shall not wither; and whatever he does shall prosper." Psalm 1:3

If someone asked you today: "What do you live for?" Could you answer with Paul, "For to me , to live is Christ, to die is gain"? Could this be your testimony as a clergy man, a farmer, a banker, a businessman, a politician, a school teacher or administration? Or a person enlisted in the military, a nurse, a doctor, a housewife, a custodian, or an engineer?

"Beloved, I pray above all things that you may prosper and be in good health, even as your soul prospers." III John 2

August 13

"But we are all like an unclean thing…" Isaiah 64:6

We thank and praise our heavenly Father for the access to the good news of the Gospel that we can use as an antidote for the filth and stench of the secular news coming at us forcefully every day from the media. I take Matthew 16:24 as an invitation from Jesus, requesting an RSVP where He said to His disciples, "If anyone desires to come after Me, let him deny himself, and take up his cross and follow Me," a trip that will end at Calvary where, with child-like faith, we lay down our sin as we nail it to that cross, flesh that smells in God's nostrils, laying down a heart "desperately wicked, and deceitful above all things." Jeremiah 17:9. It's all summed up in one five-letter Word called "grace", an undeserved gift that cannot be purchased nor worked for, "For by grace are you saved through faith, not of your own, but a gift from God, not of works, lest any man should boast," Ephesians 2:8-9. "But God, because of His great love…" Ephesians 2:4, a love that flows like they sing of the Mississippi: "old man river, He just keeps rollin' along." Or love flowing like one of those mountain streams in the Rockies, never failing, but flowing 24/7.

Reminds me of the time I was gathering eggs from the chicken coup. There he sat, a skunk, after consuming every egg from the nests, he sat there with his tail up and ready to aim and fire! What a stench, one that every vehicle driver wants to avoid at all costs out on the pavement. And nowadays, the added menace of a super-friendly skunk with rabies, ready to inject into a man, a dog, a cow, horses, or innocent wildlife.

In God's sight, all of us must appear as a "skunk" with an easily detectable odor before Jesus' pure, clean, innocent, sinless blood cleanses us in the inner man. "...we all are like an unclean thing, and all our righteousness are like filthy rags,,," Isaiah 64:6. "Instead of a sweet smell, there will be a stench." Isaiah 3:24.

But there is good news found in Romans 5:8 where the love of God steps in like a perfume, a deodorant: "But God demonstrated His own love toward us, in that while we were yet sinners, Christ died for us."

August 14

"The last of the 5000."

Many times, beginning when I was a little boy on that Montana ranch, I have seen on display the large, famous picture of the pioneer days, depicting an old, weak Hereford range cow, every rib showing, only her hide covering that rack of bones. The caption: "The Last of The 5000." In that bleak springtime, after a severe winter on the prairies, her old age also against her, she could barely stand, her eyes already sunken. Around her is a circle of hungry wolves under a dark, cloudy sky, patiently waiting for her to topple over any minute now, their meal for a day.

Like that old "Last of The 5000," some struggling, aged people have some enemies gathered around who would put them away without dignity by euthanasia, or families who just don't care about their elders; unscrupulous people who force them to live in wretched conditions; or like one hard-hearted, tight-fisted politician said: "let them die and get out of the way." An unnecessary burden like Adolph Hilter saw them in Germany under his leadership.

We hear the heart-felt plea of an aged man in Psalm 71: "Do not cast me off in the time of old age; do not forsake me when my strength fails. For my enemies speak against me. And those who lie in wait for my life take counsel together, saying 'God has forsaken him; pursue and take him; for there is none to deliver him.' Let them be confounded and consumed who are adversaries of my life; let them be covered with reproach and dishonor who seek my hurt. But I will hope continually, and I will praise You. I will go in the strength of the Lord God; I will make mention of Your righteousness, Yours only." Every man's enemies are our flesh, the world around us, and Satan.

The poet sees the faithful aged this way: "As a white candle in a holy place, so is the beauty of an aged face."

"For to me to live is Christ, to die is gain." Philippians 1:21.

This aged writer prays daily that I might live with purpose and die with dignity; God's plan for all of us.

August 15

"The ungodly are like chaff the wind blows away." Psalm 1:4

When I see the crops of grain being harvested these days, I am reminded of the intricate operation of separating the grain from the chaff I first learned about as a boy in the days of the stationary thresher, now replaced by the self-propelled combine out on the field. Harvest time is a jubilant day for a farmer, the fruition of the long awaited day of income, the blessing of his former days of planting. Therefore, it is mandatory that the good seed fill the grain bin on the farm and the chaff, the kernel's cover, be separated to save both bin room and discount at the grain elevator. So, the separation process is watched carefully by the operator, so that the sieves the grain falls onto when removed from the sheaf are set just open enough to allow the heavy kernel to fall through and elevates to a tank, while the "wind" is set just right to blow the lighter part, the chaff, out with the straw as waste.

In Psalm 1 we find God performing like a combine at harvest time as He takes the righteous aside, the grain, cleans it up, and makes it look like a nice, tall, stately tree, deep-rooted, well watered, with dark green leaves, a tree prosperous for shade, for bird's nests, for beauty, and for fruit production. "The ungodly are not so, but are like chaff which the wind drives away." Vs. 4. Like God, a combine operator is very careful not to "blow away" good grain out over the sieves, but also insistent to "blow away" all the chaff and foreign particles.

By way of parable in Matthew 13, Jesus describes how and why tares [weeds] come to mix with the good grain in the field, and then instructs in Vs 30: "Let both grow together until the harvest, and at that time I will say to the reaper 'First gather together the tares and bind them in bundles to burn them, but gather the wheat into My barn.'" A needed separation!

The choice is ours—to be a tare to be burned at His harvest or a kernel of grain to store forever in His granary called Heaven. There is definitely a separation of grain and chaff and weeds coming, our destiny depending on how each of us have handled Jesus now while there is still time. He awaits our confession: "Thou art the Christ, the Son of the living God" that Peter confessed, the rock the church is built on. Matthew 16:18.

"All the nations will be gathered before Him, and He will separate them one from another as a shepherd divides his sheep from the goats...the sheep on His right hand, the goats on the left...to them on His right... 'inherit the kingdom prepared for you'...and those [goats] will go away into everlasting punishment..." Matthew 25:32.

Will you be one of the jubilant, separated, golden kernels that fill the grain bin at harvest time, or one of the particles of chaff left in the field for the birds to devour, or a fire to burn up in the springtime, or the plow to put under after harvest?

August 16

"Home Sweet Home."

As your clay body is a home, a temple, on this earth for the Holy Spirit to indwell (I Corinthians 3:16, 6:19) is your earthly home also a temple for the Lord in worship, prayer, and the shared Word? What has your dwelling place been purposed for and dedicated to?

My childhood home on the prairies was first started by my bachelor dad in 1906, and added to in 1915 after his marriage. An unwritten, western, pioneer day "law" when you leave your rural home was to leave the door unlocked, a supply of fuel for the range, and imperishable food on the table, ready for a needy person or family in case of storm in either winter or summer. Free use of the bed and the lantern was assumed. My dad came home one time to find a deceased man lying on the floor. Western hospitality it was called, even at the risk of thieves and criminals who frequented the area, but always with deep respect for the pioneer and his family.

This morning as I studied I Chronicles 29 where King David and his people have purposely brought together every material needed for the building of the temple for worship when Solomon would reign as king, my mind went back to that boyhood home, and how it blessed people during its 65 years of occupancy. Always a place of western hospitality for neighbors and sojourners, including Native Americans and gypsies during those horse-and-buggy days. To some, it was: "My home where I hang my hat." At my mother's knee I first heard about Jesus in our home where I saw many small prayer books, leaflets, and devotions lay before my eyes, and also the time and place where I learned to pray. From that home, disciplined study on Saturday afternoon prepared me for Sunday school the next day. My wife and I occupied that same home for another twenty-two years, when it became a temple for sharing God's Word with six children; while at the same time a place for adult Bible study during the days of the Charismatic movement. It was a haven of rest for the weary, a table of food for the hungry, and a home for fun for both young and old alike. I take inventory today, and am thankful for that home, and the blessed provision that went into it.

"…for I was hungry and you gave Me food; I was thirsty and you gave Me drink; I was a stranger and you took Me in." Jesus, Matthew 25:35.

Inside our ranch house entry hung a plaque: "My home is where I hang my heart."

May the Lord Bless you today!

August 17

"My hope is in your Word." Psalm 119:147

    Would you like a bit of sweetener for your inner man's menu for today? As there are many sweeteners for the flesh's menu, and we most often settle for one favorite, so I have done this morning with the Word "hope" for the inner man. Oh, how many kidnappings have we seen in our times, where parents frantically search for their son or daughter, and find it almost impossible to give up hope, even when others give up the search. I think, too, of the people in Caribbean waters and residents of Florida this past season, how so many must surely have been living on hope, and the hope is that the hurricane will go around them or even dissipate before arriving. And for those who have evacuated, hope sweetens their day as it lingers day and night in their minds and hearts while they cling to life and a desire for the "good old days."

    I hear the Lord through the prophet Jahaziel giving hope to a helpless, terrified, fearful, people of Judah standing on the brink of being wiped out by their enemies: "Do not fear or be dismayed, for the battle is not yours, but God's." II Chronicles 20:15. That counsel was sweet music to my ear, a bright ray of hope that unloaded a heavy burden from my back one day in a severe trial of my life, when, like King Jehosophat, I had no place to turn. That Word, as I diligently searched for help, became especially alive to me, "For the Word of God is living, and powerful, and sharper than any two-edged sword. ...a discerner of the thoughts and intents of the heart." Hebrews 4:12. My Word, "life unto those who find it, and health unto their flesh." Proverbs 4:23. In life or death, our only real hope is Jesus, so that even in life's darkest hour, genuine Christians have the brightest hope, both for now and for eternity.

    In the book of Lamentations we find the prophet Jeremiah, author, witnessing unbelievable horrors, tragedies beyond himself, when the Babylonians invaded Jerusalem in 586 B.C. Solomon's temple was reduced to ruins, and with it went not only the house of worship, but also the very heart of the community. Many of us in rural America can empathize with this when we lose our school and post office for lack of population. Jeremiah's people were left with no food, no rest, no leader, no love, hope, joy, peace, or security they had known so well. But, in the very midst of their suffering and grief, God did not forsake them nor leave them, but rather inspired the prophet to write a Word of hope: "Through the Lord's mercies we are not consumed, because His compassions fail not; they are new every morning. Great is Your faithfulness." Lamentations 3:23. A fresh sweetener every morning!

"My grace is sufficient" II Corinthians 12:9. Jeremiah's sudden hope manifested here erupted because he had had personal experience of God's faithfulness, and of His promises and principals that never fail, giving extra sweetness to "Do not fear or be dismayed, for the battle is not yours, but Mine."

August 18

"Jesus Saves" the road sign read.

Destructive hurricane Charley ripped through Florida, and on its heels, devastating Francis literally blanketed the state with horrendous winds and tons of rain water, and as I write, hurricane Ivan is threatening on the western horizon, its destiny yet unknown. Why live in such hurricane-prone country, I ask myself. And then I recall, cyclones and tornados in the Midwest, terrorism in New York City, earthquakes and annual fires in the far West, blizzards and forest fires in the Rockies and upper Great Plains, and spring floods in the Red River Valley. And worst of all, the waves and fires of terrorism sweeping across the globe, as spiritual warfare daily keeps people in bondage to fear, depression, and hopelessness wherever they live.

Is there an escape? Pitiful is the man enduring the tragedies on earth today, both of the inner and outer man, without insurance or assurance. Their inner man, born dead in trespass and sin, which means out of relationship with the God of Heaven and with Jesus our Savior, open game for Satan, is well acquainted with these same kinds of tragedies as the outer man with its physical manifestations. Hopeless, and even helpless!

How shall we escape those fires of Hell for our eternal home, and the fires on the way to that ungodly destiny? The writer of Hebrews asks that same question of us in the LBV: "What makes us think we can escape if we are indifferent to this great salvation announced by the Lord Jesus Himself, and passed on to us by those who heard Him speak?" Hebrews 2:3. He announced in John 3:16: "For God so loved the world that He gave His only begotten Son, that whosoever believes on Him shall not perish, but have everlasting life."

So I find my answer to this enigma in the person and name of Jesus, manifested in the faith and testimony of those who have gone ahead, like as the three Hebrew children of Daniel 3. They were thoroughly nurtured in faith in God and in the promised Messiah from their Hebrew heritage in Jerusalem, and then tested severely under Babylonian captivity during the reign of evil King Nebucadnezzar, one who reminds me of present-day Saddam Hussein occupying that same territory. The king made an image of gold, gathered all his authorities together for a dedication, and ordered a decree that when a herald cry aloud and the instruments play in symphony, everyone shall bow down and worship the gold image; and whoever does not fall shall be cast immediately into the midst of a burning, fiery furnace, a furnace stoked up seven times hotter than usual, so hot that it killed all the attendants. Meshach, Shadrach, and Abednego refused to bow. Standing before the king, who gave them one more opportunity to bow, their faith and testimony stood firm against doubt, unbelief, and their flesh. "...our God whom we serve is able to deliver us from the burning fiery furnace, and He will deliver us from your hand, O king. But if not, let it be known to you, O king, that we do not serve your gods, nor will we worship the gold image which you have set up." Vs. 17-18—"And these three men...fell down bound into the midst of the burning fiery furnace." The king, astonished, Vs. 25: "Look,...I see four men loose, walking in the midst of the fire, and they are not hurt, and the form of the fourth is like the Son of God." Then he ordered them out, unburned, not even scorched by the flame. Christ's salvation of these Hebrew boys melted the king's heart, caused him to repent and bless their God, and in Vs. 30: "Then the king promoted Meshach, Shadrach, and Abednego in the province of Babylon."

August 19

"The widow's mite—a big thing." Luke 21:3

    Constantly, since 9/11/01, we have been taken back to "ground zero" by TV to view, amongst other things, the "little things" that became huge blessings when facilitated. I have learned along life's ways, too, that it is often the "little things" in my life that I have given or received that have blessed me most; a bereavement card, a congratulatory message, an unexpected hug, a Word of encouragement, a surprise guest, or the many unseen gestures of love of a faithful mate. I read recently of several true testimonies of the "little things" on 9/11 that saved a person's life that day when the towers came down and almost 3000 lives were lost: delayed shopping along the way to work, a failed alarm clock, school kid interruption, traffic stoppage, car failure, and taxi delay. Seems to me that Someone was Commander-in-Chief that day in many people's lives; the same One who tells us in Deut. 30:19; "I call Heaven and earth as witnesses today against you, that I have set before you life and death, blessing and cursing,; therefore, choose life, that both you and your descendants may live; that you may love the Lord your God, that you may obey His voice, and that you may cling to Him, for He is your life and the length of your days." I wonder how many times we are going to be amazed and even shocked when our life passes before us and we see the many times the "little things" in our lives are geared to a wake-up call for the lost to "come home", or "come closer" for the truly born-again. It is just another reminder to "trust the Lord with all your heart and lean not to your own understanding; acknowledge Him in all your ways, and He will direct your paths." Proverbs 3:5-6.

    From the scriptures, too, some of the "little things" have blessed me most. Two in particular: one "trusting the Lord with all her heart," and the other "leaning unto his own understanding." Talk about blessing and cursing set before them!! The little old widow we read of in Luke 21:1 laid two copper coins on the altar, all she had to her name; while others of great wealth, Jesus said: "could not together match her offering." We see that only this widow was worthy of mention in God's Word, and I am thrilled that it is there because it teaches me that in the eye of the Lord sacrificial giving counts most, that kind that cuts the flesh short and exonerates and exalts the Lord from the heart as we share our blessed gifts of time, talent, and treasure sacrificially.

Then, just the opposite in Matthew 25 where we read of a parable dealing with talents, whereby one servant was given five talents which he eagerly invested and they doubled in value. Likewise with the one given two talents which he invested wisely. These two were blessed and favorably commended, we find in Vs. 21: "Well done, good and faithful servant." But the one who had been given least of all, one talent, was filled with fear, and hid his talent in the ground for no gain. His disappointed lord severely chastened him for "leaning unto his own understanding," and we find in Vs. 30: "cast the unprofitable servant into outer darkness. There will be weeping and gnashing of teeth."

August 20

"Search me, Oh God, and know my heart; try me and know my anxieties; and see if there is any wicked way in me, and lead me in the way everlasting." Psalm 139:23-24.

"Search my heart"…for out of the heart flow the issues of life. Proverbs 4:23. "…know my anxieties…try my thoughts"…

"The Lord knows the thoughts of man, that they are futile." Psalm 94:11.

That fateful morning of April 18, 1977, when I received word of my twenty-year old son's tragic death, an automobile accident, will always be remembered, not only for the shock, but for the blessing the Lord sent my way very soon.

To that date, I had spent much time and effort in keeping my little brood of six physically and emotionally under my thumb, not as a "dictator," but as one whose heart refused to cut the apron strings and "let go and let God." It never crossed my mind that I was tinkering with a heart of idolatry. After all, aren't we supposed to love sons and daughters, even to the point of keeping them close at hand, I thought?

But listen to Jesus who spoke so gently to me from Mark 10:29: "Assuredly, I say to you there is no one who has left house, or brothers and sisters, or father or mother or wife or children or lands for my sake and the gospel's sake, who shall not receive a hundredfold now...and in the age to come, eternal life."

That day, I repented of this subtle sin; another block now in place in my faith walk with Jesus. God captured my heart as His rightful throne, the idol now laid aside. "Peace like a river" overflowed my inner man as I entered His gates with thanksgiving in my heart and praise on my lips. I discovered that an idol is anything that takes God's rightful place in a man's heart. After all, our sons and daughters are only "on loan" to us as caretakers here on earth. They are God's created property for eternity, since He has much more invested in them than we have.

August 21

"The best is yet to come."

"The best is yet to come" declared Rudy when his pastor ministered to him after his mate of well over half a century suddenly passed away. Rudy, a man well into his eighties, wheel-chair bound, was left alone for another year or two before his own glorious homecoming celebration. Apparently forgetting his own frailties, he looked ahead to meeting Jesus, with Selma by His side... "The best is yet to come."

Those of us who love this life and yet expect it to be better on the other side of the grave can concur with Jesus when He prayed in John 17:16: "They [His disciples] are not of the world, just as I am not of the world." Did you ever stop to think of the irony that to have a death there must first be life, and that God ordained that we must first apprentice on this earth in order to be a candidate for life with Jesus when this is over? After all, Paul tells us in Eph 2:1: "And you He made alive who were dead in trespasses and sins." Born spiritually into a grave, out of relationship with God, in need of resurrection right from our mother's womb. David recognized this in Psalm 30:1: "I will extol You, oh Lord, for You have lifted me up…oh Lord, You have brought my soul up from the grave…" God didn't make a few million robots to spend eternity with, but kinfolk, spirit beings, created in His own image. Here we are today in a prep school, as it were, accepting Jesus as our Savior and Lord with child-like faith; only this time and this life described as "a vapor that passes quickly." "The best is yet to come." Paul lived with a healthy balance: "For to me, to live is Christ, and to die is gain," Phil 1:21. We need balance to appreciate and enjoy the blessings of this world, while at the same time refusing to be short-sighted captives of the here-and-now. Many live only for this life, even as Christians.

We are blessed by the attitude modeled by Jesus: He enjoyed feasts and weddings. He loved little children, and compassionately provided for the needs of the multitudes. He promised abundant living, His purpose for coming, guaranteeing "the best is yet to come." Yet, He prayed longingly for His return to Heaven, a perfect example of "being in the world, but not of the world."

To find the real love, joy, peace, and security we all crave in this life requires a heartfelt surrender to Jesus whom I can hear this very moment: "If any man would come after Me, let him deny himself, take up his cross, and follow Me." Christ's journey ended at Calvary, where He gave His all for humanity. And so does our journey end there when we surrender our old self, both for now and for eternity.

We ought to make the most of life on earth by energizing our God-given gift of faith, and by investing our gifts of time, talent, and treasure in Kingdom work, knowing full well: "The best is yet to come." We wait for that wonderful Word of consolation and praise: "Well done!" from the lips and heart of Jesus

August 22

"I have been young but am now old. Yet, I have not seen the righteous forsaken, nor his descendants begging bread." Psalm 37:25.

One of my fondest memories as a very young boy on a Montana homestead that became a combination grain farm and a livestock ranch was harvest time. Lots of action, lots of men, horses and excitement. The grain farming kept all hands busy in the spring and fall time, while the livestock kept them busy in the cold, snowy winter months. I loved the four distinct seasons, but was especially fond of the harvest of the small grains, the oats, barley and wheat. An implement known as a "header", a prelude to the binder, and then the swather of today, is my first recollection of harvest. It was very simple; horse-drawn, steered by a man's body as he sat on a wide, metal seat atop a heavy shaft connected to a steel wheel on the ground. The reel and sickle fetched the grain onto a revolving canvas which carried the clippings into a horse-drawn wagon following alongside. When a wagon was full, another rolled up to replace it while the full one went to be pitched by fork into a stack. (The stack was left for weeks to go through a "sweat".) One day, weeks later, a huge threshing machine would be posted in place beside the stack and men with pitchforks would feed the grain in. The slow-moving, noisy machine separated the valuable seeds from the straw and emptied then into a horse-drawn grain wagon. When full, the grain hauler headed for a granary at the farmstead and shoveled the grain into the bin. All in a typical day's work, under the brilliant fall sunshine, the continual cloud of dust and chaff as the straw was blown into a large pile on the ground.

The slow chug and hum of the steam engine pulling the heavy belt that propelled the machine, the constant vibration of the thresher, the sweat of the worker's brow, and the special smell of harvested grain, made the colorful evening sunset of the western sky a welcome sight at day's end. Both tired, beast and man were ready for a huge meal and a cold, cold drink of fresh water.

A crude harvest it was for Ruth, too, a Moabite daughter-in-law of Naomi we read of in the old testament book of Ruth, who enjoyed a similar day of harvest for her very survival in a foreign land. Times were tough, food was scarce, and harvest very primitive like the header and the thresher in their day in America. In her search for a field to glean some leftovers, seeds missed by the harvester, widow Ruth met a wealthy farmer, Boaz, and found instant favor with him. She had hand gathered behind the reapers among the sheaves, continually, from morning until evening, resting a little in the house. Ruth 2:7. At meal time she sat beside the reapers; she ate; was satisfied, and saved some. Vs. 14. Boaz, after the meal, commanded his reapers to purposely leave grain for her to glean, making it less strenuous for the back in not having to diligently search. She gleaned until evening and then threshed out the grain from the straw by flailing. The grain measured about an ephah of barley, a strong bushel, a day's work. She stayed close beside the young women of Boaz to glean until the barley and wheat harvest ended. Vs. 23. Tired, sweaty, and thankful, she ended a day the Lord had made to rejoice in and be glad for.

August 23

"But we are all like an unclean thing…" Isaiah 64:6

"But we are all like an unclean thing, all our righteousnesses are as filthy as rags" in the sight of our holy sovereign, righteous God of heaven. The unrighteousness of an unrepentant heart reminds me of the day I stood in a repair shop in Montana where the mechanics used red-colored, tailor-made, grease rags to clean hands as they worked with grease and oil. The rags quickly became dirty and needed cleaning. As I stood there, I saw a cleaning company van pull up and the driver carried in a basket full of nice clean, folded, red-colored grease rags about the size of a bathroom washcloth. Then he went to a specific spot in the shop and filled his basket with oily, greasy cloths and took them away to clean and return the next trip back. What a wonderful service for those mechanics to enjoy! What a wonderful exchange!!

This is exactly what our Lord wants to do for us…take the old, soiled, sinful, dark, dirty, lost, corrupt heart, a filthy rag, to a cleaning shop and bring it back exchanged for a brand new, bathed, pure heart to serve a good, Godly purpose. "The heart of man is desperately wicked, and deceitful above all things." Jeremiah 17:9. Knowing this from before the beginning of time, God reminds us from Jeremiah 1:5 "I knew you before you were conceived; I sanctified you before you were born; I ordained you." I ordained you to become "a brand new creation in Christ, old things passed away, all things become new." II Corinthians 5:17. All this simply because, like the grease rags, "all your righteousness are as filthy rags." So, what can we do, where can we go, and how can we get cleansed if our "best" of the old nature is as filthy rags in the sight of God? We hear Him calling us to come to the "pool" for a bath, a place of business that is open 24 hours per day, whose address is Calvary, and there, at the foot of the cross we confess our inherent sin and need of a Savior from a truly repentant heart, and with childlike faith allow the pure, clean, innocent, sinless blood of Jesus that poured from His pierced side that Good Friday afternoon to give the inner man his first bath. And then we hear from heaven the assurance: "Come, now, let us reason together, though your sins be as scarlet, they shall be white like snow; though they are red like crimson, they shall be like wool." Isaiah 1:18. "If we confess our sin, God is faithful and just to forgive our sin, and to cleanse us from all unrighteousness," I John 1:9.

Our own old nature, self-righteousness, might deceive us and convince us that we are a "good sinner," unlike the inmate, the neighbor next door, the addict, or the merchant on main street, and are blinded to the truth of Romans 3:23: "All have sinned and fall short of the glory of God," and we allow deceit to dictate our eternal future. But God's Word tells us in Acts 4:12: "Nor is there salvation in no other name under heaven given among men by which we must be saved." Jesus, himself, tells us clearly about the great exchange in John 3:3: "...unless one is born again, he cannot see the kingdom of God." Jesus finally concluded: "I tell you...unless you repent, you will all likewise perish..." . Luke 13:2.

Let us remember that no one is too good nor too bad to qualify for salvation!

August 24

"Now the parable is this: The seed is the Word of God." Luke 8:11

In my days of driving the gravel and paved roads beside the farmstead in Montana, I noticed that birds of all sizes and breeds would perch along the edge of the road and then take flight as I drove by. One day when I was walking along that edge, I noticed kernels of grain evidently deposited there by grain trucks on their way to market. The seed lay on hard, untilled ground with no opportunity to sprout and grow. Total waste, stolen away, and devoured by the birds. But "faith comes by hearing, and hearing by the Word of God." That stony, untilled heart is taken care of when, we read in Ezekiel 36:26: "I will give you a new heart and put a new spirit within you; I will take the heart of stone out of your flesh, and give you a heart of flesh." The great exchange: a heavy, hard, cold, impenetrable heart for a light, warm, soft, penetrable one in which "I will put My Spirit," and then find a seedbed for My statutes.

In the springtime, as my drills rolled over the fields, I experienced the exact same description Jesus made of the various seed beds. On one large field, on the top of a hill, lay three or four acres of pure gravel, mixed with a bit of light sand. Too inconvenient to bypass, I drove over that ground and laid seed amongst those pebbles. Many kernels sprouted, grew about two inches high, and when the scorching sun beat down upon them, they faded away because they had no deep root, no place to go down for water. At sprouting time, the plants looked as good as any, but only days later wilted.

The most discouraging of all was the infestation of patches of morning glory, bindweed, a plant with roots deep down, and very difficult to eradicate with weed spray or with cultivation. At seeding time, they were invisible, so the grain seeds would sprout and begin life, only to be completely snuffed out by the thick growth they had to compete with, leaving spots without grain at harvest time. The same fate of many people who come to Jesus with joy, only to go out and let power, pride, doubt, success, wealth, pleasure, addictions, infidelity, and a host of other old-nature "weeds" crowd out the newly planted seed, continuing to invest their God-given gifts of time, talent, and treasure on themselves, and therefore die and produce no fruit for the Kingdom of God.

But praise the Lord, perhaps 99% of the seeds were planted in good soil, clean of weeds, properly tilled, full of moisture deep down, and nutrients from the added fertilizer to supplement nature's nitrogen from electrical storms and good old rainwater. From these fields, from this soil, we glean the big smile of joy and satisfaction on the farmer's face at harvest time, surely synonymous with that on Jesus' face at His coming harvest for that one who has allowed the seed to be planted in good soil, kept it weeded, and has patiently waited, having heard the voice of God from Proverbs 4:20-23: "My son, give attention to My Words; incline your ear to My sayings; let them not depart from before your eyes; keep them in the midst of your heart, for they are life to those who find them. And health unto their flesh."

August 25

"To everything there is a season,... time to weep, and a time to laugh, a time to mourn, and a time to dance." Ecclesiastes 3: 1,4.

On the first day of the week, Mary Magdalene came to the tomb early, while it was still dark, and saw the stone had been taken away from the tomb. John 20:1. "But Mary stood outside by the tomb weeping, and as she wept, she stooped down and looked into the tomb." Vs. 11.
The empty tomb! Jesus gone! It's for real! Her heavy heart sank to a new low!
Mary had come with spices and fragrant oils to finish preparing His body for proper burial since time had ran out on the eve of the Sabbath as He was taken from the cross. Like close friends, mates, and parents, she had mourned her loss all weekend. Can't we now imagine the shock of anticipating a pleasant blessing, only to find a severely unexpected thing, and then an empty tomb? The Jesus she loved and worshiped, the Jesus she had spent much time with, the Jesus Who had delivered her from seven demons, the Jesus she owed so much to; that Jesus now gone and His tomb empty. What shocking finality!!
But God is faithful: "Weeping may endure for a night, but joy comes in the morning." Psalms 30:5. "Now she turned around and saw Jesus standing there, and did not know Him. Jesus said to her, 'Woman, why are you weeping? Whom are you seeking?'...Jesus said to her 'Mary'...and she recognized Him... "Rabboni!" she

exclaimed. Her broken heart was comforted, repaired. She had just experienced her season to "weep...to laugh...to mourn...to dance."

Early in the morning in late **August 1995**, three weeks after my wife's passing, a beautiful day for harvest, and into my yard drove my daughter and my sister-in-law to take care of my wife's personals, a chore I had dreaded. I came home late that night, and out of curiosity, just like Mary, I headed for the bedroom and was shocked into heavy weeping and heartbreak when I saw the clothes gone, all the pairs of shoes gone, and the jewelry and knick-knacks on the dresser gone, most drawers empty, forty six years of familiarity gone, and only my skimpy wardrobe to hang in that empty closet. The room even sounded hollow. As I wept by myself, I sensed, "This is really the final "reality" of her being forever gone." "...a time to weep...a time to mourn..."

Like Mary, I sought after Jesus in prayer and in the Word, and He spoke to me from Jeremiah 29:11. "I know the thought I think toward you, thoughts of peace, not of evil; I give you a future, I give you a hope." He kept His Word, and the impossible happened: a lonely, Godly widow from far distant Iowa ventured alone out to the Rocky Mountain Bible Camp in Western Montana, and His promise, "I give you a future and a hope" became a reality as we met, became first-time friends, exchanged telephone numbers, and parted for each of our homes five days later. The rest is history, as God brought us together in marriage, both of us having stood patiently on Jeremiah 29:11. Now, "a time to laugh...a time to dance...!"

August 26

"The rough and rocky road."

It can be a bit disturbing when we are rushing down an interstate with our mind bent solely on our destination most of us would have liked to reach as early as yesterday, and suddenly a roadside sign showing two arrows side by side, indicating two-lane traffic just ahead, restricted speed, and road construction. When I think of the ultimate, purposed blessing of life God has ordained for every person ever born, each one of which He died for personally, I see that two-lane road where He first slows us down a bit while traveling south, and gets our attention by prayer and the Word as the Holy Spirit seals our relationship forever. It's like traveling south with our hand in the hand of the devil, and suddenly come crashing into a wall inscribed "Dead End," the ripened time when the Holy Spirit has been trying to get our attention. Our Heavenly Father mercifully, compassionately, gently picks us up into His arms to ease the fleshy pain of the crash as we lay aside the pain of pride, rebellion, conviction "rattling our cage," repentance calling for attention, and total surrender becoming a reality. God allows even the most severe crash to happen, since Jesus tells us in Matthew 5:29-30 that it is better that your eye be plucked out and cast away, or a right hand be cut off and discarded, "for it is more profitable that one of your members perish than the whole body be cast into Hell."

Paul, in Acts 9, was traveling fast in the lane going south one day only three miles from his destination, Damascus, when he suddenly hit a "Dead End" sign, and "suddenly a light shown around him from Heaven. He fell to the ground and heard a voice…"Saul, Saul, why are you persecuting Me? I am Jesus whom you are persecuting. Arise and go into the city." Next we find him turned around, having made a "U-Turn," and now traveling north on the opposite lane of life. Paul had heard an invitation like every one of us hears when traveling in the fast lane headed south to crash into the "Dead End" sign.

From Joel 2:13 God exhorts, commands; "Come back to the Lord, your God, because He is kind and shows mercy. He doesn't become angry quickly, and He has great love." "Come back" He says, out of your dark world of sin, death, and destruction; come back by way of the cross, assured by John 3:16: "…that whosoever believes on Jesus shall not perish, but shall have everlasting life." I hear Him saying: "Come out of that death chamber, that grave you were born into because of trespass and sin, and come back to the rightful place you were created to occupy, that place that Jesus died to bring you into, and to guarantee eternal fellowship with Him and His Father. It's back to life with the Sovereign, Holy, Righteous God of Heaven, our Creator, our Savior. "For by grace have you been saved, through faith, and raised us up together, and made us sit together in the Heavenly places in Christ Jesus." Ephesians 2:6.

We praise the Lord this morning for those who have hit the "Dead End," made the "U-Turn," and now headed for an eternity with Jesus in Heaven.

August 27

"Life mixes well with interludes!"

It was a warm, quiet, sunny, spring morning on the ranch when I suddenly heard a human whistling near-by. I looked up and saw my neighbor riding on horseback, coming toward me from the river bottom. He loved well-trained quarter horses, a comfortable saddle, and miles of rangeland he tended to frequently. The whistling spoke of the joy of life in his heart, and it spilled over into mine also, a real good lift that morning. That cowboy out on the range was one of the best matched men with his vocation I have ever known, and therefore, could truly rejoice in Psalm 118:24: "This is the day that the Lord has made; I will rejoice and be glad in it." There was a young man in the prime of life, enjoying great success in his marriage, his family, his place in life so that he just couldn't contain it that morning. Like with this man in his secular affairs, so it is with that person who is truly born into the Kingdom of God by the rebirth of the inner man who cannot contain the joy of thanksgiving and praise. God not only writes the music for our lives, but also directs the symphony of our highs and lows. "The steps of a good man are ordered by the Lord, and in his ways does the Lord find His delight. "Though he fall, he shall not be utterly destroyed, for the hand of the Lord will uphold him." Psalm 37:23-24.

Have you ever noticed that in a choral concert or a symphony of instruments that it is not unusual for certain voices or strings to stand by while others play? An interlude it is called. As I write, I am facing knee surgery and several weeks, I expect, of being "at rest," out of regular circulation, an interlude I do not welcome, But then I remember Jesus in Mark 6:31: "He said to them: 'Come aside by yourselves to a deserted place and rest awhile'." Interludes of illness, retirement or replacement can be frustrating, discouraging, or unfulfilling since we are neither ready nor willing to stop just now.

It may just be that the interludes are there to make the music in our lives sound better, just as with a concert or symphony where the quiet, slow, hushed parts put the bases to rest, while in the loud, thunderous measures the flutes, piccolos, and clarinets may rest. After a rest, and interlude, the Great Conductor motions with His baton to chime in again. Who knows the interlude just ahead in the future, the steps the Lord uses to prepare us for the next start He would introduce us to.

My whistling neighbor's unexpected visit that spring morning, a time of relaxing over a cup of coffee, was a welcome interlude, a time of refreshing for both of us; a time of interruption, a time of rest, a momentary change of direction which, like in a symphony, happens quite often on a Western ranch.

August 28

"Why are you cast down, O my soul...disquieted within me?" Psalm 42:5

It was a beautiful, sunny, warm, dry morning at the start of harvest in Montana when I came to the field where I had parked my John Deere combine the evening before. After filling the fuel tank, I lifted the hood that covered the engine to check water and oil levels, and there I found a mess...water and oil dripping freely from damaged hoses. I opened the cab door and found that fire had gutted my entire cab...anything that would burn, and had gone through the firewall of the engine compartment, had blackened the windows, and then burned out, the electrical fire that put her to rest for eternity. The droplets of water and oil of the inanimate creature matched the tears of this animate one, and together "Why are you cast down, O my soul?" Early retirement for the combine and a huge shock for me!

So it is recorded of David at his hometown of Ziklag in II Samuel: "David and his men rose early in the morning...came to the city Ziklag...burned with fires and their wives, their sons, their daughters and livestock had been taken captive. Then David and the people with him lifted up their voices and wept until they had no more power to weep." The city was burned and the families kidnapped. "But David strengthened himself in the Lord, his God." Vs. 6. I suspect a time of prayer and fasting, recalling the promises of God and his past testimonies of God's power in his life prevailed. "Then David took all the flocks and herds which they (Amalek) had driven away...and said: This is David's spoil."

I had similar blessing right away that very morning when I called my insurance agent and found that not only was my combine covered, but also the remaining acres of harvest, since I could hire another to finish; within an hour was again cutting down the grain. When I looked for a replacement combine later, I was blessed with another, the same model in excellent condition, also paid for by the insurance.

"Because of His mercies I am not consumed; His compassions never fail; they are new every morning. Great is Your faithfulness." Lam. 3:23-34.

"I will bless the Lord at all times; His praise shall continually be in my mouth." Psalm 34:1.

Even short-term trials can strengthen long-term faith!!

August 29

"And a son Samuel, was born." I Samuel 2:5

As a young farmer and rancher, I was all ears when the older generation shared their experiences and wisdom, usually at a casual gathering at a place of business in town or at the café over a cup of coffee. On one such occasion I heard the local elevator manager explain, as farmers murmured of a drought in their fields: "May is the best month for a grain field to suffer drought because the young, tender plant's roots are forced down to find moisture for their survival in the usual hot, dry July days ahead, In a wet May they are "babied" and reach out horizontally and fail to stand later stress."

I tested the truth of that wisdom for over fifty years with grain plants and found it sound; deep roots survive drought, while shallow roots fade away under stress and produce little or no harvest. Hannah of 1 Samuel illustrates well this truth in her life of having had planted early in her life deep roots of faith in God, whom she worshiped and prayed to daily. The seeds of faith planted in her young heart sprouted, took root, and sustained her throughout her severe suffering of a drought God placed upon her womb, which drove those roots deep into the heart of compassionate, merciful God, her well of strength, which culminated in a rich harvest. "…the Lord had closed her womb" Vs. 6, a time of severe drought in her life. "…as she continued praying before the Lord…", Vs.12. Her deep roots of faith in a miracle-working God and her vow to give him back to the Lord, Vs. 2—"opened her womb and a son, Samuel, was born, followed by six more children." Chapter 2:5. God then molded young Samuel into a vessel He could use in a mighty way to help usher Jesus into this world. When praying for my family, I ask God to send their faith roots deep into His own heart of love to experience a close relationship with Him so they will grow up to be strong plants because of the trials I know He will bless them to help them grow into a vessel He intended them to be at His time of giving them life. Jeremiah 1:5. "I knew you before you were conceived; I sanctified you before you were born; and I anointed you…" Deep down roots of faith keep them from being swept away when the winds of adversity prevail upon them.

August 30

"His resurrection is real!"

There must be a death before a resurrection!
Good morning to friends out there who may be looking for some good news to begin the day—and here it is, from Romans 6:5: "For if we have been united together in the likeness of His death, certainly we shall also be in the likeness of His resurrection." Good news for that one who has surrendered at Calvary, been totally forgiven of sin, truly born again, and on his way to a busy day on earth this very moment.

For the businessman or storekeeper, that often means unlocking a vault in the office to retrieve cash to prime the cash register, or personal valuables or uncompleted work from yesterday. Unless already broken into or the lock tampered with, the memorized code will work without fail. It is safe to believe in so that you can stake your life on it because the Maker's promise has proven his integrity. It works!!

There is another vault like that—man's grave—also containing a precious gem in the sight of God; just an old clay frame, but in God's eye a vault that will be supernaturally opened, and everybody within a grave will be raised up with a new form, and the spirit and soul that once inhabited that body will again inhabit—resurrected—and then face Jesus without exception, and "every tongue will confess that Jesus Christ was Lord." Philippians 2:11.

The truly born again believer will be ushered into that place prepared for the saint, Heaven. The one who refused Jesus in this life will be sent down the broad path to destruction, to forever "exist" in a place called Hell. Matthew 25. The saint will go on his way "rejoicing" while the unbeliever will go weeping, desperate, lonely, gnashing his teeth with anger and despair.

Because God says what He means in His manual for us, the Bible, and means what He says about both believer and unbeliever and about Heaven and Hell, about dying and living, it is safe to truly accept what God says in Romans 6:5 in so many words: "Die to sin with Jesus and rise to new life with that same Jesus, united as one."—truly a miracle, the best good news afloat today as we travel once more the road to the celebration of His resurrection.

August 31

"We all need someone who understands."

A store owner was tacking a sign above his door that read: "Puppies for Sale." Signs like that have a way of attracting small children, and sure enough, a little boy appeared under the store owner's sign. "How much are you going to sell the puppies for?" he asked. The store owner replied: "Anywhere from $30 to $50." The little boy reached into his pocket and pulled out some change. "I have $2.37" he said. "Can I please look at them?" The man smiled and whistled and out of the kennel came Lady, who ran down the aisle of the store followed by five teeny, tiny balls of fur. One puppy lagged considerably behind. Immediately, the little boy singled out the lagging, limping puppy and said; "What's wrong with that little dog?" The man explained that the veterinarian had examined the little puppy and had discovered it didn't have a hip socket. It would always limp and be lame. The little boy became excited, and said: "That's the puppy I want to buy." The man said: "No you don't want to buy that little dog. But if you really want him, I will give him to you." The little boy got quite upset. He looked straight into the man's eyes, pointing his finger, and said: "I don't want you to give him to me. That little dog is worth as much as all the other puppies, and I'll pay full price. In fact, I'll give you $2.37 now, and fifty cents a month until I have him paid for." The man again countered, "You don't want to buy this little dog. He is never going to be able to run and jump and play with you like the other puppies." To his surprise, the little boy reached down and rolled up his pant leg to reveal a badly twisted, crippled left leg supported by a big metal brace. He looked at the man and quietly replied: "Well, I don't run so well myself, and that little puppy will need someone who understands!"

Do we not all need someone who understands? Jesus came from Heaven to die on a cross for you and me because He understood our sin plight that only He could do something about for us, crippled from birth like that little puppy.

Here again I think of King David and his love and understanding for young Mephibosheth, a lame boy, Jonathan's son, Saul's grandson. He was five years old when his nurse dropped him while in flight. The lad grew up, lame, and one day King David ordered him to come to him, and when he came, he fell prostrate before David and said to the King: "Here is your servant." So David said to him; "Do not fear, for I will surely show you kindness for Jonathan, your father's sake...and you shall eat bread at my table continually." II Samuel 9. To servant Ziba from King David: "As for Mephilbosheth, he shall eat at my table like one of the King's sons."

Vs. 11. "So Mephibosheth dwelt in Jerusalem, for he ate continually at the King's table. And he was lame in both of his feet." Vs. 13.

Jesus, Matthew 25:40: "Assuredly I say to you, inasmuch as you have done it unto one of the least of these my brethren, you have done it unto Me."

Are you not moved today to share generously your time, talent, and treasure with the down and out people, the lame ones in spirit, soul, and body?

September 1

"...to be conformed to the image of Jesus..." Romans 8:29

It was a nice, warm, sunny, autumn afternoon, the first weekend of the school term for my first grade brother in 1933. He got an urge to ride Beauty, a kid pony, and asked me to help saddle her, which I refused, and have regretted to this day. As he rode, I followed on foot, to dad on the other side of a bayou, three quarters mile distant. At the water-soaked earth of the narrow bayou, the intelligent pony jumped across, and my brother fell into the soggy stuff with his arm clear to the shoulder. When he pulled it out, the bone above his wrist looked like an "S", and I declared: "Your arm is broken," to which he retorted: "No, it's just bent," as he wept with fear and pain. "If only he had had that saddle horn to hang onto" I shamefully thought to myself!! His arm healed quickly in a cast and a sling the Doctor put in place.

If I could trust that earthly doctor to repair a broken arm, how much more can I trust my God, the Great Physician, to reset my broken life, and at times my broken heart like He has, that I might be "conformed to the image of Jesus". Romans 8:29. His purpose for each of our lives is so well addressed in Luke 4:18, Jesus speaking: "I have been anointed to...heal the broken hearted, to deliver those in bondage, to open the eyes of the blind, and to set free them that are bruised."

The image of Jesus spells pain and sacrifice, companion, power over sin, shedding of blood to wash man's inner being clean, and to give us the hope of resurrection, as He was resurrected.

Could my brother's arm heal normally by itself? No, no more than can our hearts heal normally by themselves without Jesus as we come to the Great Physician with truly repentant hearts.

Next time I feel broken, I will not panic, but rather praise Him for one more trial that brings healing to one more ailing "heart muscle", realizing that God is at work to "conform me to His image."

Poet Hess adds this sweet aroma: "Life's fractures can be mended by faith in Christ, the Lord. At first the pain, but then the gain, and usefulness restored."

As I think of that day seventy-five years ago, I remember Romans 12:15, a perfect image of Jesus: "Rejoice with those who rejoice, and weep with those who weep."

September 2

"Make a joyful shout unto the Lord. Serve Him with gladness; come before His presence with singing." Psalm 100:1.

The old cliché, "silence is golden", is ever so true and appreciated when I am listening to the news and can use the mute button when the overly noisy advertising comes on. But to sit and watch the little pudgy guy who "just lost another loan to Ditech," in all the postures he plays, is hilarious to me, especially without sound. Reminds me of a late Saturday night when I was driving home from a harvest field, and I passed by a dance hall all lighted up. For some reason I parked alongside the road to observe for just a moment, watching couples hopping up and down and round and round, some slowly, some very fast, some young, some old, some tall, dark, and handsome, others short, stocky and bald, all seemingly in good rhythm. But I couldn't hear a sound of music playing. It was hilariously entertaining, a funny comic strip for the moment!

And now I think of the old man released from a long-term prison about dark one evening, so depressed that he headed for suicide at the bridge across town. As he walked, he began to hear the faint sound of gospel music and a piano in the background, and the music crescendoed as he came to an open church door. It raised his soul up, renewed his faith, and before the evening ended, salvaged his lost soul. Like me, he just stopped by to observe. But what a greater blessing for him than for me—one alive with sound of music, the other like a mannequin. One uplifting, the other just plain sensual and comical; one a deep-down blessing that lasted, the other simple entertainment to quietly watch and satisfy the flesh, and then vanish.

How different it was with King David when he went out and brought up the ark of God with gladness. Then, in II Samuel 6:14, "Then David danced before the Lord with all his might…and as the ark of the Lord came into the city of David, Michel, Saul's daughter, looked through a window and saw King David leaping and whirling before the Lord.…" God had lifted him up and had put a new song into his heart…"I will extol You, oh Lord, for You have lifted me up; You have not made my enemies to rejoice over me." Psalm 30:1— lifted him out of fear, anxiety, and insecurity, like as the angels did with the shepherds that first Christmas eve on the hillsides of Galilee: "and suddenly there was with the angel a multitude of the heavenly host praising God and saying, 'Glory to God in the highest, and on earth peace, good will toward men'."

This devotion comes from one who hears a new song deep down in his soul since that evening years ago when prayer over me released the Holy Spirit Who gave me a hunger for God's Word and thirst for living water that has lasted to this very hour, so that I can join with the psalmist with a thankful heart, and "Make a joyful shout to the Lord…Serve Him with gladness, and come before His presence with singing."

September 3

"The name of the Lord is a strong tower; the righteous runs into it and is safe." Proverbs 18:10.

I see a high tower like the Eiffel Tower in Paris, encircled with an impenetrable, unscaleable wall, making a huge courtyard, a wall with only one door and above it the inscription, "The door of the sheep" John 10:7; and "I am the Way, the Truth, and the Life…" John 14:6. The door that opens occasionally, opens only to that one who knocks on it to announce his faith in such word as John 3:16, being heralded from the tower, along with Romans 10:9-10. "For God so loved the world that He gave His only begotten Son, that whosoever believes in Him should not perish but have everlasting life." "That if you confess with your mouth the Lord Jesus and believe in your heart that God raised Him from the dead, you will be saved." Then and there is that void satisfied we are all born with because of inherent sin, and the cross becomes a bridge to transport us across the courtyard and into the tower's forever safety.

Milling around and around outside the huge courtyard are the 6.2 billion people on earth today, some looking for the "straight road and the narrow gate" that leads to Heaven, while most are heading down the broad path through the wide gate unto eternal destruction, worshiping false gods with foreign names.

Those milling closest to the courtyard wall out there in a dark world are those nearest the beaming light of the gospel coming from atop the tower, His name proclaimed. These are the Gentile world who have had most opportunity to enter the courtyard and run to the tower for eternal safety. They are the nations of Europe where Paul introduced the gospel that the pilgrims brought to America four hundred years ago. Like a yard light on a farmstead, or a street light on a curb, the farther away we go from that light the darker the world around us becomes. The people I see that far away, are those least exposed to Christianity, wallowing in heathenism and the influence of false gods that promise salvation by works, unlike Christianity which guarantees salvation by grace alone. "For by grace you have been saved through faith...the gift of God." Ephesians 2:8.

There is a day ahead when the exercise of man's choice will end, and the courtyard walls will vanish and the truth of Phil. 3:9 will become the final Word, "...God has highly exalted Him and given Him the name which is above every name, that at the name of Jesus, EVERY knee will bow, and EVERY tongue confess that Jesus Christ is Lord." Wise is that man who heeds God's Word: "Today is the day of salvation" while there is still time.

In the meantime, I love that most colorful part of the picture which David describes for the believer from Psalm 100: 3-5, "We are His people and the sheep of His pasture. Enter His gates with thanksgiving and into His courts with praise. Be thankful to Him, and bless His name. For the Lord is good, His mercy is everlasting, and His truth endures to all generations." Can't you just see little lambs racing, kicking up their heels across the courtyard, their satisfied hearts full of love, joy, peace, and security?

"How beautiful upon the mountains are the feet of him who brings good news…proclaims peace…glad tidings of good things… salvation…, who says to Zion, "Your God reigns!" Isaiah 52:7.

September 4

"Forever, oh Lord, Your Word is settled in Heaven." Psalm 119:89.

What a gorgeous day to be sharing from God's Word which the psalmist boldly and confidently declares in Psalm 119:89: "Forever, O Lord, your Word is settled in Heaven." Oh yes, "The grass withers and the flower fades, but the Word of the Lord endures forever." Oh, for the love, joy, peace, and security that Word, the holy scriptures, God's statues, His love letter to humanity, the Bible, puts into a believer's heart so that his testimony is one with the psalmist's heart.

"I rise before the dawning of the morning and cry for help; I hope in Your Words." Psalm 119:147, and in Psalm 119: 11: "Your Word have I hid in my heart that I might not sin against You." My friend, we need a daily heart searching because of the under-mining power of our old nature, the world about us and Satan himself to determine if our faith is real or an imitation. God addressed this in Isaiah 29:13: "These people honor Me with their lips but have removed their hearts far from Me."

During the time of the prophet Isaiah, many of the people of Israel were merely going through the motions, like many today in their repeated liturgies and masses man has concocted. I spent forty two years in lifeless motions of worship. In Isaiah 1:13 we read: "Bring no more futile sacrifices; incense is an abomination to Me… your New Moons and your appointed feasts My soul hates."

David, too, apparently made that very discovery one day about sacrifices and offerings being the important part in coming to worship, and in Psalm 4:6-8, recognized his error, manifested in Vs. 7: "Behold, I come…in the scroll of the book it is written of Me."

David convicted—"It is me, the little boy inside, that God really wants—my spirit being, that God-part of my being. "My eyes and ears You have opened, and I see the futility and emptiness of mere sacrifice and offering unless my heart is in it—unless my heart is pure in motive and my conscience clear, basking in Godly righteousness." "Search me, oh Lord, and know my heart, try me and see if there be any wickedness in me, and lead me in Your way everlasting." Psalm 139:23.

Friend, ponder your motive and enjoy your day.

September 5

"The spirit of the Lord is upon Me because I have been anointed to preach good news to the poor; to heal the broken hearted, to set the captives free, to open the eyes of the blind, and to set free them that are bruised." Jesus, Luke 4:18

This message which Jesus spoke to His hometown congregation in Nazareth was intended by Him to introduce His prophesied ministry to mankind as the prophet had declared in Isaiah 61:1: "Today this scripture is fulfilled in your hearing" Jesus, Vs. 21. The message was almost unanimously refuted in that synagogue even to the point of their wanting to destroy Him that morning. Vs. 28-29.

How different was my personal experience thirty years ago when I first heard Jesus from Luke 4:18, and the Holy Spirit quickened that truth to me. One evening I came home from a full day of field work, full of inner anger, tired, venting that anger on my twenty five year old son, who looked at me and said: "Dad, I'd like to know what goes on in your mind all day long out there in that tractor cab, as ugly as you are when you come home." My heart broke as guilt and self-condemnation, and truth overcame me, a trial that drove me into God's Word that evening and into the morning hour when Jesus became my only hope for overcoming such poisonous venom in my inner man. I was lonely, a bit depressed and ashamed until Jesus came to my rescue when I came to Him with a truly repentant heart. "If we confess our sins, God is faithful and just to forgive our sin, and to cleanse us from all unrighteousness." I John 1:9.

Sanctification was taking place in my inner man. I had just recently memorized Luke 4:18, and now stood firmly on it with child-like faith, and was set free from inner anger. Months later, in my combine cab, I realized my mind and heart had been transformed that day earlier, my freedom from that bondage a reality as "I entered His gates with thanksgiving, and His courts with praise."

"...to set free them that are bruised...". It was a pleasant, quiet afternoon at the ranch as I sat at the dining room table, praying and meditating again on Luke 4:18, and the Holy Spirit moved: "What about all those grudges, those chips on your shoulder? Write them down." I took a tablet and wrote down the names of every person—brothers, parents, friends, strangers, teachers, police, pastors, and all I could remember who had "bruised" me along life's way from early childhood. My "skin" seemed to be so thin and so sensitive. I verbally spoke forgiveness to each one from a truly, honest, repentant heart, even though many of them had passed on in the meantime. Jesus was pleased and granted me a freedom that "turned my mourning into joy" so that I could sing out with David from Psalm 30: "I will extol You, oh Lord, for You have not let my enemies rejoice over me...weeping may endure for a night, but joy comes in the morning." That joy, liberty, and freedom has lasted to this very hour.

September 6

"...And be sure your sin will find you out." Numbers 32:23.

A siege of missing sheep in central Montana caused law officers to keep special vigil for the predator. One day a highway patrol noticed a pickup-drawn trailer house going regularly down a certain highway and returning. When he stopped the driver, he asked, "What are you hauling in the trailer?" as he heard the sheep bleating, an unusual sound to come from a trailer home people usually live in. The thief was jailed and paid dearly for his "sin that found him out."

From I Samuel 15, King Saul, too, was caught in the sin of disobedience, disobeying God; and Samuel, at God's request, was sent to "catch him in the act" and spell out his fine.

God had sent King Saul on a mission: "now go and attack Amalek, and utterly destroy all that they have, and spare none, but kill both man and woman, infant and nursing child, ox and sheep, camel and donkey." Vs. 5. Temptation, the old nature flesh, arose and Saul and his people, "spared King Agog and the best of the sheep, the oxen, the fatlings, the lambs, and all that was good, unwilling to utterly destroy them." Vs. 9. "What then is this bleating of the sheep in my ears and the lowing of the oxen which I hear?" Samuel asked, Vs. 14. In self defense of his disobedience, Saul explained to Samuel: "But the people took of the plunder, sheep and oxen...to sacrifice to the Lord your God...".

Have you ever listened to Satan who tempted you to lie, cheat, steal, bluff, or engage in graft and give a portion of those tainted goods to the Lord as an offering? Or, like I heard of in Montana, a certain number of unspecified acres dedicated to the Lord at seeding time, and when harvest came, the hailed out acreage, or the shelled out wheat from wind, or the acres of poorest quality of grain cleverly became the Lord's acres. Disobedience and deceitfulness first class!!!

Samuel's God-inspired answer to Saul I like: "Has the Lord as great delight in burnt offering and sacrifices, as in obeying the voice of the Lord? Behold, to obey is better than sacrifice, and to heed than the fat rams. For rebellion is as the sin of witchcraft and idolatry. Because you have rejected the Word of the Lord, He also has rejected you from being king." What a price to pay!!!

"Ananias, with Sapphira his wife, sold a possession." Acts 5:1. "Out of a deceptive heart, they kept back part of the proceeds,...and brought a certain part and laid it at the apostle's feet." Vs. 2. You see, the church held all their possessions in common in those days, and when one sold a portion, he brought all the proceeds and laid then at the apostle's feet to distribute to the needy. Peter and Ananias, "why have you conceived this thing in your heart, You have not lied to man but to God," as revealed to Peter by the Holy Spirit. "Then Ananias, hearing those Words, fell down and breathed his last." Vs. 5. Three hours later, Sapphira, in the presence of Peter, confessed the deceit revealed by the Holy Spirit, "then immediately fell down at his feet and breathed her last." What a price to pay!!!

"Blessed are the pure in heart, for they shall see God." Matthew 5:8.

September 7

"Your Word have I hidden in my heart…" Psalm 119:11

The other night my trip across the sea of life at bedtime was disrupted by an unwelcomed guest called "insomnia", who had found his way into my boat, taunting me into the wee hours of the morning. Prayer for a pillow to lay my inner man's head on turned into worship as such Word from Psalm 3:5 poured over my soul: "I lay down and slept; I awakened for the Lord sustained me." And from Psalm 4:8: "I will both lie down in peace and sleep, for You alone, oh Lord, make me dwell in safety." Those were His Words given to me for my encouragement and edification. I seemed to imply from my heart: "Come now, Lord, let us reason together, since I trust Your Word that is running through my mind. So that now You may remove this obstacle, and put that "peace", that "sleep", into my night life."

"Return to your rest, oh my soul, for the Lord has dealt bountifully with you. Oh God, You have delivered my soul from death, my eyes from tears and my feet from falling." Psalm 116:7-8.

The real blessing was to come at 2:30 a.m. when I rose up, went to the den, and opened my Bible to Mark 4:35 where Jesus found it so easy to sleep in the boat that was being tossed and violently up and down by wind and waves. I needed a faith builder. The test of the disciples' faith in that boat with Jesus was like my test: "Are you going to believe God's Word and stand firmly, or not?

Like with me in the plight, the Word of God should have been running through their minds, a Word they could take to the bank for security, given to them before He fell asleep: "Let us cross over to the other side." Jesus says what He means and means what He says!!

It is evident that Jesus fully intended to sail to the other side… storm or no storm!! All the disciples had to do for calm and peace in their hearts as the wind and waves beat on them was to believe Jesus' words that would expel fear and doubt.

"My son, give attention to My Words; incline your ear to My sayings; let them not depart from before your eyes; keep them in the midst of your heart, for they are life unto those who find them, and health unto their flesh." Proverbs 4:20.

"Your Word have I hidden in my heart that I sin not."

September 8

"My son, give attention to My Words; Incline your ear to My sayings; Let them not depart from before your eyes; Keep them in the midst of your heart; For they are LIFE unto those who find them, and HEALTH unto their flesh." Proverbs 4:20-23 (Bold letters mine).

Someone has beautifully coined my personal testimony as to the treasure of God's Word with this bit of poetry: "Thy Word is like a deep mine, and jewels rich and rare are hidden in its mighty depths for every searcher there." Gems of truth are found deep into the Bible, and you must dig to find them as need arises. One time while cultivating a grain field, I noticed my implement lifted up and over a certain spot in the field every time I worked that spot. One day I began to dig down with a front-end loader and found an apparently huge rock that I could not budge with my tractor. I hired a back hoe operator to dig deep and soon removed a rock measuring several feet across and likewise deep.

Like that rock coming from deep into the earth, God's Word is only valuable and precious when dug from the pages of the Bible. Then does it produce a testimony of blessing—a blessing of salvation to the unsaved, and a blessing of sanctification, growth, and fruit-bearing for the man of God who is faithful and persevering in his daily digging. Two men, one a poor man from a godless background, and the other from wealth and an affluent religious environment, shared the details of their salvation recently experienced, and the wealthy man asked the poor man: "Why do you suppose you responded the first time you heard the gospel, while so many years passed before I did? (I wonder, could Luke 4:18 be the answer? Jesus, "...He, has anointed Me to preach the gospel to the poor..."). The poor man answered, "That's easy. Suppose someone came along and offered each of us a brand new suit of clothes. I'd jump at the offer, because my clothes are old and worn. But your closet is no doubt filled with the finest of suits.

So is it with salvation. You were probably satisfied with all your goodness and works, so it took you a long time to see the need for God's garment of righteousness offered to you through Christ—a long time to see your real self described in Isaiah 64: "We are all like an unclean thing, and all our righteousness are like filthy rags." I was deeply aware of my sinful condition at first sight, eager then to receive forgiveness and cleansing. "All have sinned and fall short of the glory of God." Romans 3:23. "The wages of sin is death, but the gift of God is eternal life." Romans 6:23. How David would undoubtedly sing out from Psalm 30:1, "I will extol You, oh Lord, for you have lifted me up; You have not let my enemies to rejoice over me." "Thy Word is a lamp unto my feet, and a light unto my path." Psalm 119:105.

I address you people this day as one who has been given "new clothes" of righteousness for the inner man, having been bathed in the shed blood of Jesus at Calvary with child-like faith.

September 9

"Greater is He that is in me than he that is in the world." I John 4:4.

"Dad, that car is not going to stop!" my twenty three year old son rightfully observed from the back seat when five of us in the car were returning late at night from a Rex Humbard evangelistic meeting in Regina, Sask. Highway 5, the paved road I was traveling, had the right of way, all accesses faced with a stop sign. The last I remember of the driver was his headlights and front end just ready to strike my left front fender at a terribly excessive speed, a definite death trap when someone surely on alcohol or drugs lost his judgment. The rest is history, I passed through, but with no memory, the only possibility being that God intervened with angelic force to protect us from tragedy. At home later that night, I awakened twice to the noise of clanging metal, broken glass, and screaming voices. PTL (Praise the Lord) that "Greater is He that is in me than he that is in the world"…our vehicle and occupants covered with prayer before our trip began. "The enemy has come to kill, steal, and destroy, but I have come to give life, and to give it abundantly." John 10:10. Both physical and spiritual life.

It was like that with the three million Israelites coming out of Pharaoh's Egypt, led by Moses, arriving at the Red Sea, a sure death trap as Pharaoh's army fiercely and quickly pursued them from the rear. With unscaleable high banks on either side, an impossible water depth ahead of them, an enemy in hot pursuit behind, reminds me of my own predicament just related. In either case, there was no possible safe way out but the ministering spirits sent by God for deliverance. "Are they not all ministering spirits sent forth to minister for those who will inherit salvation?" Hebrews 1:14. At the precise, correct timing, the Red Sea opened, the river bed dried instantly, and the last of the Israelites passed through just in time for God to release the waters and destroy the enemy.

"Oh Lord, I will extol You for You have lifted me up; You have not made my enemies to rejoice over me." David, Psalm 30:1-2.

"When the enemy comes in like a flood, the Spirit of the Lord raises up a standard against him" Isaiah 59:19.

From one "who's soul shall make its boast in the Lord." David, Psalm 34:2a.

September 10

"Forgiveness pays big dividends!"

This morning my mind went back to a long weekend many years ago when my sons and I saw a parcel of land for sale slip through our fingers because of a gossiping neighbor. We had agreed on the transaction on a Friday and would have sealed it on Monday. It was an especially appealing transaction for us, adjoining land we already farmed, very appealing price-wise, and actually a "big plus" for both our agricultural and livestock enterprises. Disgust, disappointment, and anger rose up in our hearts, but a trial the Lord used to bless us in the days ahead. As I searched the scriptures and prayed to be an overcomer, I heard nothing but "forgive, forgive, forgive," which I received rather stubbornly at first, and then complete surrender as I heard Jesus from Matthew 5:44: "Love your enemies, bless them that curse you, do good to them that hate you, and pray for those that spitefully use you and persecute you." And again from Matthew 6:14: "For if you forgive men their trespasses, your Heavenly Father will also forgive you. But if you do not forgive men their trespasses, neither will your Father forgive your trespasses." Fortunately, there had been no verbal exchange, which made reconciliation much easier. From a truly repentant heart, I found myself craving fellowship with that neighbor like I once enjoyed. It wasn't long until our relationship was healed, and we could compliment one another from sincere hearts once again.

We reached over the fence to bless one another as opportunity showed itself. The neighbor has passed on into eternity and I have moved 800 miles away, but our two sons today are cordial friends, blessing one another not only as they exchange greetings and pleasantries, but even work force.

"…I have set before you life and death, blessing and cursing; therefore choose life that both you and your descendants may live; that you may love the Lord your God, that you may obey His voice, and that you may cling to Him, for He is your life and the length of your days." Deuteronomy 30:19-20.

September 11

"Let not the floodwater overflow me,
Nor let the deep swallow me up.
And let not the pit shut its mouth on me." Psalm 69:15

What an appropriate, blessed work to cross my mind early in the morning of the finding of the trapped miners in West Virginia—an urgent plea for help in trouble, a bit late now, but in essence the sensitivity of faith-filled praying hearts all over America. The trapped miner's fate of yesteryear was floodwater, from which they all escaped. The miner's fate this week was encased in the goings on in the "deep" of a mountain base, the pit's mouth shut. But the same prayer in time of like trouble.

Deep water can sometimes be a problem for us as we travel the roadways of life, and like the Israelites at the overflowing, flooding Jordan, find themselves surrounded with grief or crashing waves beating upon us, and we must plead for help, standing on his promise like we find in II Chronicles 20:15: "Do not fear, nor be dismayed, for the battle is not yours but God's."

"Jacob...Israel...do not fear for I have redeemed you. You are Mine, I call you by name, so when you pass through the waters, I will be with you; and through the rivers, they shall not overflow you. When you walk through the fires, you shall not be burned, nor shall you even be scorched; for I am the Lord your God, the God of Israel, your Savior." Isaiah 43:1-3.

During the devastating drought and grasshopper infestation of the 1980's on my Montana farm and ranch, I found myself one day buried like the miners in a deep pit of financial problems that challenged my very survival, lest "the deep swallow me up." I literally lived in God's Word day and night, and alongside came an evangelist friend to pray with me. But before we prayed, he ushered me into Habakkuk 3:17-19: "Though the fig tree may not blossom, nor fruit be on the vines; though the labor of the olive may fail, and the fields yield no food; though the flock be cut off from the fold, and there be no herd in the stalls—yet, I will rejoice in the Lord, I will joy in the God of my salvation." He knew what I needed for survival.

The pitiful "why me, Lord" so ably turned into thanks and praise as I began to "count my many blessings, name them one by one:" and could then sing very soon with David from Psalm 30:1: "I will extol you, oh Lord, for You have lifted me up; You have not let my enemies rejoice over me...weeping may endure for a night, but joy comes in the morning."

There is power in praise. There is closure in praise my family found when we placed our twenty year old son and brother into the "deep" as many friends stood by and joined their voices with ours at the graveside in praise and thanksgiving so that "the peace of God which passes all understanding" could seal our hearts and minds until our meeting him in eternity.

September 12

"He, [God] frustrates the devises of the crafty, So that their hands cannot carry out their plans." Job 5:12.

Job had a "crafty" one hounding him day and night to claim his wealth, his family, his health, the loyalty of friends and a mate. But, in the middle of all his nine-month struggle for survival, God gave him powerful principal to stand on—to renew his strength day by day. You see, God could make that boast because He is our Omni-God, that One Who knows all things, is everywhere present, and has power over all other forces. Since I know the wonderful victory Job enjoyed because of God's workings of Job 5:12, I have great confidence and boldness in standing on that truth with childlike faith when I pray daily against America's "crafty" enemies within her borders and across the globe—politicians, greedy CEO's, the Casinos, Hollywood, pornography, the ACLU, the rapists and child molesters inside our borders; and the religious enemies of Christ's, terrorists sweeping across the planet to destroy America. God searches the hearts of all 6.2 billion people on earth today with an all-powerful eye, seeing the "devices of the crafty" at work, frustrating the plans of their hearts" as His people fall to their knees, daily pleading for our nation's very lifeline.

"If My people which are called by My name will humble themselves and pray, and seek My face, and turn from their wicked ways, I will hear then from Heaven, I will forgive their sins, and heal their land." II Chronicles 7:14.

Like as with Job, God can frustrate the "crafty" whose heart is bent on divorce, the teenager destroying his life on drugs and alcohol; the unreasonable boss in the workplace, the one busy with gossip stemming from a jealous, angry heart and a mouth full of lies.

From II Kings 7:3, we read of four lepers living in quarantine, and they said to one another, "Why sit we here until we die?" They arose, headed for the enemy army's camp, the Syrians, and when they arrived, they saw how God had frustrated the devices (minds) of the crafty:" ...for the Lord had caused the army of the Syrians to hear the noise of chariots and the noise of horses, the noise of a great army" Vs. 6, when there were no such noises, and when the lepers arrived, they found the camp empty: "They [Syrians]...fled at twilight, left the camp intact...and fled for their lives." Vs. 7. God frustrated the devices of the crafty so their hands could not carry out their plans to starve, by embargo, the people of Samaria.

My friend was arrested in a criminal offense which drew him with a sincere, repentant heart to Jesus, made a "new creation" out of him, and at his sentencing, prefaced by much prayer, God gave him a powerful testimony that frustrated the judge's mind and heart to release him without imprisonment,—a frustrated judge by his own confession. "For with God, nothing will be impossible." Luke 1:37.

"Trust in the Lord with all your heart, and lean not unto your own understanding; acknowledge Him in all your ways and He will direct your steps." Proverbs 3:5-6.

September 13

"But without faith it is impossible to please Him..." Hebrews 11:6.

When you use a computer, you exercise faith. As you open up an E-mail, you are manifesting faith in its workings behind the scenes to put it on the screen. Your faith is focused on that mechanical gadget. And the machine works whether you have faith in it or not. And it doesn't depend on whether you and I have little faith or much faith.

It makes me think of Jesus telling His disciples that faith even the size of a tiny mustard seed is enough to move mountains. Why? Because the FOCUS of the faith is Almighty God, and not the size of my faith that is all important.

When little teenage David challenged Goliath, a giant many times larger and stronger, well shielded, his faith was not in the pebble and the sling, but was focused on One, All Sufficient, much greater, God Himself. David to Goliath: "You come to me with a sword, with a spear, and with a javelin. But I come to you in the name of the Lord of hosts, the God of the armies of Israel...". I Samuel 17:45. His faith focused on God—the real object, not on himself. And the giant's head fell into David's hand.

When Gideon, "the least of the least", was commissioned by God to go out against thousands of Midianites, who were well stocked with weapons and horses and chariots, he was compelled to reduce his army of 30,000 men to 300 men equipped with torches inside of pitchers and trumpets in their hands. Judges 7:16. His faith was focused correctly—not on the "foolish" toys in hand, but on the power of Almighty God.

The first time I experienced that new thing called "power steering" I saw faith in its proper perspective. I severely over-steered on a street, fortunately with a concrete curb on either side. Until that moment, my faith in steering a car, pickup, truck, tractor, or combine depended on my own strength of muscles. Now, my faith was switched to mighty hydraulic power. What a blessing!!!

Then came the "cruise control" as I ventured across ND and felt so insecure, felt like I was flying, totally out of control of the accelerator as I rounded the curves and headed for stop signs. My faith now depended on automatic control, my new focus of faith in propulsion, and not my foot on the accelerator.

What it all boils down to is being careful that the object of our focus is not on our "faith in our faith," but in the giver of that precious gift—God Almighty.

"Believe in Me," I hear Him saying.

September 14

"Sow a thought and you reap an act;
Sow an act and you reap a habit;
Sow a habit and you reap a character;
Sow a character and you reap a destiny." Anon.

As I look back on my long life nowadays, I see how it has been mainly the "little" things all woven together that have made me what I am today. Oh, yes, it was the big decision of vocation, marriage, my Christian faith and one or two others that set the pace, but laced with many "little" experiences that enrich life on this earth.

"Little by little" my thoughts have made me act for good or bad.

"Little by little" my actions have become habits, by and large.

"Little by little" my habits have formed my basic character.

"Little by little" my character has had an awful lot to do with my eternal destiny.

Peter points this out in the faithful growth we need in the faith walk we have; "add virtue [to faith], to virtue add knowledge...self control...perseverance...godliness...brotherly kindness...love"—the love we find laid out in I Corinthians 13.

One April day in 1945 when my army unit passed through Nuremberg, Germany, on our way to the front lines, I saw a husky, clean, tidy, blond teenage girl picking up rubbish with her hands, thick rubble piled high on the street from the recent American bombings, and putting it in a wheel barrow, so much rubble laying there that it would have been discouraging even for a heavy-equipment operator with a dump truck. I think that if I could have relayed to her my heartfelt sentiment, facing such an impossible situation, she might have said: "Little by little I am making a difference." The portrait of real, genuine character in my mind.

A bit of nostalgia came upon me that day in Montana when I drove by a crew of men taking up forty eight miles of railroad tracks and the ties they laid on, with lots of lifelong memories attached to that run. Then, I thought, what courage and character it must have taken when Jim Hill and his crew laid that first tie on the east coast, and the second only a few inches away, finally crossing America with a vast web of railways—"little by little" as every tie and rail were laid, and fastened securely with huge spikes and heavy hammers.

In first grade arithmetic we learned that one plus one equals two, and built "little by little" on that premise through algebra, geometry, trigonometry, calculus, hydraulics, etc., to graduate an engineer. God tells us in Isaiah 28:9-10; "When will he [man] teach knowledge? And whom will he make to understand the message?...For precept must be upon precept, precept upon precept, line upon line, line upon line, here a little, there a little." To that I can say "Amen" as I have dug deep for decades for counsel, comfort, peace, exhortation, the testimony of the saints, and a satisfaction for a hungering, thirsting soul. "Little by little."

"My son, give attention to My Words, incline your ear to My sayings; let them not depart from before your eye; keep them in the midst of your heart. For they are life unto those who find them. And health unto their flesh." Proverbs 4:20-23.

May Psalm 119:11a be each of our personal testimony; "Thy Word have I hidden in my heart…" "Little by little," "line upon line." "precept upon precept."

September 15

"I must work the works…while it is day." John 9:4.

While ambling down an old Montana gravel road, I came upon the long-deserted farmstead that a high school classmate had been part of in his boyhood days. While females might be most curious to view the family living quarters, I am always curious to view the out buildings of one of those century-old, depreciating farmsteads, and in particular the barn. There I saw pens where I imagine young calves, piglets, or baby lambs spent their first days all bedded down with straw. I saw two or three stanchions still in place, used to contain a dairy cow at milking time. There were 8 x 8 stalls with hay mangers across the backside I could identify as perhaps occupied by saddle or work horses as I recognized the usual halter ties. Here and there hung horse harness parts—leather straps and tugs, horse collars, and partial harnesses, along with a familiar three-legged stool for milking time. And, oh yes, the familiar pitch fork used to carry hay and bedding into the livestock, and manure away from them. I literally saw a lifetime of hard work now silenced.

The entire Ukrainian family has now passed on, their tools and implements quietly laid aside, and their secular work completed. As my imaginary world passed before my eyes, no more days left to work, I thought of Jesus' wisdom from John 9:4: "I must do the works of Him Who sent me while it is still day." His work at hand was to heal the eyes of the man born blind, not with surgery, but with the anointing of His spittle on clay soil, applied to the eyes to test his obedience: "Go, wash in the pool of Siloam." He went, and came back seeing.

Both Jesus and the Montana farmer worked the clay to bear fruit "while it is day"—their opportunity for their physical contribution to history in their day on this earth, the day God gave them to work.

"The grass withers and the flower fades, but the work of the Lord lasts forever." Isaiah 40:8.

The farmer's work has withered and faded away, but the living testimony of John 9:4 will last forever.

September 16

"God is Love" I John 4:16.

What a reservoir of love do I find flowing out of most attendant's, caretaker's hearts at a nursing home. I have marveled and been filled with joy when I see a busy young caretaker stop momentarily to pleasantly greet an elderly man or woman. Just a touch, a hug, a kiss on the cheek, a cheery, encouraging word, a hearty smile, or a change of position for more comfort. There is no power on earth, including nuclear power, that will match the power of love to heal, produce adrenaline, or to overcome the little or big "owies" in life. The voice of love speaks to the inner man like no other voice can speak, becoming a fruit-bearer like we read of in Psalm 1:3: "He shall be like a tree planted by the rivers of water. It brings forth its fruit in its season; Whose leaf shall not wither. And whatever he does shall prosper."

If human love can be that blessed, can we fathom or imagine God's love?

"God is love." His very makeup is analogous to our clay He made us to be. His embodiment is pure, Agape love. He is clothed, housed, contained, saturated in love, "Behold what manner of love the Father has bestowed on us, that we should be called "Children of God." I John 3:1.

An elderly gentleman, suffering from early dementia, lamented the fact that he often forgets God. But, his friend assured him: "He will never forget you." This is ably manifested in Isaiah 46:4: "Even to your old age, I am He, and even to gray hairs I will carry you!..."
"For God so loved the world that He gave His only begotten Son..."

And out of that heart of love is sin-filled man made right with God, and worthy of eternal life, "For by grace are we saved through faith." Ephesians 2:8. Then that same righteous man, born out of God's love, is promised: "The righteous shall flourish like a palm tree." Psalm 92:12. And, "Those who are planted in the house of the Lord shall flourish in the courts of our God. They shall bear fruit in old age." Psalm 92:13-14.

Our human love may grow cold and old, but God's love remains steadfast, unchanging for now and for eternity. "I am God, I change not" Malachi 3:6. "Jesus Christ, the same yesterday, today, and forever." Hebrews 13:8.

His love to you today!!!

September 17

"Eye has not seen, nor ear heard..." II Corinthians 2:9

It was a moderately foggy night when I drove over the crest of a hill about one-half mile south of the well known "Bridges" oil well alongside of Highway 13. A gas-burning flame at the well sight, mixed with the substance of the fog, portrayed a beauty I have never seen before nor since—a panorama, I believe of every color known to man, beautifully woven together, too gorgeous to describe with words. I stopped and soaked up the unbelievable beauty for a long time, and wondered if that could be at least the tip of an iceberg of the beauty of Heaven, described in part in Revelation 22: "...pure water of life, clear as crystal...tree of life bearing twelve fruits, loaded with leaves. There shall be no night there, no lamp nor light of sun, for the glory of the Lord gives them light that will reign forever and ever." I believe I saw a taste of that "glory of the Lord" that night.

I believe it will resemble the snow-capped hillside of the prairies with crystal-like crust that a wintry moon shows off at twilight, the earth glistening like diamonds in a bracelet.

Is it possible to grab the finest beauty of nature here on earth and hope it is but a semblance of what we will see in Heaven when we come over the crest of that hill for the first time, a sight that will last forever?

It is written: "Eye has not seen, nor ear heard; nor have entered into the heart of man the things which God has prepared for those who love Him." II Corinthians 2:9.

September 18

"For to me, to live is Christ, to die is gain." Philippians 1:21.

This summer, as I drove down the three lanes of the cemetery in that Montana community where I spent 73 years of my life, I recognized once again the names of hundreds of pioneers and a later generation that has passed on. Sometimes I just amble enthusiastically through the tombstones and grave markers and pull from my memory bank a real long history book of people whose names are etched permanently into the gravestone markers. To me, each one has a personal testimony also etched into my heart as I watched him live out his or her life on this earth. They were tillers of the soil and ranchers, bankers, teachers, politicians, housewives, mechanics, musicians, doctors, dentists, merchants, lawyers, painters, pastors, heavy equipment operators, and many common laborers. On one stone I might see a short Bible verse. On another, a stalk of ripened grain or the head of a cow or horse, or a bar of musical notes, depicting what he or she was really remembered for. And I thought: what a complimentary would Philippians 1:21 be: "For to me, to live is Christ, and to die is gain." The kind of testimony we leave behind, etched into people's hearts as they see our name etched into a tombstone is important, not only for this short term experience here on earth, ending in a cemetery, but because of its eternal significance, bluntly put—Heaven or Hell. All depending on how we have handled that precious name and person of Jesus. "Every knee shall bow and every tongue confess that Jesus Christ is Lord." Philippians 2:6.

Paul sums it all up very well in II Corinthians 3:2: "You are our epistle written in our hearts, known and read by all men; ...an epistle of Christ...written not with ink, but by the Spirit of the living God, not on tables of stone, but on tablets of flesh, that is, of the heart."

We who are truly born again are living monuments of His grace: "For by grace are you saved through faith." Ephesians 2:8. We must stand tall, leave a Godly testimony etched into men's memory bank because the world around us is watching like I have watched others for a long lifetime, wondering, as I see a name. "Is his or her name written in the Lamb's Book of Life, lying open on the Heavenly altar? The most important engraving of all?"

I am a daily "etcher" in people's lives.

September 19

"...an inheritance incorruptible...undefiled...lasting, reserved in Heaven for you." I Peter 1:4.

How many today in America are waiting for a monetary inheritance in their family, one that will soon pass away, without any regard or concern for their eternal inheritance, a lasting one? In either case, the recipient has nothing to do with the building of the estate, or being named the benefactor. They are both handed to us on a "silver platter."

As I have watched monetary estates being handled on this earth, I have seen an analogy with the heavenly. A young couple received a thousand acres very suddenly, and then complained that the rich uncle never left cash to cover the tax. Gratitude? One young fellow, just married, was handed a large estate of land from dad and mom and managed well and has increased his holdings. Real gratitude! A middle-age couple inherited a beautiful farm and farmstead clear of debt, spent money like it was water, lived sumptuously, accumulated a monstrous debt and in a few years time went broke, and divorced, and settled by bankruptcy. Irresponsible and foolish!!

Judas Iscariot created his own inheritance by fraud and quickly found it meaningless and committed suicide, thereby squandering his heavenly inheritance as well.

So, as I have studied earthly inheritances analogous to heavenly inheritance, I am reminded of Jesus' parable of the sharing of the talents, in Matthew 25. Three men were involved: one who received five talents, one who received two talents, and one who received only one talent. Squander or invest? Prudent or foolish? Reward or rejection? The first two wisely invested their inheritance, and doubled their worth. They received the same acclaim from their master: "Well done, good and faithful servant, you were faithful over a few things, I will make you ruler over many things. Enter into the joy of the Lord". Vs. 21, 23. The third, who claimed to be afraid of his master, went out and hid his talent. "Take the talent from him...and cast the unprofitable servant into the outer darkness. There will be weeping and gnashing of teeth."

Friends, we are responsible for our gifts of time, talent, and treasure, as to how we invest while there is still time on this earth, in this life, that we may hear His commendation that day when we stand before Him: "Well done, thou good and faithful servant...enter into the joy of your Lord."

Let us remember Isaiah 40:8: "The grass withers [the earthly inheritance]; the flower fades [the glitter and glamour]; but the Word of the Lord endures forever," (a genuine, incorruptible inheritance received by faith in the resurrected Jesus, Who will live forever, unchanged). Parenthesis mine.

September 20

"But seek first the kingdom of God and His righteousness, and all these things will be added to you." Jesus, Matthew 6:33.

Greetings to everyone out there, looking at a brand new, fresh autumn day never before lived out, looking it squarely in the eye; some of you knowing precisely how you are going to spend this precious time, and some perhaps wondering: "What shall I do today?" Some of us are so consumed with work, social, political, recreational, and family schedules that we are victims of circumstances, a bygone day I well remember when chores of all kinds waited at my right and at my left. How we invest our precious God-given gifts of faith, time, talent, and treasure puts a smile of satisfaction on His face or a heavy heart in His bosom—that One who admonishes

"Seek first the kingdom...and these things shall be added...". "You take care of Me and I will take care of you" Jesus seems to tell us. "...You cannot serve God and mammon." Matthew 6:24.

I take seriously that Word "kingdom first" in Matthew 6:33—first in the morning, first in mind and heart, first in relationships, thereby shutting out that "me-first" syndrome. We cannot store up treasures in Heaven if our heart is holding tenaciously to the fleshly treasures of this world, all of which are fleeting, both for now and for eternity, never able to fill that void we are all born with, a chasm between us and our God of Heaven that only Christ and the cross can bridge.

In Africa, a trapper of monkeys cuts a hole in a case like a pumpkin, cleans out its contents, the hole just large enough for a monkey's hand to enter. The casing is filled with nuts and tied to a tree, attracting the monkey by the smell of nuts, compelling the monkey to reach inside and grab a handful. The rest of the story is history since his clenched fist full of nuts cannot physically withdraw, and his tenacious salivary glands refuse to relinquish his hold.

Dead monkey!!!

What a song of liberty, freedom and victory over lust, greed, and covetousness when we "Seek first the kingdom of God and His righteousness and all these things will be added to you."

September 21

"Trust in the Lord with all your heart, and lean not on your own understanding; in all your ways acknowledge Him and He will direct your path." Proverbs 3:5-6.

I praise The Lord this morning for that day when my faith was so quickened by this principal that it became such a part of my faith walk, my Christian life, that over a period of time it dispelled much of my fear, took away anxieties, squelched the tendency to worry, stomped out confusion, and established a certain quality and quantity of security within my soul that set me free. "It's not about me, but God," I learned. Over time, Proverbs 3:5 became a "lamp unto my feet and a light unto my path." Over time I was impressed that the trials that God puts on me, and also the trials that he allows to come upon me, and blessings He brings my way, suddenly fall into a pattern He desires for my good as I step aside and let Him direct my paths. I experienced what Paul writes in Romans 12:1: "Be not conformed to this world, but be transformed by the renewing of your mind...". No longer a spirit of jealousy, a critical spirit, nor one of competition. Fleshly pride defeated, and that me-first syndrome's neck broken. "Peace like a river" flowed over me as my inner man was truly convinced. So, I pray every morning before arising: "Oh Lord, anoint me this day with Divine power to be able to manifest my heart's desire to trust You with all my heart and lean not to my own understanding, to acknowledge You in all my ways this day, so that You may direct my paths," as promised in Psalm 37:23: "The steps of a good man are ordered by the Lord, and in his ways does He find His delight."

I don't believe that anyone has ever been more tested with the real meat of Proverbs 3:5-6 than Abraham, when in Genesis 22:2 God said: "Take now your son, your only son, Isaac, whom you love, and go to the land of Moriah, and offer him there as a burnt offering on one of the mountains I shall tell you!" I can surely hear myself from Abraham's lips: "Do you really mean that, God? This son that Sarah and I prayed for almost a century, and which You gave us at this late age, and one You promised descendants from that would number the stars of the sky or the sands of the sea? And now You are asking me to snuff out his life on top of a grill as an ordinary sacrifice? I don't understand this, God, but I will trust and obey." After a three day trip, the altar in place, the wood laid in order, Isaac bound and lying upon the wood, dad's pounding heart breaking, tears running down his cheeks, his old-nature flesh under control, Abraham raised his arm with knife in place to slay his son. Then that exciting pay-off for all this "trust" and "acknowledging God," the blessing of having laid aside that me-first syndrome, doubt, and unbelief, when he heard an angel of the Lord call from Heaven, loud and clear: "Abraham, Abraham...do not lay your hand on the lad... for now I know that you fear God, since you have not withheld your son, your only son, from Me." Just in time, as usual!!

September 22

"You have been made whole." Jesus, Luke 17:19.

Sometime ago I purposed to visit a man in the Federal prison in Yankton and another, the same day, in the state prison in Springfield. Going west from Yankton, I soon found I had to drive a long detour because three bridges were missing, new ones under construction. I was so blessed to find a "Road Closed" sign alongside the detour sign, because without a bridge, a traveler can meet sudden death or severe injury. Praise the Lord for a detour, another route.

Likewise, in our spirit world, the inner man needs a bridge. Every person is born "dead in trespass and sin", (Eph. 2:1), and thereby with a deep gulf between him and his God. Who is man's only source of light and salvation. The only bridge strong enough to carry the load across that gulf is the cross Jesus died on at Calvary. It becomes our bridge when we surrender to Jesus with child-like faith, confess our sin from a truly repentant heart, and believe that He was resurrected from the tomb. "If we confess our sins, He is faithful and just to forgive our sins and to cleanse us from all unrighteousness." I John 1:9. "For God so loved the world that He gave His only begotten Son, that whosoever believes in Him shall not perish, but have everlasting life." John 3:16.

In Luke 16 we see the picture. Lazarus, the beggar, died and was carried into Abraham's bosom, Abraham, "a friend of God", a man we know was heaven-bound when he died, his covenant with God set, his eye of faith upon the Jesus to come like as our faith is today because of His having come 2000 years ago. Therein, Abraham secured a bridge for himself to cross over into the throne room of God, his name written in the Lamb's Book of Life.

The rich man, his riches his false god, died and was buried. "And being in torments in Hades, he cried and said,..."have mercy on me...for I am tormented in this flame." Jesus. Luke 16:23-24. "...between us and you there is a great gulf fixed..." Abraham explained to him, a gulf no man can cross over either way. Vs. 26. And there is no detour, since Christ has boldly declared in Roman

14:6 "I am the Way, the Truth, and the Life; no man comes to the Father but by me."

The gulf is impassable except for the cross. Let us join our liberated hearts in a word of praise with David: "I will extol You, oh Lord, for You have lifted me up; You have not made my enemies to rejoice over me. I cried unto You, and You have brought my soul up from the grave, and have kept me alive, that I shall not fall into the pit...weeping may endure for a night, but joy comes in the morning." Psalm 30:1-3, 5b.

If you feel a vacuum, an emptiness in your inner being, be encouraged, and come to Jesus to replace that old nature flesh, and allow that cross at Calvary to bridge the gulf and fill the vacuum.

Then, "you have been made whole", healed in spirit, soul, and body.

September 23

"The thief has come to kill, to steal, and to destroy. I have come to give life, and to give it abundantly." Jesus, John 10:10.

For most people, the scenario of the three Hebrew children from Daniel 3 is so far-fetched as to be totally unbelievable. Oh yes, we can see them as part of the family of God because of their Hebrew heritage, having memorized much of the law and the old testament writings, as well as their history as a people. So, when they refused to fall down and worship a golden image of a false god like King Nebuchadnezzar demanded, it was not surprising to hear them refuse. "Thou shalt have no other gods before Me."...their first commandment taught, a clear mandate back to Moses on Mt Sinai. It's not difficult, either, to believe their verbal testimony as a resistance to the threat of sure death in a furnace, heated up seven times hotter than usual, killing the attendants. They resolved publicly: "... our God, Whom we serve, is able to deliver us from the burning fiery furnace, and He will deliver us from your hand, O King." Vs. 17. Our God is able, our God is willing!!! What faith, praise that surely blessed their Heavenly Father. "God inhabits the praises of

His people." But to be cast into the fire, bound hand and foot, and survive???

Moments later, from King Nebuchadnezzar: "Look...I see four men loose,...and the form of the fourth is like the Son of God" Vs. 25. Their bodies came through a powerless fire, hair not singed, garments intact, and even no smell of smoke. Vs. 27. I wonder how well they slept that night.

So it was for me, my wife, two grown sons, and a friend on our return trip from Regina, Sask. late one night after an evening with evangelist Rex Humbard. We were traveling west on highway #5, coming to a four-way intersection in a small town, and a stop sign on either side. As we neared the junction, my son, from the back seat, said: "Dad, that car is not going to stop." I looked left momentarily and saw his bumper only inches from my front fender. Tremendous fear gripped me, and my heart pounded, as I sped away, and his car went on through at a tremendous speed. As I later reminisced that experience, I could see us in the same predicament as the Hebrew children—literally tossed into a fiery furnace with no escape but instant death. That night I fell asleep in my bed and twice awakened, frightened, as I heard the crunching of metal, the breaking of glass, and crying out of human voices in my car. To this day, I believe the five of us went through an unavoidable crash, but came out unscathed like the three Hebrew children, and for the same reason— "the fourth Man", Jesus.

"I created you, oh Jacob, I formed you, oh Israel; fear not, for I have redeemed you; I have called you by your name, You are Mine. When you pass through the waters, I will be with you; and through the rivers, they shall not overflow you. When you walk through the fire, you shall not be burned, nor shall the flame scorch you. For I am the Lord your God, the Holy One of Israel, your Savior." Isaiah 43:1-3.

September 24

"Sufficient unto the day is the evil thereof" Jesus. Matthew 6:24.

This morning I envisioned the radio listeners up in Montana as sitting up to their spiritual breakfast table to satisfy the inner man's appetite with good news from God's Word, limited to fifteen minutes, They've heard the diner's call "come boldly before the throne of grace to obtain mercy and to find grace to help in time of need." Hebrews 4:16. I could envision them devouring, digesting, and assimilating God's Word just for today, fifteen minutes only. It reminded me of the ranchers out in the hills and valleys under the Big Sky in Montana. They learn by experience, in early winter, that when the heavy snow covers the grassland grazing, just how many bales or pounds of grain pellets to unload in a feeder or on the clean hillside for the herd's consumption for one day only, allowing for the extreme variations in the temperature. If a rancher should carry two or three day's supply into the feeding pallet, luscious, green alfalfa hay would become expensive bedding. The cow would eat her fill and then lie overnight on the extra feed. But ranchers are sensible and conservative with their feed.

So we find a situation like Moses and his family of God found immediately after crossing the Red Sea on their flight from Egypt. They found a soft manna every morning on the frost on the ground, manna from above, sufficient for one day only. God had counted his numbers and proved to be a sensible, conservative Steward, His ration came for six days only, and a fast for the seventh. Anyone who connived and cheated and stashed manna away found it was spoiled on the morrow.

In a different scenario did Paul learn that his daily "thorn in the flesh' was good for him as God reminded him: "My grace is sufficient for you...My strength is made perfect in weakness." II Corinthians 12:3. Could unlimited, rather than limited grace, have caused Paul to waste God's grace superfluously? We must be good stewards of God's daily ration of grace!

I have never seen this better manifested than with George Mueller of nineteenth century London, where he managed an orphanage of fifteen hundred boys much of his adult life, totally responsible for their keep. He never knew a single day ahead where the food for the orphans would come from. By his own testimony, there was never a meal missing on the hour it was needed. His faith in God coupled with long hours on his knees early in the morning proved the grace of God to be sufficient unto the day. Matthew 6:34.

God's grace sufficient unto the hour of need:
One pebble in David's sling, I Samuel 17:49.
Gideon's victory with only four hundred men, jars, candles, and trumpets Judges 7:20.
Invisible angels filling the hills and valleys around Elisha and his servant. II Kings 6:17.
Five loaves and two fishes to feed five thousand men and families. Matthew 14:19.
To bring Lazarus up out of the grave. Matthew 11:44.
To kill to the last man the three armies against King Jehoshaphat. II Chronicles 20:24.

September 25

"Let not your heart be troubled; you believe in God, believe also in Me. In My Father's house are many mansions...I go to prepare a place for you...I will come again and receive you unto Myself, that where I am, there you may be also...I am the way, the truth, and the life. No one comes to the Father except through Me." John 14:1-6.

The "end-time" prophets of today, men whose whole life has been dedicated to studying both old and new testament prophecies recorded in God's Word, see the day coming upon us rapidly like we see recorded in Matthew, Luke, and John. We see earthquakes, tsunamis, tornadoes, floods, and fires increasing in diverse places worldwide. Matthew 24:7.

Here in America the economy, unemployment, immorality, two wars, drugs, alcohol, divorce and politics are sources of troubled hearts.

Most people believe in God; but Jesus puts His finger on the exact cure for a troubled heart when He says "...believe also in Me." The deep-down vacuum, the empty spot deep down in every man's heart can be settled in no other way than by faith in not only the name and person of Jesus, but in His work on Calvary that Good Friday afternoon when He took every man's sin upon Himself and He became a perfect blood sacrifice that God required first under Old Testament law, the blood of animals, and then in the New Testament day of grace, a perfect human sacrifice that only Jesus could qualify for. That work, coupled with our faith in His resurrection the third day after, gives us the real essence of the "born again" experience. "Except a man be born again, he cannot enter the kingdom of God." John 3:3, 7.

"If you confess with your mouth the Lord Jesus, and believe in your heart that God has raised Him from the dead, you will be saved." Romans 10:9.

If your heart be troubled today, can you not hear the Great Physician from John 14:6: "I am the way, the truth, and the life…?"

September 26

"But he is comforted and you are tormented." Luke 16:25.

"Mickey" was my family's most loved and favorite saddle horse on the Montana ranch. She was so gentle, so smart, and willing; a "single-footer" who could cross the prairies speedily, a mare fourteen hands tall. She was as easy to ride on the range as is a rocking chair in the living room. At the 4th of July celebrations she always won the races. And on the range she worked hard and never seemed to tire. As a preschool boy, I could hardly wait for the day we boys could mount her and ride to school, "over hill and over dale." One day when she was well over twenty years old, the evidence of old age showed in her body and in her personality, her joints and legs stiffened and she hated to run anymore. Time to retire!!

On those western ranches, such a horse met one of three destinies: pamper her with good care in the stable as always; turn her out to fend for herself, to contend with the weather elements and eventually die; or, in a severe case, put her out of her misery. My dad loved Mickey and kept her same stall in the stable, nourished her with oats and the best hay, and bedded her with nice clean straw. My father-in-law, regretfully, also a horse lover, felt that he should lead his stead out by himself over a hill, and three times allowed emotion to overpower reason, and back they came, rifle unfired. Most ranchers turned them loose to fend for themselves.

As my memory recently rehearsed this long-ago scenario, I thought of Lazarus and the rich man, in a different setting, described by Jesus for us in Luke 16. What a blessing for Lazarus to age and pass on into eternity, while a terrible curse for the rich man; one taken good care of forever, the other lamentable; one's condition much improved with his demise, the other devastated.

The fate of the horses I described was in the hand of their masters for their final day on this earth. Likewise, with Lazarus and the rich man, their eternal fate was in their master's hand, Jesus or Satan. "So it was that the beggar died, and was carried by the angels to Abraham's bosom" Vs. 22. Into heaven Lazarus went!! "The rich man died and was buried" Vs. 22. The next we hear of his fate: "...being in torments in Hades..." Father Abraham, have mercy on me"... Vs. 24. "Between us and you there is a great gulf fixed so that those who want to pass from here to you cannot. Nor can those from there pass to us." Vs. 26. How final!!!

Like the rich man, we, too, are born spiritually dead. Eph. 2:1. Doomed to Hades until our God leads us to Calvary and convicts us to confess our sin from a truly repentant heart. "I will remove their stony heart from them and replace it with a heart of flesh, and I will put My Spirit within them." Ezekiel 36:26. Then that cross where Jesus sacrificed His all for humanity's sin becomes a bridge to cross over that impassable, deep gulf between every sinner and God. There, in the throne room, "I will dwell in the presence of the Lord, and abide under the shadow of the Almighty". David, Psalm 91:1.

September 27

"Coming to Him as a living stone...you also as living stones..." I Peter 2:4-5.

Can a stone, a huge rock that we see carefully placed on many lawns, have life, I wondered as I read from I Peter 2? My friend cuts stones and as he opens them, finds all kinds of beautiful colors melded together like a rainbow. Like a set of heavy bookends I observed the other day, myriad colors found when the rocks were sliced. So, to me, rocks, stones, have life created by the same God as our Creator.

Twice recently when I visited my community's cemetery in Montana, I saw huge stones, tombstones we call them, with deceased people's names engraved. And I hear Paul's writing from II Corinthians 3 to the saved people: "You are our epistle written on our hearts, known and read by all men...an epistle of Christ... written not with ink, but by Spirit...not as tablets of stone, but on tablets of flesh...the heart."

We have all watched the tousle of removing the stones on which the Ten Commandments are written, removing them from public display by court order. That's deplorable, for the stone monuments have literally written on them a celebration of Moses' Mt. Sinai trip, a celebration of righteousness on display. Proverbs 14:34 gives us a principal and a promise to heed, "Righteousness exalts a nation, but sin is a reproach to any people." Woe to America when God judges us like He did the Israelites in the wilderness, and brings wrath upon our nation!!

I give serious thought today to the engraving I am making on human hearts that they will recall when they see my name on a grave marker. My friend, that's important, not because of the short-term life and the memory to humanity only, but because of its eternal significance, HEAVEN OR HELL.

As I meander through the cemetery, I see a drunkard, a murderer, a thief, an adulteress, as I remember their familiar faces. On the other hand, a nurse, a teacher, a doctor, or a pastor who invested their entire life to bless people in their day, now lying side by side.

How well do I remember the doctor in our town who kept a horse in the livery barn in the pioneer days, and when called in the winter, hooked the horse to a "one horse open sleigh" to travel miles to a needy person. Many times poverty kept him from collecting his fee, but with complete understanding!

Every little community had its school, and a faithful teacher who taught all eight grades in one room, and was also custodian, fireman, nurse and a mother-like image to her students. In the depression days, her pay was often only a warrant, since taxes were uncollectible by the county treasurer.

I believe Paul would say of most of these testimonies as he said of his Corinthian congregation: "Do we need…epistles of commendation to you or letters of commendation from you?" II Corinthians 3:1. "You are our epistle written in our hearts, known and read by all men…" Vs. 2.

September 28

"…do this and you will live." Jesus, Luke 10:28b

A mousetrap may cause a physical death, but lack of compassion a spiritual death Jesus intimated to the lawyer who inquired: "What shall I do to be saved?" Vs. 25. Let me illustrate:

A mouse looked through the crack in the wall to see the farmer and his wife open a package. "What food might this contain?" the mouse wondered. He was devastated to discover it was a mousetrap. Retreating to the farmyard, the mouse proclaimed the warning: "there is a mousetrap in the house!" The chicken ducked and scratched, raised her head and said, "Mr. Mouse, I can tell this is a grave concern for you, but it is of no consequence to me. I cannot be bothered by it."

The mouse turned to the pig and told him: "There is a mousetrap in the house! The pig sympathized, but said, "I am so sorry, Mr. Mouse, but there is nothing I can do about it but pray. Be assured you are in my prayers."

The mouse turned to the cow and said: "There is a mousetrap in the house! The cow said: "Wow, Mr. Mouse, I am sorry for you, but it's no skin off my nose."

So, the mouse returned to the house, head down, and dejected, to face the farmer's mousetrap alone. That very night a sound was heard throughout the house, like the sound of a mousetrap catching its prey. The farmer's wife rushed to see what was caught. But, in the darkness, she did not see it was a venomous snake whose tail the trap had caught. The snake bit the farmer's wife. The farmer rushed her to the hospital and she returned home with a fever. Everyone knows you treat a fever with fresh chicken soup, so the farmer took his hatchet to the farmyard for the soup's main ingredient. But his wife's sickness continued. So friends and neighbors came to sit with her around the clock. To feed them, the farmer butchered the pig. The farmer's wife did not get well, but died. So many people came for her funeral that the farmer had the cow slaughtered to provide enough meat for all of them.

The mouse looked upon it all from his crack in the wall with great sadness. You see, each of us is a vital thread in another person's tapestry; our lives are woven together for a reason.

A chicken, a pig, and a cow DIED. "You can be sure your sin will find you out," Numbers 32:23.

"But a Samaritan had compassion on him...bandaged his wounds, pouring on oil and wine, and he set him on his animal, brought him to an inn, and cared for him." Luke 10:33-34. Later, to the innkeeper, "...take care of him...and I will repay you." Vs. 35.

Jesus said to the lawyer, " ...go and do likewise." Vs. 37. "...do this and you will live..." Vs. 28b.

The chicken, the pig, the cow, a priest, and a Levite all needed a change of heart. We find that change, even unto salvation, by grace, in Ezek. 36:26: "I will give you a new heart, and put a new spirit within you; I will take the heart of stone out of your flesh, and give you a new heart of love." God speaking.

September 29

"And the dead in Christ rise first...". I Thess. 4:16b.

We've all heard it said: "I'd like to be a mouse in the corner" at a certain time or event. Jesus set up a certain time and event in John 14:3 where He says: "And if I go and prepare a place for you, I'll come again and receive you to Myself...." I can just see the "mouse in the corner", and mice around the world in cemeteries, as curious as a cat. There, in a central spot of the community cemetery, the grass begins to move, the soil cracks, and crumbles a bit and "presto"...out comes physically the person named on the grave marker, emerging with a brand new body, a glorified body like Jesus raised up with and then ascended later into the clouds on His way back to heaven. The curious, excited mouse wonders: "Why only this grave and not that one?" Then, the little mouse remembers a word from the last funeral while he was lurking about: "For God so loved the world that He gave His only begotten Son, that whosoever believes on Him, shall not perish but have everlasting life." John 3:16. The untouched grave must be of those perishing, he concluded. "For the preaching of the cross is foolishness to those who are perishing..." I Corinthians 1:18. Then he remembers another statement to help him understand this strange phenomena from I Corinthians 15:52, when a tall, dark, handsome, pastor declared at a grave site: "...in a moment, in the twinkling of an eye, at the last trumpet...the dead will be raised...." And so, the dead in Christ will rise first, and the dead "outside of Christ" will rise later to face the great white throne judgment. Rev. 20:11. "And anyone not found written in the Book of Life was cast into the lake of fire." Rev. 20:15.

Are you a lost person today who would like to make a reservation now for the first resurrection rather than the last? I have good news for you! My heavenly Father is like a devoted shepherd of sheep who leaves his flock of 99 in their safe compound and sacrificially goes out to find that one lost lamb. Luke 15:4-6. When that lost one is found, there is rejoicing amongst the heavenly host, and an invitation to join them: "Rejoice with me, for I have found my sheep which was lost." Vs. 6.

> Then will your testimony ring out like this:
> "I've found a Friend, O such a Friend,
> He loved me ere I knew Him;
> He drew me with the cords of love,
> And then He bound me to Him."

September 30

"My Lord is on the throne."

On the ranch, I boldly planned each season's work: plant the seed, play mid-wife for the calf or the lamb, tend to the weed problem, harvest the hay and grain crops, and sell the livestock increase; each operation in its own season. Then the winter feeding and hauling grain to market, and start over again. Every day was different. But how I appreciated that the "changeless Christ", my Lord, was on the throne when: early one morning my son was taken home to Heaven, even though seeding time was at hand, and delayed; or when the nice green fields of wheat turned black overnight by grasshopper infestation; when the flood waters took out fences, corrals, and buildings one afternoon; and when the electrical fire quietly gutted my combine cab during the night at harvest time; and, oh yes, that year when the price of grain took a fifty percent drop at harvest time.

I love that phrase, "the changeless Christ", the same today as before the creation. What a truth to let linger in our hearts and meander through our minds when we search the scriptures in our times of joy and with hearts of thanksgiving and praise and find we are speaking to the same God, the same Jesus, as David or the Sons of Korah or Paul or the old testament saints whose inner man was literally exploding with ecstasy. Or, on the other hand, when trials and temptations or tribulations are so heavy, and change the course of life, and we are suddenly walking side by side with Abraham, Jacob, Joseph, Samuel, Hannah, Elijah, King David, Daniel or King Jehosophat, and we find again that we are rescued, encouraged, edified, set free by the same "changeless Christ" that they were in their life experiences.

Malachi 3:6 says: "I am God, and I change not." And Hebrews 13:8: "Jesus Christ, the same yesterday, today, and forever." Has Jesus so clearly revealed Himself to you in the scriptures that you, too, have discovered that Jesus is a "changeless Christ", sitting in control on your heart's throne this morning? John 3:16 says: "For God so loved the world that He gave His only begotten Son, that whosoever believes on Him shall not perish, but have everlasting life." It was that God Who so loved 2000 years ago that brought Paul to his knees on the road to Damascus, blinded his clay eyes to take his attention from the glamour of the flesh, and opened his inner eye to see the "changeless Christ", and experience an almost unbelievable change of heart. Was it not that same "changeless Christ" Who preached the good news to "poor" you and me, and Who healed the often broken heart, Who set us free from the captivity of sin, death, and the Devil, and Who opened the inner eye to see the cross of

Christ's death as the bridge over the gulf that separates sinner from saint, and Who performed surgery to remove the blights of bruises upon our minds, bodies, and hearts?? Luke 4:18.

The "changeless Christ"; and I hear God bellow out across the universe: "This is my Beloved Son in Whom I am well pleased. Hear Him"!!! Matthew 17:5.

The "changeless Christ": "If we are faithless, He remains faithful; He cannot deny Himself." II Timothy 2:13.

October 1

"How sweet are Your Words...sweeter than honey..." Psalms 119: 103

It was not uncommon for married or engaged GI buddies in WWII to receive a "dear John" letter, cutting off a love relationship back home. It was a devastating blow so suddenly delivered by mail. My experience was different when a female high school classmate, purely out of friendship and duty I had reasoned, wrote one letter after another. At one mail call I was pleasantly surprised when she signed her letter "love" just before her name. A "love letter" is much more palatable to receive than a "dear John" I soon realized as I matched my euphoria against another's depression.

In my shirt pocket those days was a love letter I needed and cherished most of all...a Gideon new testament, Words "sweet to my taste...honey to my mouth." I was a young, lonely GI, thousands of miles from home. A time when the psalms and the four gospels were to me "sweeter then honey" for my inner man to feast on. It was God's love letter to me personally.

So with God's love letter I've found, a myriad of varied blessings depending on my present need.

"How sweet His Words...sweeter than honey..." when He filled my heart with quantity and quality of HOPE from John 14:1: "Let not your hearts be troubled...I go to prepare a place for you...and I will come again to receive you unto Myself...that you may be there also."

"How sweet" when He filled my heart with quantity and quality of PEACE those excruciating, lonely days of widowhood: "I know the thoughts I think toward you; thoughts of peace, not of evil. I give you a future and a hope." Jer. 29:11.

"How sweet" when He shared quantity and quality of LOVE for me and for all humanity, without partially, from John 3:16: "For God so loved the world that He gave His only begotten Son, that whosoever believes in Him should not perish but have eternal life."

"How sweet" when He shared quality and quantity of earthly SECURITY from death in a potential traffic accident one night that should have sent five of us into eternity, but for the manifested mercy and grace of God, and I heard from Lamentations 3:23: "Because of Your mercies I am not consumed, because Your compassions never fail. They are new every morning; Great is Your faithfulness. Therefore come boldly before the throne of grace to obtain mercy and to find grace to help in time of need." Heb 4:16.

"How sweet" when He shared quality and quantity of JOY with me from Isaiah 1:18 after a season of repentance of Psalm 51: "Come now, let us reason together: though your sins be as scarlet, they shall be white as snow; though they be crimson red, they shall be like wool."

"How sweet" to give back to Him the praise He deserves for my salvation: "I will extol You, oh Lord, for you have lifted me up; You have not made my enemies to rejoice over me. I cried unto You, and You healed me. You brought my soul up from the grave and You have kept me alive that I should not fall into the pit...weeping may endure for a night, but joy comes in the morning." Psalms 30:1-5.

October 2

"...plant gardens, and eat their fruit." Jeremiah 29:5.

As I meditate on Proverbs 4: 20-23. I see an analogy between a spirit force at work in my heart and a physical force that a gardener enjoys.

"My son, give attention to My Word [seeds]

Incline your ear unto My sayings, let them not depart from before your eyes; [plant seeds]

Keep them in the midst of your heart [hoe, water, fertilizer]

For they are life unto those who find them, and health unto their flesh." [fruit]

That's the deep-down ambition of every farmer, including God, as He plants seeds in His garden, our heart, He plants the seeds, His Word, and reaps the fruit: life and health.

"I went by the field of the slothful, and by the vineyard of the man devoid of understanding. And there it was, all overgrown with thorns, its surface was covered with nettles," Proverbs 24:30-31b.

I farmed for forty-one years across the fence from a man "devoid of understanding" when it came to seed time, assuming mid July as good as mid May. "A little sleep, a little slumber, folding of hands to rest..." Vs. 33. He was an extremely laid-back bachelor whose arising was late morning. Then, to the café for breakfast where he read the entire Billings Gazette from front to back. Noontime soon arrived, and after a short nap and some chores about town, he would drive eight miles to his farm, and about 3 o'clock his equipment would start to move. His quitting time was one round after dark, with lights on his tractor. Often times he never harvested because there was no crop.

Could you or I be like that with Gods garden or field, our heart overgrown with weeds at seedtime; therefore hard, dry, ground, depleted of moisture to plant into? Are we an unmotivated person, perhaps even lazy, shiftless, not caring, and lacking understanding; laid back, putting off today's chores for a more convenient time, like tomorrow? The curses of the old nature, the flesh part of us, can be left to grow and smother out the intended fruit that is watered and hoed by prayer, confession, repentance, and obedience to the Lord.

"Keep your heart with all diligence, for out of it spring the issues of life." Vs. 23. Unchecked morning glory in a grain field can smother out the grain as can trivialities, greed, and other false idols left unsanctified in our hearts.

"Beloved, I pray that you may prosper in all things and be in health just as your soul prospers." III John 2.

Picture two contrasts with me of what God could reap of the seed He plants: One head of grain is two inches long, as round as a lead pencil, containing only two or three kernels; while another is five inches long, and as round as a man's thumb, with sixty to eighty kernels. Which are you? Which am I in God's sight at harvest time?

October 3

"Enter His gates with thanksgiving, and His courts with praise." Psalm 100:4.

There is nothing I cherish in my daily fellowship and communication with the Lord more than thanks and praise. I have been so blessed to hear Him from Psalm 100:3: "We are His people and the sheep of His pasture." I see myself as one of my flock of sheep on the Montana ranch at sunset, when they come home, full of grass and water, proudly displaying a nice lamb or a set of twins, and seeking a safe place to spend the night away from their predators as I shut the gate. If I could counsel them I would say: "Be thankful to God and bless His name." Vs. 4b.

How thankful that I can pray with David because I am a redeemed child of God: "Keep me as the apple of Your eye, hide me under the shadow of Your wings, from the wicked who oppose me, from my deadly enemies who surround me." Psalm 17: 8-9. And again: "I will extol You, oh Lord, for You have lifted me up; You have not allowed my enemies to rejoice over me; You have brought my soul up from the grave, and You have kept me from falling into the pit..." Psalm 30:1-3.

I thank and praise Him that I can "dwell in the secret place of the Most High, and abide under the shadow of the Almighty." Psalm 91:1. And say of the Lord that He is my Refuge in Whom I find protection and provision, my Fortress I can hide behind, my Shield Who goes before me to absorb the deadly, poisonous darts of the enemy, my Savior Who gave his body and blood as a sacrifice for my sin; "my Lord in Whom I trust with all my heart...acknowledge in all my ways, and trust to direct my paths", my One and only God, no other gods before Him.

Every person seems to be endowed with a passion to worship something or someone. How we praise God at our home daily for American parents, and to live in a nation where the preaching of Jesus Christ as Savior and Lord has been our heritage, our living, true God we worship.

Isn't it wonderful to appreciate this life today as we look toward our eternal heritage, and like Jesus, never to die, but to live forever? "His mercy is everlasting and His truth endures unto all generations." Psalm 100:5.

"I will bless the Lord at all times, His praise shall continually be in my mouth...Oh magnify the Lord with me, and let us exalt His name together." Psalm 34:1-3.

October 4

"News alert!...the bridge over the Mississippi River on interstate 35W in Minneapolis has crumbled."

How could that suddenly be, after forty years of safe travel for millions of vehicles and people? Over the Poplar River that ran past my ranch in Montana is a bridge built in the early 1900's to accommodate Model "T" Fords and horse-drawn wagons of grain hauling sixty to eighty bushels. It's a very narrow bridge with overhead structure for a suspension, sitting on concrete pillars with a roadbed of heavy wooden planks. It's still standing, but with a large warning sign at either entrance "Load Limit...4000 pounds." It gives me a strange feeling to cross over it even with a modern car or pickup that almost equals that weight.

As I think of those two man-made bridges with apparent short life expectancy, I think of another bridge, one built by God. It has been permanent, imperishable, and unchangeable now for over two thousand years; It's structurally sound enough for any truly born-again person to confidently and boldly walk over day after day into the throne room of God. I speak of the cross Calvary as a bridge, the cross Jesus gave His life on and shed His blood for our salvation, as we come to believe on Him with child-like faith. "For God so loved the world that He gave His only begotten Son, that whosoever believes in Him shall not perish, but have everlasting life."

The gulf that needs crossing over is described vividly by Abraham in Luke 16:26. "...between us [in heaven] and you there is a great gulf fixed, so that those who want to pass from here to you cannot, nor can those from there pass to us." The ungodly rich man found himself fallen into the place of torment, alienated from God permanently by a deep gulf. That "Grand Canyon" became a reality of life for all of us when Adam and Eve fell into sin in the Garden of Eden, and alienated themselves from God, dead spiritually, while yet alive physically.

Yes, we all need a dependable bridge to span that deep gulf between each of us and God from our birth "For all have sinned and fall short..." Romans 3:23. Paul puts it this way in Ephesians 2:1: "You He made alive, who were dead in trespasses and sins." And the bridge is solidly in place—that cross at Calvary when we surrender to Jesus. "For by grace you have been saved through faith, not of yourselves, it is the gift of God; not of works, least anyone boast." Vs, 8-9.

That cross spanning that unfordable gulf between God and unsaved man says to us: "I am the Way, the Truth, and the Life; no man comes unto the Father but by Me," Jesus, John 14:6.

We thank and praise God for that bridge that will carry every truly repentant person to eternity. And even now in this life, the same bridge that carried David into the throne room, into the presence of God and Jesus, seated at God's right hand since His ascension, into the "reception room" of our prayers: "I will dwell in the secret place of the Most High, and abide under the shadow of the Almighty." Psalm 91:1.

Is your bridge in place yet? Mine is.

October 5

"Seek and you shall find..." Luke 11:9
"Seek and you shall find —little by little. My version.

They were called army worms, and literally millions of them came from the east one summer afternoon, so tiny that the human eye could hardly see them individually. It was mid-1930's when they crossed our farm, appropriately named, since they crawled like marching soldiers side by side up the walls of buildings, over a steel windmill, over a vehicle, and even over a steel post, never turning to the right or left. They made the side of a red barn or granary look pure green in their march across grasslands and fields of grain, consuming the foliage slick and clean. They each ate their tiny bit so that it seemed: "United we Stand" against the fruits of nature.

Exactly fifty years later, 1985, I awakened one spring morning to find a nice stand of grain, looking good the evening before, but now totally gone, the field blackened. Newly hatched grasshoppers living in the field's grassland borders, only hours old, hardly visible, had consumed the entire crop on eighty acres. Again, "little by little" as they quickly crawled on their tiny bellies across the field.

Haven't each of our testimonies developed like that regarding God's Word? Haven't we all hungered and been put through one trial after another, as God purposed, for our spiritual growth? From Genesis 1 to Revelation 22 I have heard God speak to me "little by little" as I needed an exact Word for "doctrine, reproof, correction, and instruction in righteousness." II Timothy 3:16.

Early in my walk I heard the Lord from Proverbs 4:20: "My son, give attention to My Words, incline your ear unto My sayings; let them not depart from before your eyes; keep them in the midst of your heart; for they are life unto those who find them, and health unto their flesh." And since that day, the Lord has blessed me "little by little" as I have fed my hungry inner man like the army worms and grasshoppers took their fill "little by little."

Today I hear the prophet Isaiah asking the derelict priests and prophets: "Whom will he teach knowledge? And whom will he make to understand the message? Those just weaned from the milk? Those just drawn from the breasts? For precept must be upon precept, precept upon precept, line upon line, line upon line. Here a little, there a little." Isaiah 28:9-10.

The trials Isaiah saw facing his people as they considered claiming the land God had promised them, must have seemed as insurmountable as were the tiny worms and grasshoppers claiming many acres of crops. In either case, God expected them to each do his tiny part, showing us that "little by little" is the strategy for victory.

"Little by little seek and you shall find meat to eat and water to drink," John 4 and 6:55.

October 6

"A drink of living water." John 4.

Since my early childhood I've known two kinds of water-soft and hard water. Most wells on western farmsteads produced hard water. Our artesian well produced beautiful, soft water, so conducive to cleaning clothes or bathing, as against the hard water. To compensate for the hard water, many built concrete structures called cisterns, in their basement to accumulate captured rain water that everyone knows is soft and coveted by any housewife. To this day, even in the presence of a water softener, cistern water is used to water plants and flowers because rain water from the heavens is not only soft, but full of precious nutrients like nitrogen.

I don't know if the water from Jacob's well in John 4 was hard or soft, but I know the Living Water, Jesus, sitting on top of that well was a drink of soft water for the inner being. A Samaritan woman came to the well, totally ignorant of her need of a drink for the little girl inside of her, the real woman, a drink of Living Water. She had been born like all of us with a hard, closed heart from birth, a heart that thirsted only for the hard water of this world to satisfy her thirst, both physical and spiritual. Her hard heart, alienated from God because of inherent sin, must have grown harder with each of her five divorces and now her living in fornication, consuming the glitter of this world only.

Without her even realizing it, God was about to perform surgery on her spirit being according to Ezekiel 36:26, a preview of "you must be born again" John 3:3: "I will give you a new heart and put a new spirit within you; I will take the heart of stone out of your flesh and give you a heart of flesh." A stone, a rock is hard, heavy, cold, and impenetrable except by breaking. A heart of flesh is soft, light, warm, and easily penetrable, so that God's finger can do His mighty work as He penetrates, soaks, with Living Water.

She came in shame to the well to satisfy her physical cravings and left with her inner craving awakened and her dignity restored. It all happened in Vs. 13-14 where she believed what Jesus said: "Whosoever drinks of this [well] water will thirst again, but whosoever drinks of the water that I shall give him will never thirst. But the water that I shall give him will become in him a fountain of water, springing up into everlasting life." Jesus, the Living Water, the Word of God from heaven, poured down upon her soul, filled that "cistern" to over-flowing, and she "left her water pot, went into the city, testified of her experience, and the people followed her back to Jesus at the well."

On my farm, I've seen a heavy down-pour of soft water beat on a hard clump of soil until it is totally melted, deteriorated. So it is with Jesus, the soft Living Water, through His Word, "life unto those who find it, and health unto their flesh." Proverbs 4:2-3.

Is your soul a "cistern filled with that Living Water?

Oh, just to be soaked, without a raincoat!!

October 7

"Seek ye first the Kingdom of God"...Matthew 6:33.

"What does that sign read?" my wife quickly asked me as we breezed by a street corner, and I just as quickly answered "GARBAGE SALE" with a Minneapolis address. Fearing the worst, a gentle persuasion to stop and look over what is trash to one like me and a treasure to one like Alice, I counseled her "Honey, we don't have room even for a piece of scrap paper in our garage, so be careful."

In Matthew 6:33 Jesus addressed the stuff collector when He said "Seek ye first the Kingdom of God and His righteousness and all these things will be added unto you"—food, raiment, and housing, in proper context.

For a Christian, an idol is anything that comes between Jesus and me, anything that absorbs my time, talent, and treasure ahead of Jesus.

Think on this comical testimony for a moment. "Every fall I start stirring in my stuff. There is closet stuff, drawer stuff, attic stuff, and basement stuff. I separate the good stuff from the bad stuff, and then stuff the bad stuff anywhere the stuff is not too crowded until I decide if I will need the bad stuff. When the Lord calls me home, my children will want the good stuff, but the bad stuff, stuffed wherever there is room among all the other stuff, will be stuffed in boxes and taken to the Economy Center where all the other people's stuff has been taken. Whenever we have company, they always bring boxes and boxes of stuff. When I visit my family, they always move their stuff so I will have room for my stuff. Their stuff and my stuff—it would be so much easier to use their stuff and leave my stuff at home with the rest of my stuff.

This year I had an extra closet built so I would have a place for all stuff too good to throw away and too bad to keep with my good stuff. You may not have this problem, but I seem to spend a lot of time with stuff—food stuff, cleaning stuff, medicine stuff, clothes stuff, and outside stuff. Whatever would life be like if we didn't have all this stuff?

Now, there is all that stuff we use to make us smell better than we do. There is stuff to make our hair look good. Stuff to make us look younger. Stuff to make us look healthier. Stuff to hold us in, and stuff to fill us out. There is stuff to read, stuff to play with, stuff to entertain us, and stuff to eat. We stuff ourselves with the food stuff.

Well, our lives are filled with stuff—good stuff, bad stuff, little stuff, big stuff, useful stuff, junky stuff, and everyone's stuff. Now when we leave all our stuff and go to heaven, whatever happens to our stuff won't matter. We will still have all the good stuff God has prepared for us in heaven. Think of this good stuff today.

October 8

"He has put down the mighty from their thrones, and exalted the lowly." Luke 1:52.

One Sunday morning, an old cowboy entered a church just before services were to begin. Although the old man and his clothes were spotlessly clean, he wore jeans, a denim shirt, and boots that were very worn and ragged. In his hand he carried a worn-out hat and an equally worn-out Bible. The church he entered was in a very upstate and exclusive part of the city. It was the largest and most beautiful church the old cowboy had ever seen. The people of the congregation were all dressed in expensive clothes and accessories. As the cowboy took a seat, the others moved away from him. No one greeted, spoke to, or welcomed him. They were all appalled at his appearance, and did not attempt to hide it.

As the old cowboy was leaving the church, the preacher approached him and asked the cowboy to do him a favor. "Before you come back in here again, have a talk with God and ask Him what He thinks would be appropriate attire for worship." The old cowboy assured the preacher that he would.

The next Sunday, he showed back in for the services wearing the same ragged jeans, shirt, boots, and hat, carrying the same worn Bible. Once again he was completely shunned and ignored. The preacher approached the man and said: "I thought I asked you to speak to God before you came back to our church." "I did" replied the old cowboy. "If you spoke to God, what did He tell you the proper attire should be for worshipping in here?" asked the preacher. "Well sir, God told me that He didn't have a clue what I should wear. He said that He'd never been in this church."

"But the Lord said to Samuel, do not look at his appearance or at his physical stature,...for the Lord does not see as man sees, for the man looks at the outward appearance, but the Lord looks at the heart." I Samuel 16:7.

"Love suffers long and is kind;...love does not parade itself, is not puffed up; does not behave rudely, does not seek its own, is not provoked; thinks no evil." I Corinthians 13:4-6.

From one who loves to mingle with those old Christian cowboys!

October 9

"...they shall share alike." David, I Samuel 30:24.

In the days of WWII, I had two particular friends who were rejected from military service. One had been injured in high school days so that one leg was somewhat shorter than the other. Rejected for physical reasons. The second young man was of German heritage, having come to America with his parents in the late 1920's. People of that recent German or Japanese immigrants were refused military rights on grounds of possible treason. Rejected for loyalty reasons. Both wept as they were forced to stay back while their friends enlisted, or were drafted into the army, navy, air corps, or marines.

In the book of I Samuel, David and his army came home to Ziklag to find the enemy, the Amalekites, had raided their homes;, kidnapped their wives and children, stolen their livestock, and burned the city to the ground. The men all "wept until they had no more strength". Vs. 30:4. "But David encouraged himself in the Lord." I Samuel 30:6.

David set out with six hundred men in pursuit of the Amalekites. Along the way, a wounded Egyptian slave was found who would lead them to the enemy encampment. Because of various circumstances, like my two Montana friends, two hundred of the men could not go on, but were left behind by the Brook Besor. They were entrusted with watching over equipment, utensils, weaponry, extra clothing and such to lighten the burden for those going on. David and the four hundred man army marched on and soon found and overcame the enemy. Can't we just imagine the reunion when David and his men saw with their own eyes their captive wives and children, now set free, safe and sound? After the battle was over, there was an accounting of the material spoils, including one million animals for the victors to share.

On their return home, they came back to the ones left behind, and mutiny almost broke out in the camp when David forced the four hundred men to share the spoils equally with the ones left behind!! "I will not allow this division to happen. We are going to share."

My two rejected friends stayed behind in Montana and produced food on their farms to help feed American city folk and the "front liners" in Europe and in the Pacific theatre. Many other rejected men worked in factories, manned ships to and from the war fronts, helped build aircraft and submarines and firearms, and kept the trains running across our nation. On and on goes the list.

When it was all over, the rejects shared equally the remainder of their lives the spoils of WWII,...freedom in a nation birthed on Christian principals...America.

From one who prays daily: "God bless America" for all she does for those nations "left behind" around the world.

October 10

"They say: "you can take the boy out of the farm, but you cannot take the farm out of the boy."

So true of me after seventy-three years on a farm-ranch; and still every day finding myself choring, plowing, harvesting, haying, or driving over familiar roads and trails of yesteryear, even as I dream, awaken at night or keep busy in my new city environment. A culture shock indeed, believe me!

So it was the other morning as I was preparing a radio message for my people in Montana and south Sask., Canada, a message dealing with how the old testament saints literally rolled their confessed sins ahead annually as they celebrated the sacrifice of a bullock, a calf, a lamb, or a dove in behalf of their sins in accordance with the Levitical law requirement. It amounted to rolling their confessed sin ahead with child-like faith in that coming of the promised Messiah would make a one-time, final sacrifice with His body and blood as the prophets had recorded. They looked forward to the same sacrifice and forgiveness we look back to, executed that Good Friday afternoon on a cross at Calvary just outside Jerusalem. It was the greatest day in world history!!

While my radio message was coming together from God's Word and my own testimony, one of those "farm boy" moments flashed before my mind. I saw my familiar winter time chore of feeding cattle or sheep by carrying a big, round bale of hay to the crest of a hill by tractor and grapple fork. And then the exciting, fun part: cut the bale strings holding the hay plants together, and with a nudge of the knee, watch the 1400 pound clump of hay unroll before my eyes down the steep hill, ready for the animals to line up on either side to fill their bellies.

Then, I began to see an analogy. As those domesticated creatures consumed that rolled out feed for their personal need, even unto their very survival, and pleasure, so Jesus literally, at Calvary, consumed in His body for His pleasure and our desperate need, the sins of mankind from Adam and Eve to the last person ever to be born. As I looked down that steep hillside, I saw my last summer's investment of time, money, energy, and goods being consumed. As I looked at that nice, green, sweet smelling forage, I realized it was a sacrifice I would never see again, a wonderful, necessary blessing to a hungry herd or flock. So it was with Jesus as He looked at our sins laid out before Him, and He figuratively consumed in His body, once for all the "cup of sin" His Father poured upon his head that dark Good Friday afternoon. He consumed that sin laid out before Him for our necessary survival and pleasure, and for His glory and victory.

There at Calvary, in the person of Jesus, we see the coming together of the old testament and the new; the coming together of law and grace, and Christ the magnetic power holding them together. We see the firm manifestation of justice and love coming together once for all.

October 11

"A bruised reed He will not break, and smoldering flax He will not quench." Matthew 12:20.

Twice in my lifetime of trials, tribulations, and temptations have I been so shocked that I could not pray, and I wondered why. Oh how the body of believers must come to the side of "bruised reed" lest it be broken, and to a struggling, "smoldering wick" almost quenched. My younger brother died of suicide one beautiful October afternoon, and I was unable to pray, to storm the throne of God in my sad, unexpected grief as I traveled five hundred miles to his funeral, weeping much of the way, my best friend gone out of my life for the rest of my days.

Thirteen years later, my third son, age 20, on a balmy, warm, sunny morning in April was engulfed suddenly in a dense, heavy, fog north of Billings, Montana and destroyed by a logging truck. I could not pray, but almost immediately the Lord gave me a real vision of the boy's countenance hovering peacefully above the wreckage, separating his soul from his body, as the sound of broken glass and crumpled metal subsided, and the dust settled, and he ascended with a sober face toward heaven, a place he had claimed for his eternal home only ten months previously, a salvation his mother and I both witnessed. I appreciated so much that moment of assurance.

Recently, while sharing with Job and his grievances, I was encouraged to find that he, too, had trouble finding God at times, trying to pray under the siege of severe shock and trial. Job 1:5 says that he sacrificed and prayed daily for his family "lest they have sinned and cursed God in their hearts." He was regularly, daily in prayer, but now in Job 23:3 we read: "If only I knew where to find Him." A man who had lost all his sons and daughters, all of his material goods, bearing the terrible accusations of three friends, is now a "bruised reed", a "smoldering wick" about to be quenched. Like Job, oh how I wanted to cuddle up to God; but where could I find Him? An afflicted child just wants to hurry back to his father and hear the father's voice and see his face again, knowing full well the father will kiss the "owie" and make it all better. I felt empty of His Word, alienated from His presence, and like Job, found no consolation coming from the throne of God; and like Job, my inner man cried out:"If only I knew where to find Him."

Maybe it was just a shock, but it was very real for a day or two when nothing else mattered, as with Job, but to once again commune and fellowship with God in peace.

May this little testimony be a ray of light out there in someone's darkest night. "Weeping may endure for a night, but joy comes in the morning." Psalm 30:5.

My reed was bruised, but my joy has been restored. Praise the Lord.

"They that wait upon the Lord shall renew their strength..." Isaiah 40:31.

October 12

"Are they not all ministering spirits sent forth...?" Hebrew 1:14.

A wealthy merchant purposed to move from one city to another, a three-day trip through a lot of heavy forests inhabited by bandits. His propulsion was horses and wagons. The enemy was known to lay low in daytime and plunder by night, with outriders on horseback. The large convoy set up camp the first night before dark; and before bedtime, gathered for prayer of protection for the nighttime. The bandits appeared with intent of robbery, but found a solid, impenetrable wall around the entire campsite. The second day ended likewise, a time of prayer at bedtime. Again the bandits came and found the same solid, impenetrable wall around the camp. Persistence could have paid big dividends the third night when the bandits found holes in the wall, large enough to crawl through. But curiosity got the best of them, and at daylight they inquired of the merchant; "Why were there holes in your wall last night?" The merchant, surprised to even hear of the impenetrable wall, reasoned that on the third night everyone was so weary from travel that they had cut their prayer time short, and had not "prayed through."

"Are they not all ministering spirit?" even to the building of walls, visible to one but invisible to another? Walls of protection for the outer man like as the full armor in Ephesians 6 is to the inner man.

"God frustrates the devices of the crafty so that their hands cannot carry out their plans." Job 5"12.

"So Balaam rose in the morning, saddled his donkey, and went with the princes of Moab". He went in total disobedience to God, not waiting for the Word of the Lord. Numbers 22:21. "Then God's anger was aroused and the Angel of the Lord took His stand...as an adversary against him." The donkey, who saw the Angel in the way with a drawn sword in His hand, slipped aside into a field. Severely corrected by Balaam, she returned to the road only to find a wall on either side, and drawn sword. To get around the Angel, she pushed against the wall, crushing Balaam's foot. She received another strike on her head. A third try, and again the Angel with a drawn sword, and the donkey lay down; and another strike from Balaam's staff. "Then the Lord opened the mouth of the donkey, and she said: 'What have I done to you, that you strike me these three times?' Then the Lord opened Balaam's eyes to see the Angel standing in the way with drawn sword..."Behold, I have come out to stand against you because your way is preserve before Me...the donkey saw Me and turned aside three times. And Balaam, bowing his head, fell flat on his face, and said to the Angel: 'You stood against me, Therefore, if it displeases you, I will turn back.'"

"If we confess our sin, God is faithful and just to forgive our sin, and to cleanse us from all unrighteousness." I John 1:9

October 13

"...and I alone have escaped to tell you!" Job 1:15-17, 19.

In last week's weekly hometown paper from Montana, I eagerly looked at the special column entitled: "Seventy Five Years Ago", a selected resume of people and events in our community of 1931. An article describing the tragedy of a land embankment cave in at an open coal mine brought back a long ago memory. One late fall night my family watched and wondered about dozens of cars with headlights going south over a hill on a road across the river from us. They were headed toward the mine where two men were covered and died instantly, while a third ran fast enough to get within the length of his body from total escape. Farmers standing by to load coal, quickly uncovered him, only his hair showing. He lived. But, like Jacob at the River Jabok, he limped the rest of his days, a hip thrown out of joint. His testimony from that day to his death: "I alone escaped!"

The day when God permitted Satan to try Job to the limit, we read: "The oxen were plowing...the donkeys feeding...the Sabeans took them...killed the servants...and I alone [a servant] have escaped to tell you." Job 1:15. "The fire of God fell...burned up the sheep and the servants, and I alone have escaped to tell" Vs. 16. Another came announcing to Job: "The Chaldeans raided the camels...took them...killed the servants...I alone have escaped." Vs. 17. Another comes: "Your sons and daughters were eating and drinking...a great wind came...struck the house..., they are all dead, and I alone have escaped to tell you"...Vs. 19.

What melancholy, loneliness, and severe shock to be the only one to escape from the mine, or from Job's enemies!

I felt this one day myself in October 1964 when my youngest brother died at age 37, leaving me a lone sibling, my older brother having passed on in 1935 at age 17. My mother, too, was left alone when her eight siblings had all passed on.

Elijah, running from the threat of Queen Jezebel after his big victory on Mt. Carmel against the four hundred fifty prophets of Baal, was found resting under a juniper tree, anxious, worried, depressed. II Kings 19. After journeying forty days and nights, he went into a cave. "The Word of the Lord came to Him: 'What are you doing here?'... 'they seek to take my life, and I alone am left'" I am the last of the prophets he mistakenly reasoned until God told him of seven thousand others yet remaining.

But the saddest story in all mankind, however, came from the heart and mouth of Jesus, hanging alone on that cross at Calvary, and we hear Him cry out that dark, Good Friday afternoon: "My God, my God, why have you forsaken Me?" His first time ever of broken relationship with the Father, caused by your sin and mine. Eleven of His twelve disciples had also forsaken Him. I alone have borne the sin of mankind He must have reasoned, even though He knew His fate at His physical birth.

From one who can empathize and sympathize with one left alone.

October 14

"Blessed are the peacemakers, for they shall be called the sons of God." Matthew 5:9.

During my boyhood days on the western prairies where I saw my life as pretty casual, I often heard the phrase "live and let live" from my dad's heart, a philosophy of life, a panacea for avoiding troublesome times, and exhortation for being a peacemaker.

But then one day I learned that I am a spirit being, living in a spirit-driven world. I learned that there are two spirit forces at work against one another, Jesus and Satan, and I must choose. I heard from the prophet Jeremiah: "The heart of man is desperately wicked, and deceitful above all things". Jeremiah 17:9. I hear from God's Word "Go out against them and I will be with you." I learned there is no armor for the backside, for the runner turning his back on his enemy. I learned that "live and let live" will not always sustain itself as a real, sensible working force in this world because of the heart of unsaved, unrepentant man, man still living in his old nature all around me.

I heard "Out of the abundance of the heart, the mouth speaks, good or evil, blessing or cursing." And "out of the heart flow the issues of life." Proverbs 4:23. So, peacemaking is strictly a matter of the heart.

Wicked, jealous, King Saul's desperate pursuit of God's man of the hour, young, anointed David, is a perfect example of a situation the Christian and Jewish people are facing today. Twice, David found opportunity to draw a sword on that enemy King while Saul slept. Long before Jesus taught, David practiced as a peacemaker "But I say to you, love your enemies, bless them that curse you, do good to them that hate you, and pray for them that spitefully use you, or persecute you." Matthew 5:44.

Today, the Christian and Jewish people are the Davids of our time, being hunted down by an enemy not satisfied with "live and let live." Their Bible, the Quran, in Sarah 9:15 puts it this way: "Fight and slay the pagans wherever you find them; and seize them, beleaguer them, and lie in wait for them in every stratagem of war."

Reminds me of a sly coyote skirting the edge of a flock of sheep, with an evil eye on the fattest lamb; or a hawk soaring lazily above a flock of barnyard chickens, ready to descend and pluck a nice warm meal.

"...those who wage war against Allah...execution, or crucifixion, or the cutting off of hands and feet from opposite sides... exile from the land..." Sarah 5:33. Quran.

It's spiritual warfare, the Bible or Quran, Jesus or Allah, a global warfare between the Sauls and the Davids. It's an exact replica of 2000 years ago when they cried: "Crucify Him...release Barabbas", and the Romans nailed Jesus to the cross, a crucifixion without a cause, without a struggle, Jesus living out His own exhortation: "Father, forgive them, for they know not what they do." Luke 23:24.

"Why are you cast down, oh my soul? Why are you disquieted within me? Hope in God; for I shall yet praise Him, the help of my countenance and my God." Psalm 42:11.

October 15

"For our God is a consuming fire." Hebrews 12:29.

At the beginning of the last century one hundred years ago, my paternal grandfather and many other rugged pioneers from the East settled the untillable acres of northeast Montana. The buffalo grazing there were so few for the acreage that the grass was seemingly untouched, and stood as high as the stirrup of a mounted saddle. The settlers erected "homestead shacks", very small, and usually made of cheap lumber, the roof covered with tar paper, as were the outbuildings. Before the plow turned the soil over, there was often a terrible prairie fire, usually ignited by lightning in the fall of the year when the grass was real dry. Many farmsteads burned to the ground as the wind quickly propelled the fire, which in turn made its own vacuum or draft. A most CONSUMING fire of any burnable tinder in its way.

That lightning flashing across the heavens to bolt the earth with severe fire reminds me of the God of Heaven in Hebrews 12:29: "For our God is a consuming fire." As God had control of the earthly fire by allowing the lightening to come to earth as a consuming fire of all dry tinder in its way, so has His chastening power come from Heaven upon the heart and soul of His people as a "consuming fire." The Jewish believers were scattered, full of fear, hopeless and helpless because of their enemies and because of their wavering faith in their God to direct their paths. But the heroes of Hebrews 11 should encourage them to look back to the champions of faith, challenging them to walk in and embrace a commitment of life in faith, like their patriarchs. Immediately following the examples of faith warriors in chapter 11, the writer encourages them to settle down now, and "lay aside every weight, and the sin which so easily ensnares us, and let us run with endurance the race that is set before us." They were bothered by the weight of sin, the bondage of sin, ensnaring them, making them like the tall grass, a perfect candidate for a consuming fire from Heaven—a trial to produce discipline. As we read on, we find that God is the loving Father who disciplines His wayward child. Vs. 5-6. He is definitely a God of both love and justice. God's people, unlike the grass on the prairies, had some control over the consuming fire of God by simply confessing their sin from a truly repentant heart, and then watch God forgive them, and—"cleanse them from all unrighteousness." I John 1:9.

I believe that we learn from here that today's possessions on this earth are perishable, be it grass or the pleasures of sin; and that because our days on earth are numbered, and our "God is a consuming fire", let us serve Him with our time, talent, and treasure, and make deposits in the "Bank of Heaven" where our investment is imperishable.

October 16

"...whose trust shall be a spider's web." Job 8:14.

One time in my pursuit to read a meter outside our house, I became severely entangled in cobwebs as I parted some shrubbery in front of the meter. I felt tangled in a web, and I thought of the man Isaiah speaks of in 59:5: "they, [those separated from God by unconfessed sin] hatch viper's eggs and weave the spider's web", a web that entangles the more you work with it. The spider's web is meant to catch prey for his eating, flies that make him fat and satisfied. Such is foolish man involved in cults and false religions that require no change of heart, but only works to try to find and please God.

They flourish on lies which make them fleshly fat but spiritually lean trying to please God. They flourish on lies caught in a deadly web, which is skillfully made, a maze of delicate threads, sometimes miles of them in a large, completed web. To see it in daylight against the sun is a beautiful array of perfection. Are not many of the cults and anti-Christian religions appealing on the outside? I Samuel 16:7 says "...for man looks at the outward appearance, but the Lord looks at the heart." Polished lies and deceptions.

The honey bee reaches out to the live alfalfa flower from which to gather his wax, but the spider weaves her web from her body, her abdomen. Such are the humanists and New Agers of our day who claim man has it all in his own being, including salvation. A spider lays out its own foundation to build on with no reliance on the grace of God like the bee. But, oh so frail is the web, no match for a strong wind, a maiden's broom, nor my shirt sleeve as I cleared my face with one simple swipe. The web cannot stand the tests, nor can the cults or false religions founded by dreamers of old whose bones lie still today in an earthen grave, without hope beyond today. We praise God this morning for Christianity whose foundation is Christ, One who died, was buried, but on the third day resurrected and very much alive today and in the business of setting men free from entanglements of the web of sin, death, and the devil.

We sing with David this morning from Psalm 30: "I will extol You, oh Lord, for You have lifted me up. You have not made my enemies to rejoice over me. I cried unto You and You healed me, You brought my soul up out of the grave, and You have kept me alive, that I should not fall into the pit. As saints of Yours, we praise You this morning and give thanks at the remembrance of Your holiness... weeping may endure for a night, but joy comes in the morning."

Praise God for morning...resurrection times for the saints!

October 17

"Rescue the perishing, Care for the dying...", a chorus by Fanny Crosby

This morning when I awakened, I began to wonder, "Why is it so easy for me to weep big tears when I see little children of any color or race starving, or in any way being neglected?" Why am I shocked and saddened and down-hearted even with tears when I learn of a couple I love, now coming to end their marriage in divorce? I can weep easily when I visit a nursing home in Montana and see old-time friends so dysfunctional in body and mind. The other evening I sat a long time watching the horrendous pictures on TV of healthy, innocent, brave, young men lying dead on a beach in the South Pacific during WWII days, or the English channel bloodied by the terrible battle of D-Day in June 1944. It is so easy to shed a tear, and so natural, at the graveside of a relative or friend when the reality of their final departure from my life really hits me. When someone has hurt me in the business, social, or family worlds, its easy to shed tears of shock, anger, hopelessness and despair.

While all this was passing through my mind and heart, I had to ask myself an honest question: "Why it is so easy to shed tears in times of sorrow over all these fleeting, earthly, fleshly, natural happenings while it is so unlikely to do likewise when we know someone is not yet truly born-again, not yet right with God, still living in their eternal death every man is born into, on their way to Hell for eternity? I once saw a very young married couple at Christ for the Nations Bible school in Dallas, Texas, weep over the lost in black Africa as they set sail on a three-year program to go to Africa and deliberately minister salvation to the unsaved. I envied them for their sincere, deep-down, heart-felt concern as I went back to my ranch in Montana, back to normal life. "Why"? I asked myself then, and again this morning...why am I so burdened about people's earthly concerns, which certainly are not to be neglected nor belittled, and yet so unconcerned about millions of lost souls that will soon leave this world of suffering and enter into an eternity of far worse suffering in Hell, without Jesus? Maybe I'm just too nice, too naïve, too considerate of their freedom to choose, a disguise for being a coward, full of fear.

I pray daily for an especially sensitive, Holy Spirit led grief over lost souls as I hear the great commission from Jesus' own lips; "Go into all the world and make disciples of all nations, baptizing… teaching…and lo, I am with you" Matthew 28:19-20.

Let us pray for opportunity to share time, talent, and treasure, God's gifts to us who believe in Jesus.

Let our heart's desire be one with Fanny Crosby's chorus; "Rescue the perishing, Care for the dying."

October 18

"I was lost in sin, trapped."

It was a very dry, windy, late autumn evening, and the dark, cloudy Montana sky lighted up like fireworks, starting many prairie fires over a huge range land, leaving nothing in their paths but that which will not burn. Even a small town burned to the ground that night, leaving only steel bins and some farm machinery in its wake. Custer's battlefield in southeastern Montana burned off one day, also, its first fire ever, and uncovered untold secrets of what may have happened in that battle well over a hundred years before. A century ago, when my grandfather settled in northeast Montana, the dreaded grass fires sometimes left only a steel hay rake unscathed.

As a ground fire on earth proves that which will not burn, so does the fire of the Holy Spirit while passing over the inner man prove that which will not burn as a man is truly born again. Listen, as I share from Isaiah 43:1: "I created you, oh Jacob, and I formed you, oh Israel; do not fear for I have redeemed you, you are mine, and I call you by name, so that when you pass through the waters I will be with you, and through the rivers, they shall not overflow you. When you walk through the fires you shall not be burned, nor shall the flame scorch you, for I am the Lord, your God, the Holy One of Israel, your Savior."

More than once when I have been under fire in spirit, soul, body, finances, or relationships, I have stood with child-like faith on II Corinthians 10:13 for my escape, my extinguisher: "No temptation has overtaken you except such as is common to man; but God is faithful, Who will not allow you to be tempted beyond what you are able to stand; but with the temptation will make a way of escape, that you may be able to bear it." Thrice, even Jesus could prove this; once after His forty days of fasting in the wilderness, and Satan tempted Him three times and He overcame by the power of the Word. Again, in the Garden of Gethsemane: "Father, if there be any other way." And finally, that dark Good Friday afternoon when angels ministered to Him on the cross. Next time you are in a fire, my friend, remember that you are in good company, this temptation is common to your fellowman, and is known by Jesus. The fire of the Holy Spirit burns off the dross, and presents to Jesus a lily-white brother or sister "...though your sins are as scarlet, they shall be white as snow; though they be as crimson red, they shall be like wool." Isaiah 1:18.

"For we do not have a High Priest Who cannot sympathize with our weaknesses, but was in all points tempted as we are, yet without sin." Hebrews 4:15.

"I will extol You, oh Lord, for You have lifted me up, and have not let my enemies rejoice over me. Oh, Lord my God, I cried unto You, and You have healed me. Oh Lord, You have brought my soul up out of the grave; You have kept me alive, that I should not go down to the pit...weeping may endure for a night, but joy comes in the morning." Psalm 30: 1-5.

Praise the Lord! This is morning time for the truly redeemed!

October 19

"Your daughter is dead." Luke 8:49.

From Luke 8:49 we read: "Your daughter is dead." A shocking message for Jairus to receive while begging Jesus to come to her bedside with healing. His shock, grief, and anguish became mine, likewise, when early in the morning of April 18,1977, my son-in-law shared with me: "Lee never made it to Billings." While driving in a very dense fog, a huge truck loaded with lumber swung into my son's driving lane and demolished his brand new Luv pickup, instantly snuffing out his life. Empathy, coupled with sympathy, is a wonderful panacea to come alongside a grieving mother, dad, mate, brother or sister. Praise the LIVING Word of God that without exception, as we search it with zeal for help, a panacea in any kind of disaster, we will find scripture we can learn from and empathize with. Such was Jairus' experience for me. His daughter was twelve years old, dying from an illness. My son was twenty years old, now dead from an accident. My shock and regret lined up with Jairus' desperation we read of from Vs. 41: "...And he fell down at Jesus' feet and begged Him to come to his house..." I literally felt likewise as I immediately thanked and praised Jesus for that night only ten months previous when Lee went to an altar and accepted Jesus as his Savior while his mother and I sat by in witness. Now He has taken him home, a young man who had recently shared with a classmate: "I can hardly wait to get to Heaven." A certain security gripped my inner man while I departed and spent alone an hour or so walking around the farmstead, observing mementos I could tie him to, like the vehicle transmission lying on the shop floor, or the yellow racing car behind the garage with a bumper sticker: "In case of the rapture, this car will be unmanned." I saw his private lodge he had built on stilts in a ravine, just in case of flood waters. I walked on the graded road he had constructed with a contractor's heavy equipment left in our yard. I walked through the shop door he had just put in place. He was the center of my whole life for days and weeks as I "tied" him to one work or memory after another.

From Luke 8:54 we read: "...He, [Jesus], took her by the hand and called, saying, 'little girl, arise', and then her spirit returned and she arose immediately," Immediately upon hearing of Lee's death, I saw him hovering over the vehicle out there on the prairie, and the dust settled and the sound of glass and metal crushing vanished, and he soberly ascended upward in the spirit.

My son, Jairus' daughter. The same Jesus. Two opposite results. But the same comfort "Because of Your mercies I am not consumed, because Your compassion's never fail; they are new [yes fresh] every morning. Great is Your faithfulness." Lamentations 3:22-23.

October 20

"For this child I prayed." Hannah, I Samuel

When I pray daily for my descendants—sons and daughters, their mates, and the grandchildren to the fourth generation—I always am reminded of how much more love God has for them—His agape love against my human love—and how that He created them and died for them, a feat I could not do for any real purpose, nor am I asked to do. How much more He has invested in them than I have!!!

One day when I was studying in I Samuel about Hannah, I realized that my family is only a loan from God to enjoy for now, to pray for, to sacrifice for, and to literally give them back to God like Hannah did at weaning time with her son Samuel. After years of tears, humiliation, despair and loneliness, her life was turned into joy as she prevailed in prayer year after year; and then was moved to make a vow with God; "I will give him to the Lord all the days of his life..." I Samuel 1:11. God needed a Samuel on the scene of that day, and opened her womb so that "Hannah conceived and bore a son" Vs. 22. "...I will take him, that he may appear before the Lord and remain there forever." My heart fills with joy when I boldly and confidently pray for my offspring and lift them up to the very throne of God so that He may "search them and know their hearts, try them and know their thoughts, and keep them in His way everlasting." Psalm 139:23. I love Hannah's humble testimony of Vs. 27-28: "For this child I prayed, and the Lord has granted me my petition I asked of Him. Therefore, I also have given him to the Lord; as long as he lives he shall be given to the Lord. So, they worshiped the Lord there."

Like as with Hannah, when I pray for my children my faith rises up and I am filled with a Godly measure of love, joy, peace, security, assured that my descendants are saved only by the power of God working in them by the Holy Spirit. Romans 1:16. God's hand and heart are moved by my prayer and supplication. What a consolation to have confidence and boldness when I read of Paul and the jailer in Acts 16:3 "Believe in the Lord Jesus Christ and you will be saved, you and your HOUSEHOLD." A heavy responsibility on me as head of the household.

October 21

"Shall the one who contends with the Almighty correct Him?" Job 40:2a.

A married couple I knew very well were blessed of God in every facet of life—an excellent marriage, an inherited farm (debt-free), a beautiful, healthy family, talents galore, and high respect in the community. One day, addictions, the glitter of the world, foolish, excessive spending, cost them their marriage, their farm, their machinery, their health and stability, and the coziness of a family relationship. The husband, convicted by the Holy Spirit, repented and took the blame on himself. The wife angrily asked:"Why? Why did not God spare us from all this rather than let us be destroyed?" Then, by her own testimony, she stood out in a field, in the wide open spaces, under a big sky, and shook her fist at God, as though threatening and condemning Him for their sad state of affairs. The husband, to this day, is a secure, joyous, peaceful man, fully restored to God—a mystery, a miracle, a testimony of God's love to the unlovable. The wife continued to contend, to argue the Word of God, and be proud enough to defy God as she passed into eternity. "Shall the one who contends with the Almighty correct Him?" Recently, a man in dire straits in his marriage, asked me: "If God is so great, why doesn't He write on that wall right now what I should do this very afternoon? And again, if He is so powerful, why doesn't He come down with a strike of lightning and strike down this enemy of mine?" "He who rebukes God, let him answer Him." Job 40:2b.

At times, Job acted like a little child scolding his parent, a case of role reversal. My Bible says that "no creature is greater than his Creator." "The steps of a good man are ordered by the Lord, and in his ways does God find His delight. Though he fall, he shall not be destroyed, for the hand of the Lord will uphold him." Psalm 37:23-24. While "casting all your cares upon Him for He cares for you," we should be in a spirit of expectancy, submission, repentance, and teach ability.

Recently, I told an angry, proud, contentious, spiteful, pity-filled man, complaining of his abuse, that he should think of all Jesus endured as He simply trusted His Father through it all, including Gethsamane, even to the point of dying on a cross, totally innocent. "Shall the one who contends with the Almighty correct Him?"

October 22

"Life and death are in the power of the tongue, and they that love it shall eat of its fruit." Proverbs 18:21

They that speak life with their tongues from a heart bent on life — the positive, up-building, encouraging, constructive, shall know and experience life, and be blessed by life's fruit. And just opposite for those crepe hangers, the negatives, the ones who see and speak only darkness, and they shall eat of that fruit—death.

God immediately sets the perfect pattern for SPEAKING life and bearing fruit of life in Genesis 1, where nine times: "Then God said:" and brought forth light, firmament, waters, grass, moon and stars, aquatic creatures, birds, cattle, creeping things, man and food.

Jesus: "The thief has come to kill, steal and destroy; but I have come to give life, and to give it abundantly." John 10:10. Graphically illustrated when two of the twelve spies, Caleb and Joshua, in Numbers 13 came back with a positive report regarding life on the other side of the Jordan river in the "promised land," the "land of milk and honey," encouraging the Israelites to cross over, believing God's promise to direct their paths, empower them unto success. The enemy spoke destructive Words through the ten negative spies, which kept them in the wilderness, a land of no fruit bearing, a land of only death for the next forty years, having put fear of the giants and walled cities into their hearts. "But the men who had gone up with him [Caleb] said 'We are not able to go up against the people'." Numbers 13:13. "Those very men who brought the evil report died by the plague—but Joshua and Caleb remained alive." Numbers 14:32-38. At the end of the forty years in the wilderness, Caleb, age 85, is still speaking life and enjoying the fruit of life when he said in Joshua 14:10: "...and now, here I am this day, eighty-five years old,...as strong this day as I was when Moses sent me [as a spy]; just as strength was then, so now is my strength for war...for going out and coming in." What a testimony of spoken life into a fruit-bearing person. "Give me this mountain...it may be that the Lord will be with me, and I shall be able to drive them [enemies] out as THE LORD HATH SAID." Vs. 12, emphasis mine. From that day, victory after victory bore them much fruit because they both spoke life and loved life, and the Lord honored their positive word.

"They that love death shall eat of its fruit." "Barzaillai, a very aged man, eighty years old...a very rich man..." II Samuel 19:32, was invited by King David to cross over the River Jordan once more with him, on the way to Jerusalem, answered: "Your servant will go a little way across the Jordan with the King...Please let your servant turn back again, that I may die in my own city, and be buried by the graves of my mother and father...And when the King had crossed over, he kissed Barzaillai and blessed him, and he returned to his own place"—to die and be buried in the family plot. He died, the fruit of his spoken word coming from a tired, negative heart. II Samuel 19.

One day, Condoleeza's dad, a wise, Godly man, took her, an afro-American child, to the streets outside the White House, the chambers of Congress, and the Pentagon, and literally spoke life into her future; "One day, you can be here if you so desire." What a positive word for a black girl of her day!! Today, she is Secretary of State, and, rumor has it, a potential candidate for the future.

October 23

"They called him "Kraut-an-hour-Schauer."

Henry was my neighbor's hired hand on the farm, drafted into the army early in WWII. He not only earned the title, but also the most coveted military honor; the Congressional Medal of Honor. Henry was a rather timid, quiet, bashful, reserved fellow, but one day on European soil, stepped out of his "cocoon," walked deliberately from his unit with his MI rifle in hand and a full ammunition belt, and stood in the wide open, unprotected field for seventeen hours, picking off enemy soldiers, one after another as they appeared and shot at him, but somehow missed that determined patriot who seemed to be supernaturally protected. His reward was seventeen Germans in seventeen hours—"Kraut-an-hour-Schauer."

In II Samuel 23 we read of the "pea-patch" patriot, Shammah, whose story is much like Henry's. Shammah was an enlisted man in King David's army, constantly fighting against the Philistines. One day: "The Philistines had gathered together into a troop where there was a piece of ground full of lentils. Then the people fled from the Philistines. But he [Shammah] stationed himself in the middle of the field, defended it, and killed the Philistines. And the Lord brought about a great victory." This sounds like Joshua, or Gideon, or David against Goliath.

In our nation today we have such men standing up on radio, TV, in the courts, in the legislatures, and yes, on the fields of battle fighting against legalized abortion, gay-rights demands, corruption in high places, syndicated crime on our streets and in our very homes, standing against God's rejection from public places, including our schools in a land where guaranteed freedom of honoring that which made America so great. "Not by might, not by power, but by My Spirit says the Lord of hosts." Zechariah 4:6. I can just see Shammah standing firm, and I can hear him declare to his enemies: "This is my pea-patch, and you cannot have it." "When the enemy comes in like a flood, the Spirit of the Lord will raise up a standard against him." Isaiah 59:19.

If He will use and empower Henry, Shammah, Joshua, David, and Gideon to protect His "pea-patch" on this earth, He will do likewise with you and me as we stand firmly on His Word—"Powerful, living, and sharper than a two-edged sword." Hebrews 4:12. "It is written" Jesus told Satan while being tempted, and then quoted appropriate scripture and overcame the enemy. "The sword of the Lord" is God's Word that we thrust into the bosom of the enemy.

October 24

"Oh Lord God of our Fathers, are You not God in heaven, and do You not rule over all the kingdoms of the nations, and in Your hand is there not power and might, so that no one is able to withstand You? Are You not our God...? ...And now here are the people of

Ammon, Moab, and Mt Sier…coming to throw us out of Your possession…will You not judge them…for we have no power against this great multitude…nor do we know what to do, but our eyes are upon You." II Chronicles 20:6-12.

What a faith builder as we empathize with that people in our present global warfare in which America is the primary target. Our borders on both north and south are wide open, with non-sympathizing, non-cooperating nations of either side. Our shorelines on the east, south, and west are wide open to enemy entrance.

We never miss a single day at our home but that we know and confess to our Lord that man alone is not capable, that there are too many holes in our shields, and not able to cope alone with an enemy, inside and outside our borders, bent on destroying Christianity with its beautiful inherent blessings of liberty and freedom. But, we pray in full faith in such a Word from God's heart found in Job 5:12: "He frustrates the devices of the crafty, so that their hands cannot carry out their plans." Can you believe that with me, with child-like faith as you pray?

Child-like faith in a Word like Job 5:12, coupled with one coming from Nehemiah, chapter 1, make a winner for us like as He showered upon King Jehosophat and his people from II Chronicles 20:24: "So when Judah came to a place overlooking the wilderness, they looked toward the multitude, and there were dead bodies, fallen on the earth. No one had escaped."

Nehemiah, in chapter 1, prayed like we must pray: "Your servants confess the sins of America, which we have sinned against You. Both my fathers house and I have sinned…"

Friends, we have the full armor we need: God's promise, His principal from Job 5:12 coupled with our confession of sin which brings forgiveness and with forgiveness "the healing of our land." II Chronicles 7:14.

"The effective, fervent prayer of a righteous man avails much." James 5:16b.

October 25

"You cannot serve God and mammon." Matthew 6:24.

    The wealthy old farmer, pretending complaint, while really bragging, said to me: "I am giving fifty percent of my income to the government for taxes." Then he waited for my sympathy or compliment, I am not sure. I suggested that he, a regular church goer, give to the Lord's work and thereby cut his tax considerably. He replied "I just as well give it to the government as to the Lord," intimating that in either case he cannot keep it for his own pleasure here and now. One night, only a short time later, he collapsed on his kitchen floor, and at age 84, passed on into eternity without realizing that the true measure of a man's wealth is the treasure we have in heaven — the deposits we have sent ahead to the heavenly bank where God is the president, the board of directors, and the caretaker of the account in a safe that only He has the combination needed to open it one day when we come face to face with Him.

    A young man of the sixteenth century said to his older Christian friend, Philip: "I am finally going to get to law school this fall." Phillip said: "Then what?" "Then I shall become a lawyer." "And then?" "Then I shall earn lots of money, buy a country home, marry a beautiful woman, and lead a delightful life," "And then?"...he realized there would be a final "and then", and that he had not reckoned with that final phase, and had only the glitter of this world and life here and now without any concern or sight of the glamour of the world to come, building his life only on temporal values. "Gone With The Wind", a 1938 Hollywood production...gone with the prevailing wind when that "numbered" day reaches down and takes its toll.

    Many in America today are building huge estates they are trusting in for their future. But listen to the counsel Jesus has for each of us from Matthew 6:19: "Do not lay up for yourselves treasures on earth, where moth and rust destroy, and where thieves break in and steal; but lay up for yourselves treasures in heaven...for where your treasure is, there will your heart be also...no man can serve two masters, for either he will hate the one and love the other, or else he will be loyal to the one and despise the other. You cannot serve God and mammon."

It is not the matter of "sizing up the estate," but of letting the estate size me up!

October 26

"Encourage one another."

Good morning friends—every one of you, I'm sure, in need of encouragement to bless your walk today. Some may be weary from long hours of hard work; others with weakened or hurting bodies; others lonely; others, a broken relationship; while others are suffering economic hardship. Broken hearts!! We all need encouragement, including yours truly, one who seeks such encouragement each morning from God's Word—"A lamp unto my feet, a light unto my path." Psalm 119:105. "Life unto those who find it [God's Word], and health unto the flesh." Proverbs 4:23.

Now since we each know that we need encouragement, it behooves us then to reach out and be an encourager to those around us. "The afflictions of the righteous are many, and the Lord delivers him out of all of them." Psalm 34:19. Will He use me or you today, submissive to His calling? "I know the thoughts I think toward you, thoughts of peace, not of evil; I give you a future and a hope." Jeremiah 29:11. That's the Word that carried me, a lonely widower, to a blessing of "mighty things you do not know." Jeremiah 33:3b.

There is a story of an eccentric old man who carried an oil can with him wherever he went, to apply to the hinge of a squeaky door or a stiff gate he may pass through. He simply made life more pleasant and encouraging for those who passed through those same doors or gates after him that day.

Some people we meet carry burdens, longing for the oil of a sympathetic or empathetic Word, "The Lord has anointed Me... to give them beauty for ashes, the oil of joy for mourning." Isaiah 61:1,3, speaking of Jesus, the promised Messiah to come. Some are in despair and fear and are tempted to throw in the towel. Just one drop of oil—encouragement, could restore their hope.

Think of how much Jesus must have felt that same need that last week of His life before Good Friday, and especially in the Garden of Gethsemane the eve before his crucifixion where He sweat drops of blood as He prayed and agonized. He had arranged for Peter, James, and John to come alongside and pray with Him. Then I hear His most pitiful, mournful cry: "Simon, are you sleeping? Could you not watch one hour?...the spirit is ready, but the flesh is weak." Mark 14. "Then He came the third time and said to them: "Are you sleeping?" How many opportunities we miss because we are insensitive!

The greatest encouragement I get in time of severe trial is remembering how my Savior suffered for me because He loves me unconditionally. It is encouraging to know that I have never suffered like my Jesus did at Calvary. And the best encourager I can be is to share His Word, good news, with a people who are fearful, dismayed, and burdened, a Word I hear from II Chronicles 20:15: "Do not fear or be dismayed, for the battle is not yours, but God's."

From God's heart—to my heart—to your heart, my friend—BE ENCOURAGED!!

October 27

"Weeping may endure for a night, but joy comes in the morning." Psalm 30:5.

My farmer neighbor in Montana was known as "Wild Bill." Upon his return home after his service in WWII—a very ambitious, energetic, prosperous farmer in the springtime, summer and fall time, the "busy season", and also in the winter, the "off season", as a gambler, a consumer of booze, and a fighter on the street or in the bar. Small-town gambling bored him. So he sought out the big cities and their dens of iniquity. One such trip of about twelve hundred miles brought him to a motel room where he found a Gideon Bible in his night stand as his only reading material that late evening, having decided to rest and hit the "big time" stuff on the morrow. By midnight, having been sorely convicted of his lost, sinful life by the power of the Holy Spirit as he read God's Word, he was kneeling by his bedside with a truly repentant heart, and with tears flowing like a river so that his bedding was soaked. He came to that city of sin as a condemned, lost, guilty, unforgiven sinner, but by morning experienced II Corinthians 5:17: "If any man be in Christ Jesus, he is a brand new creation, old things passed away, all things become new." The den of iniquity left behind, he headed for home in the morning, the answer to his mate's and her church's faithful prayer year after year.

"Weeping may endure for a night, but joy comes in the morning"—the joy of salvation, his name written in the Lamb's Book of Life, and at his passing years later, a room waiting for him in Heaven. "Let not your heart be troubled; you believe in God, believe also in Me. In My Father's house are many rooms...I go to prepare a place for you...I will come again and receive you to Myself, for where I am, there you may be also." John 14:1...

"Weeping may endure for a night, but joy comes in the morning." "Wild Bill" was now ashamed of his sin-intimated name, and his testimony rang out like David's in Psalm 6:6 in a similar grief now turned to victory: "I am weary with my groaning; all night I make my bed swim, I drench my couch with tears. Let all my enemies be ashamed and greatly troubled; let them turn back and be ashamed suddenly."

"Weeping may endure for a night, but joy comes in the morning", because God's Word is "living, powerful, and sharper than a two-edged sword; piercing even to the division of soul and spirit and joints and marrow, a discerner of the thoughts and intents of the heart." Hebrews 4:12.

Praise God for the morning time when the SON rises up, never to go back down, confirming Nehemiah's testimony: "The joy of the Lord is my strength." Nehemiah 8:10.

May that same joy be your strength today, too, my brother or sister in the Lord!!

October 28

"I tell you, unless you repent, you will all likewise perish." Jesus, Luke 13:3-5.

Only nine Words, a repentant heart, and perhaps ten seconds of time made the difference of heaven or Hell for the thief on the one cross beside Jesus that Good Friday afternoon at Calvary. He cried out after sensing something magnetic about Jesus which compelled him to simply pray: "Lord, remember me when You come into Your kingdom." Nine Words! Jesus replied: "Assuredly, I say to you that today you will be with Me in Paradise." On the other cross a disgruntled, disturbed, vocal thief who "rode it out" and died, undoubtedly with Hell as his eternal address.

Hell is described in scripture as a place of eternal darkness, loneliness, depression, and unbelievable pain, "weeping and gnashing of teeth forever. I can just imagine those last seconds of reality for those sent down the "broad path to destruction," the unbeliever whose destiny is just as much in the hands of God as is the believer's destiny. "It is a fearful thing to fall into the hands of the living God." Hebrews 10:31. "For our God is a consuming fire." Hebrews 12:29.

"God works in mysterious ways His wonders to perform." Reminds me of how He used a talking donkey in Numbers 22 to bring Balaam to repentance. It seems that Israel moved in on King Balak's territory of Moab, "and Moab was exceedingly afraid... they were many...Vs. 3. King Balak called for Balaam, a noted seer, and begged him to come, "for I know that he whom thou blesses is blessed, and he whom thou curses is cursed..." Vs. 6. Just think of coming to God for counsel and power to curse His people Israel, God's chosen people. Balaam disobeyed God's Word to him, rose early one morning, saddled his donkey, and went to King Balak. "Then God's anger was aroused...and the angel of the Lord stood in the way...against him" as he traveled down the road and met the God-planted angel. Three times the donkey saw the angel and made severe moves to side-track him, one time crushing Balaam's foot against a wall, and each time taking a severe beating from Balaam, fuming over the stubborn beast. "Then the Lord opened the mouth of the donkey..." and in self-defense he vocally reasoned with his rider for mercy, until the Lord opened Balaam's eyes to see the angel the donkey had seen and had veered from. "And Balaam said to the angel of the Lord: I have sinned...Now therefore, if it displeases you, I will turn back" Vs. 34.

"Except you repent, you shall likewise perish." What impossible ways has God used to bring man to repentance, forgiveness, and salvation!!

October 29

"...My Words...life unto those who find them, and health unto all their flesh." Proverbs 4:20-23.

Life and health, two key reasons explaining why we were at the café, ushered to our table by a pleasant waitress, and handed a menu for our consideration. Under my breath: "Why so many choices, so much variety, so difficult to make a choice?" Then I noticed as I scanned, my taste and salivary buds beginning to work, and soon a decision made because of a pleasant past experience with that same meal. My decision (breakfast, lunch, or dinner) is based a whole lot on nourishment. "Junk food" I can easily forfeit. Do we not all eat food to sustain our earthly life, satisfy the flesh, the outer man, while being ever so conscious of our health?

One day on my return home from the café, Proverbs 4:20 streamed through my mind so freely, and I thought: "What an inviting, commanding Word for the infilling, satisfying for the inner man's hunger, just as meat and potatoes just were to my outer man. Then I thought of that long menu I had just chosen a meal from. I sensed Jesus as that Waiter Who ushers us to the table. I felt the inner man's hunger pains. But what about the menu I can choose from? What am I hungry for today? Petition or praise? Then I picked up a little Gideon new testament and I opened the cover and here's the menu I found:

A list of 31 references under "Where to find help, when:"

A list of 37 teachings of life's problems. Take your pick, depending on your day's problem.

A list of 48 portions on "Christian Virtues and Character."

Then, the frosting on the cake for those hungry for singing praise and thanksgiving. Dessert, a list of 7 well loved hymns. And finally a copy of the Lord's Prayer. What a complete menu for the nourishment of a soul craving life and health!

I can just imagine from studying Psalm 51 how hungry, convicted David was satisfied as God anointed him to plea for his redemption after falling into a heinous sin. Likewise for us in a like need, the satisfaction of a lonely, guilt-ridden heart, a way back into the grace of God by confession of sin from a truly repentant heart. "Life and health," the inner man's hunger pains satisfied:

"Have mercy upon me, O God.
Blot out my transgressions.
And cleanse me from my sin.
Purge me with hyssop,
Wash me, and I shall be whiter than snow.
Make me to hear joy and gladness,
Create in me a clean heart, O God,
Restore to me the joy of Your salvation,
And uphold me..."

Then, when the inner man is well fed and once again nourished with life and health, forgiveness for David and fruit following:

"I will teach transgressors Your ways,
And sinners shall be converted to You."
"My son, give attention to My Words,
Incline your ear unto My sayings,
Let them not depart from your eyes,
Keep them in the midst of your heart,
For they are life to those who find them,
And health to all their flesh." Proverbs 4:20-23"
From one who enjoys the blessings of either menu.

October 30

"...seek My face and turn from your wicked ways..." II Chronicles 7:14

"Hang up your phone and I'll call you back in ten minutes", echoed the young man's voice from twelve hundred miles away when I asked for help with my "naughty" computer. John, an experienced, sharp, learned man in the computer world had helped me set up the machine months before. We agreed on a certain word to call my password, a word that enabled him to come directly into my computer and read it as though he were sitting in front of the windows. I trusted him one hundred percent with the sharing of that password along with myself. When minutes later he called back and reported the problem was now fixed.

I see myself as that complicated computer, so perfectly engineered, but needing fixin'. Then I heard from Jeremiah 33:3; "Call upon Me, and I will answer you and show you great and mighty things you do not know." I called upon John and he did likewise, showed me great and mighty things I did not know.

When I need help in the spirit, soul, or body, I hear His invitation from Hebrews 4:16: "Let us therefore come boldly to the throne of grace, that we may obtain mercy and find grace to help in time of need."

One day evangelist Paul persuaded me from Ephesians 2:1 that I was a "naughty" complicated, out-of-commission creature: "...born dead in trespass and sin." Needing fixing. Jesus just could not use me the way I was. It just wouldn't work. My energized gift of faith, my password, lay alienated from God because of inherent sin, but allowed Jesus to see deep down into my heart, that which needed repair. Conviction, confession, and repentance came forth at the nudging of the Holy Spirit, Who spoke God's Word into my inner man: "For by grace are you saved through faith, not of yourselves, but it is the gift of God, not of works, lest anyone should boast." "I will give you a new heart and put a new spirit within you; I will take the heart of stone out of your flesh and give you a heart of flesh. I will put My Spirit within you." Ezekiel 36:26-27.

I gave a few seconds of time to the Man on the "phone", God's Word from heaven. He found the problem instantly when He came into my "naughty" being through my password called "faith". "So then faith comes by hearing and hearing by the Word of God." Romans 10:17.

I'm so glad He called me, saw my need for fixin', energized the password, and fixed my inner being for eternity. Praise the Lord.

October 31

"Then the Lord God closed the door...". Genesis 7:15 LBV.

We exited our plane, only to find our next flight's gate a very long distance away and very short time to make our connections. My mate's vascular problems demanded for us a quick find of an electric car or a wheel chair for her. Precious time quickly elapsed and along came a large, young, strong, foreign lady more than able and willing to help, assuring us along the way: "I get you there", as she almost ran while pushing the wheel chair. About the time we could see the gate, the door closed. What a shock!! The boarding clerk, however, saw us just in time, and opened the door for us, while asking the crew to wait. We were blessed and relieved.

As we thanked and praised the Lord, two other times in history came to mind when we recalled the door of the ark in Noah's day, and the five virgins who needed oil in their lamps and on return found the door to the wedding shut, never to open. In either case, I can imagine the desperate pleas as they knocked frantically on a closed door, with no later "flight" as a way out.

In Noah's day, the door slammed shut on all but eight people, and they "missed the boat" because they ignored over one hundred years of warning, preaching, that landed on deaf ears, the ears of people who didn't care, "leaning unto their own understanding."

On the contrary, "the ten virgins took their lamps and went out to meet the bridegroom" Matthew 25:1, "But while the bridegroom was delayed, they all slumbered and slept." Vs. 5. Like with many of the Christian world today, apathy set in and five of them, unprepared, found no time to fill their lamps with oil, analogous today with those depending on mental assent, but with no Holy Spirit dwelling within. "And while they went to buy oil, the bridegroom came...and the door was shut." Vs. 10.

"My son, give attention to my Word...it is life unto those who find it and health unto their flesh." Proverb 4:23. Give attention to the preaching, the teaching, and the reading of God's Word, so that we and our families will be ready for the day when God says: "Fear not, for I am with you; I will bring your descendants from the east, and gather you together as a family from the west. I will say to the north, 'Give them up' and to the south. 'do not hold them back!' Bring My sons from afar, and My daughters from the ends of the earth." Isaiah 43:5-6.

It behooves us to listen to Noah's preaching, and to prepare with lamps full of oil (Holy Spirit) lest Jesus should return tonight and shut the door forever.

November 1

"...the Lord has set apart for Himself him who is godly." Psalm 4:3b

Susan, a young wife and mother, had been taught about the rapture of the believers one day when Christ would return and take her home, either out of the grave or from the face of the earth, if still living, at His coming. She firmly believed Paul's first letter to the Thessalonians where in chapter 4 she believed; "For the Lord Himself will return from heaven with a shout, with the voice of an archangel, and with the trumpet of God. And the dead in Christ will rise first. Then we who are alive and remain shall be caught up together with them in the clouds to meet the Lord in the air. And thus we shall always be with the Lord." Vs. 16-17.

One warm, pleasant, summer day, Susan drove to the neighboring town in Montana to shop, to eat out, and to enjoy a free time by herself and her young son. Upon returning home in later afternoon, as she testified to me, she found her husband absent, and no cell phone in those days. She called her parents to chat with them, and got no answer. She called several of her Christian friends and not one was home to answer. She called our number and got no response. Then she began to panic as the possibility of the rapture might have come and she was "left behind". I've tried to imagine the anxiety of one like Susan with childlike faith now so blatantly energized, a coveted faith for many of us.

Whether we have experienced this or a similar feeling is not so important. What is so vitally and absolutely important is that we know we are ready like Susan knew she was. When we have once truly accepted Jesus as our Savior and have made Him Lord of our life, we will find ourselves daily anticipating the excitement of His "coming in the clouds with a shout, with the voice of an archangel, and with the trumpet of God."

"Be still and know that I am God; I will be exalted among the nations; I will be exalted in the earth." Psalm 46:10.

I know He's coming!!

November 2

"The stone had been rolled away." Mark 16:24

As I write today, there are just thirteen days until election day in America, Nov 4, 2008. Ever since 1936, I've been keenly interested in political campaigns; first as a sixth grade student engaged in our classroom in a knock-down, drag-out debate over candidates Franklin Roosevelt and Alf Landon. Our class was pretty much evenly divided in support, and, believe it or not, free to engage politically, unlike classrooms of today. It was fun, and educational, manifesting boldly the freedom of speech in line with our constitution. I've followed with keen interest fifteen campaigns, and have seen the presidency change hands twelve times. I've seen a first glimpse of socialism with FDR; then a first Catholic with JFK, and now today, a first black man in the running, Barrack Obama. Since the "woman's suffrage" law of 1919, we have seen two females run as vice president.

There is one issue foremost in all fifteen presidential campaigns—the pocketbook. In the second place, I've seen wars and moral issues most at stake.

Since 9/11/01 the issue of terrorism, spiritual warfare across the globe, twice the economy, and wars on two fronts, a day when the whole world, it seems, has become so small, and interrelated. Yes, today's issues are so different, and have put a sense of fear on many hearts, like I've never known before, about like the women approaching the tomb.

The removal of the dark cloud hanging over America, and in fact, most of the world today, reminds me of the women spoken of in Mark 16. They headed for the tomb where Jesus' body lay, carrying ointment for His body. As they came near the place of burial, the practical difficulty of moving the heavy rock that sealed the door brought them unnecessary anxiety. Their fears were groundless, since the rock was already removed by angelic power sent from on High.

Since you and I cannot see what place God has for America in these end-days, anymore than could they see how the rock was removed, it behooves us to listen as He encourages us from His Word.

November 3

"The Lord does not see as man sees." I Samuel 16:7.

On January 20, a young, tall black man was inaugurated as the 44th president of the USA. He's an educated, wealthy attorney whom millions of Americans thought of as "presidential" by the way he talked, acted under pressure, and how he presented himself physically and emotionally on world-wide television. As election day approached, the man of the world trusted the polls that favored Obama to win, while the man of God trusted God by standing on Romans 13:1: "...For there is no authority except from God, and the authorities that exist are appointed by God" Romans 13:1, sometimes baffles us!

Ed Smith, a Montana rancher friend, candidate for Governor, lived in sparsely populated eastern Montana. He was a tall, stately, rugged-looking man with only high school education, but with uncanny business brains, immeasurable wisdom, and common sense. He built his holdings from meager grassroots. As a long-time senator, he always refused to make a "deal" or "trade horses" to get his bill passed, saying: "If my bill will not stand on its own merits, let it go down." He was a man of great integrity, his Word as good as gold. In his run for Governor, he lacked money, population, and a smooth, polished debate. His opponent, with lots of family wealth, a city dude with a law degree and a smooth demeanor, won the race, and was eventually exposed as a "gay", with a yearn for shoplifting. Romans 13:1 sometimes baffles us!

Abe Lincoln, a rugged-looking, very large, comely man from out in western pioneer country, debated the elite, wealthy, educated, well dressed Douglas of eastern urban society, and won the debate handily, and on to the White House. Romans 13:1 sometimes baffles us!

I Samuel 16 shows us how God sailed through the "primaries" to anoint a replacement for King Saul. "...Samuel...I am sending you to Jesse, for I have provided Myself a King amongst his sons,... invite Jesse to the sacrifice feast..." . And then God consecrated Jesse and his sons. After Jesse made seven sons to pass before prophet Samuel, Samuel said: "The Lord has not chosen these." But the Lord said to Samuel, "Do not look at his appearance or his physical stature...for the Lord does not see as man sees, for man looks at the outward appearance but the Lord looks at the heart." Youngest son, David, tending the sheep at home, was brought in. Of the youngest and smallest brother the Lord said: "Arise, anoint him for he is the one." Romans 13:1 sometimes baffles us!

Romans 8:28 settles it for me: "For we know all things work together for good for those who love God, and are called according to His purpose."

November 4

"Whatsoever you do, do as unto God."

Good morning to each one who has awakened to once again play out this day a certain role of life in your important little corner of the world. Believe me friend and neighbor, you and your effort are important in the eyes of God.

We are so mindful of this during the coming election year when millions feel their little one vote doesn't count, so they stay home. But statistics show us many elections in our nation's history where only a vote or two made a big difference. But most important it is an attitude of the heart our Lord sees and frowns on in a nation. He purposely established to give us that wonderful, coveted, powerful, responsible chore that has a potential of dividing our course in history. God has put each of us exactly where we are in the day we live in history, and He depends on each of us to play our part in the victory.

A place kicker on a football team sees very little playing time compared with a quarterback. But oh how many games are won by just those three points he put through the goal posts from far out in the field, simply because he played his little part well.

I see this played out at "Living Word Free Lutheran Church" every Sunday morning where just a small, dedicated group work like beavers at JFK elementary school gym to set up the chairs, and altar, a pulpit, the flags, wrestling mats on edge to make a cozy setting, and the sound system. God is blessing them for their zeal, their enthusiasm and their attitude that "little things count", and one of these days a congregation housed in their own church and with a full time pastor.

Sometimes we are prone to reason that who we are and what we have to offer is insignificant. But let us not forget that a little bit given unselfishly, freely, unreserved in to the hand of Jesus can accomplish as we see in John 6 with five loaves and two fish, and the disciple asked Jesus: "but what are these among so many?" A short prayer, God's blessing and five thousand men were fed with twelve basketfuls left over.

I often think of the little boy's mother who perhaps, put the lunch together, just a little daily chore to care for her loved one on a special outing for the day. Little did she ever know that her little insignificant part would be recorded in God's Word, the Bible, and be read and preached about and become such a blessing for faith building as long as civilization lasts on the earth.

What a tremendous 'little' contribution to a people in need, a little job she faithfully took care of as a loving mother, a job well done enough for God to honor and bless, and maybe one day hear Jesus say, "Well done thy good and faithful servant, enter into the kingdom prepared for you.", a rich reward for sharing her time, talent, and treasure God has blessed her with.

November 5

"...I am the door of the sheep..." John 10:7

The cattle were still out on their fall grazing pasture when the snow started to fall that early winter morning. I loaded my 4-wheel-drive pickup with hay bales and ventured from the pavement out into the large acreage in search of the cattle. By the time the feeding was complete, on the far end of the pasture, a severe blinding snowstorm had emerged, causing me to lose my orientation, especially since I had to contend with contoured fields. Suddenly, as I drove aimlessly, my only hope of finding my bearing sprang up before me...a round steel grain bin I knew the exact location of. The door of the bin I knew was facing south, and I had to drive easterly to get back on the pavement, one and a half miles from home. When one knows which direction is south for sure, east is easy to calculate. I thanked and praised God for that door that became my physical salvation from the snowstorm.

The old man had spent all of his adult life in prison, and was now released in the evening, his time paid in full. As the prison door closed behind him, and the dark night before him, fear, depression, and despair hit him like a winter blizzard as he stood there with no possessions but the clothes on his body, and no potential for a brighter day ahead. He was severely lonely as he made a decision. The prison was located on a hill on the south edge of town. The old man knew there was a river on the north end and a bridge over the water. He headed north toward suicide. On his way, he began to hear faint refrains of music, and the farther he went, the louder the music that began to speak to his heavy heart and lighten his load. Soon, he approached an Assembly of God church with its door wide open, only inches off the sidewalk. His soul was being so bathed that he stopped to soak up all he could as he stood listening in that open doorway. The Holy Spirit invited him to come in and fill the empty seat in the back pew. That lively gospel music warmed his spirit so that the preaching of the Word and lifting up of the name of Jesus could convict him of his sin and need for help, and drew him to the altar to surrender his life to Jesus. Praise God for that open door that saved the old man's lost soul during that most stormy evening in his life.

That day when Jesus looked up into the tree and called Zacchaeus to come down, He became the "door" that that sinner could enter into and find direction and peace in his soul's stormy life as a dishonest tax collector. Luke 19:5.

So, we find that whether it's a granary door, a church door, or the door of the sinner's heart, His claim "I am the door of the sheep" to be valid, filled with hope, love, joy, peace and security for the lost man.

From one who is glad Jesus found me when I was lost.

November 6

"The wages of sin is death..." Romans 6:23

One sunny summer afternoon, I strolled slowly but carelessly out of the grocery store, my eyes attracted by something afar off, and I suddenly descended from a severe, well marked, step onto the pavement. I lost my balance and tried desperately to remain upright. Some distance away, however, I fell flat on my face, bent my glasses, and immediately looked around to see if anyone saw me, a usual first impulse we all contend with. Almost instantly, about a dozen people rushed to me, one a friend who asked: "Dale, are you alright?" Modesty and pride rushed on to the scene from my soul, and I was totally embarrassed! As I drove home, I thought of another time when I stumbled and fell out in a Montana pasture, miles from civilization, and once again I automatically looked around to see if anyone was in sight. Two extremes, one with a lot of people around, and again all by myself, but the exact same reaction, embarrassment, modesty, and pride! While musing over this, I wondered: "Am I as proud, modest and embarrassed when I stumble into sin before the Omni-eye of God? While strolling along, do I not sometimes stumble into sin when my eye sees afar off things like lust, greed, covetousness, and idolatry?

And here I am reminded of Achen from Joshua 7. Joshua had led his people in to a battle where God had commanded to destroy everything except that which was reserved for the Lord's treasury. But Achen, an Israelite soldier, fell flat on his face in his own privacy, evidently not concerned, and ignorant of anyone watching. Achen had taken some loot for himself and the all-seeing eye of God made the Lord angry at what He saw, not only angry at Achen, but also with the entire nation of Israel. Sin can have a domino effect, beginning with the sinner and its effect reaching out to family, friends, and even to a city and a nation. The Lord said to Joshua: "Get up off your face." Vs. 7-10. Speaking of Achen, God said: "I said, 'It [loot] was not to be taken, and they have not only taken it, but they have lied about it, and have hidden it among their belongings'."

"Then Joshua and all the Israelites took Achen, the looted silver, the robe, the wedge of gold, his sons, his daughters, his oxen, donkeys, sheep, his tent, and everything he had. And the men of Israel stoned them to death, and burned their bodies…". "The wages of sin is death." I find my daily prayer, a shield of protection to help keep me from falling flat on my face into sin, from Psalm 139:23: "Search me, oh Lord, and know my heart; try me and know my thoughts, and see if there is any wicked way in me; and lead me in Thy way everlasting."

"You can be sure your sin will find you out." Numbers 32:23.

November 7

"…Go up you baldhead! Go up you baldhead!' II Kings 2:23

>   Once upon a time, there was a pastor,
>   And of his sense of humor, a master.
>   To illustrate his point in church one day,
>   I plainly heard him say: as he looked at me,
>   "Some people have hair and some don't, you see"
>   Some people laughed, and me, too, I'm proud to say,
>   As I thought "I'll get even some day."
>   About that time, Luke 3:11 flowed through my mind,
>   Where it says that if you have two of a kind,
>   And your neighbor has none,
>   Share, so that you each have one.
>   As I looked at the pastor's heavy, two-tones head of hair,
>   I quoted to him the verse regarding the coat to spare,
>   And assured him I saw, (in fine print), that also means "hair".

From II Kings 2, I read of another "baldy" named Elisha. He had just performed a miracle of purifying the city's water supply. "...the water bad and the ground barren." Vs. 19. Elisha took salt and poured it in at the water's source, and said: "Thus says the Lord: 'I have healed the water; from it there shall be no more death or barrenness.'". "...and as he was going up the road, some young youths came from the city and mocked him, and said to him: "Go up, you bald head! Go up you bald head! Vs. 23. "So, he pronounced a curse on them in the name of the Lord. And two female bears came out of the woods and mauled forty two of the youths." Vs. 24.

Oh, Pastor friend, I love you so much,
Not a curse I bring, but a blessing as such.
As for your lush head of hair, I could covet,
But will accept what the Lord gave me, and love it.
To the Lord be pleasing; to me just teasing!

November 8

"...He who dwells in the secret place of the Most High..." Psalm 91:1.

Whenever I come into the presence of the Lord at prayer time, I picture myself like David came in Psalm 91:1 where "He who dwells in the secret place of the Most High [God's throne room], and abides under the shadow of the Almighty." The invisible God must dwell in a cloud above to make a shadow as His glory shines brighter than the sun on earth. Or like Isaiah describes the same experience in 6:1: "...I saw the Lord sitting on a throne, high and lifted up, and the train of his robe filled the temple."

Have you ever heard Him ask: "Would you like to enlarge your ministry, your knowledge of truth, your love for Me?" I like the way Jabez prayed with child-like faith to God in I Chronicles 4:10: "Oh, that You would bless me indeed, and enlarge my territory, that Your hand would be with me, and keep me from evil, that I may not cause pain." And God granted Jabez his request.

We see how the saints of old enjoyed such wonderful blessing in coming into an intimate presence to worship God, just like I experience every morning as I arise and begin my walk with Psalm 139:23 in the presence of God: "Search me, oh Lord, and know my heart; try me, and know my thoughts, and see if there is any evil way within me..." Innate sin can block my fellowship with God like Isaiah confessed: "...woe is me...for I am a man of unclean lips..." After confession from a truly repentance heart, we can enjoy the freedom of Isaiah 1:18: "...though your sins be as scarlet, they shall be white like snow. Though they be crimson red, they shall be like wool."

Last November 6 we ambled through many rooms of the Billy Graham Library in Charlotte, N.C., and heard many of his recorded messages as he covered literally the whole world in his lifetime. One day later we could have seen him in person, celebrating his 90th birthday, and could have enjoyed the mind of Job in the same setting with Jesus: "For I know that my Redeemer lives...and that He shall stand on earth...in my flesh I shall see Him." Job 19:25.

Dwelling with Him in the Spirit today, but in His very presence tomorrow.

November 9

Psalm 18:10 says: "The Name of the Lord is a strong tower, the righteous runs into it and is safe."

I see here a tall watchtower like we see along a coastline, a brilliantly lighted tower in the center of a courtyard, around which is a very high wall no man can scale, pass through, nor dig under. That wall has only one door, plainly visible to those who hear the call from the tower. Milling around the outer perimeter day after day, a lifetime for most, are the billions of people on earth looking for something or someone to fill an empty void inside, a void caused by lost man being out of relationship with the righteous, holy God of Heaven, his creator.

Those nearest the wall are closest to the light, like as we Americans with our Christian heritage. The further out ones soon fade into total darkness, like a deer passing through a lighted farmstead and on into the night. Some nations far out are in total darkness because the light hadn't reached out that far yet. It is very noticeable that every so often the door opens and a joyful saint enters the courtyard with thanksgiving in his heart and with praise on his lips, having heard the watchman's call and having seen the beckoning arm: "Behold, I stand at the door and knock; if any man hears My voice and opens the door, I will come in to him and dine with him and he with Me." The call is clear and the response is positive. It is no wonder that in spite of the light and the call and the beckoning arm, that so many, day after day, blindly pass by the door, since Jesus Himself said: "Only a few will enter therein." The prophet Isaiah, looking forward to that hour and its blessing in chapter 65:19 tells us: "The sound of weeping and crying will be heard no more." But the saint has found in Jesus, the strong tower, his refuge, his fortress, his shield, his Savior. His Lord, his One and only God—"The way, the Truth, and the Life, the only way to the Father in Heaven." His thankful heart, full of praise, will know no more weeping, no broken friendships, no poverty, famine, peril, persecution, slander, pain, death, nor bereavement. No more fear, now taken over by love, joy, peace, and security. No more trials, tribulations, temptations, nor storms, but now a sunlight that never dims nor sets behind the horizon, a drink of water from the River of Grace flowing out of the heart of God, never to run dry. No more "grass that withers nor flower that fades." But rather the weeping willow, now a palm branch-victory—and weeping eyes now turned into bright pearls of eternal joy and bliss.

"What a day that will be when my Jesus I shall see,

And I look upon His face—the One who saved me by His grace.

When He takes me by the hand, and leads me through the Promised Land,

What a day, what a glorious day that will be!"

November 10

"I will extol You, oh Lord, for You have lifted me up", David. Psalm 30:1.

A positive testimony we all love to hear; lifted up out of the muck and the mire of the glitter of the world, "out of the grave", no longer alienated from God. My friend went the other way, his eye on the glitter of the world. He grew up in a Bible-believing home, in church and Sunday school every Sunday, graduated at the top of his high school class, was one of the very best farmers in the community, a man with a brilliant mind and sound business head. At midlife, boredom overcame him, and he started inhabiting the local pub, and before long was an alcoholic, never to recover. Early one morning I knocked at his door, and when he answered, I was shocked to see his bloodshot eyes, his old, old, wrinkled face, and his hand shaking, waiting for that early morning "shot." What bothered me the most was his testimony that leaked out from the bar: "If I'm going to believe that there is a heaven, someone is going to have to come back from there and tell me so." His early day faith in Jesus now gone for good as he passed away shortly thereafter.

In his day of boredom, he put his hand in the hand of Satan, whereas if he had chosen Jesus and the Christian way of life he would probably have heard: "My son, give attention to My Words; incline your ear to my sayings; let them not depart from before your eyes; keep them in the midst of your heart, for they are life to those who find them, and health unto their flesh." Proverbs 4:20.

Thomas, one of the twelve apostles who walked with Jesus for three years, had trouble believing the good news that Jesus was resurrected, and now alive again amongst them. "Unless I see in His hands the print of the nails, and put my finger into the print of the nails, and put my hand into His side, I will not believe." John 20:25. Unlike my friend, God called His bluff.

After eight days, the Lord appeared to Thomas, showed him His scars, and told him to stop doubting and believe. Thomas was convicted, abandoned his doubts, and said confidently: "My Lord and My God"...a beautiful, positive testimony of faith.

Could you be one who believes in God but shuns Jesus with unbelief in His work on the cross? I hear Jesus pleading from John 14:1: "Let not your heart be troubled, you believe in God, believe also in Me."

"Lord, I believe; help my unbelief." Mark 9:24, a praying father.

November 11

"I am proud to be an American!"

As a very young boy on the Montana ranch, I discovered that we were literally surrounded with proud, very proud, WW I Veterans as they paraded on main street and into the old Rex theatre in their uniforms, to celebrate Armistice Day. I was proud of my three uncles who "went to the war" in 1917, a war fought on European soil, declared to be "a war that would end all wars." I remember two songs in part that they sang as they marched, "He found a rose in Ireland," on the light-hearted romantic flavor, and promise in another, "We won't come back 'til it's over, over there' as they sang in cadence.

Armistice Day was that day when leaders of the involved nations gathered at Versailles, France, just outside Paris to sign the cessation of World War I fighting. They purposely signed on the 11th hour of the 11th day of the 11th month, November 11, 1918. My uncanny, wholesome pride to be an American these past decades became deeply rooted as I watched those WW I veterans on Armistice Day and Memorial Day celebrations.

We take time to honor our veterans, especially those who paid the ultimate price with their lives. And here I think of Jesus from John 15:13, "Greater love has no one than to lay down his life for his friend." May we never forget to honor and praise from a thankful heart for Christ who died on that cross at Calvary that Good Friday afternoon, gave His all and shed His blood for a dying world. On Easter Sunday we remember and celebrate His resurrection, guaranteeing us of the same hope.

"Praise God from whom all blessing flow, praise Him all creatures here below, praise Him above ye heavenly host, praise Father, Son, and Holy Ghost."

November 12

"He descended into Hell." Jesus, Apostle's Creed

On the Monday morning following Palm Sunday, as usual, I visited with the disc jockey while waiting for my broadcast time over KCGM radio in Montana. She had a problem on her heart: "What does it mean in the Apostle's Creed where it says that Jesus "descended into Hell? How could that be?" I assured her that it does not mean physically, but rather His soul, His spirit, His inner man. Like with any of us when we die physically, our spirit is going to leave that old clay and return again into a glorified body like as with Jesus when He arose from the tomb on Easter morning. The inner man will reenter on the day of resurrection, the day we are called from the earthen grave with a glorified body. "How could I be sixty years old and miss that all these years?" she asked. Maybe I am partly to blame, since she was in my Sunday School class in her Junior High years.

I quoted his purpose in that decent from Colossians 2:15: "Having disarmed powers and principalities. He made a public spectacle of them, triumphing over them in the victory He had on the Cross." This was a special work, a special blessing the genuine man of God could enjoy all the days of his early life, a blessing the unsaved does not enjoy, all a part of the blessing of the grace of God accomplished on that cross at Calvary.

This is why we claim Jesus as our Refuge in Psalm 91:2: "I will say of the Lord, He is my refuge and my fortress; my God in Whom I will trust." He is a special protection for the saved like as with the wildlife and birds out on the prairies, finding their way into a "refuge" erected by the State Fish and Game Department. It is a heavily fenced, boldly claimed as a refuge, warned by signs on the fences "No Hunting", a special area with lots of water and foliage. I've noticed that the wildlife seem to have a special peace about themselves while in there, a sense, it seems, of security. I now understand what Paul means when he so often uses the phrase "in Christ", a refuge He guaranteed when He descended into the bowel of the earth with supernatural power and glory.

From one who appreciates those three days Jesus spent in the bowels of the earth!

November 13

The road to Emmaus

On my occasional return to the ranch in Montana, I am quickly inclined to take a trip on the graveled, county road leading west, down "memory lane." Back in the "early" days, it was this road that led us to the wide-open grazing lands to the west. It was the "road to town" for the Silver Star community to the south. It carried me to my first grade country school a mile away by foot, by saddle horse, or by horse-drawn wagon, buggy, or sleigh. Along the road were our closest neighbors, most of them with large families we boys enjoyed. It was on that road I walked in high school days to pray, meditate for a speech class, to dream, to imagine, and to enjoy the freedom of the Big Sky country. There I practiced driving in my pre-license days. I knew every half-mile marker, and have used those distances as a mental measure of distance down to this very day. It was on that road that my brother and I cried and pleaded with our foster dad in the summer of 1930, when both our parents had major medical problems at hospitals far away. We begged old Pete to stop at our house and let us stay there. But to no avail, as he wept with us, having been a real foster child himself as a boy in Minnesota. It was that road that carried our farm equipment to a tract of land three miles away; and fenced on both sides, provided a good trail for us horseback riders to haze our cows to pasture and back. Many summer evenings, my wife and I drove that road very slowly, just to enjoy the cool evening, and to admire our crops and the neighbors'. From a field I was working, I'd often see a cloud of dust arise from the road, and very often it was Lois with a dinner, a milk shake, or an errand she had run to help me out, like a repair. My seventy-three years of living along that old gravel road etched some deep memories into my mind and my soul.

I wonder if that Emmaus road we read of in Luke 24 wasn't like that to Jesus and his disciples, one of the dusty trails that carried them to and fro, out into the mountains, along the lakes, and in and out of Bethlehem, Bethany, and Jerusalem.

There were two men walking on the road to Emmaus after Christ's crucifixion. They were unnecessarily grieving at the loss of a dear friend, someone they loved, someone who had been taken from them. Looking back, they weren't sure when or where, but at some point they realized someone had joined them, a companion to walk with. He talked, but mostly listened. At their invitation, Jesus dined with them. "He took bread, blessed, and broke it, and gave to them. Then their eyes were opened and they knew Him." Vs. 31-32. He then vanished. The very One they had hoped to see again! HE IS ARISEN!! Their cloudy, gloomy day turned quickly to a bright, sunny evening, even though they may not have understood all the details he had recited for them that afternoon.

The gravel road in Montana and the dirt road to Emmaus have had their play in people's lives, but nothing to compare with that road we find in John 14:6 where Jesus says: "I am the Way, the Truth, and the Life, no man comes to the Father but by Me." The only road to eternal life.

November 14

"Rejoice with those who rejoice, and weep with those who weep." Romans 12:15.

As a conservative Christian American, I find it easy to "rejoice with those who rejoice, and to weep with those who weep." Setting politics aside, when Governor Sarah Palin came on stage with a Down's syndrome baby boy in her arms and a broad, proud smile on her face, I rejoiced with tears of joy. And I am not ashamed. Even having known about this condition early in her pregnancy, she chose to carry the baby and to refuse abortion. I rejoice for such character! "How he has changed our lives. We love him so much," a testimony of love and compassion coming form an honest heart, a testimony I could rejoice over.

But when her political enemies came on forcefully with smear and shame and untruths, even to suggesting Sarah's young daughter as the "real " mother, just for political gain, I found a time to weep.

A dad I once read of in similar situation said to his hecklers: "I am glad the Lord gave the child to me and not to you." Praise the Lord!

As Sarah and this dad accepted a disabled son as God's gift to them, so King David was pleased to show love, compassion, kindness, and mercy on a young crippled man, Mephibosheth, we read from I Samuel 9. David said to the son of David's friend: "Do not fear, for I will surely show you kindness...for the father's sake... Mephibosheth...shall eat bread at my table always." Vs. 7, 10. "So Mephibosheth dwelt in Jerusalem...continually eating at the king's table. He was lame in both feet" Vs. 11.

Good news! Time to rejoice with a crippled man and his compassionate friend.

Someone once asked Jesus of a blind man: "Who sinned, this man or his parents?" John 9:3. Jesus answered: "Neither this man nor his parents sinned..." But rather, we might hear and rejoice from Exodus 4:11: "Who has made man's mouth? Or who makes the mute, the deaf, the seeing, or the blind? Have not I, the Lord?" That settles it for me!!

From one who can testify with joy that "every good and every perfect gift comes down from above..." James 1:17.

November 15

"...the sheep of my pasture," Psalm 100:3.

November days are "roundup days" on the Montana ranches, that day when for many families, mom and dad, sonny and sister mount their favorite steed to go out into the hills and valleys, sometimes with a neighbor or two, and bring in the proud cows with a large calf alongside that makes every rancher satisfied with his long months of hard work now turning into his annual income. As they near the corral, there is crowding, some frightened calves trying to escape, human voices encouraging the animals, lariat rope in hand, ready for action, and lots of cow-calf bellowing as they come to this abnormal experience. The cows and calves are separated—the cows to go back out to the pasture, the calves to market, a separation that reminds me of Jesus in Matthew 25—"sheep to the right" to go on living eternally and "the goats to the left, down the broad path to destruction."

On Pentecost Day in Acts 2, we find Jesus, too, rounded up a multitude of "offspring"—Jews—"And suddenly there came a sound from Heaven, as of a rushing mighty wind...and when this sound occurred, the multitude came together and were confused..." What a brilliant roundup! The wings of angels His steed! The "corral" was filled with a captive audience, and Peter, standing up with the eleven, raised his voice and said to them... God's Word, his lariat in hand, an anointed message that pierced their hearts as Peter lifted up Jesus, whom they had crucified, admonishing them: "Repent, and let every one of you be baptized in the name of Jesus Christ for the remission of sins; and you shall receive the gift of the Holy Spirit..., and that very day about 3000 souls were added to them"—to the body of believers.

Jesus rounded them up, corralled them, sorted them, and took in a harvest of 3000 souls for eternity; good interest on His investment as their names were written in the Lamb's Book of Life.

"It was for the joy that was set before Him that He endured the cross." Hebrews 12:2.

November 16

"...and be sure your sin will find you out." Numbers 32:23.

My daily journey to a certain hay meadow one season took me through a long-ago deserted farmstead wherein stood an old dilapidated wagon box overloaded with scrap iron and other refuse. Such "junk" never appealed to me, but one day an urge caused me to stop and look. There lay in plain sight a nice crowbar that I suddenly "needed" for a particular purpose. The spirit of covetousness overcame me and I took the bar without any reservations. All went well until years later, during a time of spiritual renewal, and I heard the Lord say: "...be sure your sin will find you out," and that which I had taken so lightly years earlier the Holy Spirit brought to my attention. I had learned to pray Psalm 139:23: "Search me. Oh Lord, and know my heart; try me and know my thoughts, and see if there is any wicked way within me..." Thus I confessed my sin from a truly repentant heart, as conviction and confession can be frightening; but it's also cleansing. I am praying yet that one day I may find that bar and return it to the old dilapidated wagon box. Nothing else, good or bad, about that haying experience can I remember.

God let me off much easier than He did Achan, of the tribe of Judah, we read of in Joshua 7. God promised and provided victory for the Israelites, under Joshua's leading, to overtake Jericho by a certain strategy they carried out to the letter. But God's command to take no loot, no bounty, from the enemy, "but that the silver and gold and the utensils of bronze and iron will be dedicated to the Lord, and must be brought into His treasury." Joshua 7:9. "But there was sin among the Israelites. God's command to destroy everything except that which was reserved for the Lord's treasury was disobeyed. For Achan took some loot for himself, and the Lord was very angry with the entire nation of Israel..." "...they have not only taken loot, but then lied about it, and have hidden it among their belongings." Vs. 7:11. "Joshua sent some men...and found stolen goods. They brought it to Joshua...The Lord will now bring calamity upon you... [Achan], and the men of Israel stoned them to death, and burned them...". Achan lost his life, the silver, the robe, the wedge of gold, his sons, his daughters, his oxen, donkeys, sheep, his tent, and everything he had. Vs. 7:24 (my version).

"For the Lord knows the way of the righteous, but the way of the ungodly shall perish." Psalm 1:6.

Praise God for the day of grace: "Though your sins be as scarlet, they shall be white as snow; though they are red like crimson, they shall be like wool." Isaiah 1:18, fulfilled.

From a sinner saved by grace.

November 17

"He shall be like a tree planted by the rivers of water...and whatever he does shall prosper." Psalm 1:3.

One Sunday morning at Abiding Savior, I, for some reason, took a special time to study and meditate in detail on a wonderful, quite large work of art on cloth, sitting on a stand beside the pulpit, with the inscription: "Take root and bear fruit." It consists of a beautiful tree full of branches bearing fruit, standing tall, its roots plainly exposed below ground level. "Take root and bear fruit." It said to me: "plant a seed, watch it sprout and take root as the tree grows upward, reaching toward the light of the heavens, its branches ready to "bear fruit."

The idea for the art work came from Grace, a retired lady in our midst who has put her time, talent, and treasure together to bless Abiding Savior with not only this work, but with many tapestries, at appropriate times and seasons. Pastor Flaa announced early this year of 2009 that our theme was to be: "Take root and bear fruit." So, Grace, a beautiful woman of faith, a true servant, so willing to serve the Lord in her special capacity, created a work to add a luster to our worship center, to keep the theme constantly before our eyes, to be a weekly reminder of our theme which our pastor has so ably expanded on from the pulpit. I am sure that Grace is getting much richness and satisfaction in these later years by sharing with us who cherish her work, and with the Lord Who just might have a complimentary word like: "Well done, thou good and faithful servant."

And then there was Dorcas, a disciple in Joppa, who was "always doing good and helping the poor." Acts 9:36. She found meaning in life through following Christ. Dorcas died, leaving a beautiful legacy: "...all the widows stood around him [Peter] crying and sharing the robes and other clothing that Dorcas had made..." Vs. 39. This humble, simple, devout, dedicated lover of Jesus is never mentioned again in the Bible, but her powerful testimony of "doing good and helping the poor" lives on because she had invested abundantly her time, talent, and treasure.

"For to everyone who has, more will be given, and he will have abundance." Jesus, Matthew 25:29.

From one who believes that an unselfish investment of time, talent, and treasure will reap big eternal dividends.

November 18

"For with God nothing will be impossible." Luke 1:37.

One November afternoon, out on the prairies of Montana, five miles from our farmstead, my son and I had corralled our cows and calves. We separated them and sent the calves to an Iowa feeder and the cows back out to pasture. It was then time to disassemble the large portable corral of steel panels. We placed them carefully side by side into our stock trailer. Having loaded twenty of them, our carrying was quite distant. So I suggested that we tie them with a rope to the wall and drive up a distance. My son suggested he could stand beside them and keep them from falling over. I drove ahead carefully and slowly, but they tipped, and I found him pinned to the wall at his throat, stifling his windpipe. I tried two things to free him, without success, from a load that weighed thirteen hundred pounds. Finally, his desperate plea, "I can't breathe" drove me to my knees, to crawl under the leaning load. As soon as I rose up with my back to lift that load of steel, the panels stood upright and he was freed. "For with God nothing is impossible." Even for a man of small statue.

"...I have set before you life and death, blessing and cursing; therefore, choose life, that both you and your descendants may live." Both for now and for eternity will he live!

As I reflect on this real-life experience, what I saw when I heard the son's cry, and I ran to the end gate of the trailer, is the same tragedy God saw when Adam and Eve fell into sin. He saw them pinned against a wall of Hell, pleading for help, help to lift the load of sin and death. He had promised that "...for in that day you shall surely die." Genesis 2:17. "...between us and you is a great gulf fixed, so that those who want to pass from here to you cannot, nor can those from there pass to us." Luke 16:26.

From the day of Abel and Cain, God had used the sacrifice of the blood of an animal to "cover" the sins of Old Testament saints, cover until the coming of the promised Messiah. God had a plan to lift the deadly weight of sin from the trapped man, not for the cover of sin, but for the remission, the removal, by the blood of a perfect sacrifice. So it was, Jesus, endowed with pure, clean, innocent, sinless blood of his Father, would come to earth in the flesh (John 1:14) and go directly from the crib at Bethlehem to the cross at Calvary. There was He crucified, His side was pierced, His heart stopped, the load of your sin and mine borne in His body. He was then placed in a borrowed tomb. On the third day after He was resurrected by the power of God, One now with power to likewise resurrect each of us who would come to Him with child-like faith, confess our sin from a truly repentant heart, and believe that He was resurrected.

As God gave me supernatural physical strength to lift that steel and free my son, so has Jesus lifted the weight of every man's sin so that his inner man could live, not die, but set free forever.

November 19

"Search me, oh Lord, and know my heart..." Psalm 139:23

In the days of old, before milk came out on the market in paper cartons, pasteurized and homogenized for store sale, dairymen used a one quart round glass bottle with a large base and a small "neck", rising up form a smooth, rounded curve. Fresh milk, after proper cooling and a few hours of setting still, would automatically separate into two parts as the "cream", the best part, arose to the top. The line of separation was visible, and ranged from two inches in depth to perhaps five inches, depending largely on the breed of the dairy cow. The big, heavy Holsteins brought lots of gallons of milk, but so high cream line in the neck of the bottle. The tiny Jersey cow produced less milk but several inches of cream in the bottle.

As an analogy, I see the glass quart bottle of milk symbolizing the heart of man, plainly visible in God's sight. Some hearts contain large quantities of the glitter of this world, and consequently a high "cream line" in that heart. In I Corinthians 6:9 Paul describes some glitter like this: "fornication, idolatry, adultery, homosexuality, sodomites, thieves, covetous, drunkards, revilers, and extortioners, which will not inherit the kingdom of God."

The worldly people are the big, tough, rugged ones endowed with an uncontrollable dose of the "me-first syndrome" of life who see "the preaching of the cross as foolishness." I Corinthians 1:18, while Jesus declares from Matthew 16:24: "If any would come after Me. Let him deny himself, take up his cross, and follow Me."

On the other hand are the lowly, humble, repentant, meek Jersey-like, producing an abundance of "cream", the valuable fruit of the

Spirit: "love, joy, peace, patience, kindness, faithfulness, gentleness, and self-control." Galatians 5:22-23.

"Give and it shall be given to you: full measure, pressed down, shaken together, running over shall men give into your bosom..." Luke 6:38.

"Search me. Oh Lord, and know my heart; try me and know my thoughts; and see if there be any wicked way within me..." Psalm 139:23.

Where does God find the "cream line" in your heart and mine—high or low in the neck of the bottle?"

Oh, to be a little Jersey with all that good stuff in my heart!!

November 20

"...My sheep know My voice." John 10:4.

I called, I bleated, I whistled, I begged, and pleaded for my flock of 450 female sheep to come, follow me out of the corral as I stood outside the wide open gate. I even enticed them with grain pellets, and finally one jumped over the imagined "barrier", an extended shadow of a tall wooden post, and the others followed, every one, however, jumping over that shadow to the last sheep! It was a comical sight and not because they were "female" nor because they were "sheep", but because of their inherent instinct did they tickle my funny bone.

I recently read of another flock of fifteen hundred sheep where one jumped off a forty five foot cliff, and one by one, all followed, killing the first five hundred head, the last one thousand saved by falling on the soft, wooly, dead bodies. Stupid?? No, instinct.

The Bible often refers to us human beings as sheep: "We are His people, the sheep of His pasture." Psalm 100:3. "All we like sheep have gone astray..." Isaiah 53:6.

In a church in Montana, a couple had left the "glitter of this world" crowd with all the carousing and drinking and free lifestyle, and had surrendered to Jesus. The day of the high school divisional basketball tournament was approaching, so my wife and I naively invited them to now be a part of our party at the motel, at the games, and at the café, assuming that their worldly crowd would now be left behind. They said they were not going. But when we arrived at our motel miles away, they drove up with their same old click, endorsing the same lifestyle of old.

Sometimes we "sheep" get easily distracted, fall over the cliff with the old crowd rather than listen to the good Shepherd: "I am the good Shepherd; and I know My sheep, and am known by My own." John 10:14.

From a "little lamb" following the "Big lamb", Jesus.

November 21

"I will joy in the God of my salvation." Habakkuk 3:18-19.

In the early fall of 1939, the western sky quickly darkened, and soon a black cyclone tunnel was seen racing down Police Creek in Eastern Montana. At a certain spot, the cyclone veered directly into the Christensen farmstead, where it removed the home's roof and planted it in the nearby grove of trees. Particles of straw were supernaturally driven into a concrete step. Food perishables daily stored sixty feet underground, under the windmill, were lifted up and set on the ground unharmed. Other parts of the yard were badly damaged. Olene stood in the home's doorway without injury, while Knudt was in town, about twenty miles away. A concerned neighbor went to meet him on the road, to spare him the shock of driving into the mess unawares. Neighbors flocked in to help the beleaguered couple in many ways. Being people of character that they were, they refused a cash gift from the community, since no one could really afford to help financially after the decade of drought and depression of the 1930's.

Reminds me of King David and the shocking sight he and his six-hundred man army came upon when they came home to the city of Ziklag for a few days of R & R. They were shocked to tears when they saw their city burned to the ground, and their livestock and families gone, taken by the enemy. "They wept until they could weep no more." I Samuel 39:4. "But David took strength from the Lord." Vs. 6. "Then David asked the Lord: "Shall I chase them?

Will I catch them?" And the Lord told him: "Yes, go after them, you will recover everything…" Vs. 9.

David asked of an Amalekite casualty along the way: "Can you tell me where they went? He answered: "I will guide you to them." David and his men, guided perfectly, "rushed in…and slaughtered the enemy…no one escaped." "David got back everything they had taken." Vs. 19.

Whether it is a cyclone, a burned up city, or a rampage of kidnapping, I hear His great promise from Jeremiah 33:3: "Call upon Me and I will answer you, and show you great and mighty things you do not know."

"Your trial is one common to man, but God is faithful, Who will not allow you to be tried beyond what you are able to stand, but will with the trial make a way of escape that you might be able to bear it." I Corinthians 10:13.

"Though the fig tree may not blossom…And there be no herd in the stalls, Yet, I will rejoice in the Lord; I will joy in the God of my salvation." Habakkuk 3:17-18.

From one who has learned to "Count it all joy when you fall into diverse trials…" James 1:2.

November 22

"Choose you this day whom you will serve." Joshua 24:15.

On **November 22**, 1963, Lee Harvey Oswald learned of the route President J. F. Kennedy would travel from the airport through Dallas to his meeting place. Oswald went ahead, entered a book store depository with rifle in hand, and positioned himself before a window overlooking the caravan. At a precise moment, the expert rifleman looked through his scope, fired a shot at the open car and assassinated the President of the U.S. of America. Concealed behind a wall, Oswald's heart's intent was to kill, a feat that backfired on him only a few days later when he was mercilessly murdered outside the jail.

What a contrast when we look at Luke 19 and read of Zacchaeus who also knew of a Man's caravan route about two thousand years ago. He also ran ahead, but to perch in a tree, to look down upon the King of Kings, not concealed because of a sinful heart, but out in the open where Jesus could look up and see him, a man waiting to confess his sin from a truly repentance heart, a heart that would bring new life, not death. While Oswald shut himself up into death, Zacchaeus opened himself up unto life.

"And when Jesus came to the place, He looked up and saw him, and said unto Zacchaeus, make haste and come down...So he made haste and came down, and received Him joyfully. Then Zacchaeus stood and said to the Lord: "Look, Lord, I give half of my goods to the poor; and if I have taken anything from anyone by false accusation, I restore four-fold." "And Jesus said to him, 'Today salvation has come to this house.'" Vs. 5-9.

We see spiritual warfare undoubtedly bring eternal death to one and eternal life to the other. "The cowardly, unbelieving, abominable murderers...shall have their part in the lake which burns with fire and brimstone, which is the second death." Revelation 21:8. "He who overcomes shall inherit all things, and I will be his God, and he shall be My son." Revelation 21:7.

"For the Lord knows the way of the righteous, but the way of the ungodly shall perish." Psalm 1:6.

Thank you, Jesus, for life!

November 23

"As for me and my house, we will serve the Lord." Joshua 24:15.

"...choose for yourselves this day whom you will serve..." So, that surely explains for me why a Pastor's home turned out one son to follow his daddy's footprints, and another to become an atheist. Unbelievable!! All the more to bear out a basic truth of New Testament scripture: each of us is responsible for his own salvation!

How well I remember my childhood days on the Montana prairies the trails with a "Y" always calling for a choice "which way shall we go?" was often asked.

A beautiful Christian family I once knew had two sons almost the same age. One chose life on the high road, and became a pastor, a pianist-organist, adept with gospel music, a Godly husband, and father who enjoyed long years of good health and a golden opportunity to serve the Lord, and a nice retirement along a peaceful lake. His brother, walking down the same road in childhood, chose the low road at the "Y" along the way. He married, learned to play guitar and thrived well on the century-old cowboy songs. Adultery and fornication tempted him and cost him his marriage, and infidelity on the wife's part cost him his second divorce. All this left him homeless, financially destitute, and broken health in later years.

I've often wondered: Genes? Breaks in life? I believe it's found in Deuteronomy 30:19: "I have set before you life and death, blessing and cursing. Therefore, choose life, that both you and your descendants may live." "My son, give attention to My Words...life unto those who find them and health unto their flesh." Proverbs 4:20.

The walk begins at our birth, when our hand is clutched tightly into Satan's hand because "All have sinned and fall short..." Romans 3:23. Alienated from God! Then one day Jesus comes along that same road and tells us: "I have chosen you" and at the fork in the road we drop Satan's hand and grasp the hand of Jesus...a decision that leads to heaven for eternity rather than Hell. We've chosen the high road.

From the heart of the song writer: "Turn your eyes upon Jesus, look full in His wonderful face, And the things of earth will grow strangely dim, In the light of His glory and grace.

From the one who chose Jesus at the "Y" in the trail.

November 24

"Give thanks at the remembrance of His holiness on Thanksgiving Day."

On this Thanksgiving Day, let my imagination take me back to what history has taught me about the hearts of those few pilgrims in that first year here in America— 1620-1621. They had lost half of their people, had undoubtedly spaded raw prairie, perhaps raked it smooth, and manually placed every seed of their gardens. It was a day to day sustenance, and enough to store, perhaps in the ground, for the winter ahead along America's eastern shoreline. As they gathered to pray, praise and give thanks to their Almighty God, I can see one bringing a beet, another a parsnip, head of cabbage, a squash, a few potatoes and other mature goodies, some would be preserved for the cold winter ahead.

I can imagine that as they came together with their tangible blessings in hand for the body, that suddenly there arose an explosion of thanks for the soul, perhaps from Psalm 100, "Make a joyful sound all of you people. Serve Him with gladness, come before His presence with singing...We are His people, the sheep of His pasture. Enter His gates with thanksgiving and His courts with praise...His mercy is everlasting. His truth endures unto the end of the ages." Praise the Lord in spirit, soul and body.

"I will bless the Lord at all times, His praise shall continually be in my mouth...Come, let us magnify the Lord. Let us exalt His name together." Psalm 34.

May our thanksgiving season this year be prompted from a genuine heart of thanks and praise like as with that first Thanksgiving, and anointed with a quantity and quality of love, joy, peace, hope, faith and security in our Lord Jesus Christ.

November 25

Jesus, My hero!

At a springtime outing at Eagle's Nest in Montana, my High School senior year, my Eagle Scout classmate, "Bumps" rescued another from drowning in a river. Only a few months later, while operating a Browning Automatic machine gun in the Battle of the Bulge in WWII Europe, he was killed in action at age nineteen. His bones are still lying on that battlefield now sixty-five years later. "Bumps" is a hero first class, his only recognition, however, a picture in his uniform with an obituary in his little home-town newspaper. Thousands of others also sacrificed their lives as HEROES for American freedom.

After hearing for weeks the two words "hero" and "icon" as complimentary to a "hip-hop, bebop" addict whose only prominence and contribution was to make an "S" formation of his body and kick up his heels like a punter on a football team, I looked those two words up in my sixty-five year old college dictionary and found this: Hero: "A man honored after death by public worship because of exceptional service to mankind, and usually held to be, in part at least, of divine descent." Icon: "An image or representation. In the early church, the image of Christ, the Virgin Mary, or a Spirit.

To the believer in Jesus, there is only one real hero or icon to worship even now two thousand years after His death and resurrection. He's alive!! He was a hero from day one...born a humblest of birth, His arteries running full of pure, clean, innocent, sinless blood, destined to sacrifice for all mankind, "that none should perish, but have everlasting life" John 3:16. A Hero, an Icon, for those of us who have moved out of the flesh where "weeping may endure for a night, but now have joy in the morning." Psalm 30:4. Truly born-again because of Jesus and His work at Calvary.

My Hero lay in a tomb, wrapped in cloths, to be resurrected on the third day after, while the man of the flesh is buried in a gold plated casket, to be lifted up at the White Throne judgment. My Hero that I worship has spared me from that final, deadly judgment, having taken it upon Himself, My Hero!!

Airplanes full of people from all over the globe came to worship a dead man, while we believers, at prayer and praise time, enter the throne room in heaven in the spirit, where "we dwell in the secret place of the Most High and abide under the shadow of the Almighty God, and say of the Lord, Jesus seated at the Father's right hand: "You are my Refuge, my Fortress" Psalm 91:1, a live Jesus now housed in a glorified body rescued from the tomb, now ascended back to His Father.

Earthly, fleshy, "heroes" come and go, but my Hero Jesus: "...the same yesterday, today, and forever." Hebrews 13:8.

November 26

"...God loves a cheerful giver." II Corinthians 9:7.

While trying to barely exist during the "great depression" of the 1930's, accompanied by almost a decade of severe drought in Montana, Clara's husband divorced her. He left her to support a teen-age son, and to somehow pay off $3000 of delinquent tax held against the small farm, more than the farm's worth. She lived fourteen miles from town, had no vehicle, no machinery, and only a milk cow for livestock. Ways and means were tough for all her neighbors, too, in those days. But her three closest ones shared their love and resources to help her through. One planted her wheat crop, another took care of her usual meager harvest, and a third assured her of transportation for grocery and household shopping.

Upon his graduation from high school, her son stayed by her, and they gradually prospered as it started to rain in 1938, and WWII helped agricultural people to prosper so that by war's end, a new, small tractor, and a pickup were bought and paid for, after that decade of severe trial.

From John 3:17-19, I see the real heart of her three neighbors described: "But whoever has this world's goods, and sees his brother in need, and shuts up his heart from him, how does the love of God abide in him? My little children, let us not love in word or tongue, but in deed and in truth, and shall assure our hearts before Him."

"Give, and it shall be given unto you: good measure, pressed down, shaken together, and running over will men give into your bosom, for with the same measure that you use, it will be measured back to you." Luke 6:38.

As for me, I hear Jesus blessing and praising the three helpful neighbors: "Inasmuch as you have done it unto one of the least of these, my brothers, you have done it unto Me." Matthew 25:40.

November 27

"...let him deny himself...and follow Me..." Jesus. Matthew 16:24

It must have been a hard pill to swallow for Ted Turner and his ex-wife Jane Fonda who were expelled from that restaurant in Manhattan, Montana, celebrities held not highly in southern Montana, where the tycoon had thousands of precious acres and much influence. They came into a crowded restaurant which has no reservations, but with tasty steaks, and many ranchers and wives waiting for a seat. The hostess informed them that they would have to wait in line for forty-five minutes. Jane curtly asked "Do you know who I am?", and the lady said "Yes, but you will have to wait forty-five minutes. Then Jane asked for the manager, and he greeted her pleasantly, and this time both of them asked "Do you know who we are?" "Yes, but we cannot put you ahead of these who have been waiting so long." Then, Ted asked to speak to the owner who asked them "Do you know who I am?" "I am the owner of this restaurant, and a Vietnam veteran. Not only will you not get a table ahead of my friends and neighbors, but you also will not be eating in my restaurant tonight, nor any other night. Good bye!" "Montana, Montana, glory of the west..." her state song proclaims.

I gather from Mark 10:35 that it was that same "me-first syndrome" that caused James and John, the sons of Zebedee, to boldly make a similar request of Jesus when they said: "Teacher, we want You to do for us whatever we ask." Sounds like the same old-nature heart we are all born with, and deal with until Jesus does His work within our hearts. "You must be born again." Jesus. John 3:3. "And He said to them, what do you want Me to do for you?" "They said to Him, "Grant us that we may sit, one on Your right hand, and the other on Your left, in Your glory." "But Jesus said to them: "you do not know what you ask. Are you able to drink the cup that I drink, and be baptized with the baptism which I am baptized with?" Vs. 38. "They said to Him: we are able." "Jesus said to them...to sit on My right hand and one on My left is not Mine to give, but it is for them for whom it is prepared." "And when the ten heard it, they became greatly displeased with James and John." Mutiny in the camp, eh?

Whether it is in Montana or Galilee, we hear Jesus from Matthew 16:24: "If any would come after Me, let him deny himself, take up his cross, and follow Me." Those who do will confess their sin from a truly repentant heart, and be set for life both for now and for eternity.

November 28

"When you pass through the waters I will be with you..." Isaiah 43:2.

The crowd was small, the June afternoon was warm and pleasant, and the Spirit of the Lord was present as we sat on the bank of the Hungary Horse River in the mountains of western Montana, sharing with one another. It was Bible Camp time come again. I heard a young widowed mother tell of how she, her husband, and their daughter had been out on a lake in Williston, N.D. area on a boat that capsized and deposited them into the waters, without life jackets. Only the mother could swim, and was therefore forced to make a quick decision: to save the husband or the daughter. Her mother instinct forced her to save the daughter, while watching the husband flounder for life, only to drown. I thought: "what a shock; what a shame." I was blessed to see no bitterness or anger in her heart, but rather a strong testimony of how her faith in Jesus sustained her through her days of grief and sorrow. No remorse or guilt for the decision she had made. When nothing else made sense, she still had Jesus! "Lord, where shall we go? You have the Words of eternal life." Peter, John 6:68.

In her behalf I heard the Lord as in one of my plights along life's way: "Do not fear nor be dismayed, for the battle is not yours but God's...position yourself, stand still, and you will see the salvation of the Lord." II Chronicles 20:15-17.

When I rehearse this lady's testimony, I am reminded of Isaiah 43:1: "...Fear not, for I have redeemed you; I have called you by name, you are Mine. When you pass through the waters, I will be with you; and through the rivers, they shall not overflow you. When you walk through the fires you shall not be burned, nor shall the flame scorch you. For I am the Lord, your God, the Holy One of Israel, your Savior."

"I know the thoughts I think toward you, thoughts of peace, not of evil; I give you a future, I give you a hope." Jeremiah 29:11. "I will bless the Lord at all times; His praise shall continually be in my mouth..." Psalm 34:1.

November 29

"Give and it shall be given unto you...as you measure it out it shall be measured back to you." Luke 6:38.

    There he sat, riding the bicycle next to me at the exercise center, always decked out with ear phones and a CD playing country music, totally aloof to anyone around him. I tried to befriend him, without success, until one day when he took the phones off, looked me in the eye, and gently asked my name, announcing to me with a handshake that his name is Jerry. The silence, the aloofness, was broken and he shared that he was suffering from deep depression, that he was once severely addicted to alcohol, three times divorced, with a son and daughter who had rejected him, hardly having seen them since their infancy. He called himself a "loner" as I had guessed, and blamed only himself for it all. I loved the man from a sorrowing heart, and soon we became close friends, a blessing I could see he needed and hungered for.
    One day I felt comfortable in talking about spiritual matters, only to find a man, raised Catholic, reaching out desperately with child-like faith in prayer, which both Alice and I were more than ready to share with him. One day at the dinner table when Alice and I joined hands to pray, he quickly reached over and laid his hand on ours. Jerry was loosening up and enjoying our company and attention, now like a normal person. Suddenly, for several days we missed him, only to find him in a nursing home after a stay in a local hospital. With joy in our hearts we found reconciliation with his son and daughter, who were moving him to a northern Minnesota town, into assisted living quarters. A time of sharing Jesus and prayer and God's Word and a copy of the scriptures enriched all three of our lives.

From Luke 10 we read of a man lying and bleeding on the road to Jericho. A Samaritan came upon him, saw his desperate need, bandaged his wounds, helped him on to the saddle horse and took him to a local inn, cared for him for a season, spent his own money, and left him for a day or two with the innkeeper, only to return and finish the work.

"So which was neighbor to him who fell among the thieves? He who showed mercy on him." The Jesus said: "Go and do likewise."

"...Let us magnify the Lord and exalt His name together..." Psalm 34:3.

November 30

"...for man looks at the outward appearance, but the Lord looks at the heart." I Samuel 16:7.

When my elderly dad suggested in March 1946 that I take over the farm and ranch, my first negative consideration was my God-given small physique. But when I considered neighbors of old, B. J., Pete, Dave, Art, Alfred and others, I was encouraged as they seemed to cope very well with hard work, each built with my statue. I fared well, too, but soon welcomed the milking machine for the dairy, the grain auger at the granary to replace the shovel, the hay baler on the meadow to replace the pitch fork, the truck to haul grain to replace the horse and wagon, the combine to replace the binder and the threshing machine, the front-end tractor loader to replace the manure fork, and electricity to replace the kerosene lantern, to say nothing of the compete revolution in the household world.

God's Word from I Samuel 17, where comparatively "tiny" David, anointed of God as he took on huge giant Goliath, who was decked out with full body armor, has encouraged me many times. The Israelites were severely besieged by the enemy Philistines, to the point of such fear that the "big boys" hid out in caves, King Saul and his people completely stymied before the taunting of giant Goliath: "So David prevailed over the Philistine with sling and stone and struck the Philistine and killed him. But there was no sword in the hand of David. David ran and fell over the Philistine, took

Goliath's sword and drew it out of its sheath...cut off his head...and the Philistines fled." I Samuel 17:50-51. "It's not the size of the man in the fight, but the size of the fight in the man that counts."

If young David's faith, built up by his shepherding years where he killed a bear and a lion with his bare hands, could serve him so well, now why can't the same living God Who never changes, miraculously strengthen any of us who pray and trust Him when He promises in Jeremiah 33:3: "Call upon Me and I will answer you and show you great and mighty things you do not know."

"I can do all things through Christ Jesus who strengthens me." Paul, Phil 4:13.

"God is our refuge and our strength, a very present help in trouble." Psalm 46:1.

December 1

"Keep the unity of the Spirit in the bond of peace." Ephesians 4:3.

I found great pleasure sitting in the big gymnasium in Great Falls, Montana, in March 1979, watching my home-town Spartans win so easily the "B" class basketball State Championship. They had put together excellent talent, good height, experienced coaching, and best of all a spirit of unity. There was no grandstanding at the scoreboard, but many times an unselfish sacrifice in behalf of a team mate. Referees and coaches spoke of them as being the best team in Montana that year, all because of a totally unselfish attitude in every player, playing together in "a bond of peace."

How well I remember the hundreds of miles my mate spent riding backwards in the front seat, her arms clinched solidly over the front seat as she achieved "unity of the spirits in the bond of peace" when the six sons and daughters, behaving in their old nature, chose to act otherwise.

My wife and I were unusually well blessed when we opened the door of the Friendship Baptist Church to deliver a Gideon message, and immediately Deacon "so-and-so" one after another, came with a cordial welcome to join in their worship service. Women came forth freely as we ambled toward the sanctuary, and finally the pastor with a warm welcome and a resume of where I fit in the agenda, with five to ten minutes as I wanted or needed. I don't believe it was because I was a Gideon that gave us that warm welcome, but mutual friendship with our Lord and Savior, Jesus. The spirit of love and unity literally saturated the gathering as they all seemed so important to the service in song, prayer, and lots of Amens and Halleluiahs.

From Nehemiah 2:17, we read, Nehemiah speaking; "You see the distress we are in, how Jerusalem lies in waste and its gates are burned with fire. Come and let us build...that we will not be a reproach." Then they said; "Let us rise up and build...Then they set their hands to this good work." Many men from many families found their place for restoration. Twenty two times I found the words; "Next to him or next to them," as they harmonized like as a symphony, each one a part to play.

"So we built the wall, and the entire wall was joined together... for the people had a mind to work." Nehemiah 4:6.

Like the Championship basketball team, and like the Black Baptist Congregation, they kept the unity of the Spirit, in the bond of peace.

December 2

"They laid him in a manger." Luke 2:7.

Because my parents lived near the county seat in Montana, I was born in the Dahlquist Hospital, under the careful attention of a doctor and nurses. But many rural mothers gave birth at home, under the care of a midwife, she was called. Most families were long miles from town, so that when mamma would advise her husband that the time for the baby's birth was at hand, it was dad's time to hitch up the horses to a sleigh in the cold of winter, or to a one-horse-buggy in fair weather days. It was actually traditional for each community to have its own midwife, most often a former nurse now married to a farmer-rancher neighbor. I can just see that Big Sky, it's called, loaded with bright stars on a clear, cloudless night.

How different it was for Mary, the one selected by God to carry Jesus in her womb so that He might satisfy His Father in becoming a perfect sacrifice for the redemption of lost man, born dead in trespass and sin—"The Word made flesh."

Mary's hour for deliverance found her in the busy, busy crowded city of Bethlehem, where there was no room in the town's inn; no available doctor or hospital, and no midwife there in the stable except the rough hands of carpenter Joseph in that uncomfortable straw bed in the midst of bleating sheep, bawling calves, and restless camels, all crowded together to expel body heat for the stable. Baby Jesus arrived, and they "wrapped Him in swaddling cloths and laid Him in a manger," a clean place for His physical protection.

What a most humbling maternity for both Mary and her Son, known throughout history as the "King of Kings and the Lord of Lords," the most famous Man of all time, destined to do the most needed work He accomplished on that cross at Calvary and His resurrection on the third day after.

"Turn your eyes upon Jesus, Look full in His wonderful face. And the things of earth will grow strangely dim, in the light of His glory and grace."

December 3

"Suffer the little children to come unto Me." Jesus, Luke 18:16.

"Then the little children were brought to Him that He might put His hands on them and pray…Let the little children come to Me, and do not forbid them, for of such is the kingdom of God." Luke 18:15-16. Therein lies the meat of the King of our heavenly government toward little children…"save them and bring them to Me for prayer…and deny them not."

Wherein lies the heart of a president and a majority of lawmakers who constructed and voted for Roe vs. Wade in 1973? Or the heart of a president and lawmakers who stood by the shameful, disgraceful "partial-birth" law of 2009? I'm so thankful that I cannot hear the heart-wrenching "cries" of maybe fifty million babies all at one time, babies like Lincoln once was, or Martin Luther, or Apostle Paul, or Billy Graham, or the countless doctors, architects, statesmen, musicians, athletes, or the millions of just ordinary folks, like our mothers and dads.

Jesus, too, could have been one of them as an infant, along with many babies ordered to be killed, but the wise men from the East failed to listen to wicked, jealous King Herod who said to them out of a scheming, murderous heart: "Go and search carefully for the young Child...bring Him back to me that I may come and worship Him also." What a hypocrite!! Reminds me of the wicked heart of the partial-birth doctor, supported by government law, would destroy a perfectly normal baby by denial of care for a helpless little one. Where is their conscience?

"Behold, an angel of the Lord appeared to Joseph in a dream, saying: "Arise, take the young Child and His mother, flee to Egypt, and stay there until I bring you Word; for Herod will seek the young Child to destroy Him." Vs. 13.

Oh, what a sad eternal future for the abortion clinic personnel, and the Planned Parenthood people when the truth of Revelation 21:8 kicks in: "But the cowardly, unbelieving, abominable murderers...shall have their part in the lake which burns with fire and brimstone, which is the second death."

"Search me, oh Lord, and know my heart. Try me and know my thoughts, and see if there be any wicked way within me..." Psalm 139:23-24.

"My son, give attention to My Words...life unto those find them, and health unto their flesh." Proverbs 4:20.

December 4

"To him the doorkeeper opens..." John 10:3.

The old cliché says: "You can take the boy from the farm, but you cannot take the farm from the boy." I see myself as a good testimony of that quote, since not a day passes even now in my senior years but that I find myself "returning" especially to the old farmstead in Montana. There was the big barn, and on either end a wide, heavy, wooden, sliding door hanging on a track, sometimes frozen tight to the guide on the bottom, making it impossible for a little boy to open without help. This little boy's memory rehearsed that enigma the other day when I ushered my cart of groceries toward the exit at Hy-Vee, and the big door automatically opened quickly.

And here I think of another door of two thousand years ago that also opened automatically and quickly. That door was supernaturally opened by angelic power, a power that never fails because with God nothing is impossible. We find in Acts 13 that Peter, imprisoned, and tied with chains, needed and was blessed with that automatic door opener we find in Vs. 10: "They [Peter and the angel] passed the first and second cell blocks and came to the iron gate to the street, and it opened for them of its own accord! So they passed through and walked along together for a block, and the angel left him." Chapter 13:10, LBV.

I can hardly wait for the day when this old farm boy joyfully leaves the farm forever, to enter that automatically opened door to an eternal place called heaven, to walk the streets of gold with Jesus, Who has promised: "I will never leave you nor forsake you." Hebrews 13:5.

That big door will automatically open for either a little boy or an old grandpa!!

December 5

"Here I am, Lord, send me." Isaiah 6:8.

The daylight never ended one evening shortly after WWII on the streets in my hometown in Montana. The switch turned on and the usual dark streets became brilliantly lighted as the newly installed, high-powered bulbs kicked in. Two of my imbibing neighbors sat in the corner pub on Main Street away into the night, and upon returning home, told their wives that it never got dark in town last night!

The suddenness of the unexpected and brilliance of the light reminds me of Saul on the road to Damascus. In his possession were papers giving him and his accompanying crew permission to wipe out a final remnant of the men and women of the "Way", the Jesus people, and bring them to Jerusalem. Acts 9:1. Like the people in Montana, living in physically dark streets, Saul and his men were living in a dark, unlighted world spiritually. "And as he journeyed, he came near Damascus, and suddenly light shone around him from heaven." Vs. 3. Can you picture the brilliant, unexpected light that filled the heavens above? The glory of God it was, proudly lighting as lost man's "main street."

It must have been like a sudden lightning and thunderstorm, causing Saul to hit the dirt and hear an invisible, loud, voice, the voice of Jesus: "Saul, Saul, why are you persecuting Me?...it is Jesus whom you are persecuting..." Vs. 5. The sudden blow had blinded his eyes, and they led him into Damascus. Three days of blindness and fasting and along the way, "Lord, what do You want me to do? ...here I am, Lord." Vs. 6, 10.

Then the blessing of heavenly "rain": "...for he is a chosen vessel of Mine..." "Jesus, Vs. 15. The "lightning and thunder and heavy rain" now over, and Paul became the greatest anointed apostle of all time to the Gentile world. Praise the Lord that we of European descent, down to today, could be the recipients of such blessing!!

From one who, like the blind young man Jesus healed: "I once was blind, but now I see." John 9:25.

December 6

"The secret place of the Most High." Psalm 91:1.

That evening years ago when I sat down to memorize Psalm 91, I received a double blessing unexpectedly, a blessing I craved and needed. The minute I read: "He who dwells in the secret place of the Most High..." I immediately received a memorable picture of the throne room of God, as if I had just snapped it with a camera. I found the place where I wanted to cuddle up to God and Jesus when, in the throne room, where I could come to with praise, prayer, thanksgiving. Until that evening, I was never sure of, nor satisfied with the various mental images I had conjured up. At times, it was like throwing my prayers to the wind, with no solid grasp as to where they would find God.

Then David wrote: "Shall abide under the shadow of the Almighty..." and here, knowing that God is invisible, I saw Him in all His glory and power hovering overhead in a cumulus cloud, since it takes an object to make a shadow, like as on a sunny day, when a cloud passes between the sun and the earth...a shadow. Not only the privilege to dwell "in the secret place", a large room, the throne room of God, but to look up into that cloud hovering over, and be that close to the majestic, loving, powerful God of heaven. I thank the Holy Spirit indwelling me for lifting me up in the spirit, up to that throne room even though my feet are still planted on earth. When I come to that room, I always seem to be alone, with all His attention, even though in His Omni-being He may be listening to millions of others with the same attention.

"Seated at the right hand of the Father" we read of Jesus after His ascension. Sure enough, as I look around, there is Jesus, physically seated, so that when we assemble to worship on Sunday morning, we can all gather around Him in the Spirit, and fellowship with our Lord in person.

David continued with verse 2 "I will say of the Lord: He is my refuge and my fortress, my God in whom I will trust."

A wild-life refuge on the open prairies of Montana is an acreage specifically set aside for animals and birds to find perfect protection; fenced with many barbed wires, and always with ample water and grass, and "no-hunting" signs plainly displayed on the fences. The wild-life seem to sense their place of safety, and inhabit it much of the time during hunting season. So, when Paul writes over and over "in Jesus", I feel like the protected wild-life, since "He is my refuge."

When I see Jesus as "my fortress" in verse 2, I see my inner man hiding behind His unlimited stature, about like the Rock of Gibraltar would by a perfect fortress for my body in time of earthly warfare.

"Let us magnify the Lord and exalt His name together." Psalm 34:3.

December 7

December 7, 1941, Pearl Harbor.

A day which I can well remember, quickly awakened America from a twelve-year slumber, known as the "Great Depression." It was a surprise attack by Japan's air force on America's Navy huddled in the Hawaiian port of Pearl Harbor, demolishing much of our Navy, killing almost three thousand Americans on that quiet, early Sunday morning. Recent immigrants of German and Japanese blood were immediately put under close scrutiny by the U. S. Government. Almost overnight factories in America began to turn out planes, submarines, rifles and ammunition as well as naval vessels and ground vehicles and airplane carriers. Men went to war and women filled their places on the home front. America's economy mushroomed overnight, causing lots of changes in our overall daily life. Soon after Pearl Harbor, we went to war also with Germany. I can well remember the Monday morning of December 8th when our high school assembled in the gymnasium to hear President Franklin Roosevelt, by radio, asking Congress for permission to go to war against Japan immediately.

Volunteers stepped forward to serve in the military, while millions more qualified for draft according to the "Conscription Act of 1939."

The sudden shock of attack and the immediate, unhesitating response, reminds me of when King David and his warriors came home from battle to find their city, Ziklag, burned to the ground, their families kidnapped. David and his men "wept until they could weep no more." Then, like President Roosevelt, David turned to his government, God Himself, "shall we pursue the enemy?" "Pursue them and all will be restored," David and his men pursued and soon returned home with their families intact. As America enjoyed V-J Day in September 1945, so King David and his men won their man-to-man war.

"Weeping may endure for a night, but joy comes in the morning." Psalm 30:5.

December 8

"...He is my refuge and my fortress...in Him will I trust." Psalm 91:2.

Our faith in God becomes set in concrete when we pass through one trial after another. I believe we get a feel of this from God's speaking to Israel through the prophet Isaiah in chapter 43:1, where the Lord reminds them of how He had worked faithfully in their lives in miraculous ways. He said: "I created you, oh Jacob; I formed you, oh Israel. Do not fear for I have redeemed you; you are Mine, I call you by name. When you pass through the waters I will be with you; and through the rivers, they shall not overflow you. When you walk through the fires you shall not be burned, nor shall the flames even scorch you; for I am the Lord your God, the Holy One of Israel, your Savior."

What a faith builder for them and for us today. They, nor we, have come upon the scene incidentally, but as God purposed. Their Old Testament sacrifice for sin, coupled with their faith in the coming day of grace through Jesus, redeemed them; and made them personal friends with their Father. He reminded them of His blessing of how they crossed over the Red Sea, and also the Jordan River with springtime waters overflowing the banks. Then, how the three Hebrew children fared well in the heated-up furnace where Jesus was truly their refuge.

"Praise God from whom all blessings flow..." That's what we are doing at our house since the Friday afternoon in Montana when, on our way home, a tall, bay horse came onto the pavement just far enough ahead to give us time to completely stop and avoid a tragedy. Four hours later, on interstate 94, east of Billings, we drove into a blinding rain and hail storm, and again our Refuge helped us out of the line of traffic, "just in time."

"I sought the Lord and He heard me, and delivered me from my fears." Psalm 34:4.

From one who finds assurance in "trusting the Lord with all my heart...and acknowledging Him in all my ways..." Proverbs 3:5-6.

December 9

"Eli, Eli, Iama Sabachthani?" Matthew 27:46.

It was a terrible shock to the Montana community when they heard of the recent widow's death by suicide. She, her late husband, and two young sons had migrated from Europe in the late 1920's, acquired a farm, struggled with learning the English language, and fell immediately into the Great Depression and the dust bowl days of the 1930's. They fared well, and hard work and good management of the prosperous WWII days gave them opportunity to enjoy financial prosperity by the time he suddenly passed on in the mid 1950's, leaving a hopeless, lonely widow who soon chose death over life. As a very young man, I had trouble understanding how lonely a widow's life can be until I experienced it myself some forty years later. How a person's innate power of self-preservation could be so extremely uprooted, I wondered. When unbearable silence filled her home, her lover's companionship missing forever, fear and insecurity found no comfort or pleasure in the financial wealth she now had, no one to share it with.

Her lonely days on the prairies of Montana remind me of Jesus' lonely hours He bore in dark Gethsemane on the eve before His crucifixion and on the cross at Calvary that Good Friday afternoon.

In the Garden of Gethsemane we hear Him pleading "If it be possible, let this cup pass from me…," and His disciples fell asleep when He needed them and it seems depended on them to pray at a distance with Him. Before the evening was over, Judas, the disciple's treasurer, betrayed Him for a cache of silver as he identified Him to his enemies. They were standing by to bring Him to death on a cross at Calvary very soon. Before it was over, already betrayed by Judas, found ten of the remainder denying Him, scattered for fear of their own flesh, sending Jesus to the cross with only John present. Jesus gave John the responsibility of caring for Mary in her deep sorrow at the foot of the cross that dark Good Friday afternoon. Jesus had to bear it alone until after his resurrection when He met the deserters face to face, loved them, forgave them, and assigned them with a mission to "Tend my sheep, Feed my lambs."

Surely, His loneliest, darkest hour He suffered was when the cup of sin was poured on His head by God the Father, who of necessity turned his back on Jesus, and Jesus cried out "Eli, Eli, Lama Sabachthani" "My God, My God, why have you forsaken me?" His one and only time of enduring the shock and pain and loneliness of a moment of separation from God, His Father, who demonstrated how that He always turns His back on sin, even on His sinless Son.

He died, "gave up His spirit," but the scripture turns on a bright light when we read; "It was for the joy that was set before Him that He endured the cross." "The veil was rent from top to bottom" that afternoon, giving Jesus the pleasure of knowing perhaps millions of people would therefore spend eternity with Him in Heaven.

"To God be the glory."

December 10

"I need you, I want you." Jesus' plea.

A very catching billboard sign of WWII days flashed across my memory bank this morning, a sign I saw on top of a building in Minneapolis, in the country along the highways, or in the vacant lots in towns across America. It depicted "Uncle Sam", standing tall, all decked out in red, white, and blue, with that matching stovepipe hat, leaning forward with a serious look in his eye and a long finger pointing at passersby, with the inscription: "I want you." It was a plea for the young people to enlist in the military services of their country. I see a like finger pointing at you and me from Heaven, with the inscription: "I want you. I need you." One little person like you and me God wants to enlist in His earthly Kingdom's army.

It has always been that way, beginning with Adam and Eve whom he created to begin populating the earth. Then came Noah to save the human race in the days of the flood. Abraham was called out of the land of Ur to build a special, set-aside family of believers in God, to enter into eternal covenant with God. Moses, called by God from the backside of forty years of herding sheep in a desert, was wanted and needed to deliver God's people out of Egyptian slavery. Redeemed harlot, Rahab, living on the wall of Jericho, saved her family simply by obedience with a red cord she hung on the wall, David killed giant Goliath and helped his nation to move on from their enemy. Esther's plea for her people kept them from being destroyed. Gideon destroyed the thousands of Midianites with only three hundred men, jars, candles, and trumpets. On top of Mt. Carmel, Prophet Elijah confronted alone the 450 false prophets of Baal, and proved the power of the living God of Heaven, the

One Who alone empowered each of these warriors of His army on earth...needed, wanted, called out of everyday life right here.

Are you willing to enlist, become anointed, and used where you are needed, simply because one little you or I can make a difference?

A century ago D. L., Moody was won to the Lord by a Sunday school teacher; evangelist Torrey by his Mom's prayers; and Muller of England by a friend. We see here the preciousness of just one person God used to increase His fold. I see that long finger and stern look in the eye of Jesus today, saying to us personally: "I need you. I want you." "If any would come after Me, let him deny himself, take up his cross, and follow Me." Mark 8:34. That one will end up at Calvary, where he will be willing to surrender all. That's the roadmap!

December 11

"And to the...church of Thyatira..." Revelation 2:8.

"...I have a few things against you...that woman Jezebel...to teach and seduce My servants to commit sexual immorality, and eat things sacrificed to idols." Revelation 2:20. The church of Thyatira Jesus accused. And who is the Church? Is it not we who profess to be believers in Jesus as our Lord and Savior, the family of God on earth today? Is there fornication, adultery, homosexuality, lesbianism, and pornography in any of our lives today? Jesus reveals there is immorality as such.

"I gave her time to repent of her sexual immorality, and she did not repent." Vs. 21. "Except you repent, you shall perish." Jesus, Luke 13:3.

We shower daily to cleanse our outer man with water, while we allow the inner being, the soul, the real eternal me to go without a bath day after day, and it creates a stench in the nostrils of God. What a blessing to man and glory to God when both the clay and the inner man are bathed daily.

Jesus' pierced side is the "faucet" out of which pure, clean, innocent, sinless blood flows to purposely wash us clean of sin as we come with a truly repentant heart, with childlike faith to the foot of the cross, a daily chore. In my personal daily routine I begin with Psalm 139:23-24: "Search me, oh God, and know my heart, try me and know my thoughts, and see if there be any wicked way within me..." A search brings conviction, and conviction repentance, and repentance forgiveness, so that "though your sins be like scarlet, they shall be as wool." Isaiah 1:18. "As far as east is from the west, so far has He removed our transgressions from us." Psalm 103:12.

Because of forgiveness and deliverance, the fruit of a truly repentant heart, we hear further from Jesus in Revelation 2:26: "He who overcomes and keeps My work until the end, to him will I give power over the nations..."

Therein is found our daily ration of hope, love, joy, peace, and security we all seek and need.

From one who would join hand and heart with Paul: "I die daily." I Corinthians 15:31b.

December 12

"Jesus interceding for us..." Romans 8:43.

A constant daily disciplined part of prayer at our house in our devotional time these days since 9/11/01 is that our Omni-God whose eye sees every movement on earth as well as the secrets of every heart, will detonate, put to naught, cancel out or muffle every devious plan of any enemy on our soil or on foreign soil to further destroy or terrorize our people, our bridges, our dams, our airplanes, our nuclear tanks, our railroads, our Statue of Liberty, or any of our memorabilia or business buildings in America. We claim with child-like faith Job 5:12: "God frustrates the devices of the crafty so that their hands cannot carry out their plans."

But how exciting for us disciples of Jesus, the truly born again, with child-like faith, to know that He is 24 hours a day interceding for us to the Father Who responds in times of our dire need by sending ministering spirits, angels from the very throne of God, for our edification and for our protection. Romans 8:34 says of the risen Christ: "...who is even at the right hand of God; Who also makes intercession for us."

I am always reminded of this when I hear Jesus in Luke 22:32: "I have prayed for you." Note the Words of comfort and encouragement to Peter here when Jesus says: "Simon, Simon, Satan has asked to sift you as wheat, but I have prayed for you, Simon, that your faith will not fail." As I look back over the many good things that have happened in my life, my salvation, my marriages, my hunger and thirst for God's Word, etc. I just know it had to be Jesus praying for me, and all I had to do was "Trust Him with all my heart and lean not unto my own understand; acknowledge Him all in my ways, and He will direct my paths."

God put severe limits on Satan's trial of Job's faith. Jesus said literally to Peter: "I have prayed for you, I have protected you already; I have gone to court as your advocate and offered a counter piece in your behalf even before accusation is made." O, how many wonderful escapes we are someday going to see where we would have been destroyed in spirit, soul, body, finances, and relationships, but Jesus, our Omni-God, with the great power, diverted the enemy and his cunning devise.

I remember well the mine fields they were called in Europe during WWII, where two of my Montana comrades lost a limb each in Italy. The mines, mini bombs buried and disguised underground were laid out in paths that the enemy knew would have to be traveled, and laid out with such system that they could not be purposely avoided without detonating. There was no warning of their whereabouts but only a fearful dread, which is still there today where boys and girls play on grounds once planted to mines, but which were overlooked in the post-war days of clearing the minefields.

December 13

"You will find a Babe wrapped in swaddling cloths, lying in a manger." Luke 2:13.

For the Christian church, December ushers in the advent season, starting four weeks of preparing the inner man for celebrating our Savior's birth. The root word for Advent connotes "a coming," the first time at his birth in Bethlehem, and the second as we anticipate

His return to take His church home. "For the powers of the heavens will be shaken. Then they will see the Son of Man coming in a cloud with power and a great glory. Now when these things happen, look up and lift up your heads, because your redemption draws near." Luke 2:26-28.

In my early days, high school sweethearts faced the shame of an illegitimate pregnancy, back when fornication and illicit sex relations were seldom. Oh how rapidly the gossip passed from one to another in that small western town. The kids married, raised a family and celebrated over sixty years of good marriage. Such it must have been for Mary and Joseph, betrothed to one another in a tiny Galilean village when Mary was found pregnant. The announcement coming to her by an angel, "Rejoice, highly favored one; the Lord is with you; blessed are you among women." "Then the angel said to her, do not be afraid, Mary, for you have found favor with God." Luke 1:28-30.

Jesus' mother had to be a virgin for the matter of purity, and she had to be supernaturally impregnated by God in order for pure, clean, innocent sinless blood to flow through His body, to become a perfect sacrifice for mankind's sin, a sacrifice that would satisfy His Father. "That Holy One who is to be born will be called the Son of God..." Vs. 35.

Then Mary said; "Behold the maidservant of the Lord! Let it be to me according to your Word." And the angel departed from her. Luke 1:38.

"For with God nothing will be impossible." Luke 1:37.

December 14

"Praise God from Whom all blessings flow."

One morning after my six weeks of tender, loving care from countless people, while giving my broken hip time to mend, I was in prayer, praise and heartfelt thanksgiving and suddenly Matthew 10 burst forth from my memory and it seemed as though the whole ordeal came into real perspective as I rehearsed verses 29-31, where Jesus spoke to my heart, "Are not two sparrows sold for a copper coin? And not one of them falls to the ground apart from your Father's will. But the very hairs of your head are all numbered. Do not fear therefore, you are of more value than many sparrows." What a faith builder when we sometimes, as a child of God, unfairly deem ourselves as insignificant and worthless in the eye of God. NOT SO!!

An anonymous writer puts it this way, "If God sees the sparrow's fall; paints the lilies, short and tall; gives the skies their azure hue; will He not then care for you?"

As a six-year old boy in 1932, I lay by myself in a hospital after surgery in a room overlooking north Main Street. Suddenly the old blue square Chevrolet drove by, our family car, and I watched it make a "U turn" and stop by the hospital door. My lonely heart leaped with joy, and Mom and Dad entered my room. My inherent security had arrived. As I looked for my parents seven decades ago, today I watch for Jesus to appear in the clouds with a shout, and the blast of a trumpet, to take me to my eternal home with Him. I Thessalonians 4:16-17.

Home Sweet Home!!

December 15

"I wish above all things that you prosper...even as your soul prospers." III John 2.

Even now after twelve years of retirement from the Montana farm, I can hear the pleasant voice of the John Deere dealer on the other end of the phone when I would call in time of trouble or need on my tractor or combine, and hear his opening remark: "What can I do for you today?" It was his trademark that pleased every farmer who ever called him, whether a small farmer, a pauper, with not too much apparent future to the dealer, or an old man ready to retire, with like potential for the future, or the successful middle-aged farmer with a large acreage and much future potential...he treated all alike, his question was sincere, and he prospered year after year. We could sense his heart, his empathy as he gently queried "What can I do for you today?"

In Matthew 20 we find two blind men sitting along a road, hearing that it was Jesus and a large crowd passing by, and then cried out: "Have mercy on us, oh Lord..." In a sense the same cry I came to the John Deere dealer with in time of trouble on a nice, pleasant, warm day in the field, losing precious time. After their second desperate plea, Jesus stopped and said: "What do you want Me to do for you?" Vs. 32, "Lord, that our eyes may be opened." Vs. 33. "So Jesus had compassion...touched their eyes, and immediately they received sight, and they followed Him." Vs. 34. In a sense, "Lord, can you be my "fixer-upper," my repair man, so that I can get going on this nice day?"

Then, from my own personal experience in my day of severe trial, I heard Jesus from Luke 4:18: "The Spirit of the Lord is upon Me because I have been anointed to preach good news to the poor; to heal the brokenhearted; to set free those that are in bondage; to open the eyes of the blind; and to set free them that are bruised..." My faith muscle was exercised, and blessing came to me.

Just as I called on the implement dealer in full faith, and with good success in my worldly need, I've called on Jesus with like success in my inner man's need. In either case, music to my ear: "What can I do for you today?"

"I know the thoughts I have towards you, thoughts of peace, not of evil; I give you a future and a hope." Jeremiah 29:11.

From one who loves to hear God from Jeremiah 33:3: "Call upon Me and I will answer you, and show you great and mighty things you do not know."

December 16

"For to me to live is Christ, and to die is gain." Philippians 1:21.

In a cemetery in Montana is a family plot with room for four graves. One headstone reads simply: 7-19-1950, a premature son who lived only three hours. On another: 1-8-1957—4-18-1977, a son saved ten months before his death. On a third, 9-25-1924—8-6-1995, my wife, a mother, a child of God. The fourth is still open: 2-3-1926—waiting for my occupancy.

The question…"How do you live your 'dash?'" —an anonymous writer. "I read of a man who stood to speak at a funeral of a friend. He referred to the dates on his tombstone, from his beginning…to the end. He noted at first the date of his birth. And spoke of the following date with tears. But he said that what mattered most of all, was the dash between the years.

> "For the dash represents all the time
> That he spent alive on earth.
> And now only those who loved him
> Know what that little time line is worth.
> For it matters not how much we own, the cars,
> The house, the cash.
> What matters is how we live and love,
> And how we spend our dash.
> So think about this long and hard,
> Are there things you like to change?
> For you never know how much time is left,
> That can still be rearranged if we could just slow down enough,
> To consider what is true and real,
> And always try to understand the way other people feel.
> And be less quick to anger,
> And show appreciation more,
> And love the people in our lives like we have never loved before.
> If we treat each other with respect,
> And more often wear a smile,
> Remembering that our special dash
> Might only last a while.
> So when your eulogy is being read,
> With your life's actions to rehash,
> Would you be proud of the things they say?
> About how you spent your dash?"

I hear Jesus: "If anyone would desire to come after Me, let him deny himself, take up his cross, and follow Me." Matthew 16:24.

He meant: to be delivered of that me-first syndrome we all are born with. Nail your old nature flesh to a cross, it's purpose. Then follow Me to Calvary; repent and be bathed in My pure, clean, innocent, sinless blood in the inner being. "And though your sins be as scarlet, they shall be white as snow; though they be crimson red, they shall be like wool." Isaiah 1:18.

"Except you repent, you shall perish." Luke 13:3. "But if you confess your sin, God is faithful and just to forgive your sin and cleanse you from all unrighteousness." I John 1:19.

Let us consider that long dash from the womb to the tomb! It's do or die; it's heaven or hell.

December 17

"Victory in Jesus..." a favorite chorus.

Last fall, in my hometown in Montana, the football team, practically all senior boys, won a state championship and a beautiful, big, coveted trophy. That day, for most of the spectators, will pass by as a fleeting moment, but for the coaches and for those senior boys, that victory and that season will linger on and become firmly etched into their lives as a real trophy along life's trek on this earth.

In the Word of God we find men like Jacob, Moses, David, Gideon, Paul, and the disciples coming home also with nice big trophies they won after a tough, grueling season of wrestling with the flesh until the forgiveness of sin came their way, and the gift of faith they exercised brought them an eternal trophy, salvation. Read about them in Hebrews 11. And their victories of long ago are still being remembered, recorded in God's Word, and etched deep into my heart and the hearts of many.

The boys who won the state football championship made a good choice earlier in their high school days when they chose to go out for football and chose to be teachable in the techniques of the game as they listened to coaches. It was their earlier choice that put them on the gridiron at an exact time for an exact win. In Mark 8:34 we hear from the lips of Jesus: "Whoever desires to come after Me, let him deny himself, take up his cross, and follow Me." Here's a choice we all have: "do we want to be on the team or not?"

At every football game, the home spectators stand in support on the side where the coach and relief players stand, and the opponent across the field. Picture with me now that Good Friday afternoon and Jesus' invitation to come along. That One Who came from Heaven in the flesh, walked directly from the manger in Bethlehem to a cross on Calvary, just outside of Jerusalem. On one side stands the crowd, jeering, enticing, laughing, mocking, teasing, and commanding. On the other side of the testy competition stands a lone peasant, a carpenter's son with swollen lips, black eyes, bleeding head and back, and a lofty promise we just read from Mark 8. The fickle, hypocritical crowd calls for acceptance, compromise, the easy way out, Barabbas! The other promises a cross, a grueling trial, a matter of life or death for now and for eternity. One side supports flesh and a "flash in the pan", while the other offers a gift of faith that "none should perish, but all who believe on the cross, everlasting life." The evil crowd of that day, like that same crowd today, says: "Follow us, the huge majority, and fit yourself into the New Age and humanism." Jesus promised: "Follow Me and be one of the few that stand out head and shoulders above the crowd." The world promises to please the flesh and remain lost, but Jesus promises to save, to resurrect from the grave we are all born into. I hear God asking each one of us, since we are each responsible for our own salvation and walk following: "which is your choice: the crowd or Christ?" The trophy is heaven or hell for eternity.

December 18

From the pen of an anonymous writer:

> "If Jesus came to your house"

Yes, if Jesus came to your house to spend a day or two...
    If He came unexpected...just dropped in on you...
Oh, I know you'd give your nicest room to such on honored guest
    And all the food you'd serve to Him would be the very best...

And you would keep assuring Him you're glad to have Him there,
    That serving Him in your home is joy beyond compare,
But when you saw Him coming, would you meet him at the door
    With arms outstretched in welcome of your heavenly visitor?
Or, would you have to change your clothes before you let Him in?
    Or hide some magazines and put the Bible where they'd been?
Would you turn the radio off and hope He hadn't heard?
    And wish you hadn't uttered that last loud hasty Word?
And would you hide your worldly music, and put some hymn books out?
    Could you let Jesus walk right in, or would you rush about?
And I wonder, if the Savior spent a day or two with you,
    Would you go right on doing the things you always do?
Would you go right on saying the things you always say?
    Would life continue as it does from day to day?
And would your family conversation keep up its usual pace?
    And would you find it hard each meal to say a table grace?
Would you sing the songs you always sing and read the books you read?
    And let him know the things on which your mind and spirit feed?
And would you take Jesus with you everywhere you planned to go?
    Or maybe, would you change your plans for just a day or so?
Would you be glad to have Him meet your very closest friends?
    Or hope that they would stay away until His visits ends?
And would you be glad to have Him stay forever on and on?
    Or would you sigh with great relief when He at last was gone?
Oh, it might be interesting the things that you would do.
    If Jesus came in person to spend some time with you!"

Every time I read the Christmas story from Luke 2, I am disturbed a bit in the softest part of my heart when I read the sad, sad part of the true scenario: "there was no room in the inn." In Bethlehem, for a woman heavy with child to lie down and rest after a long tiresome trip, and, in fact, no place to lie down and bear her child in a comfortable bed. Could not the innkeeper have given her his room for the night? What would I have done? What would I have done? Because of his choice, the innkeeper missed out on the most important, most necessary, most significant human birth in history. The innkeeper made his choice, and now I have to ask myself: "What if Jesus came to my door today—would I let Him in?" In my many years of knocking on the door of a friend, a neighbor, a relative, or a stranger, of being, in fact, on either side of the door, the one knocking and the one opening, I have experienced both the cozy invitation to come in and fellowship over a cup of coffee, and also the cold kind where the door is utterly guarded, lest I should make a move to enter. I have also had to make the choice of being friendly, hospitable, understanding, or choose to shut the door in his face, be friend or foe. So it is with our hearts when we hear Jesus knock and we make a choice to open, invite Him in from a hospitable heart with child-like faith, or shut the door and say "no". The choice, registering an eternal effect, has been made—Heaven or Hell!!

December 19

"Go and do thou likewise." Jesus, John 10:37.

The story is told of a Christian soldier who was home on furlough. He was rushing to catch his train when he ran into a fruit stand on the station platform, knocking most of the piled-up apples to the ground. The young boy who operated the stand tried to pick up the scattered fruit, having difficulty. The apologetic serviceman put down his luggage and started collecting the apples. He polished each one and put it back on the counter. So impressed was the boy that he asked gratefully: "Soldier, are you Jesus?" With a smile, the soldier answered: "No, but I am trying to be like Jesus."

From Luke 10:30 we read of another" spilled box of apples"...a man beaten and robbed, left half dead, bleeding severely, lying on the Jericho road. Unlike the soldier, a Priest and a Levite looked at the matter of life and death, hardened their hearts, and in the busyness their "me-first syndrome" ushered them by on the other side of the road. The third man, a Samaritan, by nature a "soldier" in God's army, stopped, quickly analyzed the situation, and began to "pick apples": "A certain Samaritan...saw him...took compassion on him...bandaged his wounds, pouring on oil and wine...set him on his own animal, and took him to an inn, and cared for him. The next day, on his departure, he took out two denarii, gave them to the innkeeper, promised to come back and repay the innkeeper for any more cost. Go and do likewise." Jesus Vs, 33.

What a wonderful investment of time, talent, and treasure, gifts of God!!

"Give and it shall be given unto you, full measure, pressed down, shaken together, running over shall men give into your bosom; for as you measure it out it shall be measured back to you." Luke 6:38.

December 20

"...let him deny himself..." Matthew 16:24.

There I sat on the turning lane with flashers blinking, and with heavy traffic on four lanes on Minnesota Avenue in Sioux Falls, as my transmission failed. As I stood by my car waiting for a police car to drive by, a handsome young man pulled in ahead of me and asked: "Can I help you?" I was thrilled to ask him to call AAA from my card, since I could not read it well in the twilight. Almost immediately a police car pulled in behind me with flashing lights. I had it made!! The young, kindly, concerned civilian moved on, the AAA truck soon arrived, hauled the ailing car to a repair shop, and the police took me home. Praise the Lord, I thought to myself.

Unless someone would come along, I felt hopeless and helpless, much like the man we read of in John 5: "For an angel went down into the pool and stirred the water; and whoever stepped in first was made well of his infirmity. Now a certain man who had an infirmity for thirty-eight years was there...he said to Jesus, 'Sir, I have no man to put me into the pool when the water is stirred, but while I am coming, another steps down before me.'"

How many times in thirty-eight years did hundreds of people exercise that "me-first" syndrome we all are born with an abundance of? Was there not even one who would say to himself, "I'll encourage this hopeless, discouraged man this "stirring of the water" time, and wait for the next one for myself?"

"...let him deny himself..." and bask in the sunlight of I Corinthians 13:4-5: "Love suffers long and is kind; love does not envy; love does not parade itself, is not puffed up, does not behave rudely, does not seek its own...thinks no evil...".

"...love your neighbor as yourself." Romans 13:9b.

One day Jesus, the Good Neighbor, stepped out of the busy lane of traffic, and said to the man: "Rise, take up your bed and walk. And immediately the man was healed," healed by that One Who never knew that "me-first" syndrome.

December 21

"We fall into temptation when we don't stand against it." A quote.

"Blessed is the man who walks not in the counsel of the ungodly, nor stands in the path of sinners, nor sits in the seat of the scornful... He shall be like a tree...that brings forth its fruit in due season, whose leaves shall not wither; and whatsoever he does shall prosper...The ungodly are not so, but are like chaff which the wind blows away... for the Lord knows the way of the righteous, but the way of the ungodly shall perish." Psalm 1:1, 3-4, 6.

Jacob had one son of each: Joseph the righteous one and Judah the wicked. Watching the two brothers handle the temptation of lust is like watching a soap opera on TV. Joseph handled it like a man of God, while Judah fell to the way of the world and the flesh. "The steps of a good man are ordered by the Lord, and in his ways does the Lord find His delight." Psalm 37:23.

Such was Joseph, sold as an Ishmaelite slave, taken to Egypt and one day, while doing his daily household chores in Potiphar's home, when his wife desperately pleaded for young, handsome Joseph to sleep with her. Fornication reached out to grab him, but Joseph escaped the temptation and God eventually blessed him with a high position in Pharaoh's government, such blessing that eventually saved his family from starvation during a seven-year famine.

"For we know that all things work together for good for those who love God, and are called according to His purpose." Romans 8:28.

In Genesis 38 we find that the wicked son, Judah, married a Canaanite woman, sired three sons, meddled in their lives, and made an ugly mess not pleasing to God, to the extent that the Lord killed his first two sons, "since they were wicked." Vs. 7, 10.

Judah's wife died, and soon lust burned in his body and he laid with his veiled daughter-in-law, mistaken for a prostitute on a street corner, "Surely You set them in slippery places; You cast them down to destruction." Psalm 73:18.

The history of Joseph and Judah shows us that temptation itself is not the problem, but how we handle it...succumb or scatter!!

"Your Word have I hidden in my heart, that I might not sin against You." Psalm 119:11.

Even Jesus was tempted, but did not sin, "As it is written..."

December 22

"The steps of a good man..." Psalm 37:23.

Good morning, friends, with whom I would share a personal testimony all summed up in one short verse of that brief New Testament book called "Jude." Only one chapter, where in verse 24, I personalize and read like this: "And now all glory to Him alone is God, who saves me through Jesus Christ my Lord, and He is able to keep me from slipping and falling away."

I think here of a pastor friend and his wife who slipped off the icy pavement in the Rockies of Western Montana, and headed for a long, disastrous, steep descent into the canyon a thousand feet below; but rather found themselves in the grasp of a strong cluster of pine trees that quickly resisted their fall to sure death.

That was a physical miracle, and in Psalm 37:23-24, David speaks of a like tumble spiritually. "The steps of a good man are ordered by the Lord, and in his ways does the Lord find His delight; though he fall, he shall not be utterly destroyed; for the hand of the Lord will uphold him."

When my friends were physically saved by a cluster of pines, they were blessed with opportunity to live on even to this very day, with thanksgiving pouring from their hearts and praise to God from their lips. Likewise, the fallen of Psalm 37:23 is given the option once more to confess and repent from the heart, and find: "He is able to keep me from slipping and falling away." Jude 24. And should I slip and fall, He is willing and able to stop me from destruction.

David, the apple of God's eye in his day, fell into lust, which resulted in adultery, an illegitimate birth, the murder of an innocent man, and finally the premature death of a son. Like a string of standing dominoes fall, tragedy struck when David fell into deep sin. However, David's confession, coming from a truly broken, repentant heart we read of in Psalm 51, was his way back to God, "for the hand of the Lord will uphold him," that One "who would not that any should perish, but all should come to everlasting life".

Praise God this morning for the gift of child-like faith that makes all this possible for "whosoever will."

December 23

"To set the captives free..." Luke 4:18.

One Christmas greeting I received from up Montana way thrilled me more than all the others combined, in that it contained the testimony of a young man's recent salvation experience, a neighbor boy I had lost tract of. He testifies:

> "Drinking had been a way of life in high school, getting worse in college...reckless and out of control, I consumed life. Twenty traffic tickets and $10,000.00 of associated expenses...pace quickened...martial arts, fighting, divorce, credit card spending, no regard for others, growing debt, seeking approval, too many one-night relationships, hedonistic pleasures pursued purely for fleshly thrill." The answer?—Jesus. Could He accept me with my past? Should I expect only His wrath? I learned the Biblical truth that no matter how often I slapped His hand away He was still there waiting to forgive me. I surrendered completely and was radically transformed; now, true friends, unconditional love, obedience instead of rebellion, blessings instead of

cursings, depth of character, trust, acceptance, redemption, washed clean, no longer an empty void within, set free. I had finally found the One I could trust completely with no fear of rejection or need to prove myself. I have lived more of life in the last three years than in the first thirty six."

"I will give you a new heart and put a new spirit within you; I will take the heart of stone out of your flesh and give you a new heart, and put a new spirit within you. I will put My Spirit within you." Ezek. 36:26-27.

"As far as east is from the west, so far have I removed their transgressions from them." Psalm 103:12.

What a wonderful transformation accompanied that heart of true repentance! Like Zachaeus when he met Jesus: "Look, Lord, I give half of my goods to the poor; and if I have taken anything from anyone by false accusation, I restore fourfold." As I reflect on this young man's testimony, and on that of Zachaeus, Paul, and even King Nebuchadnezzar, I am reminded of real life illustration I passed through in my first year on the ranch. It was a hot, dry, sultry July day in 1946, and about noon ugly, black, heavy rain clouds started rolling in from the west. It started to rain about one o'clock, and it rained heavily for four hours, an accumulation of about eight or so inches of water. That afternoon, I stood in the south doorway of our barn which sat on a ledge above the valley below. Down the valley came the torrent of flood water from miles away to the west, headed for the Poplar River to the east. As I stood there, I saw the flood water rise up to the doorsill, and as it ran furiously by, it took with it every shelter, every pole and post, every fence and feed lot, and even the manure and grass down to a hard-pan—a 100% cleanup of over forty years buildup—all gone, washed clean like the sin of a repentant heart now made ready for the chore of rebuilding and starting over again, a man's heart now ready to sing out with David from Psalm 30:1: "I will extol you, oh Lord, for You have lifted me up, You've not made my enemies to rejoice over me, You have brought my soul up from out of the grave, and you've kept me alive, that I should not fall into the pit..."

December 24

"God loves a cheerful giver." II Corinthians 9:7.

While on my daily walk today, the Lord drew from my memory bank an experience I believe has been most instrumental in forming my outlook on stewardship in my life, an experience that touched my heart so dearly that I developed a weeping eye in the inner man for giving sacrificially. It was in the afternoon of December 24, 1936, when I went to our rural mailbox and found a large, soft package addressed to our family. Under the heavy, dark sky on that wintry afternoon, my heart leaped with joy when I saw my uncle's name on the return address, and I just knew it was a Christmas gift. You may wonder about my ecstasy. 1936 was the midst of tough times for our country, and in Montana, the midst of a severe drought, which forced the sale of livestock and kept the grain bins empty one more year. Christmas gifts were just not a necessity nor a need in those days; at best a want at our house, where, without that package that precise hour, our Christmas would have been very barren and empty, gift-wise. I will never forget the tan zipper jacket for me and another for my younger brother. The dreaded emptiness of that evening was filled with my uncle's generous spending on a needy family. He was single at the time and had a break or two than put him in better position than most of us.

Jesus loves and blesses sacrificial giving. Is there really any other, from the heart? The widow's two mites placed on the altar drew the only recorded attention that day, and down to today, when Jesus, standing by, said to His disciples: "Assuredly, I say to you, that this poor widow has put in more than all those who have given to the treasury, for they put in out of their abundance, but she, out of her poverty, put in all she had, her whole livelihood." I sometimes wonder if the rich ones gave only their tithes and Jesus was more concerned about the other 90%. I really believe we are more accountable for the offerings than the tithes.

I thank and praise the Lord to this day for the seed He planted in my soul, a lesson I learned from the generosity of my uncle on my tenth Christmas, 1936. That bleak Christmas planted a tender spot in my heart for the depraved, which has implanted the Godly pattern for sacrificial giving, going without something in order to bless another in need, a reason for joy like Jesus had when He gave sacrificially at Calvary: "It was for the joy that was set before Him that He bore the Cross." The saved ones who would spend eternity with Him. God loves a cheerful giver, and rewards with immeasurable hope, love, joy, peace, and security that we all crave along life's way.

December 25

"Away in a manger, no crib for a bed..." a favorite Christmas hymn.

One springtime evening in the 1930's on the Montana ranch, I noticed a hen quietly park herself into a vacated manger in the barn. Upon investigation, expecting a peck on my hand, I found her nest had several eggs in it. "She must be a setting hen", I concluded. You see, God had created her to plan for a brood of chicks after the eggs were fertilized, laid, and made ready for twenty-one days of incubation as the faithful, hopeful hen's body would be that perfect incubator by setting on the eggs, and keeping them warm, to hatch and bring forth physical life, a baby chick.

At this Christmas season, according to God's Word, I see how God, like that setting hen, had a plan to bring joy to his heart, when He secretly impregnated a virgin named Mary, by the power of the Holy Spirit, with a baby boy, gave her nine months of gestation, and then the birth and a manger to place Him into. Like with the mother hen, God was cognizant of the unsanitary surroundings, and of the disturbances, like maybe a mouse or two, the neighing of a horse, the bleating of a sheep, or even the baying of a camel, the animals whose bodies heated that stable that chilly, winter day in Bethlehem of Judea. As the hen was far from her normal home, the coop, so Mary gave birth far from her home in Nazareth.

As I was blessed in that Montana barn to be able and responsible to lift each baby chick out of the manger after a day or so of hatching, with maybe a dozen chicks to grow up and one day be a "bread of life" on our dining room table, so it was with Mary, blessed and responsible to lift Jesus out of the manger, "bread of life" for lost man's spirit, his salvation. How blessed can be the fruit of a manger!!

Jesus, the "Word, was made flesh and dwelt amongst men" John 1:14. "This is the bread which came down from heaven...not as your father's ate the manna and are dead. He who eats this bread will live forever". Jesus, John 6:58.

One day early in my life "He knocked...and I opened the door..." Revelation 3:20...and then He promised: "He who eats My flesh and drinks My blood abides in Me, and I in him." Jesus, John 6:5-6.

From one who loves that "meat" for my inner man "a good and perfect gift from above." James 1:17.

December 26

"Love your neighbor as yourself..." Mark 10:27.

Immediately after Germany surrendered in May 1945, my 16th armored division was deployed to eastern Czechoslovakia, and camped a few yards from the Russian border. We were to help take care of the destitute, displaced people WWII had brought on. At naïve age twenty, I regarded Russians as friendly allies, but soon experienced the birth date of the cold war when our kitchens and living quarters were raided very often. After the war, I soon learned that capitalism and communism were incompatible. We heard Stalin's boast "We'll overtake America without firing a shot." Many people along the Canadian border built bomb shelters, stashed full of groceries, fuel, and other immediate necessities of life. My family was not one of them, but a radical, belligerent neighbor was, to the fullest extent. One day I suggested that since I was not so resourceful, what would he do if he saw my destitute family walking up that last mile to his home. He quickly told me that he would destroy us.

What a contrast when God is involved. Lonely Elijah, hiding out beside the Brook of Cherith, because of a severe drought, saw the brook go dry, and heard the Lord: "Arise, go to Zerephath...and dwell there...And when he came to the gate...a widow was there gathering sticks, and he called to her: "Please bring me a little water in a cup"...and as she was going, "please bring me a morsel of bread in your hand." After informing Elijah that she had only enough for herself and her son, and then would die, he insisted she serve him first. Then he explained, in her desperate situation: "For thus says the Lord God of Israel: 'the bin of flour shall not be used up, nor shall the jar of oil run dry until the day the Lord sends rain on the earth.'" God kept His Word, and still more blessing besides, when Elijah later prayed over her dead son, and he was resurrected back to life.

Millions since have seen God keep His Word from Luke 6:38: "Give, and it shall be given unto you, full measure, pressed down, shaken together, running over shall men give into your bosom, for as you measure it out, it shall be measured back to you." "Let him deny himself...and follow Me." Matthew 16:24.

Great rewards are promised for those who will deny themselves; give food to the hungry, water to the thirsty, a home for a stranger, clothes for the naked, a visit to the sick and the imprisoned, "Assuredly I say to you, that inasmuch as you have done it to one of the least of these my brethren you have done it unto Me." Matthew 25:40.

December 27

"Who is leading who?"

I asked the young lady trying to keep pace with the large dog on her leash. They were both putting their "best" into that joyful experience.

While doing field work with my tractor on the Montana farm, I often found myself a couple miles from my pickup at evening time, going home time. I loved to walk in those days before my knees started to rebel; and to make good time, I would practice the scout pace I had learned as a high school Boy Scout where I could walk briskly for fifty paces and then jog for fifty, easily covering a mile in twelve minutes or less, never grudging my trip. Did you ever notice that most street walkers are slender people?

Walking was man's first means of self-propulsion. And here I think of Prophet Elijah the day after his mountain-top experience with the prophets of Baal we read of in I Kings 18. In a day long tussle between the power of the false god and the 450 prophets of Baal and the God of heaven, Elijah represented; the prophets of Baal were easily defeated, and Elijah and his warriors put them all to death. Queen Jezebel appeared on the scene with anger and retribution on her heart to the extent of seeking out and killing Elijah within twenty four hours. An angel of the Lord brought food to Elijah and we read in 19:8 "...he ate and drank, and went in the strength of that food forty days and forty nights..." and undoubtedly walked many miles away from Jezebel and toward God, his safety net, whom he met in a cave. Such was a physical blessing he needed by that long walk.

What a pleasant contrast we read of in Genesis 5:23-24, "So all the days of Enoch were three hundred and sixty five years. And Enoch walked with God, and he was with God, for God took him home." This describes Enoch's close communion with God daily. Literally walking by His side like two lovers strolling through the park. Enoch evidently had an obedience that God appreciated in the corrupt culture of that day surrounding them. We read of only two men in God's Word who entered into heaven without physically dying: Enoch and Prophet Elijah, who was taken up in his chariot.

May your testimony and mine be like the hymn writer sings it out:
"He walks with me and He talks with me,
And He tells me I am His own;
And the joy we share as we tarry there,
None other has ever known."

December 28

"Behold how good and how pleasant it is for brethren to dwell together in unity." Psalm 133:1.

"God bless America, land that I love," especially how history has taught me of the solid unity they enjoyed while they placed one plank after another into the greatest constitution in all of time. I've read that some planks were debated and prayed over for three weeks until they had unanimous support for passage. Some were of the Christian faith while others were not, but allowed for the sake of unity, to build a constitution of common sense for all in the generations to come. To them, separation of church and state had no intent of being exclusive for some, dividing our people, but working in a spirit of unity.

After their mother passed away, the four sisters of my wife's family gathered one afternoon, took care of the knick-knacks sitting around, the jewelry articles, the memorials hanging on the walls, a matter of give and take, and they left as united as ever, love and respect as solid as ever. I was proud of them.

Family unity blesses God, and brings glory and honor to His name. But disunity like we find in Luke 15, caused by self-pity and jealousy undoubtedly, brings a curse and condemnation from the Lord. The prodigal brother had left home with his inheritance in hand. He foolishly squandered it all in riotous living. He later confessed his "sin from a truly repentance heart" desiring to return to his father and be considered now a servant rather than a son.

His jubilant father said "no," and ordered his servants to "bring out the best robe and put it on him, and put a ring on his finger, and sandals on his feet. Bring the fatted calf here, kill it, let us eat and be merry." Vs. 22-23.

Now the older brother came home from the field, inquired about the merriment and soon lost his temper, feeling slighted and cheated, breaking family unity, even as Dad tried to reason with him: "Son, you are always with me and all that I have is yours."

Oh, what a heart full of love and forgiveness could have done for family unity!

December 29

Got caught!

Yep, my brother and I found where the old gray cat had birthed her new litter, in the haystack of the barn mow on the old Montana ranch. We had made it very evident to her of our delight in fondling those several blind kittens. Later that day, while playing in the farmstead yard, we looked up and found the gray mamma cat proudly carrying a kitten by her teeth from the barn to another hide-away across the yard, her escape from an unwelcome "enemy."

Today, seventy five years or so later, that memory flashed back, a secular memory I can easily relate to in a spiritual testimony of years later. I see myself born into visibly enemy territory for my inner man because of the inherent sin I, like every person, inherited from our first parents, Adam and Eve. I was born naturally into the wrong nest, a birth that guaranteed eternal death unless someone would come, like as with the gray mother cat and move me from a world of death, darkness and despair, to a place of life, light and restoration.

Jeremiah 1:5 proves God's urgency in this matter, where he says: "Before I formed you in the womb I knew you; before you were born I sanctified you; I ordained you a prophet to the nations." As a prophet, Jeremiah was to serve God, share the good news of the gospel with his peers of that day, a message we of New Testament times hear from the lips of Jesus: "You must be born again." John 3:3, 7. One day I heard that message preached, my gift of faith was exercised and the Holy Spirit "moved" my inner man from my place of birth, darkness, death, destruction, to a new home of life, light and restoration. As the kittens grew rapidly, physically in their new home, I too, grew rapidly, spiritually in my "new home."

"The Spirit of Truth, whom the world cannot receive because it neither sees Him nor knows him; but you know Him for He dwells with you and will be in you." John 14:17.

I'm glad my enemy "who came to kill, steal, and destroy" (John 10:10) got caught and I got moved.

December 30

Polls measure popularity.

Polls, polls, polls, have become a fairly accurate scientific way of gauging what is going on in the hearts and minds of people as we found in the recent election. They appeared to have some influence on the money spending, to advertise, especially in the close races. It was interesting to see how volatile they were at times, sometimes severe up and down on a particular candidate, and would surge and then fall back. Elections in my boyhood days, especially the national ones, were more exciting as we sat by the radio anticipating the win or loss. In 1936, FDR's second term, no one dreamed for such a landslide when he carried forty seven of that day's forty eight states. Exciting as the pre-ultra sound days of awaiting the gender of the baby a mother was carrying. I believe that it was the late 1940's before we heard of the first Gallup poll in an election.

What if a news media like we have today had followed Jesus two thousand years ago, and had recorded all the ups and downs of His popularity? On the night of His birth, the Shepherds on the plains around Bethlehem would have exalted him in the polls. But not much later His own people rejected Him, and down went the poll of popularity! Up they would climb at his age twelve when He displayed unusual wisdom in the temple before the elders, Jesus asking: "Wist you not that I be about my Father's business?"

But oh what a drop in the polls early in His earthly ministry when He healed a man on the Sabbath. He didn't measure up to the legalists! Down go the polls. Then came the day when selfish humanity showed its best to raise the polls when Jesus supernaturally took fish and loaves, and by praying for God's blessing, He had enough to feed five thousand men and their families. Popularity once again.

The polls continued to show Jesus as a popular candidate when on Palm Sunday He rode like a King on the back of a selected donkey in to Jerusalem, the people placing wreath and branches on the ground before Him. Joyfully singing praises unto Him as a triumphant King. Polls soaring high. But by Friday one disciple had betrayed Him, and the fickle crowd cried out "Barabbas, Barabbas!" The polls slumped drastically so that by Good Friday afternoon only John, Mary, his mother, and the other Marys stood alone at the foot of the cross to watch him suffer. The polls continued to fall until Easter morning when the polls rose higher than ever when Jesus arose from the grave, never to die again, giving every born again Christian that same hope.

Today His benefactors can proudly sing: "Turn your eyes upon Jesus, Look full in His wonderful face, And the things of earth will grow strangely dim, In the light of His glory and grace."

"For I know that my Redeemer lives and He shall stand at last on the earth." Job 19:25.

December 31

"Though I know not what awaits me—
  What the future has in store,
  Yet I know that God is faithful.
  For I have proven Him before." Anon.

On this last day of the year, as I look to the morrow, I remember, by analogy, my teen-age years at Metigoshi Lake, N.D. Boy Scout camp, where I was housed in a tent over a hill from Metigoshi, a place called Icogowan, and how this "early bird" in me awakened at sunrise, beckoning me to run over the hill and through the trees and cobwebs to the breakfast table, as the sun shone gorgeously on the big, clear, quiet lake—the birth of a new day for swimming, canoeing, bird studying, hiking, life saving; and as the day wore on, the confectionary and the crackling evening camp fire, songs and fellowship. What a treat for a Montana boy coming from the treeless "dust bowl", the severe drought of the 1930's, a land without a single lake, not even a man-made one like we enjoyed decades later, a land of wilderness. To me, each new day at camp signaled the end of one exciting time, challenge, accomplishment, and good fellowship, only to give away to the beginning of a new one just as exciting. Such I see the passing from 2008 into the New Year 2009.

I muse today over the old year's problems and struggles, its fun and joy, its weeping and its rejoicing, and they became a dim memory when I think of getting a fresh start like every morning was at scout camp.

It must have been something like that for Joshua and his people as they stood on the dark wilderness side of the Jordan River, maybe on the west side with the sunset behind them and the sunrise of a new day before them, glistening on the waters of the overflowing

Jordan banks, on the brink of Psalm 30:5, "Weeping may endure for a night, but joy comes in the morning."

Behind them lay forty years of murmuring and complaining, disobedience and faithlessness in the desert without trees or lakes or productiveness. Ahead was land of milk and honey that God had promised them after their Red Sea crossing, but which they failed to take hold of. Besides a land of milk and honey, like many of us believers in Christ know ahead for the new year, they had God's promise, like we, that He would be with them: "Do not be afraid, nor dismayed, for the Lord your God is with you whenever you go." Joshua 1:9.

And so it was with King Jehosophat, his face to the enemy as he heard from the Lord: "Do not fear or be dismayed, for the battle is not yours but God's." II Chronicles 20:15. That makes a new day, a new year, so palatable—"God with me."

The bright, eastern sunrise daily lifts us up with a measure of hope, love, joy, peace, and security we've never known before when we learn to "Trust the Lord with all your heart and lean not unto your own understanding. Acknowledge Him in all your ways and He will direct your paths." Proverbs 3:5-6.

"Praise God from whom all blessings flow, Praise him all creatures here below"—my personal doxology as this old year passes into eternity.